D0857619

Performance Zoning

Performance Zoning

Lane Kendig

with

Susan Connor, Cranston Byrd, and Judy Heyman

Planners Press
American Planning Association
Washington, D.C.   Chicago, Illinois

WILLIAM MADISON RANDALL LIBRARY UNC AT WILMINGTON

This book is dedicated to Wilma and Heather
and to all those who provided encouragement,
assistance, or criticism as performance zoning
has evolved.

Copyright 1980 by the American Planning Association
1313 E. 60th Street, Chicago, Illinois 60637

All rights reserved.
ISBN 0-918286-18-2
Library of Congress Catalog Card Number 79-93346
Printed in the United States of America

Contents

HT169
.6
.K462

222165

Publisher's Foreword

Early zoning ordinances, prepared for cities which were already built up, have tended to ignore an important factor: that land, as a natural resource, deserves protection. Moreover, buildings may deserve protection. This can be accomplished when development is prohibited on land that contains unstable soils.

Planners also have become disenchanted with zoning concepts that, under widely varying circumstances, force identical requirements on developers. In response, some communities have adopted performance-oriented land use regulations. However, these new approaches usually have simply been added onto zoning and subdivision ordinances, which follow an essentially traditional approach to regulation.

Lane Kendig, in his work at two different planning agencies, has over the past decade developed a new approach to these problems. Planners who have been exposed to this work in the form of agency reports and conference presentations have responded enthusiastically to the ongoing enterprise. We here at the APA also have watched the development of these concepts with great interest.

Now we are extremely pleased to publish "Performance Zoning," a book that contains not only an explanation of the basic concepts of performance zoning, but also a model ordinance. The ordinance has been prepared for Lake County, Illinois, and can be adopted by other county governments and local municipalities. We believe that the ordinance contains concepts and approaches which can be adopted by planners throughout the nation. These planners need only study their own local environmental conditions to discover which concepts are directly transferable and which need modification. Most important, by using the basic approaches outlined in this book, planning agencies can save staff time and money when designing new ordinances.

The APA is most grateful for permission to publish this book and thanks the Lake County Department of Planning, Zoning and Environmental Quality, the County Board of Lake County; and the U.S. Department of Housing and Urban Development.

About the Authors

Lane Kendig is the Director of the Lake County Department of Planning, Zoning, and Environmental Quality, Waukegan, Illinois, and former Director of Community Planning with the Bucks County Planning Commission, Bucks County, Pennsylvania, where he first developed performance zoning.

Susan Connor was a Planner/Lawyer with the Lake County Department of Planning, Zoning, and Environmental Quality.

Judy Heyman is an Associate Planner in the Advanced Planning Section of the Lake County Department of Planning, Zoning, and Environmental Quality.

Cranston Byrd was the Deputy Director for the Planning and Zoning Section of the Lake County Department of Planning, Zoning, and Environmental Quality and is presently Director of Community Development and Planning, City of North Chicago, Illinois.

Acknowledgments

Over the past decade, as I sought to develop a comprehensive performance zoning ordinance, I have become indebted to many people who have assisted me in its evolution: Carter Van Dyke, Walter Evans, Mike Frank, Bruce Fowler, John Kellogg, Jeff Osterman, John Skibbe, and John Wahlen—all of whom worked on early performance zoning ordinances in Bucks County, Pennsylvania. I am also indebted to Larry Appelson, Nancy and Scott Hedburg, Chris Miller, Mary Otting, Terry Sedik, and Sheel Yajnik-Raval of the Lake County (Illinois) Department of Planning, Zoning, and Environmental Quality. These individuals have done research on specific types of performance controls, or they have worked with local officials to adapt performance zoning to individual municipal needs.

One individual, Franklin C. Wood, must be singled out above those whose work contributed to the performance zoning ordinances that preceded this book. During my years in Bucks County, Franklin allowed me the freedom to develop new ideas, despite their potential for controversy. He provided a climate conducive to innovation that has, in large part, made it possible for me to explore new methods of zoning.

Research of legal issues and encouragement from David Callies and Cliff Weaver have been a great help. They should be absolved of any errors I have made.

Kenny Parson's, Ruth Paulsen's and Peter Bayard's assistance in providing finished graphics was also key to the completion of this work, as was the editorial work of David Novak and Alma Dean Kolb. My gratitude is extended, too, to Karen Hall, Jeanne Leska, and Barbara Christiansen for their perseverance and patience in clerical assistance.

There are a number of performance zoning ordinances in force in Bucks County communities. The elected and appointed officials in those communities have provided valuable input that has resulted in improvements for which I am grateful.

I would especially like to acknowledge the support of county board members in Lake County, who have enabled this research to take place and gave permission for the publication of this book.

Much of this research on Performance Zoning has been funded over the years by the U.S. Department of Housing and Urban Development; the Commonwealth of Pennsylvania; the County of Lake, Illinois; and the County of Bucks, Pennsylvania. The model ordinance and introduction to performance zoning contained herein was funded with Community Development Block Grant funds. That assistance has been invaluable.

Last, but not least, I wish to express my gratitude to the American Planning Association for making it possible to publish this book.

Lane H. Kendig

Part One

The Concept of
Performance Zoning

Introduction

In city and suburb alike, planners, elected officials, and citizens look to zoning to control their destiny. Zoning has long reigned as the premier tool in the planner's arsenal. This has been the case since 1916, when New York City adopted perhaps the first comprehensive zoning ordinance. By 1926, the U.S. Supreme Court had put to rest all doubt that zoning enactments which restricted an individual's right to develop private property were a constitutional exercise of a community's police power. In "Village of Euclid vs. Ambler Realty Company," the court upheld the validity of an ordinance scheme (later referred to as "euclidian zoning") which divided all the municipality's area into separate zoning districts, specified uses permitted in each district, and prescribed minimum lot, area, and bulk requirements for all permitted uses. Today, with rare exception, "euclidian" or "conventional" zoning exists in the cities, villages, and counties of this country which have adopted zoning. The theory of this approach is that the separation of land into separate districts allows sorting groups of land uses on the basis of their compatibility. This sorting is based on the likely or predicted effect of any particular land use rather than on the actual performance of any example of such a use. As a corollary to the separation of uses, regulations related to the bulk area and other details of all permitted uses are prescribed for each district. The intent of the zoning restrictions is to protect the public health, safety, and general welfare in as many ways as there are regulations.

Although the history of euclidian zoning in America spans more than six decades, its promise as an effective land use measure for the implementation of plans has not been fulfilled. Zoning has failed to protect the environment: forests have been felled, floodplains and marshes have been filled (often with serious flooding consequences), and agricultural land has been destroyed. While public opinion often casts developers in the villain's role, the truth is that zoning has failed to prohibit such activities and often encourages them. Conventional zoning has not prevented our arterial highways from being choked by strip development. Indeed, the inventiveness of zoning specialists has regularly produced ordinances which contain "highway commercial" or "highway service" districts in order to legitimize their failures to protect our arterial roads. The nemesis of planners, "urban sprawl," is not due to an absence of planning and zoning; it is "zoned sprawl." Most suburban communities have been developed under zoning, and large-lot zoning districts have encouraged urban sprawl. The supreme indictment is that people are now fleeing the older suburbs, just as

they do nineteenth-century cities that predate zoning. They are fleeing what zoning has wrought. Yet, surprisingly, as they move they bring with them the same zoning tools that permitted their previous environment to become less than desirable. In this process the rural environments that attracted them are inexorably destroyed.

The failures of traditional zoning indicate a need to explore alternative ways of regulating land-use development. This book provides a dramatically different, comprehensive approach to zoning which enables a community to plan for its future population, while safeguarding the natural, social, and economic qualities that have made it an attractive place in which to live. "Performance zoning" has been developed to address areas of regulation where conventional zoning has failed. Unlike the traditional approach, it does not organize uses into a hierarchy which is then used to protect "higher" uses from "lower" ones. Rather, it imposes minimum levels of "performance" by setting standards which must be met by each land use. The performance approach to the imposition of zoning regulations was first taken in the early 1950's to regulate noise, smoke, dust, and other nuisances associated with industry.[2]

Several attempts to modify the conventional ordinances and PUD provisions for municipalities in Bucks County, Pennsylvania, proved to this author that a more radical approach was necessary. To provide flexibility and control, the author began work on a performance zoning ordinance. The first of these ordinances taking a more comprehensive performance approach has been in effect since 1974 (in Bucks County, Pa.). These ordinances retain traditional zoning districts but impose performance standards for site design, residential land uses, and many environmental concerns. Meanwhile, some municipal officials were questioning the need for all those residential districts, and thus arose a second generation of performance zoning ordinances which boiled all the residential districts down to a single district. Performance standards took complete control of intensity, and the first attempts to apply performance standards to nonresidential uses were made.

This book presents a third-generation performance zoning ordinance, one which eliminates conventional zoning district designations and replaces them with far fewer and more important district distinctions. The ordinance regulates all permitted uses and structures as a function of the particular, and frequently measurable, "by-products" that each use is likely to have. These by-products may vary for the same use (e.g., "office") depending on the intensity of that use proposed by the developer.

In the first part of this book, the major failures of zoning will be explored and the important issues and constraints of any regulation system identified. The major components of performance zoning will be outlined, and the way in which it operates will be illustrated. The second part comprises a model performance zoning ordinance developed in Lake County, Illinois. The final part contains a more detailed explanation of the ordinance's development and information about its use in and adaptation to different jurisdictional settings.

Why Performance Zoning?

The year 1966 will be a significant one for American Planning. It marks two anniversaries: the beginning of the fifth century of the oldest city in the United States and the ending of the fifth decade of comprehensive zoning. It is a nice question which is less obsolete—the St. Augustine plan of 1565 or the comprehensive zoning ordinances of the country based on the New York City Zoning Resolution of 1916. The quaint, narrow streets of the old Spanish town serve at least to attract the tourist dollar; the quaint, narrow provisions of our zoning ordinances, judging from current comments, attract only the lawyers.

John Reps, *Requiem for Zoning*[3]

Zoning was developed to protect the public health, safety, and welfare by preventing the misuse and overcrowding of land and by protecting individuals from adverse impacts of neighboring land uses. For a variety of reasons, including both theoretical inadequacies and poor administration, traditional zoning has consistently failed to provide the protection it was intended to guarantee.

Planning and law journals abound with criticism of conventional zoning. Often, such criticism elicits the knee-jerk response that "zoning is alive and well." This reaction is understandable because, dead or alive, zoning remains the major planning tool available to local government. Nevertheless, the criticism is usually well deserved: the time for a new approach to zoning is here.

One of the most instructive ways to evaluate the performance of conventional zoning is to examine its development over time in a specific area. This may be done graphically by comparing the zoning ordinance map of a community as it appeared some years ago with a contemporary one. The illustrations on the adjoining page depict changes in the zoning map of Bensalem Township near Philadelphia.

The results are typical of what has occurred throughout the nation, particularly in developing areas close to a relatively developed community. Initially, the township consisted of seven districts which were located to implement long-range land use plans. In a mere twenty years, however, the number of different zoning districts has increased to a point where they are no longer logically separate entities, and rezonings have thoroughly wreaked havoc with the original land use policy plans.

BENSALEM TOWNSHIP   1954

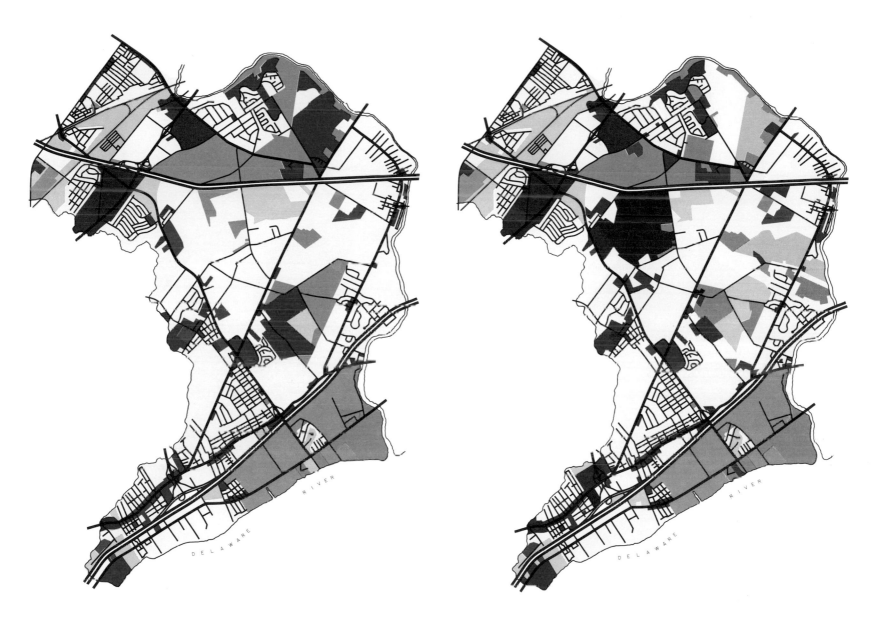

BENSALEM TOWNSHIP   1968   BENSALEM TOWNSHIP   1975

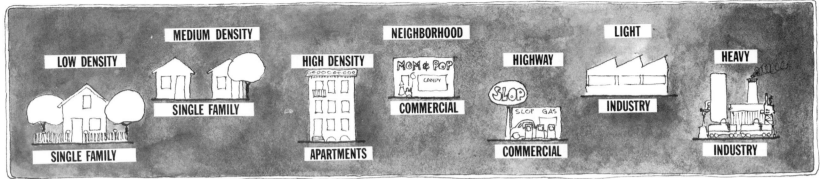

SINGLE FAMILY — LOW DENSITY
MEDIUM DENSITY — SINGLE FAMILY
HIGH DENSITY — APARTMENTS
NEIGHBORHOOD — MOM & POP — COMMERCIAL
HIGHWAY — SLOP — SLOP GAS — COMMERCIAL
LIGHT — INDUSTRY
HEAVY — INDUSTRY

HIGHEST
BEST

LOWEST
WORST

LAND USE HIERARCHY

Theoretically, zoning is based on a hierarchy of land uses. The degree of incompatibility of any two uses depends on how far apart they are on the hierarchical scale illustrated above: the farther apart, the more incompatible are two uses as neighbors. Zoning districts are intended to separate incompatible uses and thereby prevent any lower use from substantially harming a higher one. Traditional zoning, then, seeks to delineate areas in which residential ("higher") uses are permitted and areas in which industrial ("lower") uses are permitted. A sketch of an ideal new town at the time zoning was first adopted provides an interesting comparison with Bensalem Township; note the juxtaposition of land uses that occurs in practice as compared with the theoretical separation.

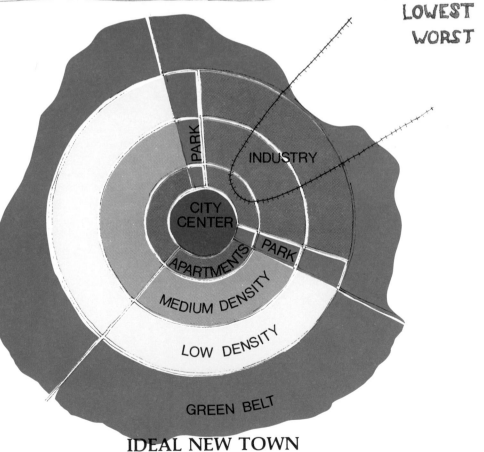

IDEAL NEW TOWN

There are three major reasons that conventional zoning has failed to meet the expectations of land use planners. The first is the proliferation of zoning districts. As the number of districts grows, it becomes increasingly difficult to distinguish among them; as the distinctions become less clear, the purpose of any given district becomes blurred, and the formal distinctions themselves become less defensible. An increase in the number of districts also results in fewer uses being permitted in any single district, which decreases the likelihood that an available site will be properly zoned to match a developer's needs. This in turn increases the probability that a zoning amendment will be sought.

A second problem is that conventional zoning has been administered as an ad hoc reaction to proposals initiated by the private sector rather than as an implementation tool of public policy. This is a problem of considerable magnitude. In Lake County, Illinois, for example, the zoning ordinance and zoning district boundary lines were comprehensively revised in 1966. In the past thirteen years, 695 petitions for rezoning have been sought and 399 (57 percent) have been granted. In addition there were over one thousand rezonings through annexations to villages. Planning implies that something is built according to a plan; the ad hoc zoning process in which a community must react to proposals which are not in the plan virtually insures that the plan will not be followed. This type of problem is exacerbated by the number of competing interest groups which play some role in almost any rezoning: planners, the zoning board (in some states), elected officials, developers, and neighbors. Moreover, a high turnover of local governmental personnel interferes with the development of "institutional memory" and continuity of the plan's implementation.

Finally, the legal requirement that all land within a jurisdiction be zoned (if land is zoned at all) presents a problem. As a result of this stricture, land—particularly in suburban growth situations—is often zoned for very low density in spite of the jurisdiction's full knowledge (and intent) that the zoning will be changed as developmental pressures increase. The use of a low density zone as a holding zone not only casts suspicion on both the real purpose of low density districts and on the zoning ordinance as a whole, but has also led to additional complications. As people build in these low density areas, they create pressure to maintain them at that density, regardless of the areas' suitability in terms of the jurisdiction's overall plans and needs.

The failure of conventional zoning aside, there are some valid reasons to mix land uses. Private developers who control land use on large parcels support this concept: they often carefully provide for mixed uses. This phenomenon undermines the basic assumption of traditional zoning that different uses must be physically separate or distant from one another in order to protect themselves from each other. The traditional goal of a balanced community implies a wide range of land uses interacting with each other to create a healthy environment.

Zoning is supposed to protect landowners from the adverse impacts of adjoining land uses. Historically, it has not achieved this, because conventional ordinances do not contain standards to protect adjoining landowners. The success or failure of conventional zoning depends on the process of designating the boundaries of a zoning district. Vernon Township's conversion of rural area to a suburban area containing seven municipalities shows the result of such decisions (see illustration). It is similar to the Bensalem example shown on pages 6 and 7.

VERNON TOWNSHIP   1939

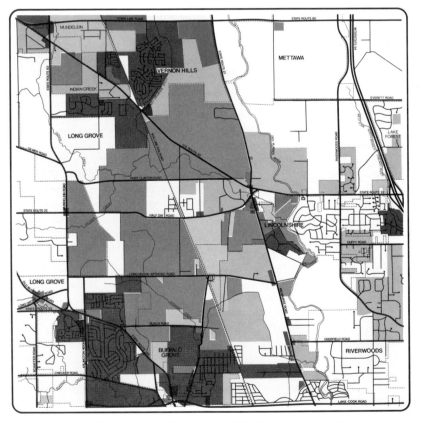

VERNON TOWNSHIP   1978

Ad hoc decisions cannot successfully protect all interests because decision makers are always required to choose between two conflicting interests: the neighbor who wants the neighboring property to remain vacant or to be developed to a use no higher than his, and the developer who wants a higher intensity use. One *must* win; the other *must* lose. In one situation the developer reaps a "windfall" return, and the neighbor does not receive protection. If the neighbor is protected, the developer suffers a "wipeout," The history of conventional zoning has been to restrict more narrowly the use of land, thereby forcing more ad hoc decisions and exacerbating this problem.

The illustration demonstrates this conflict as it typically occurs. A landowner desirous of developing a property with frontage on a major highway proposes a zoning change which would permit that development. The developer contends that the busy road and shallow depth render the subject property unsuitable for the residential uses which are permitted. But the illustrated property contains a grove of mature oak trees, all of which may be destroyed if the property is developed as requested by the developer. The adjacent property owners, all concerned with variables such as congestion, noise, dirt, and environmental degradation, argue against the change. The rules of zoning do not allow the decision makers latitude to find a middle ground. Consequently, local officials or the courts must award victory to one side despite the valid points of the other.

The failings of conventional zoning have been demonstrated. Each problem, even if it were the sole problem, would be serious. In combination they are fatal. Years of fine tuning and supplemental additions to the basic technique have not worked. Accordingly, radical departures from tradition are necessary. The performance approach to zoning is one such departure.

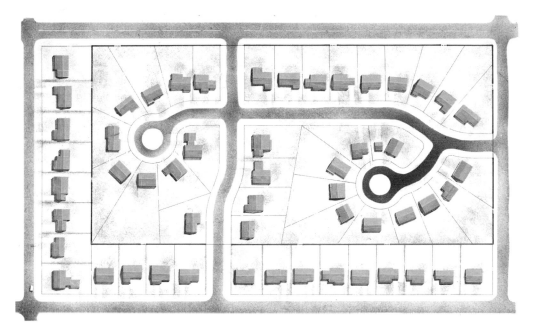

DEVELOPMENT (Existing Zoning)

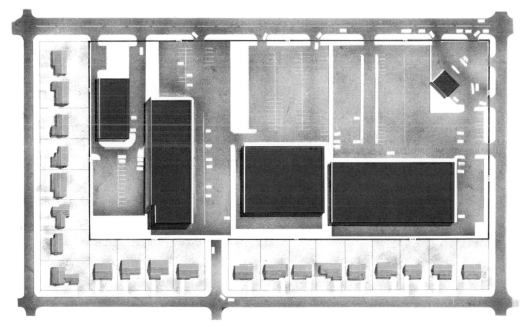

COMMERCIAL DEVELOPMENT (Zoning Change)

11

Variables

The size, shape, and natural resource features of a site constitute constraints which have direct implications for its development potential within either the conventional or the performance approach to zoning. Descriptions of each of these variables, together with an explanation of their consequences for development, follow.

Size

The size of the site affects its design. The smaller the site, the greater the probability that the road length per dwelling unit and the impervious surface ratio will increase and that density will drop. A smaller site is more difficult to lay out because the minimum ordinance requirements for street frontage and lot area may not be provided efficiently. The probability of having to provide lots larger than a required minimum or of inefficient block layout increases as site size decreases.

The accompanying illustration shows a decrease in density necessitated by a smaller site. Road length per dwelling unit increases dramatically, and impervious surfaces are slightly increased compared to the illustrated example of a larger site. In economic terms, the result of this difference is either that the cost of the land must be adjusted down or that each unit will cost more on a small tract than on a larger one.

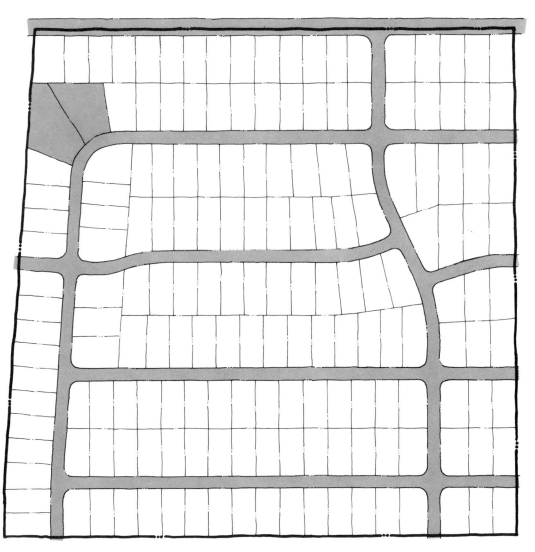

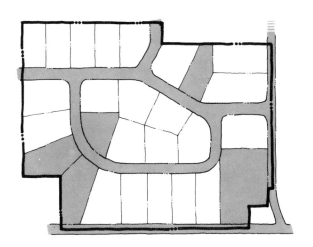

SMALL SITE

Density   1.77 du's/Ac

Length of Street/DU   94 ft.

LARGE SITE

Density   2.09 du's/Ac

Length of Street/DU   64 ft.

Shape

The shape of a property has a significant impact on how efficiently it may be utilized. It is often difficult to develop an efficient street network on an irregularly shaped site, which in turn leads to a wasteful lotting arrangement. Odd, irregular, or oversized lots may result.

The accompanying illustrations demonstrate that road length per dwelling unit is likely to increase while density declines on an irregularly shaped property, when compared with the similarly sized but regularly shaped site on the preceding page. This makes each lot in the development costlier and the increased street length may mean more expensive maintenance in future years.

IRREGULAR SITE

Density   1.96 du's/Ac

Length of Street/DU   67 ft.

15

Natural Resources

Natural resources or limitations such as floodplains or wetlands are obvious constraints on the development of a site. The presence of these features may dramatically alter the development potential of a site. A natural resource which cannot be developed always has the effect of reducing the buildable area. Further, the location of the resources on a site may create an irregular shape with unusable corners or render access to portions of a site difficult. The result is a reduction of density and an increase in street length per dwelling unit.

A number of resources require protection. Every book and course in land planning or site design emphasizes the need to work with the environment and to avoid construction in unsuitable areas. Because the presence of resources tends to reduce density and increase street length per dwelling unit, there are intense economic pressures working against environmental protection.

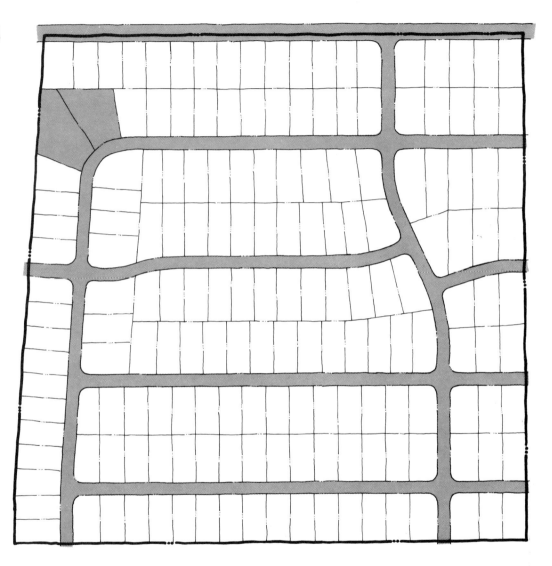

UNRESTRICTED SITE

Density   2.09 du's/Ac

Length of Street/DU   64 ft.

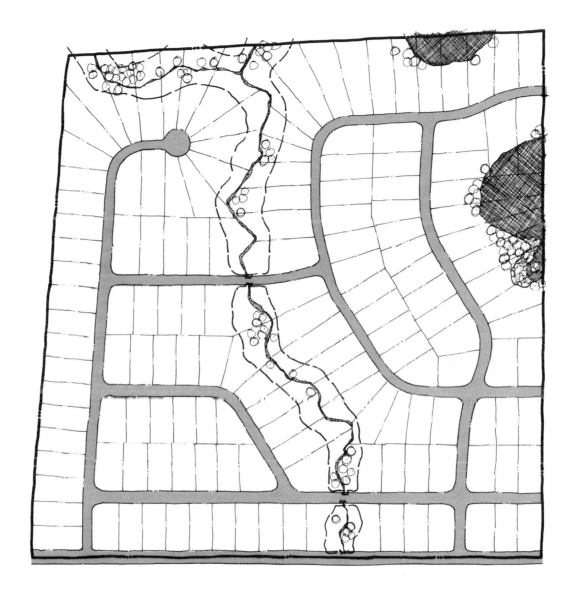

RESOURCE RESTRICTED SITE

Density	1.73 du's/Ac
Length of Street/DU	75 ft.

It should be noted that all three of these variables can affect a single site. Hence, very few sites can be built to the densities specified by zoning. All too often present zoning is deemed restrictive because the site cannot be developed to its full potential. In reality, the full potential of a site is a function of its unique properties, its size, shape, and the presence of natural features. A study of subdivision plats shows that, when compared with an optimal site, one with no wasted space, the average site plan is only 81.1 percent effective. Sites actually built under the conventional Lake County ordinances ranged from 56.5 to 97 percent efficient.

The accompanying illustrations demonstrate how dramatically the efficiency of an ideal site can be altered by modest changes in the variables just described.

Developers often initially avoid properties that are difficult to develop because of size, shape, or resource limitations. The developer correctly assesses the site's limitations, and the landowner usually fails to adjust the asking price accordingly. As time passes and land becomes scarce, these parcels become more marketable. The landowner, aware of both general inflation and scarcity, actually increases the asking price, although from the performance perspective the market should operate to make these sites less valuable. The result of price inflation is that zoning changes to permit more intense development are sought.

Traditional zoning encourages landowners to expect an artificially high price for irregularly shaped properties. When land becomes sufficiently scarce, the relative inefficiencies pale and the developers seek to change the zoning restrictions in order to compensate for natural limitations of sites. Performance zoning views each piece of land as unique—as a function of its size, shape, and natural features—and requires both developer and landowner to assess its uninflated development potential, including its liabilities.

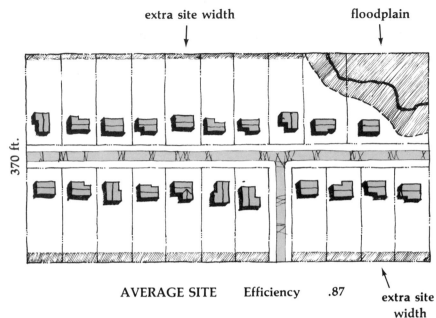

extra site width   floodplain

AVERAGE SITE   Efficiency   .87   extra site width

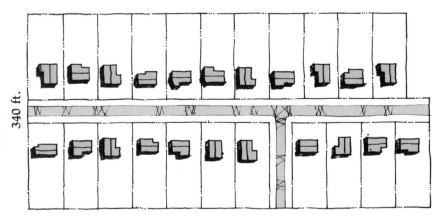

IDEAL SITE   Efficiency   1.00

Design

Design professionals, architects, landscape architects, and land planners are trained to strive for creative excellence. Zoning militates against this end because it creates rigid rules that restrict creative solutions and usually result in mediocrity. Zoning regulations are often based on a fear that something thought to be undesirable will occur if a particular regulation is not imposed. Because those who normally draft zoning provisions are planners, lawyers, or other professionals who do not understand design, creative design solutions are often prohibited. The first step toward rectifying this inadequacy must be an understanding of design.

Conventional Cookie-Cutter Design

1. The cookie or lot

3. Place streets and double row of cookies, then repeat

4. Make adjustments for resources and remaining areas

2. Start a row of lots along road

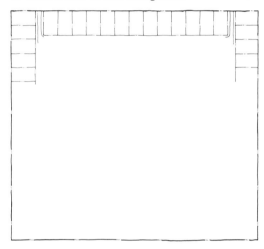

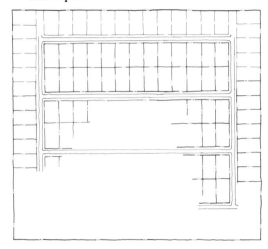

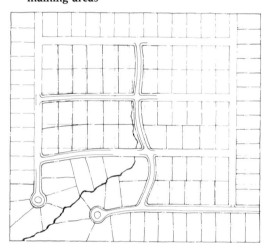

Conventional zoning regulations rigidly specify a minimum permitted lot size for each zoning district. Because almost any deviation from the specified minimum involves a reduction in density and therefore an economic penalty to the developer, minimum lot size requirements foster a recurring practice of laying out subdivisions with little or no attention to principles of good design. In order to maximize density, the developer designs (to use the term loosely) by laying out a row of minimum sized lots along one property line. The process is repeated and streets inserted until the site is filled. This technique ignores natural features of the land in single-minded pursuit of maximizing the number of lots in the development.

5. Rework design for greater efficiency

6. The final plan

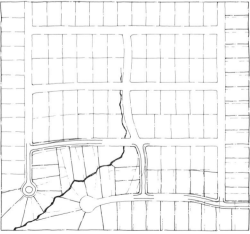

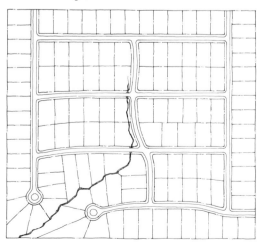

Good Design

Good design begins with an analysis of the natural and environmental assets and liabilities of a site. Variables such as topography, drainage, vegetation, views, amenities, and access should be considered. In the performance zoning approach, this analysis, rather than a fixed minimum lot size permitted virtually anywhere and everywhere on the site, should set the parameters of how and where development may be permitted.

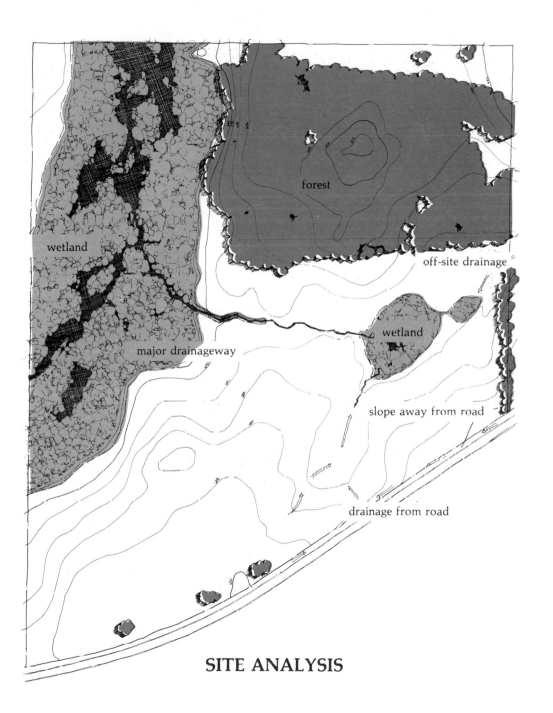

SITE ANALYSIS

Generally the designer begins by working with the site analysis to determine areas best suited to certain uses and to develop major circulation routes.

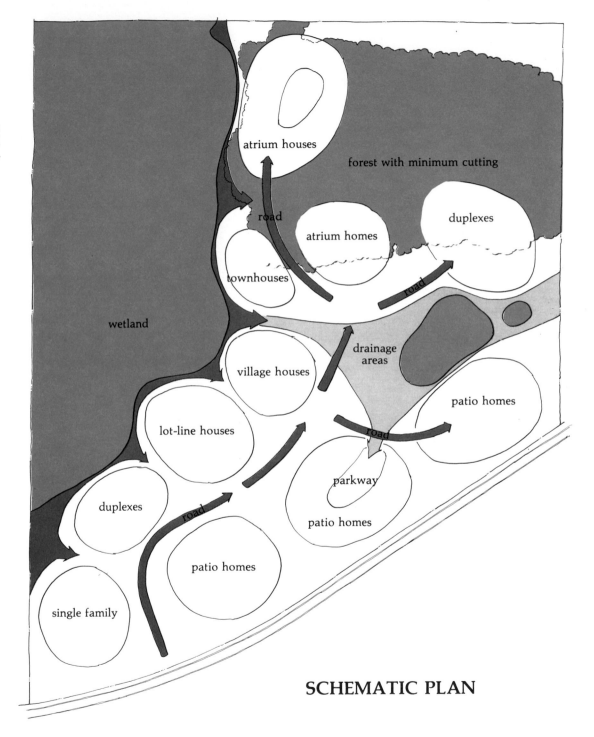

atrium houses

forest with minimum cutting

road

duplexes

atrium homes

townhouses

wetland

drainage areas

village houses

patio homes

road

lot-line houses

road

parkway

duplexes

patio homes

road

patio homes

single family

SCHEMATIC PLAN

Lastly, the designer refines the siting of individual land uses and minor roads. The result is a site plan that fits the site rather than fights it—still seeking to maximize profits (e.g., providing a mix of dwelling-unit types that results in much the same density as would have resulted from a cookie cutter approach).

FINAL PLAN

CONVENTIONAL ZONING

Conventional zoning often promotes bad design because of its rigidity. The standards it sets become the lowest common denominator, with mediocrity in design a predictable result. In order to maximize his profits under these standards, the designer is almost compelled to employ a cookie-cutter design, which gives to suburbia its "little boxes made of ticky-tacky." Conventional zoning also results in uneconomical layout and waste when a portion of a site does not conform to its inflexible standards. Finally, it encourages natural resources to be bulldozed, often literally, so that they may be converted into developable area.

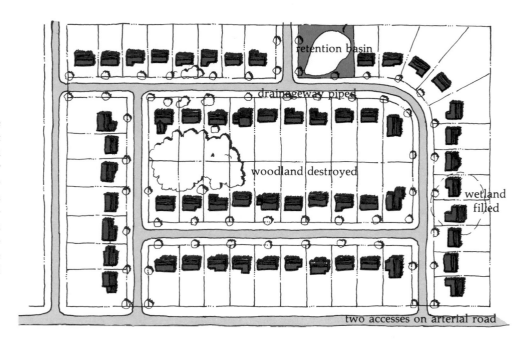

PERFORMANCE ZONING

Good design is predicated on freedom, flexibility, and creativity. Performance zoning was developed to permit the designer to implement these values. The increased flexibility of performance zoning enables the landowner to work with the constraints of the site and to buffer adjoining uses and roads; it provides a necessary protection for the welfare of the community without depriving the developer of a profitable return. The illustrations contrast the layout of a property under conventional and performance zoning.

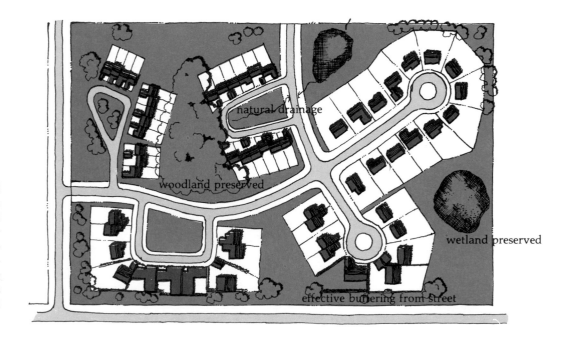

The Standards

The performance approach to zoning regulates development mainly on the basis of four variables: open space ratio, impervious surface ratio, density, and floor area ratio. The first two standards apply to all land uses, whereas density is applicable only to residential uses. For nonresidential uses, the floor area factor is utilized in place of density. This section illustrates the aspects of development which each of these standards controls. It demonstrates the advantages of using these standards to evaluate the performance of a development.

Open Space Ratio

TO CALCULATE, DIVIDE ACRES OF OPEN SPACE BY GROSS SITE AREA

$$\frac{6.8 \text{ Ac}}{20.5 \text{ Ac}} = .33$$

The open space ratio measures the proportion of a site, excluding land occupied by private lots or road rights-of-way, which remains undeveloped and is specifically designated as open space. It is intended to benefit the neighborhood or community as a whole in contrast to private open space, which is solely for the enjoyment of the individual lot owner. The purpose of open space is threefold: it protects natural resources or features, provides recreational area, and sets the character of an area.

The protection of the environment is an essential element of planning. The open space ratio enables performance zoning to protect sensitive natural areas. Conventional zoning has been unable to preserve open space, largely because its standards of minimum lot size are rigid and because its definition of open space includes private front, rear, and side yards. These intensively used areas, in the center of which homes are placed, cannot function to protect resources.

As population density increases, residents of a community require more, relatively large, land areas for recreation. Private yards do not suffice. A minimum open space ratio ensures adequate areas for play.

Lastly, open space is a measure of community character. The migration from city to suburb, from old suburb to new suburb, and from urban areas to rural areas stems at least in part from dissatisfaction with the prior community's character. Open space is a critical element of character, as anybody who has watched citizens protesting a zoning change can attest.

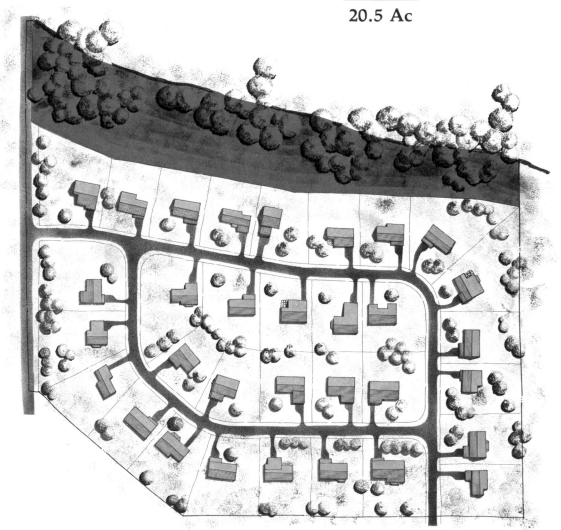

Impervious Surface Ratio

Impervious surface ratio, the second principal measure of land use intensity, is the proportion of a site occupied by impervious surfaces. These are surfaces which do not absorb rain and include all buildings, roads, sidewalks, patios, parking areas, and any area paved in concrete or asphalt. Conventional zoning ordinances have often used building coverage to limit the intensity of use, but this is a poor surrogate for impervious surface because it so frequently underestimates such coverage.

Impervious surfaces critically alter the natural environment. Besides the obvious increase in stormwater runoff, there are many other related adverse environmental impacts. The increase in runoff leads to flooding, declining stream flows during drought, and increased water pollution. In addition, extensive impervious surface coverage can disturb the water cycle by drastically reducing the same amount of rainfall available to recharge the aquifers which replenish water supplies. Impervious surfaces alter the microclimate of an area by increasing summer heat. In intense urban areas this heat buildup contributes to the temperature inversions which create hazardous health conditions.

TO CALCULATE, DIVIDE ACRES OF IMPERVIOUS SURFACE BY GROSS SITE AREA

$$\frac{5.4 \text{ Ac}}{20.5 \text{ Ac}} = .26$$

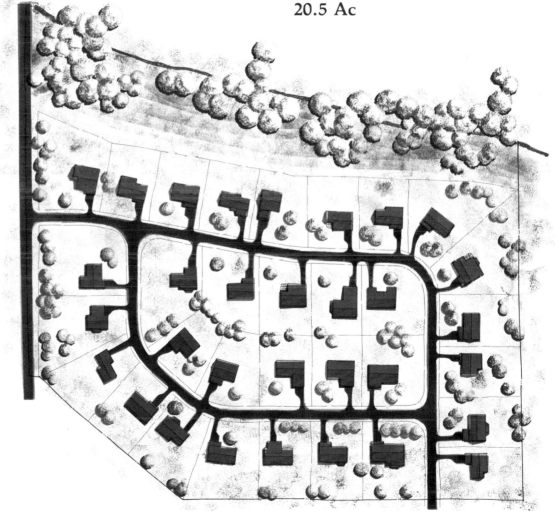

Density

Density is a measure of residential land use intensity which is expressed as the number of dwelling units per acre. In conventional zoning, density may not be explicitly stated as a standard, but it nevertheless is dictated by a minimum required lot size and other dimensional requirements. In performance zoning, density is explicitly stated as the number of dwelling units per acre. The ordinance uses the term "density factor," which is the measure of the number of dwelling units per acre of net buildable land, rather than "gross density," the number of dwelling units on the entire site, the measure with which planners are most familiar. The reason for this is that gross density cannot accommodate variations in the physical site. The density factor is a direct measure of the impact of a given development on road systems, community facilities, schools, and services.

TO CALCULATE, DIVIDE THE NUMBER OF DWELLING UNITS BY GROSS SITE AREA

$$\frac{32. \text{ du's}}{20.5 \text{ Ac}} = 1.56 \text{ du's/Ac}$$

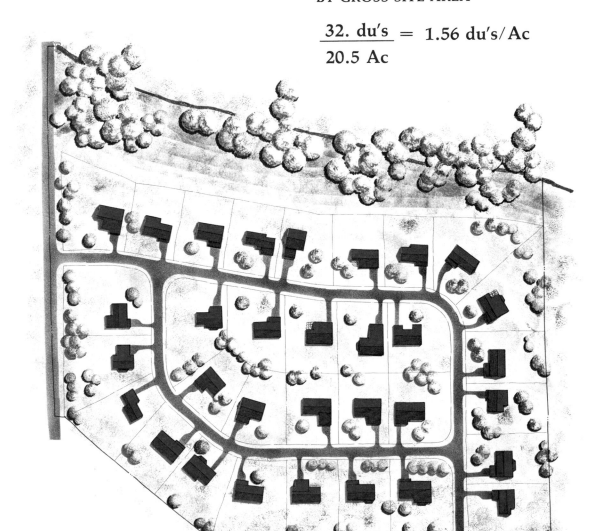

Floor Area Ratio

Floor area ratio is a nonresidential land use intensity measure analogous to density. It compares the floor area of a building with the total area of its site. Floor area is the sum of the areas of the several floors of the building or structure. The floor area ratio has been used in many conventional zoning ordinances. It is a useful indicator of the impacts of land use and one which provides the flexibility appropriate to the considerable diversity of nonresidential uses.

TO CALCULATE, DIVIDE THE AREA OF ALL FLOORS BY GROSS SITE AREA

$$\frac{24{,}000 \text{ sq. ft.}}{46{,}400 \text{ sq. ft.}} = .52$$

The following illustrations show the application of the standards to both conventional and performance zoning on the same site.

It is possible to develop an infinite variety of performance districts. The districts defined by conventional zoning ordinances can be translated into performance zoning districts. This will alter the manner in which a district is described but not the character or design of land developments built under performance zoning.

It is also possible go beyond the conventional and to rethink the use of land. A designer may be given more freedom to work with nature and to develop land plans that are outstanding living environments. In this instance the intent is to develop an environment that makes the most of its site.

Gross Density	1.91 du's/Ac
Open Space Ratio	.00
Impervious Surface Ratio	.20

CONVENTIONAL ZONING
15,000 sq. ft. lots

Gross Density	1.91 du's/Ac
Open Space Ratio	.40
Impervious Surface Ratio	.16

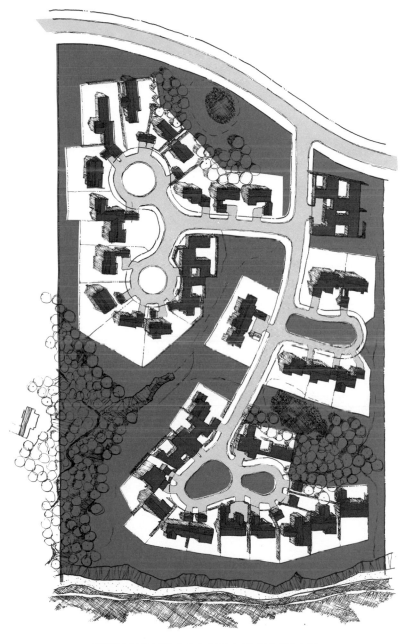

PERFORMANCE ZONING

Gross Density	3.53 du's/Ac
Open Space Ratio	.50
Impervious Surface Ratio	.15

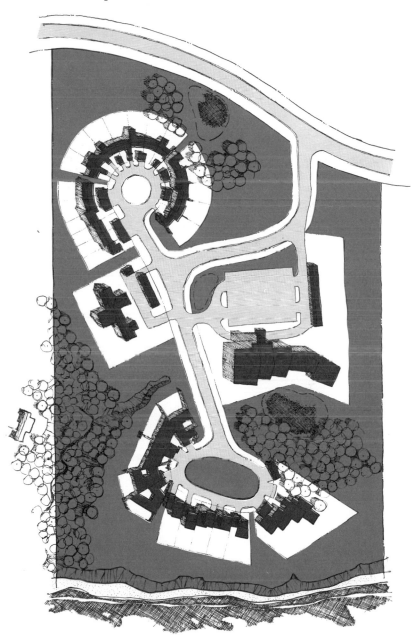

PERFORMANCE ZONING

Site Capacity and Land Use Intensity

Planners have always been concerned with the relationship between the carrying capacity of the land and the zoning regulations applicable to that land. Carrying capacity is an ecological term which defines the composition of a community of living things that can achieve a balance in a given environment. While balanced natural systems have considerable recuperative powers, upsetting them can have adverse effects on most of the system's species. For example, the desertification of North Africa is caused by human interference in the formerly natural balance and results in malnutrition and starvation for human populations.

This section reviews the ways in which the concept of carrying capacity can be applied to, and made an integral part of, zoning regulations. It suggests an alternative and more precise method of measuring land use intensity.

The site capacity calculation uses the open space ratio as a standard to insure protection of the natural environment in a dependable and consistent fashion. This performance approach differs from the conventional resort to "arm twisting" which has arisen because of lack of formal ordinance standards designed to meet this imperative.

Conventional Zoning—District Selection

In conventional zoning, the primary mechanism employed to protect the environment is large lot zoning. The theory of this approach is simply that the more resource limitations a site has, the relatively larger the lot requirement should be in order to reduce the damage done by roads, drives, buildings, and utilities. Conversely, denser zoning classes should be permitted where there are fewer environmental limitations. For many resources the protection provided is illusory.

Conventional zoning's reliance on lot size alone to protect the environment adequately is fraught with difficulties. The conventional approach does not work well, for example, with floodplains (restricted site illustration). Conventional zoning either prohibits development or allows filling, which destroys the floodplain. There is continual tension between the developers and a community's environmental concerns. Lot size is at best an indirect means of solving a problem which can be regulated much more directly and sensitively.

The conventional method has been ineffective in the past. With most resources, the developer will seek to encroach to the maximum extent possible in order to achieve maximum intensity. The performance approach takes a larger than lot-by-lot perspective in regulating environmental degradation. It strives to permit maximum development and and at the same time to protect resources by requiring a site capacity rather than a lot capacity analysis of developmental constraints. Unlike the conventional approach, performance zoning takes into account the fact that natural resources are often present only in scattered, small areas that can only be dealt with in conventional zoning by resorting to spot zoning.

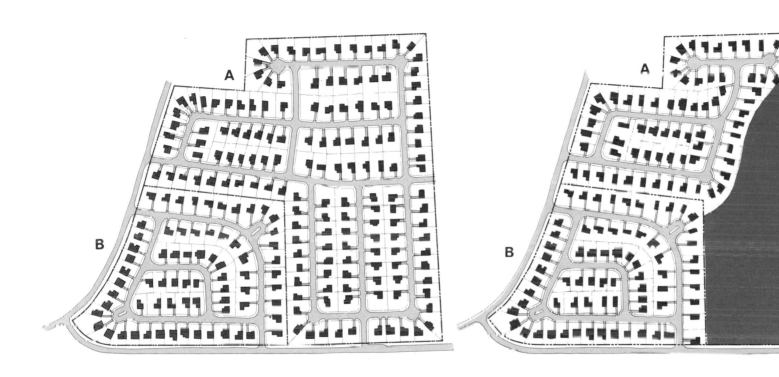

UNRESTRICTED SITE

Site A
Average Lot Size–11,138 sq. ft.
Gross Density–3.91 du's/Ac
Density Factor–3.91 du's/Ac

Site B
Average Lot Size–11,997 sq. ft.
Gross Density–3.91 du's/Ac
Density Factor–3.91 du's/Ac

RESTRICTED SITE

Site A
Average Lot Size–11,138 sq. ft.
Gross Density–1.64 du's/Ac
Density Factor–3.91 du's/Ac

Site B
Average Lot Size–11,997 sq. ft.
Gross Density–3.91 du's/Ac
Density Factor–3.91 du's/Ac

Density Zoning

Clustering, in various forms, has long been the preferred means of resource protection. In density zoning, both easily buildable and restricted properties are permitted equal gross densities (see illustration), provided that they are in the same zoning district. The resultant density factors (densities on the buildable land) can be quite different.

The system will always protect the resources. Density zoning is fairly workable, so long as the percentages of resource limitations in the sites of a district do not vary greatly. When the differences become large (as shown in the illustration), the impact on the adjoining land use is similar to granting a zoning change which might significantly increase the density of the buildable site. Note that the contrasts in lot size on the two illustrations are similar but reversed. Although the system does protect the environment, intense clustering often juxtaposes different densities, thereby decreasing protection of the neighbors. Another disadvantage is that the value of land is totally dependent on zoning, not on the suitability of the site.

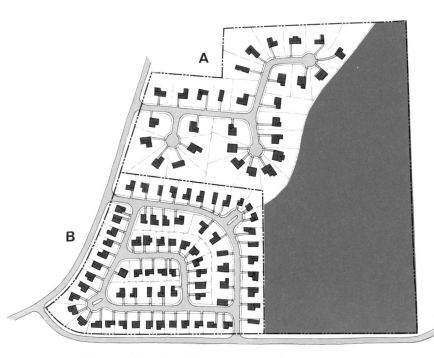

DIFFERENT ZONING

Site A
Average Lot Size–26,887 sq. ft.
Gross Density–.67 du's/Ac
Density Factor–1.66 du's/Ac

Site B
Average Lot Size–11,997 sq. ft.
Gross Density–3.91 du's/Ac
Density Factor–3.91 du's/Ac

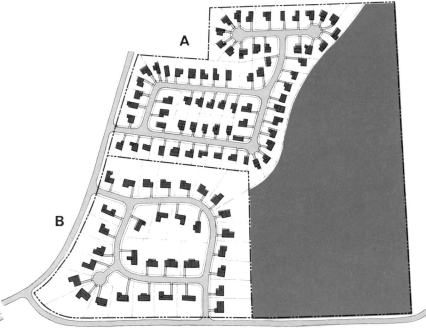

DENSITY ZONING

Site A
Average Lot Size–11,138 sq. ft.
Gross Density–1.64 du's/Ac
Density Factor–3.91 du's/Ac

Site B
Average Lot Size–26,244 sq. ft.
Gross Density–1.64 du's/Ac
Density Factor–1.64 du's/Ac

Performance Zoning

Performance zoning is based on the use of a density factor which applies only to buildable land. The intensity of use on any piece of buildable land within a zoning district is held constant, although the gross density may vary depending on the characteristics of the individual property.

Performance zoning protects the environment by specifying developmental limits on a resource-by-resource basis. For example, no disturbance of a very unstable or rare resource is permitted, whereas some level of disturbance of a less sensitive feature may be allowed. This approach avoids the device of numerous, small zoning districts to provide different levels of resource protection. By setting a maximum use intensity (density factor) on the buildable portion of a site, this approach ameliorates conflict between that portion of the site and less intensely developed neighboring property. It is a rational system in which value relates to the physical characteristics of the site, not just to a page in the zoning ordinance.

On the following pages, the five steps in the site capacity calculation will be illustrated.

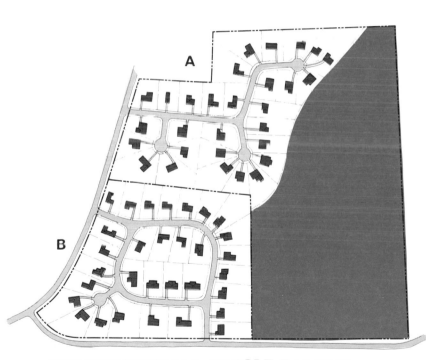

CONVENTIONAL SINGLE FAMILY

Site A
Avg. Lot Size—26,887
Gross Density—.67 du's/Ac
Density Factor—1.66 du's/Ac

Site B
Average Lot Size—27,100
Gross Density—1.66 du's/Ac
Density Factor—1.66 du's/Ac

PERFORMANCE ZONING

Site A
Gross Density–1.35 du's/Ac
Density Factor–3.36 du's/Ac
Open/Space Ratio–.6

Site B
Gross Density–2.36 du's/Ac
Density Factor–3.36 du's/Ac
Open Space Ratio–.30

Site Capacity Calculation

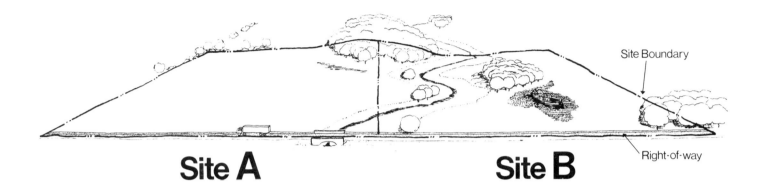

Site A   **Site B**

Site Boundary

Right-of-way

1. Base Site Area

Certain portions of tracts may not be usable for the activities proposed for the site. These are subtracted from the site area to determine base site area.

		SITE A	SITE B
Take:	Gross site area	20.6 acres	20.6 acres
Subtract:	Land within ultimate right-of-way or easements	−.6	−.6
Subtract:	Land for bufferyard area	−.84	−.84
Equals:	Base site area...................	19.16 acres	19.16 acres

NOTE: The illustrations assume that the developer elected to provide the ten foot wide bufferyard from among the options available for the required B bufferyard.

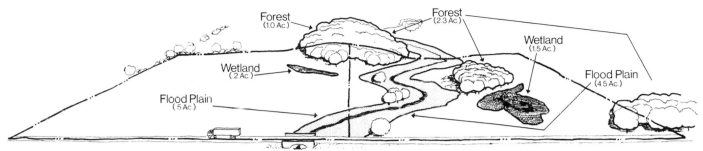

Forest
(1.0 Ac.)

Forest
(2.3 Ac.)

Wetland
(1.5 Ac.)

Wetland
(.2 Ac.)

Flood Plain
(4.5 Ac.)

Flood Plain
(.5 Ac.)

Site A Site B

2. Resource Protection Land

All land within the base site area shall be mapped and measured for the purpose of determining the amount of open space needed to protect it.

Resource	Open Space Ratio	SITE A		SITE B	
		Acres of Land in Resource	Resource Protection Land (Acres in Resource × Open Space Ratio)	Acres of Land in Resource	Resource Protection Land (Acres in Resource × Open Space Ratio)
Floodplains	1.00	.5	.5	4.5	4.5
Wetlands	1.00	.2	.2	1.5	1.5
Natural retention area	.90				
Steep slope (25% or more)	.85				
Forest	.80	1.0	.8	2.3	1.84
Pond shore	.80				
Lake shore	.70				
Steep slope (15–25%)	.70				
Steep slope (8–15%)	.60				
Total Land with Resource Restrictions		1.7		8.3	
Total Resource Protection Land			1.5		7.84

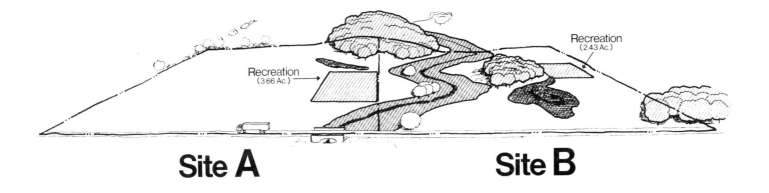

Recreation
(3.66 Ac.)

Recreation
(2.43 Ac.)

Site A

Site B

3. Recreation Land

While some of the open space required by the zoning district may serve as resource protection land, the specific intent of this section is to provide for usable public or common open space as near to each unit as possible. Thus, there is a need for guidelines to insure that a minimum amount of land is provided for this purpose. Therefore:

		SITE A	SITE B
Take:	Base site area	19.16	19.16
Subtract:	Total land with resource restriction	−1.7	8.3
Equals:	Total unrestricted land	17.46	10.86
Multiply:	Total unrestricted land by recreation factor ×	.10	.10
Total recreation land equals.		1.75 acres	1.03 acres

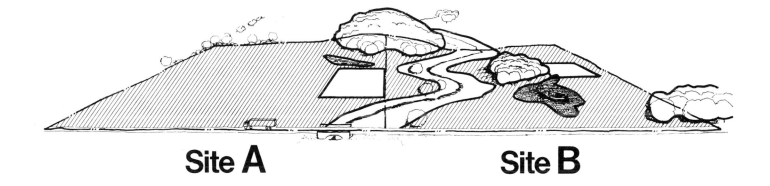

Site **A** Site **B**

4. Determination of Site Capacity

Individual site capacity is found by calculating net buildable site area. For residential uses, the maximum number of permitted dwelling units is determined by multiplying net density by net buildable site area. The calculations for the illustrated sites are as follows:

		SITE A	SITE B
Take:	Total resource protection land	1.5	7.84
Add:	Total recreation land remaining to be provided	1.75	1.09
Equals	Total open space	3.25	8.93
Take:	Base site area	19.16	19.16
Multiply by:	Open district space ratio*	.35	.35
Equals:	Minimum required open space	6.71	6.71
Take:	Base site area	19.16	19.16
Subtract:	Total open space or minimum required open space, whichever is greater	6.71	8.93
Equals:	Net buildable site area	12.45 acres	10.23 acres

*Each zoning district has minimum open space requirements as described in its zoning regulations. In this example, it is 40 percent (.4).

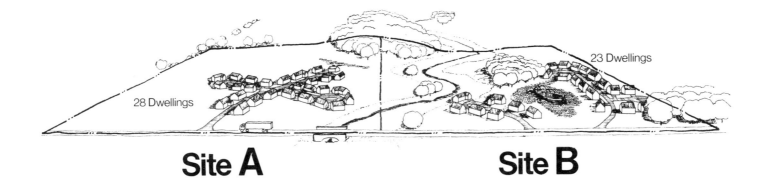

28 Dwellings

23 Dwellings

Site A   Site B

5. Determination of Number of Dwelling Units

		SITE A	SITE B
Take:	Net buildable site area	12.46	10.23
Multiply by:	District maximum density factor	2.25	2.25
Equals:	Number of permitted dwelling units (do not round up)	28.0 du	23.0 du

Rational Land Valuation

In a free market economy the buyer will pay most for that product which, all other things being equal, provides the greatest return. Thus, a farmer seeking a new farm evaluates the soils to determine the land's productivity. The example below compares two 100-acre farms.

Farms A and B are both 100-acre properties. Farm A has good soils and may be expected to yield 9,710 bushels of corn. Farm B has areas of untillable land, and its soils are generally less productive. It would yield only 6,890 bushels of corn.

If a fifty cent profit per bushel is the farmer's estimated return, Farm A will earn $4,855 and Farm B $3,445. Using a very simplistic calculation, this means that an acre of A and B would yield $48.55 and $34.45 per year, respectively. Based on this land valuation system, the farmer should pay more for the more productive farm (A); however, neither conventional zoning nor density zoning results in such a rational system of land valuation. In each, land value is essentially established by turning to the page in the zoning ordinance which indicates the permitted density: the higher the developmental intensity permitted on a parcel, the greater its price in the market place, regardless of the use to which the buyer intends to put the property. Accordingly, both conventional and density zoning discourage distinctions among sites based on their buildability. Performance zoning, through the site capacity calculation, diminishes the intensity permitted on a site having constraints which render some of it unbuildable. To this extent, the calculation operates to deflate price in a rational manner related to site capacity. Thus, a developer would look critically at the land rather than at the zoning book before determining what he can pay for the property, just as the farmer does.

Bufferyards

Noted architect Frank Lloyd Wright succinctly captured the essence of the bufferyard concept when he observed that "greenery hides a multitude of sins." A bufferyard is an area of plantings surrounding a land use which screens or blocks vision, noise pollutants, or other negative by-products associated with that use. In the case of very intense uses abutting considerably less intense ones, structural components such as fences or berms may be required of a bufferyard.

Because of the bufferyard requirement, performance zoning is able to accommodate the values of both the developer and the adjacent landowner. The developer has considerable flexibility to build at very different land use intensities on any particular site, but all neighbors to the development are protected—literally "buffered"—from the consequences of the more intense use "next door."

Purpose

It is obvious that bufferyards provide visual barriers which block out the glare of lights, signs, and other visual nuisances. In addition, planted buffers function in two ways to block noise. Distance and plant material reduce the intensity of noise, and wooded areas introduce the background sounds of trees, wind, and birds. While these background noises do not actually reduce noise, they make it less noticeable and therefore less annoying. Buffers also shield the source of the noise from view, which tends to distract attention from the nuisance and thereby minimizes its perceived impact. They may also serve as a protective or safety barrier, insofar as they block physical passage. Finally, relatively heavily planted buffers reduce air pollution, dust, dirt, and litter. Greenery in urban areas may make important contributions to better air and aid improvements of water quality.

ACCESS

NOISE

LIGHT & GLARE

AIR POLLUTION

Flexibility

The bufferyard must be flexible. A single standard for all uses or even for any given pair of uses can both impose unnecessary hardship on the developer of a particular parcel and also lead to monotony. Within each class of bufferyard, a developer may choose from several options. Because different land values and plant material costs are introduced, the developer is given flexibility to make cost tradeoffs in deciding which option to select. Depending on the size of the parcel, this flexibility may become extremely relevant. As shown in the accompanying illustration, even a narrow bufferyard can impose a considerable developmental constraint on a small site. On a large parcel, however, the developer will lose little buildable land.

50 ft.

CONSTANT BUFFERYARD

38% buildable   69% buildable

89% buildable

MAJOR DIFFERENCE–LARGE BUFFER

SMALL DIFFERENCE–SMALL BUFFER

Variables

There are four basic variables in the bufferyard design: distance, plant material, plant density, and land forms. A combination of all these factors was used to develop each bufferyard required by the ordinance and, because each element performs a different function, a different combination of elements is specified for different juxtapositions of uses. For example, far more and denser planting is required between a residential use and an industrial use than between a residential and small office use. In the case of an extreme disparity between adjacent land uses, structural bufferyard elements such as walls or berms may be required.

DISTANCE

PLANT MATERIAL

PLANT INTENSITY

LAND FORMS

Hierarchy

Zoning has historically arranged uses in a hierarchy. While there may be no consensus about where in the hierarchy a given use falls, there is considerable agreement about the nature of the highest or best and the lowest or worst uses.

A hierarchy of uses is essential in order to evaluate the impact of the lower of two neighboring uses on the higher one. Obviously, the severest problems or nuisances result when the uses are at opposite ends of the hierarchy. Thus, performance zoning specifies the bufferyard required between two uses only after having classified the uses hierarchically. The greater the distance between uses on this scale, the larger and more densely planted the buffer must be.

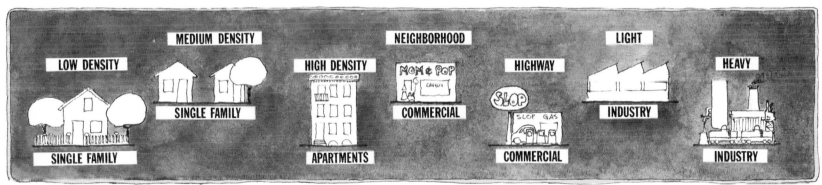

HIGHEST
BEST

LOWEST
WORST

Determination of Buffer

The following procedure must be followed in order for a developer to know what bufferyard will be required at all perimeters of a site:

1. All adjoining uses must be identified. This information should be recorded on the site plan.

2. The land use intensity class of each adjoining use must be identified. The table of land use intensity classification performance standards (Section 4602 of the model ordinance) must be consulted for this determination. Part of this table (for commercial and residential uses) is shown.

3. The proposed use and its land use intensity must be determined. The table of required bufferyards must then be consulted to determine the letter designation of the bufferyard required between the proposed use.

4. The bufferyard to be used is selected from at least three alternatives. The landowner chooses the option whose mix of plant material, distance, and structures best meets the requirements of the site.

1.

ADJACENT EXISTING CLASS II USE

20' H Bufferyard

ADJACENT VACANT LAND

15' Bufferyard G

PROPOSED CLASS VI USE

15' Bufferyard G

ADJACENT VACANT LAND

NO BUFFERYARD REQUIRED

ADJACENT EXISTING CLASS V USE

10' Bufferyard C

ADJACENT EXISTING CLASS VIII USE

10' Bufferyard E

ADJACENT COLLECTOR STREET RIGHT-OF-WAY

3.

Proposed Land Use Class

	I	II	III	IV	V	VI	VII	VIII	IX	X
I	none	Ag	Ag	Ag	Ag	Ag	none	none	none	none
II	Ag	B	C	D	D	E	G	H	I	J
III	Ag	C	B	D	D	E	G	H	I	J
IV	Ag	D	C	B	D	E	G	H	I	J
V	Ag	D	D	D	none	none	C	D	E	E
VI	Ag	E	E	E	none	none	none	C	D	D
VII	none	G	G	G	C	none	none	none	C	C
VIII	none	H	H	H	D	C	none	none	none	B

--Adjacent existing Land Use Class--

4.

REQUIRED PLANT UNITS / 100'

4 Canopy Trees

6 Understory Trees

24 Shrubs

12 Evergreens/Conifers

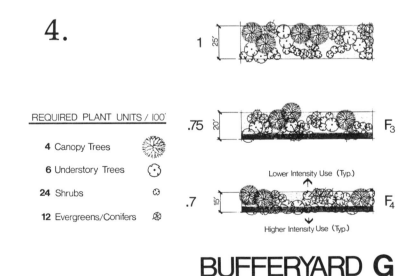

1 — 25'

.75 — 20' — F₃

Lower Intensity Use (Typ.)

.7 — 15' — F₄

Higher Intensity Use (Typ.)

BUFFERYARD G

Housing

In a conventional zoning ordinance, varying sizes or types of housing are permitted only in different zoning districts, unless the developer makes the unlikely choice of developing at a lesser intensity than permitted. Faced with a fluctuating housing market, the developer is forced to seek a zoning change in order to take advantage of economic shifts. Any such amendment entails considerable problems and costs.

A lot of a given size can produce a totally different environment as the size and scale of units placed on it change over time. Lots that in 1950 looked spacious with homes of 1,100 square feet appear congested in 1979 with homes of 2,401 square feet.

Performance zoning seeks to solve both of these problems. Its keys are that all housing types are permitted in each zoning district and that there are performance criteria for each type of dwelling unit.

Single-Family Detached

This is the housing type to which most Americans aspire. Its principal feature is that the house is roughly centered on the lot and has large front and rear yards and narrow side yards. The large yards make it especially attractive to families with children.

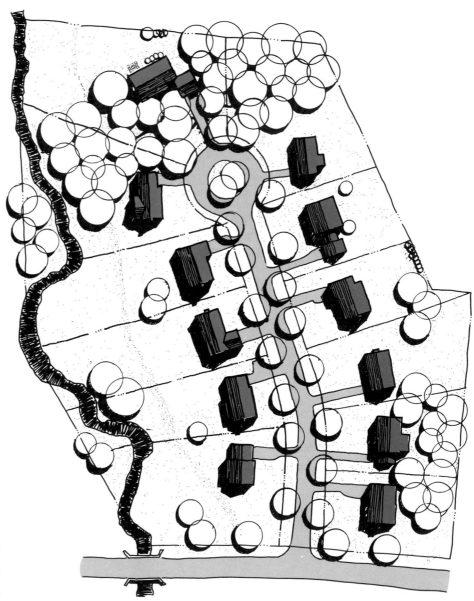

DENSITY	1.55
OPEN SPACE RATIO	.00
IMPERVIOUS SURFACE RATIO	.16

Lot-Line House

The lot-line house is a single-family detached unit which, instead of being centered on the lot, is placed against one of the side lot lines. This makes the side yard usable and requires less land than a house centered on its lot. The front yard, which is seldom used, may be substantially reduced.

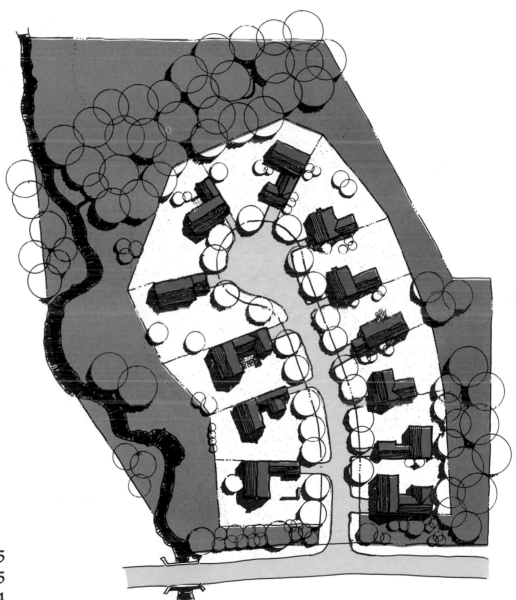

DENSITY   1.55
OPEN SPACE RATIO   .55
IMPERVIOUS SURFACE RATIO   .14

Village House

There are numerous old single-family detached houses built on very small lots in the historic towns and villages New England and areas such as Bucks County, Pennsylvania. The village house is a modern descendant of these units. It is placed close to the street to maximize the rear yard; alleys are encouraged to reduce the visual impact of the auto on streets. The result is a lot which is smaller than that of the lot-line house. Specific architectural or landscape standards are required for the street yard(s) of the house. Research on historical houses of this type indicates that landscape features provide the charm, scale, and privacy that permits their location close to the street.

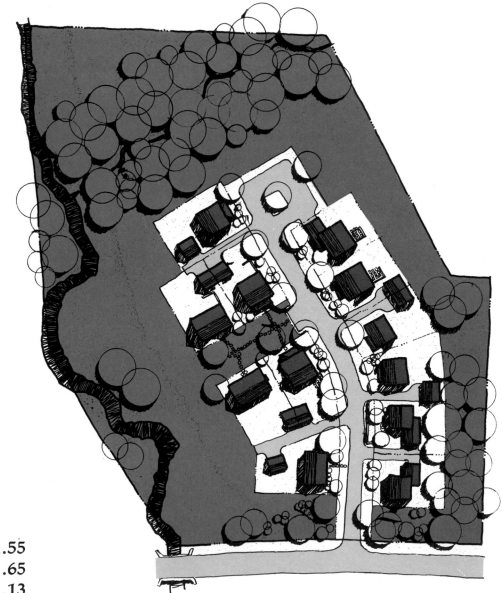

DENSITY	1.55
OPEN SPACE RATIO	.65
IMPERVIOUS SURFACE RATIO	.13

Twin House

The twin house is a semi-detached, single-family house, which is connected along a common party wall to a similar unit. Each structure has only two dwellings. Space is saved by eliminating two side yards.

DENSITY   1.55
OPEN SPACE RATIO   .72
IMPERVIOUS SURFACE RATIO   .13

Patio House

The patio house is a single-family detached or semi-detached unit. It is built on a small lot enclosed by walls which provide privacy. If the walls are ignored, its layout may be similar to either the lot-line or twin house; thus, it may be built either as a detached or semi-detached dwelling. The patio house appeals to those who want privacy without the maintenance of a larger yard.

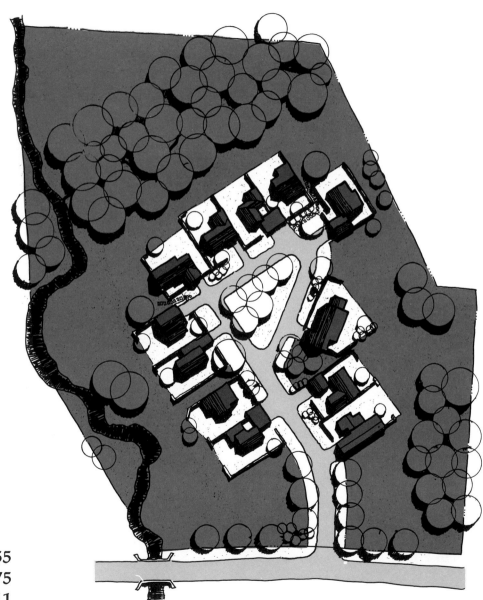

DENSITY   1.55
OPEN SPACE RATIO   .75
IMPERVIOUS SURFACE RATIO   .11

Atrium House

The atrium house is similar to, though distinct from, the patio house. It differs from the patio house in three respects: it has a smaller lot and yard, it is an attached unit, and it is a single-story unit. A small private yard is surrounded by the house and its walls; privacy is guaranteed. It appeals to persons without children who want privacy and do not want a maintenance responsibility. It is ideal for the elderly, because it is a single-story home with minimal exterior maintenance responsibilities.

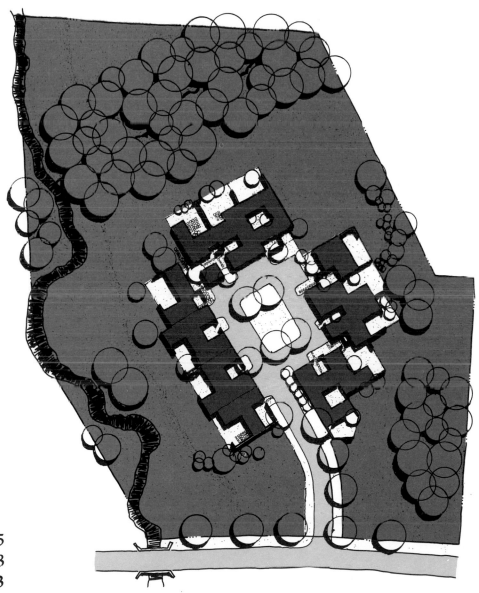

DENSITY	1.55
OPEN SPACE RATIO	.78
IMPERVIOUS SURFACE RATIO	.13

Weak-Link Town House

This single-family attached dwelling is a variation of the town house. It is distinguished by the fact that each unit has both a one-story and a two-story portion. The units are wider than conventional town houses and are on larger lots. They present a facade resembling single-family detached homes and therefore provide a greater sense of the individual unit identity.

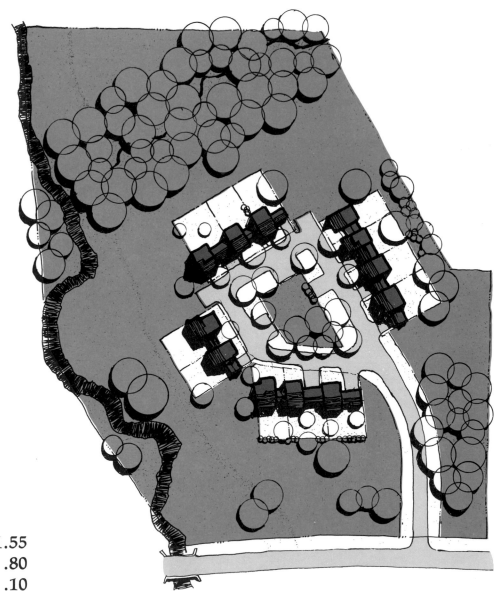

DENSITY	1.55
OPEN SPACE RATIO	.80
IMPERVIOUS SURFACE RATIO	.10

Town House

The town house is a form of single-family attached dwelling in which units share common side walls and are often designed in rows (although good design attempts to deemphasize the "lined up" appearance). Yard areas are small, and privacy requires careful protection.

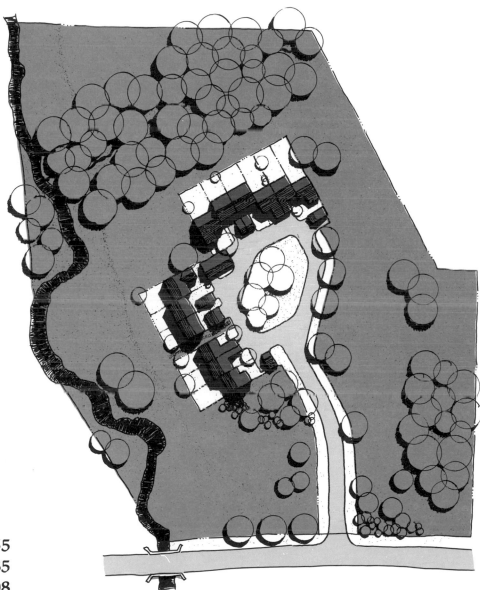

DENSITY	1.55
OPEN SPACE RATIO	.85
IMPERVIOUS SURFACE RATIO	.08

Multiplex

The multiplex is either a single-family attached unit or a multi-family unit. There are a variety of configurations: attached as a row, attached back to back with each unit the corner of a square, or with some units on the first floor and others on the second. Dwelling units may have individual or shared outside access. Small patios or balconies provide outdoor living space. A well-designed multiplex may look like a large, single-family detached unit. Multiplexes can provide either individual unit ownership or rental units.

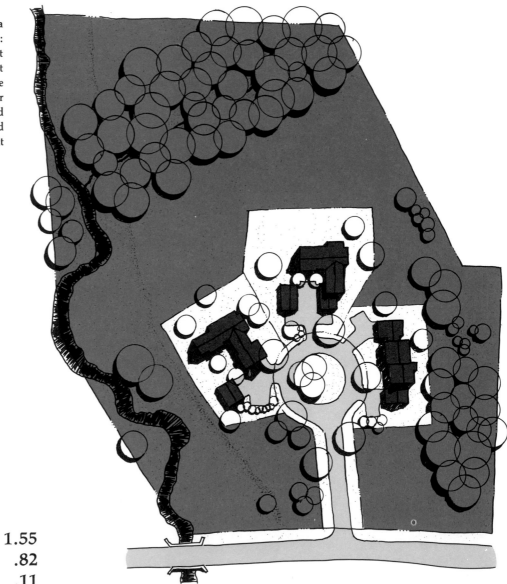

DENSITY   1.55
OPEN SPACE RATIO   .82
IMPERVIOUS SURFACE RATIO   .11

Apartments

Apartments are multi-family housing. Dwelling units share a common outside access. Ownership is not a factor in this type of unit, which may be either rental or condominium. Apartments appeal to single individuals and families without children.

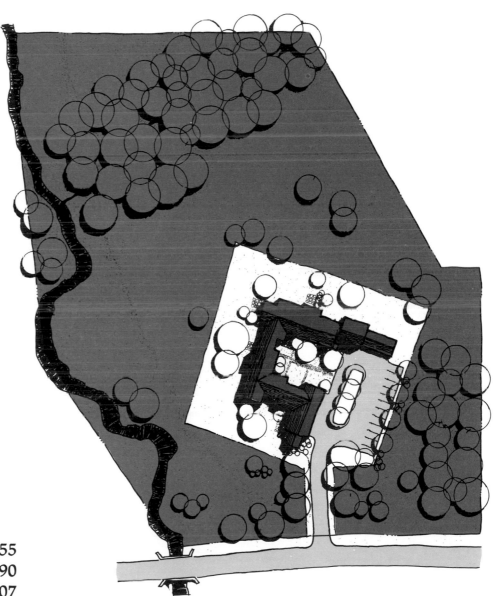

DENSITY	1.55
OPEN SPACE RATIO	.90
IMPERVIOUS SURFACE RATIO	.07

Housing Cost

It is obvious that by permitting and encouraging all types of housing units, performance zoning provides more flexibility for the private market to provide housing for the broadest sector of the market. A significant cost reduction as compared to conventional zoning is the elimination of the necessity for zoning changes to permit such a developmental mix. In many suburban communities the zoning change or annexation process may last a year. The costs are unnecessary; they do not provide a better lot or larger house. Any such costs make attached housing types less competitive.

A second problem is the relationship of lot size and dwelling unit. When zoning was introduced in many suburban communities, homes were often scaled to fit on the respective lot sizes while the lots had some spaciousness. Rising expectations as to the number of required rooms and size of a home have increased housing sizes, and inflation has forced many to opt for smaller lots. The result is developments that seem crowded and congested. In addition, lower cost housing has been forced out of the market place.

Homes on 70 foot lot 1950

Homes on 70 foot lot 1978

Variable Lots

Performance zoning specifies floor area ratio and maximum on-lot impervious surface standards for each type of dwelling unit. This means that larger dwellings require larger lots. The system thus maintains scale by automatically adjusting site size to building bulk. It also acts as a pricing mechanism, since density and therefore land costs are altered as the dwelling size increases. This is an incentive to maintain a broader market for homes.

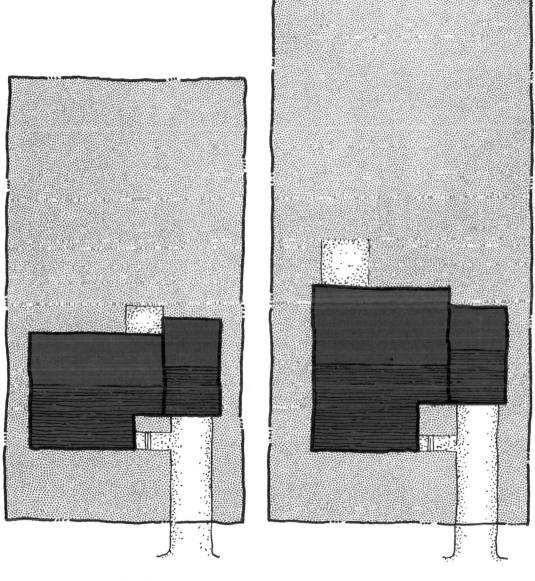

1800 sq. ft. house   2400 sq. ft. house

Scale of Development

In conventional zoning, large scale projects of a single housing type have been encouraged because they involve the rezoning of large parcels of land. Performance zoning encourages a smaller scale mix of land uses which reduces land use conflicts and deemphasizes the project character of the development. A 100-acre apartment project is suburbia's equivalent to Pruitt-Igoe and breeds resistance to further rezonings.

Transportation

A major concern of citizens is the elimination of traffic congestion. Busy roads attract certain land uses and by doing so increase the problem of congestion. Conventional zoning has not solved this problem. Performance zoning attempts to control development in a way that prevents increased traffic congestion. A related transportation concern is the cost of required roadway improvements, both to the homeowner and to the environment. The performance approach provides a comprehensive basis for insuring the functioning of road systems at acceptable levels and for a sharing of the costs of roadway improvements by the private sector whenever it proposes a development which causes a significant impact on the roadway system.

The transportation section of the ordinance also imposes street width standards which vary depending on the type of street involved and the intensity of use located on the street. This approach works to the mutual advantage of the developer and the public in general. It insures adequate road width for safe vehicular movement and on-street parking, yet does not demand excessive and costly width for roads which have low traffic volume or which serve uses not requiring on-street parking.

Road Classification System

In performance zoning, a roadway classification system is developed based on the ultimate function of a road, regardless of its present traffic volumes. The classification system has four major components: freeways, arterial roads, collector roads, and residential streets.

Expressways are roads intended to serve interstate or high speed, high volume urban traffic. They bypass urban centers or lead to urban cores. Access to expressways is limited to other expressways and arterial roads. Arterials are roads of regional importance or the main roads of a community. Access to arterial roads is limited solely to regionally significant land uses and collector roads. Collectors are minor roads that provide access to nonresidential land uses and connect residential streets to the system's arterial roads. Access to collector roads is forbidden to individual residential uses in order to prevent congestion. Residential streets provide access to individual residential properties.

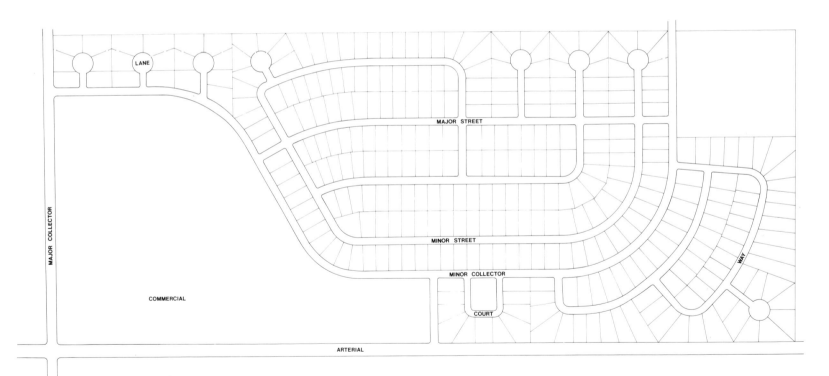

Arterial Streets

The arterial road network of an area is determined when the rural road system is initially established. Lake County, the area for which the model ordinance was developed, is a typical example. Despite a population increase from 120,000 to 430,000 between 1940 and 1978, the arterial network has barely changed: only sixty miles of roadway have been added to the initial system. Given this record of limited new construction, the protection of the existing road network is essential. Therefore, control over access to these roads and provisions for upgrading and widening them are made a developmental constraint or requirement.

The historically limited improvement of these thoroughfares has rendered the capacity of the arterial road network to support development very small. Studies in Lake County reveal that even in rural areas the capacities of the arterial network allow densities of no more than two dwelling units per acre. Thus, it is not surprising that the rural roads of two or three decades ago have become today's urban arterials with traffic volumes in excess of 20,000 cars per day.

A problem with the classification system used by planners and engineers to determine road type is that it is based on existing traffic volumes. Thus, roads are not classified as arterials, which should have limited access, until traffic volumes are high enough for congestion to be present. Once a pattern of free access is established, the community's only recourse is to build a bypass. Planners have long recognized that controlling access to such roads can ameliorate problems of congestion and limited capacity. Performance zoning preclassifies roads and controls access to arterial roads. This permits higher speeds and fewer turning movements, which lessens the probability of accidents.

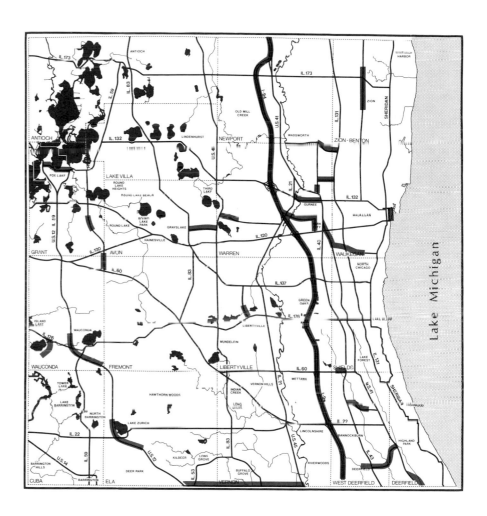

LAKE COUNTY–NEW ROADS, 1939–1979

A problem with the classification system used by planners and engineers to determine road type is that it is based on existing traffic volumes. Thus, roads are not classified as arterials, which should have limited access, until traffic volumes are high enough for congestion to be present. Once a pattern of free access is established, the community's only recourse is to bypass. Planners have long recognized that controlling access to such roads can ameliorate problems of congestion and limited capacity. Performance zoning preclassifies roads and controls access to arterial roads. This permits higher speeds and fewer turning movements, which lessens the probability of accidents.

The performance approach to transportation problems may require private developers to assume the responsibility of providing some of the roadway improvements necessitated by a development. Smaller uses need only provide deceleration lanes at their entrance and collector roads to adjoining properties. Land uses which by virtue of their scale and traffic-generating rates will lead to congestion in other superblocks must make improvements beyond their boundaries.

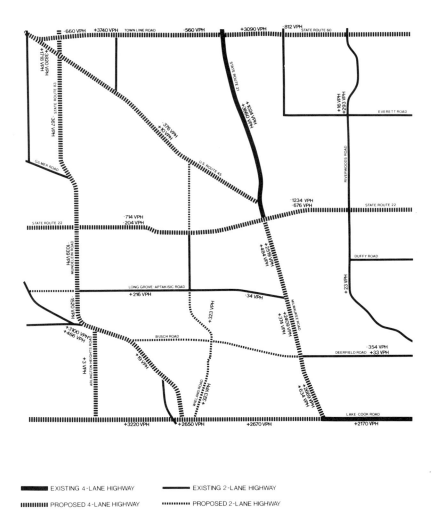

▬▬▬ EXISTING 4-LANE HIGHWAY	——— EXISTING 2-LANE HIGHWAY	
‖‖‖‖‖‖ PROPOSED 4-LANE HIGHWAY	•••••••• PROPOSED 2-LANE HIGHWAY	

Note: Where two capacities occur the more limiting one is based on intersection capacity.

VERNON TOWNSHIP–ROAD CAPACITY

Residential Streets

Residential streets provide direct vehicular access to individual dwelling units and accommodate the overflow parking needs which individual lots cannot.

Too large a roadway is environmentally undesirable. The large impervious areas increase stormwater runoff and thereby prompt flooding. The washoff from streets pollutes streams and lakes. The same surfaces store heat. The microclimate is altered, becoming hotter and dryer. Such alterations make city living less comfortable than rural living. Excessively wide roads and easements also require unnecessary destruction of the environment. Forested areas are especially sensitive to such destruction.

In addition to the general negative consequences of excessively wide roads, oversized residential streets cause particular problems. First, they add to the cost of a house without providing more living space. Wider roads also encourage higher speeds. This threatens the safety of children and pedestrians in a residential area.

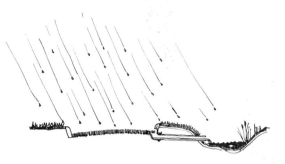

Storm Water Run-off

Micro Climate

Safety

Environment

Factors Affecting Street Width

Because of the aforementioned concerns, an attempt to minimize residential street widths was part of performance zoning. The residential street standards imposed by the model ordinance are specified for five different levels or types of residential roads. These are distinguished on the basis of the number of dwelling units served by each and their respective traffic volumes. More specifically, residential street width is affected by four variables:

Traffic volume (the number of vehicles which travel a street per day). The fewer the vehicles, the narrower the road may be. Fewer cars meet or pass each other.

Design speed (the speed for which a road is designed). At slower speeds, drivers have more time to react to traffic situations and can therefore more easily avoid collisions. Accidents at low speeds are less damaging. Thus, roads may be narrower as design speeds decline.

Parking. When a residential street is to serve the overflow of off-street parking areas, at least one extra lane of roadway width is required. Whether a street will be used to provide parking is a function of the residential density and the extent of off-street parking provided.

Lot width. Lot width affects the need for on-street parking: lots which are wide and large require less on-street parking.

These variables form the basis for developing variable street width standards. Where meetings of two vehicles or types of vehicles are infrequent, a single paved lane with improved shoulders may be adequate. As volume and design speed increase, more lanes must be added. Similarly, as lot width decreases, more parking on streets occurs; this necessitates the addition of two parking lanes.

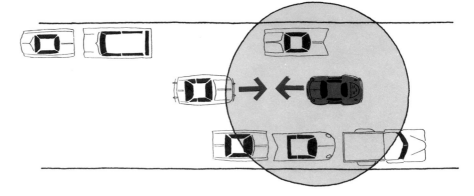

Meeting on single lane

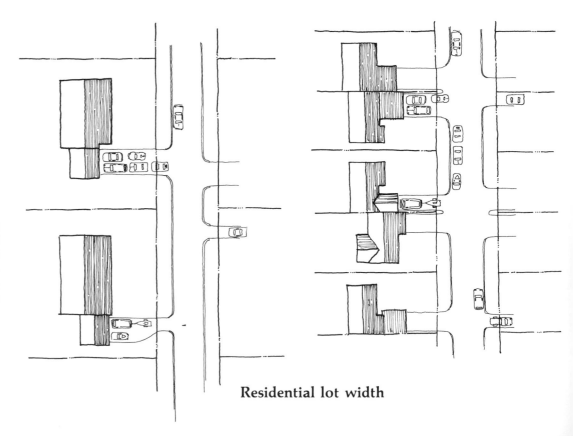

Residential lot width

32 foot cartway   20 foot cartway

Both conventional and performance zoning street standards yield streets
which adequately accommodate the traffic, but the characters of the two
streets are much different. The conventional approach demonstrates the
application of an undiscriminating "city" standard to suburban conditions.
With performance zoning, the streets are adequate, not overbuilt, and both
environmentally and aesthetically more desirable.

Performance Standards for Streets

The following illustrations show the variable road width standards for
residential streets. The standards provide adequate safety without creating
a city environment in the suburbs.

STREET TYPE number of du's design speed	TWO WAY WITHOUT CURBS 60 feet R/W unless otherwise specified				
	LANE < 7 10 mph	**COURT** 7–14 10 mph	**WAY** 15–30 15 mph	**MINOR STREET** 31–115 20 mph	**MAJOR STREET** 116–160 25 mph
street frontage abutting lots 120 ft or more	40 ft R/W 10 ft	40 ft R/W 13 ft	40 ft R/W 15 ft	44 ft R/W 17 ft	 19 ft
90–119 feet	14 ft	17 ft	19 ft	21 ft	23 ft
60–89 feet	17 ft	20 ft	22 ft	24 ft	26 ft
less than 60 feet	23 ft	26 ft	30 ft	32 ft	34 ft
no lots taking direct access	10/17 ft*	13/18 ft*	15/18 ft*	17/21 ft*	20/22 ft*

*The second number is the required width for the forty feet of these roads from where they intersect with a higher order road.

Putting It All Together

Having discussed a number of problems addressed by performance zoning which the conventional approach has ignored, or which the two systems approach very differently, we now provide several illustrations of new developments that may result within the performance framework. The illustrations are intended to represent a wide range of possibilities spanning rural to highly urban situations.

Zoning Districts

The following sections describe the zoning districts which are proposed by the model ordinance. These districts are significantly fewer than in the typical conventional ordinance. They are separately defined along functional lines; generally, each accommodates many more uses than the traditional zoning district. As described elsewhere, traditionally zoning districts tend to proliferate—many small towns have in excess of twenty districts—and there appears to be no logical functional distinction among them.

Because performance zoning's districts are designed very carefully on the basis of use distinctions, geographical considerations, and community fiscal and planning policy, they must be mapped with special care. Thereafter, there should be minimal rezoning, because the initial zoning will have already been designed to accommodate all development for the long range (approximately twenty-five years) at locationally appropriate sites.

Wilderness District

A wilderness area is an extreme example of a functionally distinct zoning district. It is obviously not a district required by all jurisdictions. The wilderness district is intended to maintain the land within its boundaries in a very pristine state in order to preserve plant and animal species which deserve special attention or which are valuable to the area. Consistent with the purpose for this district, it is required to be kept in open space except for 2 percent of its area, which may be used to accommodate development (structures) consistent with wilderness conservation. The district must be mapped to include all areas requiring such protection.

The accompanying illustration shows a wilderness district in which residential development is permitted only at the most minimal density: the open space ratio is .98. This protects the wilderness, yet allows the owner to receive a return on his investment. Note that all development is concentrated near the road, thus maintaining the wilderness character of the land.

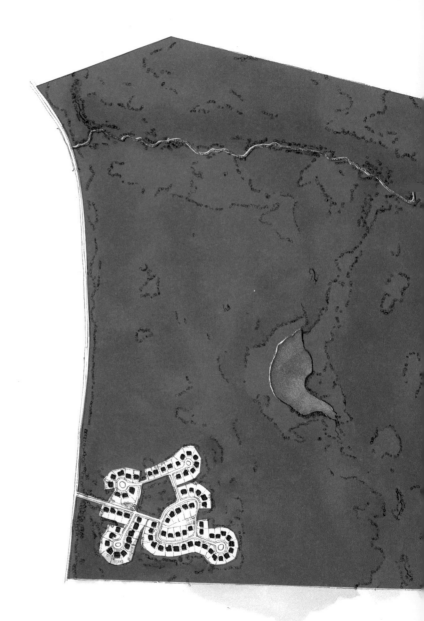

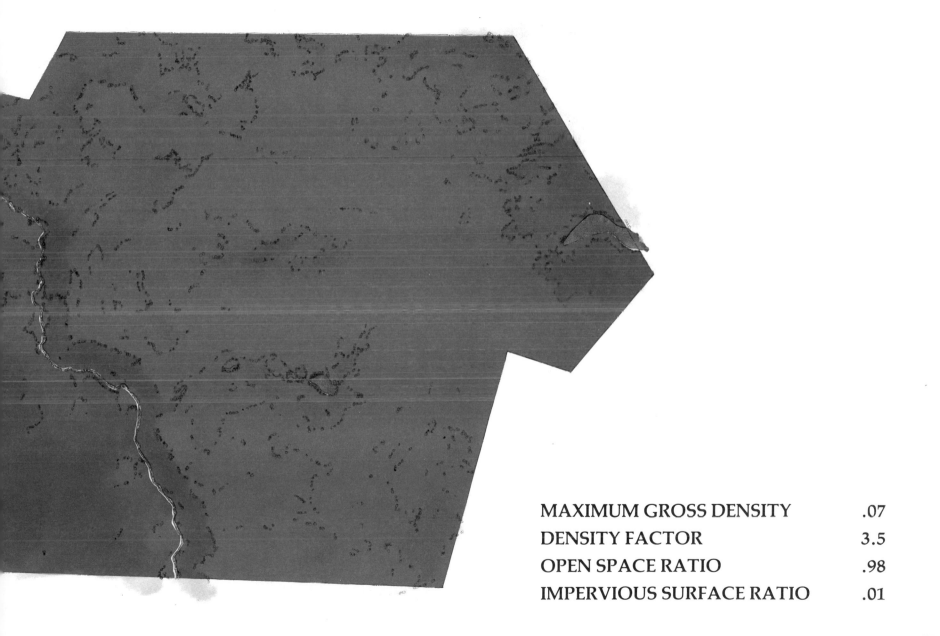

MAXIMUM GROSS DENSITY   .07
DENSITY FACTOR   3.5
OPEN SPACE RATIO   .98
IMPERVIOUS SURFACE RATIO   .01

Agricultural District

The agricultural district is mapped on the basis of the presence of productive agricultural soils. Its purpose is to preserve that agricultural land for agricultural uses. This purpose differs from that for which conventional agricultural districts may be zoned, namely, to "hold" land from development until a later point when the market is ready to develop the area for residential subdivision or other urban uses. In order to preserve agricultural uses, this district requires a .90 open space ratio and limits impervious surface coverage to .5 percent of the site. The accompanying illustration depicts an actual fifty-acre tract developed under the performance zoning ordinance of Buckingham Township, Pennsylvania. This tract had previously been zoned to permit its development at a density of one unit per acre. After being rezoned to the performance zoning agricultural district, the land was developed by its owner within the constraints of the new regulations. Of the original fifty acres, approximately forty were preserved as an agricultural use (nursery), and the owner developed and sold ten dwelling units (one of which was a preexisting barn which was converted to a residence). The landowner received an economic return on this development which equaled the value asked for the property when it was zoned for the fifty one-acre lots which prior zoning regulations would have permitted.

MAXIMUM GROSS DENSITY	.22
DENSITY FACTOR	2.2
OPEN SPACE RATIO	.90
IMPERVIOUS SURFACE RATIO	.50

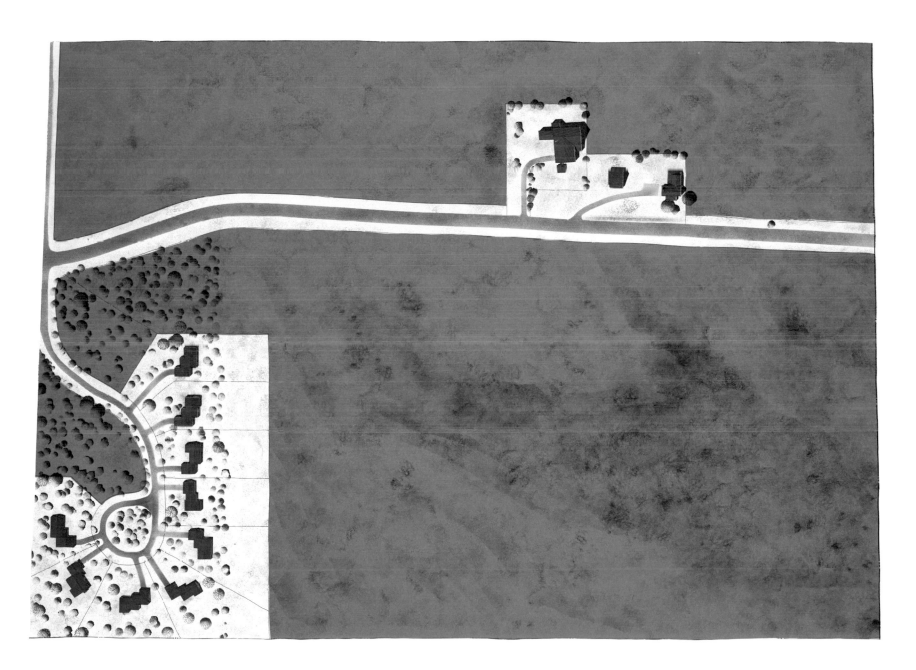

Conservation District

The conservation district is intended to preserve natural resources. The illustration is a staff proposal of how development could be accommodated on a beautiful and sensitive site. The site slopes steeply from the stream valley toward a ridge line (located at the top of the page). The hillsides and stream are heavily forested and covered with boulders. Units have been placed to minimize the disruption of an area of great recreational and scenic value.

The clusters on the lake and on the right hand side of the illustration were placed in natural clearings. This site had often been discussed as a county park site. Under traditional zoning, only outright condemnation could preserve it as public open space. Under the performance approach, which allows the landowner the right to develop uses and receive commensurate economic return, the large expanse of open space can be insured without the public having to pay the landowner for that space and without removing the property from the public tax rolls.

MAXIMUM GROSS DENSITY	1.0
DENSITY FACTOR	6.6
OPEN SPACE RATIO	.85
IMPERVIOUS SURFACE RATIO	.06

Rural District

The rural district is designed to preserve a rural land use pattern by allowing low density residential units. In the long term, the district will provide land which may be converted from the rural designation to a development district. For this reason, land uses permitted in this district and the standards applicable to it are designed so that future, more intensive development is not precluded. The accompanying figure illustrates a development in which the developer elected to construct residential units on lots of 10,000 square feet under a performance zoning ordinance rather than to develop one-acre lots, which the applicable ordinances also permitted.

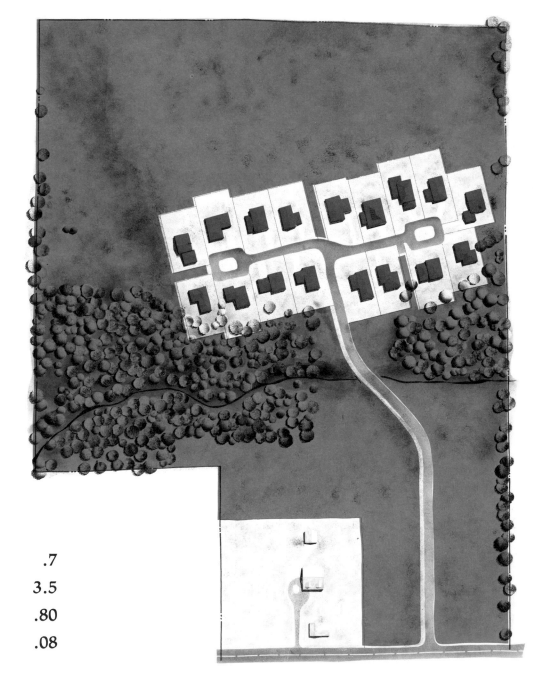

MAXIMUM GROSS DENSITY	.7
DENSITY FACTOR	3.5
OPEN SPACE RATIO	.80
IMPERVIOUS SURFACE RATIO	.08

Estate District

The estate district is designed to accommodate low density, exurban residential development. The permitted density, therefore, is quite low and the development permitted will generally not benefit from public capital expenditures (which would not be cost-efficient at the permitted density). The accompanying illustration depicts a plan which was developed as an estate-type planned unit development using a performance zoning approach. The permitted density was one unit per two acres. The development was designed to protect resources and conserve the open character of the area. This was largely accomplished by the use of restrictive (open space) easements to preclude the future development of areas shown on the illustration as open space.

MAXIMUM GROSS DENSITY	.48
DENSITY FACTOR	.96
OPEN SPACE RATIO	.50
IMPERVIOUS SURFACE RATIO	.08

Development District

The development district is intended to be the area which will accommodate most of the development necessitated by growth of a jurisdiction. It is planned to be the focus of capital improvements and services. It permits medium density residential development as well as commercial, institutional, and some industrial uses.

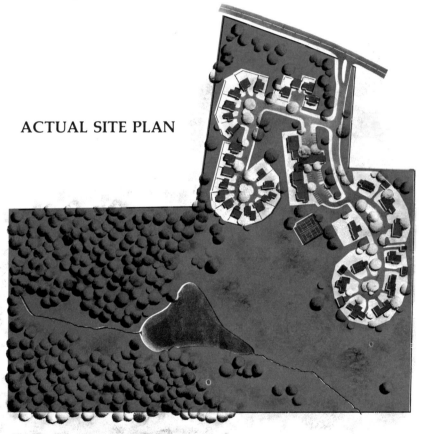

ACTUAL SITE PLAN

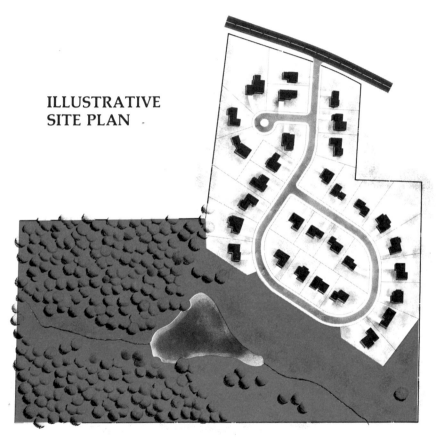

ILLUSTRATIVE SITE PLAN

MAXIMUM GROSS DENSITY	.75
DENSITY FACTOR	1.70
OPEN SPACE RATIO	.56
IMPERVIOUS SURFACE RATIO	.56

MAXIMUM GROSS DENSITY	1.59
DENSITY FACTOR	4.83
OPEN SPACE RATIO	.67
IMPERVIOUS SURFACE RATIO	.8

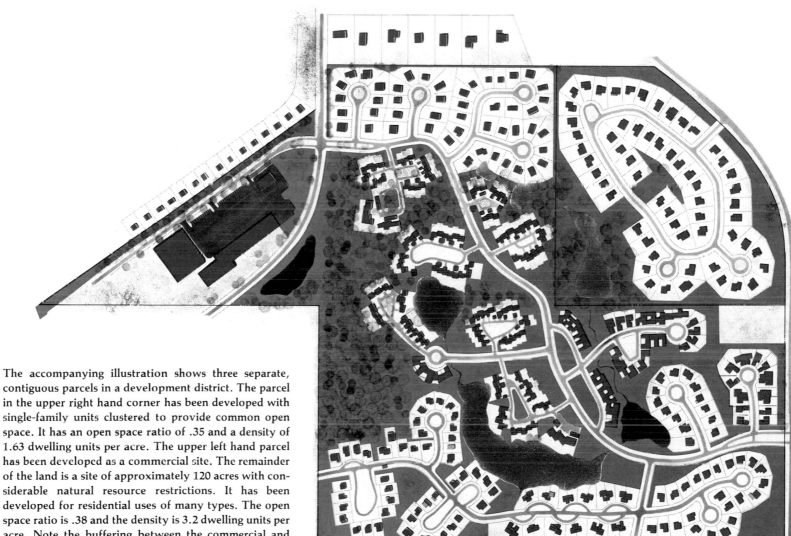

The accompanying illustration shows three separate, contiguous parcels in a development district. The parcel in the upper right hand corner has been developed with single-family units clustered to provide common open space. It has an open space ratio of .35 and a density of 1.63 dwelling units per acre. The upper left hand parcel has been developed as a commercial site. The remainder of the land is a site of approximately 120 acres with considerable natural resource restrictions. It has been developed for residential uses of many types. The open space ratio is .38 and the density is 3.2 dwelling units per acre. Note the buffering between the commercial and residential uses and the controlled access (which necessitates the installation of a frontage road) required of the commercial development.

Development District

MAXIMUM GROSS DENSITY	2.00
DENSITY FACTOR	4.00
OPEN SPACE RATIO	.50
IMPERVIOUS SURFACE RATIO	.18

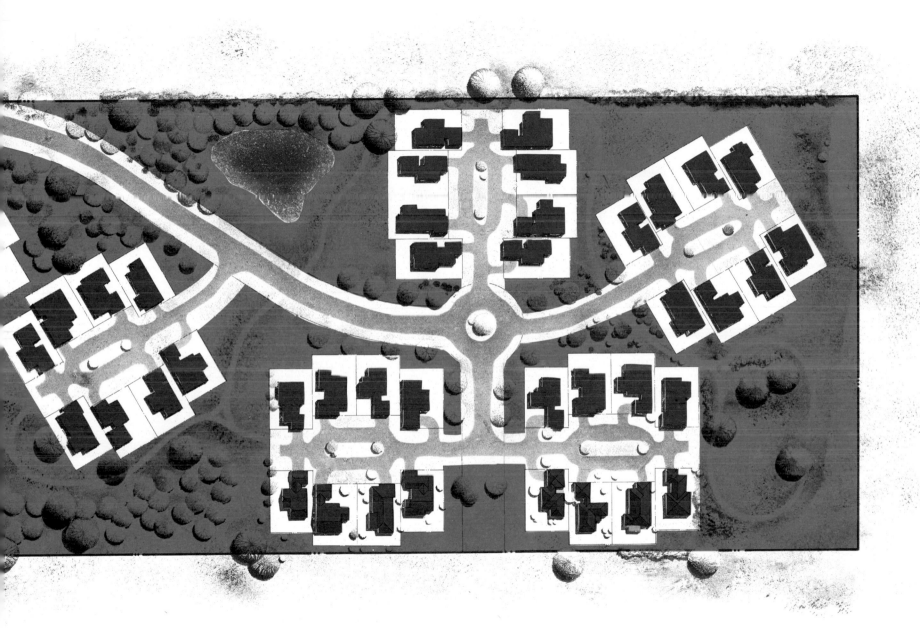

Urban Core District

The urban core district includes areas which are presently urbanized or are expected and planned to become so. The district provides for centers and uses of regional or community importance and consequently includes a full range of public improvements.

The accompanying illustrations show a typical strip commercial development produced by conventional zoning and the hypothetical development of the same area as a performance zoning urban core district. The contrast illustrates how an area which usually develops into a congested and undesirable strip under traditional regulatory schemes could have been developed much better using the performance approach: quality of the environment is improved, the integrity of roads is preserved, yet the same uses which are presently within the strip are there at the same locations. Very significantly, the residential uses in the performance approach are protected from the several nuisance impacts of adjacent nonresidential uses. No such protection is afforded by conventional regulations.

The illustration on the facing page shows a shopping center and residential development on the outskirts of a small town. Note the mix of housing types and the provision of bufferyards and open space for recreation in this proposal.

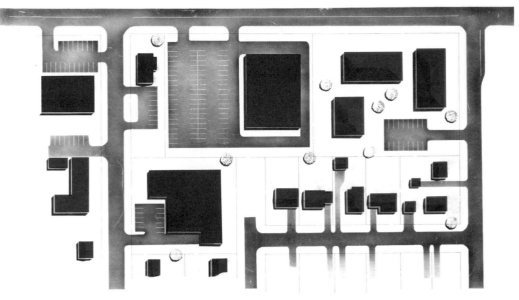

TYPICAL URBAN DEVELOPMENT

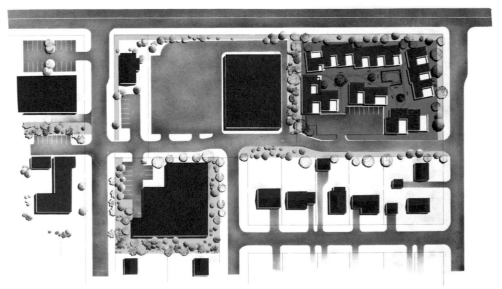

URBAN DEVELOPMENT UNDER PERFORMANCE ZONING

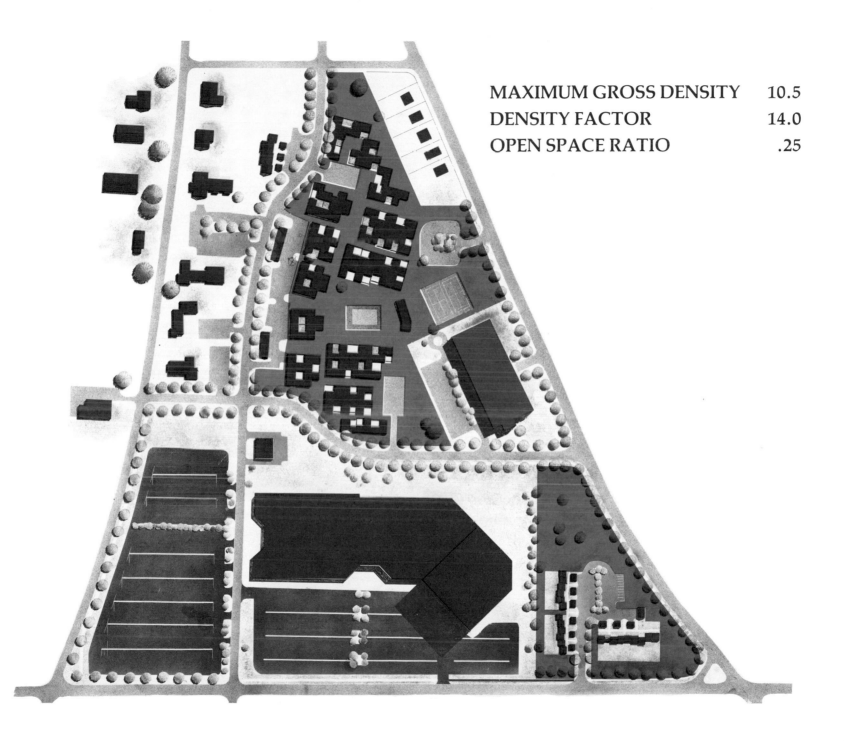

MAXIMUM GROSS DENSITY 10.5
DENSITY FACTOR 14.0
OPEN SPACE RATIO .25

Summary

The districts illustrated on the previous pages cover a wide range of environments. The conservation district site can be used to summarize most of the advantages of performance zoning to both the public and private sectors. Conventional zoning would substantially destroy the environment, an outcome not without costs to the developer. Construction on a boulder-strewn, forested hillside results not only in considerably higher costs but also in inefficient design; at most, 57 percent of the dwellings possible on an ideal site of similar size can be placed in the conservation district, and the actual efficiency could be lower since the soils are very poor for on-site disposal.

Conventional One Acre Lots

Theoretical Gross Density	1.00
Actual Gross Density	1.00
Open Space Ratio	.84
Efficiency	1.00

Large-lot zoning is the technique most municipalities would use to preserve such a site. Because the site has difficulties, there will always be pressures to rezone. The municipality must argue that the large-lot zoning protects the resource while the developer argues that economics prohibit development.

Performance zoning protects the environment and enables the developer better to utilize the site. Improvement costs are substantially reduced by avoiding lengthy roads. The landowner has flexibility of dwelling types, and units will be buffered from roads. It is in the best interest of the community, the builder, and the consumer that sites be built under performance zoning.

Performance Zoning	
Theoretical Density	.87
Gross Density	.5
Open Space Ratio	.84
Efficiency	1.00

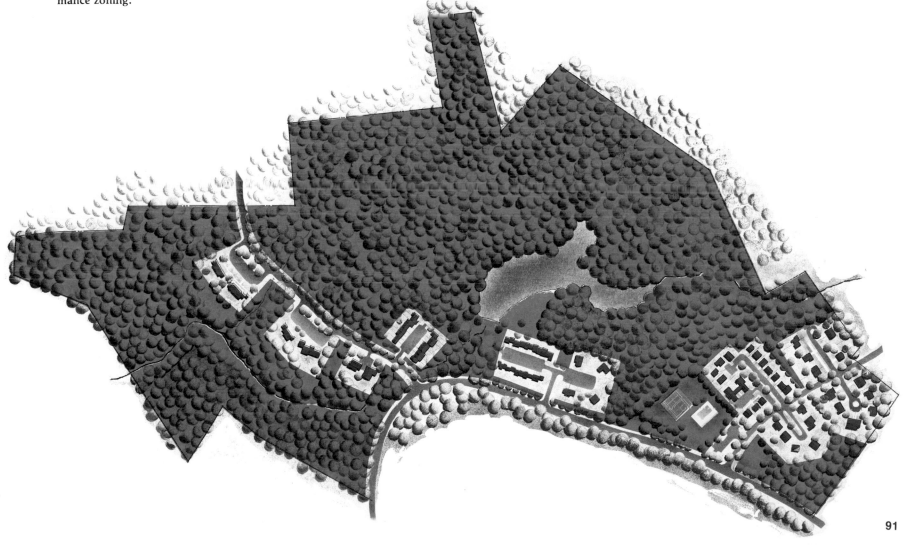

Part Two
Model Ordinance

Table of Contents

Article I. Title, Purpose, and Jurisdiction.

Section 1000. Title.

This ordinance shall be known as and may be referred to as the "(Municipality) Zoning Ordinance."

Section 1001. Legislative Intent.

In enacting this zoning ordinance, special notice has been taken of the fact that the goals of citizens and landowners of (Municipality) often conflict or compete. In the light of this situation, the first consideration has been to devise technical solutions which minimize or eliminate conflicts exacerbated by the prior (Municipality) zoning ordinance. The prior ordinance regularly forced a "winner-take-all" solution to the resolution of conflicts between neighbors or adjoining property owners. Whenever a proposed use encountered objections, the (Municipality) Board or the courts had only two choices: either to permit the use, to the detriment of the objectors, or entirely to prohibit it, to the detriment of the landowner who proposed it. Whenever a use was permitted (usually by virtue of a rezoning), the preexisting adjacent users were unprotected from any of its negative impacts. This ordinance has been designed to protect and accommodate both competing interests. This has inevitably, and properly, led to some form of compromise. In arriving at these compromises, every possible consideration has been given to the public interest, individual property rights, and externalities. While compromise implies mutual concessions or losses, it also implies — and this ordinance has been designed to provide—mutual gains and benefits. It is the goal of this ordinance that both the burdens and the benefits which it, like any scheme of public regulation, implies be rationally and fairly distributed among the citizens and property owners of (Municipality). The regulations contained in this ordinance are based on extensive analysis of the consequences of the regulations imposed by the previous (Municipality) zoning ordinance and the costs and benefits, to all affected parties, implicit in the regulations imposed by this ordinance.

Commentary: All zoning cases pit either a landowner and the public interest or two landowners against each other. There is substantial judicial precedent for the proposition that it is the legislature's role to determine the best path for land use to follow; in this instance, (Municipality) has devoted a substantial effort to finding equitable solutions to conflicts. Every effort has been made to make uses a matter of right subject to performance criteria capable of nondiscretionary, objective administrative evaluation, thus reducing the number of times that ad hoc decisions need be made. This greatly increases the potential uses or choices available to individual property owners. The ad hoc decisions which conventional zoning ordinances frequently necessitate appear to reduce the certainty of protection to neighbors and to increase the potential for adverse impacts to (Municipality). This ordinance contains performance criteria intended to insure that neighbors are protected from adverse impacts. The ordinance also contains performance criteria to protect the community's general welfare. Zoning districts are few in number, and each has a clearly different purpose. Distinctions between districts are significant and based on (Municipality's) Comprehensive Plan. The districts are sized to be adequate to handle (Municipality's) long-term needs and must be regularly updated as time passes. Where performance criteria severely limit the use of properties, the ordinance has gone to considerable extremes to provide the landowners with a range of choices, flexibility, and options for development.

Section 1002. Commentary.

Throughout this ordinance subsections prefaced *Commentary* are included. Each commentary is included and intended as an official statement of legislative finding or purpose. Whenever a section or subsection of this ordinance is deemed to require clarification, explanation of its intent, or further elaboration, that section is followed by a commentary. The commentaries have been legislatively adopted together with the more formal text of the ordinance. They are intended as a guide to the administration and interpretation of the ordinance and shall be treated in the same manner as other aspects of legislative history.

Section 1003. Purpose.

The purpose of this ordinance is implementation of the (Municipality) Comprehensive Plan and the promotion of the health, safety, and general welfare of the present and future inhabitants of (Municipality) by:

A. Giving effect to policies and proposals of the (Municipality) Comprehensive Plan.

B. Dividing the unincorporated area of (Municipality) into districts according to the use of land and buildings, the intensity of such use (including bulk and height), and surrounding open space.

C. Protecting and preserving (Municipality's) agricultural industry and the prime agricultural soils essential to the conduct of this industry.

D. Providing methods to implement Article XI of the Constitution of the State of Illinois which declares that the public policy of the State and the duty of each person is to provide and maintain a healthful environment for the benefit of present and future generations by providing standards to control the amount of open space and impervious surfaces within a development; to control the intensity of development in areas of sensitive natural resources or natural features in order to reduce or eliminate adverse environmental impacts.

E. Controlling and regulating the growth of (Municipality), concentrating development in areas where adequate sewerage facilities, roads, and schools can be provided, and limiting development in areas where these facilities are not and should not be provided.

F. Regulating and restricting the location and use of buildings, structures, and land for trade, industry, residences, and other uses.

G. Providing standards for all types of dwelling units so that all the people may have access to decent, sound, and sanitary housing in accordance with the goals of the Federal Housing Act of 1949, among which is the provision of adequate zoning to meet a fair share of the region's housing needs.

H. Lessening the danger and congestion of traffic on the roads and highways, limiting excessive numbers of intersections, driveways, and other friction points, minimizing other hazards, and insuring the continued usefulness of all elements of the existing highway system for their planned function.

I. Securing safety from fire, panic, flood, and other dangers.

J. Providing adequate privacy, light, and air.

K. Protecting the tax base by facilitating cost-effective development within (Municipality).

L. Securing economy in local governmental expenditures.

M. Conserving the values of property throughout (Municipality).

N. Protecting landowners from adverse impacts of adjoining developments.

Each purpose listed above serves to balance the interests of the general public of (Municipality) and those of individual property owners.

Section 1004. Interpretation.

This ordinance shall be interpreted, whenever an administrator or the judiciary is called upon to do so, in conformance with the purposes intended, by the (Municipality) Board, to be served by its enactment. The intent of the standards and supporting definitions is to protect both individual property owners and the general public from adverse impacts which might otherwise be the result of a proposed use. To this end, those called upon to interpret this ordinance shall proceed as follows:

A. Determine the public purpose(s) of the standard(s) with respect to which an interpretation is required.

Commentary: Before any zoning interpretation is made, there must be an explicit identification of the purpose(s) for which the regulation was initially imposed. Each zoning regulation is intended to protect the interests of both present and future neighbors and the general public. Each standard is developed as a regulatory response to an identifiable negative impact or potential. A sound interpretation of any such standard cannot be insured without a careful analysis of the end to which the regulation is directed.

B. Determine the actual impact of a proposed interpretation.

Commentary: There is a critical distinction between an interpretation which provides a greater degree of design freedom to achieve a permitted land use and an interpretation which permits a new or not previously permitted use or which allows a use to be enlarged or have its intensity increased beyond the degree specified in the ordinance.

C. Determine that the proposed interpretation will insure a just balance between the rights of the landowner and all others who will be affected by that person's land use proposal.

Commentary: If an interpretation merely would allow a design solution which is more flexible, albeit slightly different from the one expressly stated, and if it results in no less a degree of protection to any affected party, such an interpretation may be appropriately made. Any interpretation which would result in any identifiable loss of protection or which would increase the nuisance potential of any use should not be made by an administrator. Any interpretation which will result in any loss of protection or increase in intensity beyond that already permitted should only be made when the party interpreting the ordinance has the power to impose additional restrictions or conditions to protect the public and exercises this power.

Commentary: This ordinance has been carefully designed to avoid the necessity of making ad hoc decisions about whether the interest of a landowner or the public interest should prevail: it has sought to balance those interests. All required interpretation should do likewise. This section recognizes that there is a tension inherent in the regulatory approach in that minimum standards must be set in the context of typical or anticipated development. It is not intended that such regulations frustrate good design, but some approaches by good designers which are quite atypical and therefore neither envisioned nor expressly regulated by this ordinance's standards are probably inevitable.

An example of the way these rules of interpretation are intended to be applied is presented here. The example involves the term "bedroom" and standards which vary as a function of the number of bedrooms per dwelling unit. A person called on to interpret this ordinance may be required to determine the standard applicable to a home which its developer describes as having four bedrooms and one "den" or "study." The first step is to determine why each such standard is expressed in terms of the number of bedrooms. The reason is that this number provides a basis for regulating lot size, private yard area available per person, the number of parking spaces, or the size of a septic system. These are all important purposes which protect the health (septic systems), safety (adequate off-street parking), and welfare (the yard size, based on the number of expected inhabitants). An interpretation that the den can and will be used as a bedroom will insure that all these public interests are protected. Were the interpretation to be that the room labeled a den was not a bedroom but was in fact later used as one, the standards applicable to septic field, parking, and lot area would be inadequate. The judgment to be made is whether the room is likely to be used as a bedroom (based, e.g., on its location within the unit and with respect to closets and bathrooms). An extra "nonbedroom" might still require a larger lot but not more parking or a larger septic field. As a pre-

requisite of accepting a room as a den, there must be assurance that it cannot readily be used as a bedroom. This approach is often little more than the exercise of common sense. It insures the integrity of the ordinance and does not hamper or unduly limit the landowner's use of the land.

Article II. Definitions.

Section 2000. Purpose.

It is the purpose of this article to define words, terms, and phrases contained within this ordinance.

Section 2100. Word Usage.

In the interpretation of this ordinance, the provisions and rules of this section shall be observed and applied, except when the context clearly requires otherwise:

A. Words used or defined in one tense or form shall include other tenses and derivative forms.

B. Words in the singular number shall include the plural number, and words in the plural number shall include the singular number.

C. The masculine gender shall include the feminine, and the feminine gender shall include the masculine.

D. The word "shall" is mandatory.

E. The word "may" is permissive.

F. The word "person" includes individuals, firms, corporations, associations, trusts, and any other similar entities.

G. The word "(Municipality)" means (Municipality), (State).

H. The words "(Municipality) Board" mean the Board of Commissioners of (Municipality).

I. The words "Planning Commission" shall mean the (Municipality) Regional Planning Commission.

J. The words "Recorder" and "Recorder of Deeds" shall mean the (Municipality) Recorder of Deeds.

K. In case of any difference of meaning or implication between the text of this ordinance and any caption, illustration, or table, the text shall control.

Section 2200. Abbreviations.

The following abbreviations are used in this ordinance and are intended to have the following meanings: DF (density factor), FAF (floor area factor), ISR (impervious surface ratio), OSR (open space ratio).

Section 2300. Definitions.

When used in this ordinance, the following terms shall have the meanings herein ascribed to them:

Abutting. Having a common border with, or being separated from such common border by, an alley or easement.

Access. A means of vehicular approach or entry to or exit from property.

Acre. Forty-three thousand, five hundred and sixty (43,560) square feet.

Agricultural soils, prime. Those soils which are best suited for the production of food, feed, and other crops. Prime agricultural soils meet the following criteria: (1) they have an adequate moisture supply, either by natural rainfall or irrigation, and have good water-storage capacity; (2) they have a mean annual temperature and growing season necessary for high crop yields; (3) they are neither too acid nor too alkaline for vigorous plant growth; (4) the water table is either lacking or so deep that it does not adversely affect plant growth; (5) the soils are neither very salty nor high in sodium; (6) they are not flooded more often than once in two years during the growing season; (7) they do not have serious erosion hazards; (8) they have a permeability rate of at least .06 inches per hour in the upper twenty (20) inches; and (9) the surface soils are not so stony as to hinder farming operations with large machines. The following are prime agricultural soils: Miami silt loam, Montmorenci silt loam, Harpster silty clay loam, Sawmill silty clay loam, Elliott silt loam, Pella silty clay loam, Martinton silt loam, Del Rey silt loam, Morley silt loam, Ashkum silty clay loam, Beecher silt loam, Dresden loam, Fox loam, Peotone silty clay loam, Aptakisic silt loam, Saylesville silt loam, Mundelein silt loam, Barrington silt loam, Montgomery silty clay, Odell silt loam, Corwin silt loam, Markham silt loam, Zurich silt loam, Wauconda silt loam, Grays silt loam, Wauconda and Beecher silt loams, Grays and Markham silt loams, Zurich and Morley silt loams, Wauconda and Frankfort silt loams, Aptakisic and Nappanee silt loams, Zurich and Nappanee silt loams, Barrington and Varna silt loams, Mundelein and Elliot silt loams.

Alley. A thoroughfare either used as such or shown on any recorded description of the subject parcel(s) which is not more than thirty (30) feet wide and which affords only a secondary means of access to abutting property.

Apartment. A dwelling unit contained in a building comprising more than three (3) dwelling units, each of which has an entrance to a hallway or balcony in common with at least one (1) other dwelling unit.

Appeal. A means for obtaining review of a decision, determination, order, or failure to act pursuant to the terms of this ordinance as expressly authorized by the provisions of Article IX.

Arterial road or street. A roadway so designated by Sections 4703 and 4704.

Attic. That part of a building which is immediately below, and wholly or partly within, the roof framing.

Basement. A portion of a building located partially underground, having less than fifty (50) percent of its clear floor to ceiling height below grade.

Base site area. A calculated area; see Section 4301.

Beach. The strip of land between the edge of Lake Michigan at a point five hundred and eighty (580) feet above mean sea level and the upland line of partially stabilized vegetated soils which are not affected by wave action; or between the same edge of Lake Michigan and the toe of a bluff.

Bedroom. A room marketed, designed, or otherwise likely to function primarily for sleeping.

Bluff. A land form having a slope in excess of thirty (30) percent which terminates in Lake Michigan, its beaches, or any artificial land including its associated erosion hazard area. The erosion hazard area consists of one of the following: the 100-year high risk erosion area, as prepared by the Illinois State Geological Survey for the Illinois Division of Water Resources, or, in areas which study indicates are stabilized, the area of the bluff and that area defined by a thirty (30) percent slope drawn from the toe of the bluff inland.

Bufferyard. A unit of land, together with a specified type and amount of planting thereon, and any structures which may be required between land uses to eliminate or minimize conflicts between them.

Building. A structure built, maintained, or intended for use for the shelter or enclosure of persons, animals, or property of any kind. The term is inclusive of any part thereof. Where independent units with separate entrances are divided by party walls, each unit is a building.

Building, accessory. A building which (1) is subordinate to and serves a principal structure or a principal use, (2) is subordinate in area, extent, and purpose to the principal structure or use served, (3) is located on the same lot as the principal structure or use served except as otherwise expressly authorized by provisions of this ordinance, and (4) is customarily incidental to the principal structure or use. Any portion of a principal structure devoted or intended to be devoted to an accessory use is not an accessory structure.

Building front. That exterior wall of a building which faces a front lot line of the lot.

Building line. A line on a lot, generally parallel to a lot line or road right-of-way line, located a sufficient distance therefrom to provide the minimum yards required by this ordinance. The building line delimits the area in which buildings are permitted subject to all applicable provisions of this ordinance.

Building, principal. A building in which is conducted, or in which is intended to be conducted, the main or principal use of the lot on which it is located.

Caliper. A measurement of the size of a tree equal to the diameter of its trunk measured four and one-half (4.5) feet above natural grade.

Cartway. The paved portion of a road or street.

Cellar. A portion of a building located partially underground having more than fifty (50) percent of its clear floor to ceiling height below grade.

Collector road or street. A roadway so designated by Sections 4703 and 4704.

Comprehensive Plan. A composite of the (Municipality) Comprehensive Plan, all accompanying maps, charts, and explanatory material adopted by the (Municipality) Board, and all amendments thereto.

Corner lot. *See* Lot, corner.

Curb cut. *See* Access.

Caretaker's residence. A dwelling unit which is used exclusively by either the owner, manager, or operator of a principal permitted use and which is located on the same parcel as the principal use.

Dedication. The transfer of property interests from private to public ownership for a public purpose. The transfer may be of fee-simple interest or of a less than fee interest, including an easement.

Density, gross. The quotient of the total number of dwelling units divided by the base site area of a site.

Density factor. An intensity measure expressed as the number of units per net buildable site area (as calculated pursuant to Sections 4304 and 4305). It is the density on the buildable portion of a site.

Design deviation. A standard, alternative to and providing more flexibility than, than the one otherwise required by this ordinance for residential development. The ordinance specifies certain requirements as a precondition for the use of the deviation standard. See Section 5400.

Developer. The legal or beneficial owner(s) of a lot or parcel of any land proposed for inclusion in a development, including the holder of an option or contract to purchase.

Development. The division of a parcel of land into two (2) or more parcels; the construction, reconstruction, conversion, structural alteration, relocation, or enlargement of any buildings; any use or change in use of any buildings or land; any extension of any use of land or any clearing, grading, or other movement of land, for which permission may be required pursuant to this ordinance.

Drainage. The removal of surface water or groundwater from land by drains, grading, or other means. Drainage includes the control of runoff to minimize erosion and sedimentation during and after development and includes the means necessary for water-supply preservation or prevention or alleviation of flooding.

Drainageway. Minor watercourses which are defined either by soil type or by the presence of intermittent or perennial streams. The following areas are drainageways: (1) areas with soils, as delineated in the *Soil Survey of (County)* by the Soil Conservation Service, of the following types: Houghton Muck (103), Sawmill silty clay loam (107), Pella silty clay loam (153), Ashkum silty clay loam (232), Peotone silty clay loam (330), and Granby loamy fine sand (513); (2) the land, except where areas are designated as floodplain, on either side of and within sixty-five (65) feet of the centerline of any intermittent or perennial stream shown on the U.S. Geological Service's *Hydrologic Investigations Atlas*; (3) the land, except where areas are designated as floodplain, on either side of and within sixty-

five (65) feet of the centerline of any intermittent or perennial streams shown on soil survey maps of (Municipality) prepared by the Soil Conservation Service.

Dunes. Narrow ridges of sand, approximately parallel to Lake Michigan, characterized by sparse vegetation and low fertility. The following areas, which fit this general description, are dunes: (1) areas of Plainfield sand, mapped as (V54) by the U.S. Department of Agriculture, Soil Conservation Service, which lie less than 596 feet above mean sea level and are adjacent to Lake Michigan; (2) areas of beach sand mapped as (367) by the U.S. Department of Agriculture, Soil Conservation Service, which are vegetated and lie more than 576.8 feet above mean sea level; (3) any unmapped areas of sand or sand loam which lie less than 596 feet above mean sea level and are elevated so that the depth to the water table is at least three (3) feet.

Dwelling. Any building or portion thereof which is designated or used for residential purposes.

Dwelling, single-family detached. A dwelling designed for and occupied by not more than one (1) family and having no roof, wall, or floor in common with any other dwelling unit.

Dwelling unit. A room or group of rooms, providing or intended to provide living quarters for not more than one (1) family.

Dwelling, attached. Three (3) or more adjoining dwelling units, each of which is separated from the others by one (1) or more unpierced walls from ground to roof.

Dwelling, multiple family. A building designed for or containing two or more dwelling units, sharing access from a common hall, stair, or balcony.

Dwelling, semi-detached. Two (2) dwelling units, each of which is attached side to side, each one (1) sharing only one (1) common wall with the other.

Easement. Authorization by a property owner of the use by another and for a specified purpose of any designated part of his property.

Erosion. The detachment and movement of soil or rock fragments by water, wind, ice, and/or gravity.

Erosion hazard area. An area so designated by map in the Illinois Coastal Zone Management *Geological Atlas of the Coastal Zone. See* Bluff.

Exterior storage. Outdoor storage of fuel, raw materials, products, and equipment. In the case of lumberyards, exterior storage includes all impervious materials stored outdoors. In the case of truck terminals, exterior storage includes all trucks, truck beds, and truck trailers stored outdoors.

Family. One (1) or more persons related by blood, marriage, adoption, or guardianship, or not more than five (5) persons not so related, occupying a dwelling unit and living as a single housekeeping unit.

Fast food restaurant. *See* Restaurant, fast food.

Filling. The depositing on land, whether submerged or not, of sand, gravel, earth, or other materials of any composition whatsoever.

Floodplain. Floodplains may be either riverine or inland depressional areas. Riverine floodplains are those areas contiguous with a lake, stream, or stream bed whose elevation is greater than the normal waterpool elevation but equal to or lower than the projected 100 year flood elevation. Inland depressional floodplains are floodplains not associated with a stream system but which are low points to which surrounding lands drain.

Floor area. The sum of the gross floor area for each of a building's stories measured from the exterior limits of the faces of the structure. The floor area of a building includes basement floor area and includes attic floor area only if the attic area meets the (Municipality) Building Code standards for habitable floor area. It does not include cellars and unenclosed porches or any floor space in an accessory building or in the principal building which is designed for the parking of motor vehicles in order to meet the parking requirements of this ordinance.

Floor area factor. An intensity measure expressed as the ratio derived by dividing the total floor area of a building by the net buildable site area. It is the floor area ratio measured on the buildable area of the site.

Floor area ratio. An intensity measured as a ratio derived by dividing the total floor area of a building by the base site area. Where the lot is part of a larger development and has no bufferyard, that lot area may be used instead of the base site area.

Forest. Area containing mature woodlands, woodlands, and/or young woodlands.

Garden center. A place of business where retail and wholesale products and produce are sold to the retail consumer. These centers, which may include a nursery and/or greenhouses, import most of the items sold. These items may include plants, nursery products and stock, fertilizers, potting soil, hardware, power equipment and machinery, hoes, rakes, shovels, and other garden and farm tools and utensils.

Garage. A deck or building, or part thereof, used or intended to be used for the parking and storage of motor vehicles.

Gas station. An establishment providing sales of vehicle fuel and such services as lubrication, oil and tire changes, and minor repairs. This use does not include paint spraying or body fender repair.

Greenhouse. An enclosed building, permanent or portable, which is used for the growth of small plants.

Gross density. *See* Density, gross.

Group dwelling. The residence of a group of six (6) or more persons, not related by blood, marriage, adoption, or guardianship and living together as a single housekeeping unit.

Height of structure. The vertical distance measured from the lowest ground elevation to the highest point on such structure.

Home occupation. A business, profession, occupation, or trade conducted for gain or support and located entirely within a residential building, or a structural accessory thereto, which use is accessory, incidental, and secondary to the use of the building for dwelling purposes and does not change the essential residential character or appearance of such building.

Hotel. A building or group of buildings used, or intended to be used, for the lodging of more than ten (10) persons for compensation.

Impervious surface. Impervious surfaces are those which do not absorb water. They consist of all buildings, parking areas, driveways, road, sidewalks, and any areas of concrete or asphalt. In the case of lumberyards, areas of stored lumber constitute impervious surfaces.

Impervious surface, on lot. The total amount of impervious surface which is present on a lot.

Impervious surface ratio. A measure of the intensity of land use which is determined by dividing the total area of all impervious surfaces on a site by, in the case of residential uses, base site area or, in the case of nonresidential uses, by net buildable site area.

Intensity class, land use. A measure of the magnitude and negative impact of a land use on the environment and neighboring land uses (see Sections 4601 and 4602).

Junkyard. Any land or structure used for a salvaging operation, including but not limited to the storage and sale of waste paper, rags, scrap metal, and discarded materials and the collection, dismantlement, storage, and salvage of two (2) or more unlicensed, inoperative vehicles.

Kennel. Any place in or at which any number of dogs are kept for the purpose of sale or in connection with boarding care or breeding, for which any fee is charged.

Lakes and ponds. Natural or artificial bodies of water which retain water year round. A lake is a body of water of two (2) or more acres. A pond is a body of water of less than two (2) acres. Artificial ponds may be created by dams or may result from excavation. The shoreline of such bodies of water shall be measured from the maximum condition rather than from the permanent pool in the event of any difference.

Lot. A parcel of land undivided by any street or private road and occupied by, or designated to be developed for, one (1) building or principal use and the accessory buildings or uses customarily incidental to such building, use, or development, including such open spaces and yards as are designed and arranged or required by this ordinance for such building, use, or development.

Lot area. The area contained within the boundary lines of a lot.

Lot corner. A lot abutting two or more streets at their intersection.

Lot frontage. Lot width measured at the street lot line. When a lot has more than one street lot line, lot width shall be measured, and the minimum lot width required by this ordinance shall be provided, at each such line.

Lot line. A line bounding a lot which divides one lot from another or from a street or any other public or private space.

Lot line, rear. That lot line which is parallel to and most distant from the front lot line of the lot; in the case of an irregular, triangular, or gore-shaped lot, a line twenty (20) feet in length, entirely within the lot, parallel to and at the maximum possible distance from, the front line shall be considered to be the rear lot line. In the case of lots which have frontage on

more than one road or street, the rear lot line shall be opposite the lot line along which the lot takes access to a street.

Lot line, side. Any lot line other than a front or rear lot line.

Lot line, street. In the case of a lot abutting only one street, the street line separating such lot from such street; in the case of a double frontage lot, each street line separating such lot from a street shall be considered to be the front lot line, except where the rear yard requirement is greater than the front yard requirement in which case one of two opposing yards shall be a rear yard.

Lot of record. Any validly recorded lot which at the time of its recordation complied with all applicable laws, ordinances, and regulations.

Lot width. The mean horizontal distance between the side lot lines measured at right angles to those side lot lines at the building line. Where there is only one side lot line, lot width shall be measured between such lot line and the opposite lot line or future right-of-way line.

Maintenance guarantee. A guarantee of facilities or work to insure the correction of any failures of any improvements required pursuant to this ordinance and regulation, or to maintain same.

Minimum floor elevation. The lowest elevation permissible for the construction, erection, or other placement of any floor, including a basement floor.

Mini-warehouse. A building or group of buildings in a controlled-access and fenced compound that contains varying sizes of individual, compartmentalized, and controlled-access stalls or lockers for the *dead* storage of a customer's goods or wares. No sales, service, or repair activities other than the rental of dead storage units are permitted on the premises.

Mobile Home. A transportable, single-family dwelling intended for permanent occupancy contained in one unit, or in two units designed to be joined into one integral unit capable of again being separated for repeated towing, which arrives at a site complete and ready for occupancy except for minor and incidental unpacking and assembly operations, and constructed so that it may be used with or without a permanent foundation. For the purposes of determining standards which apply, a distinction is made between doublewide units mounted on a permanent foundation which shall be considered a single-family home and shall be regulated by the provisions of Sections 5200A and 5200B(1) or (3), and singlewide units which are permitted only in mobile home parks.

Mobile home park. A mobile home park is a performance subdivision containing mobile homes. Such a facility shall meet all requirements for performance subdivisions listed in Section 4203.

Motel. *See* Hotel.

Net buildable site area. A calculated area; see Sections 4304 (residential uses) and 4305 (nonresidential uses).

Nonconformity. *See* Article VI.

Nursery. An enterprise which conducts the retail and wholesale sale of plants grown on the site, as well as accessory items (but not power equipment such as gas or electric lawnmowers and farm implements) directly related to their care and maintenance. The accessory items normally sold are clay pots, potting soil, fertilizers, insecticides, hanging baskets, rakes, and shovels.

On-site. Located on the lot in question, except in the context of on-site detention, when the term means within the boundaries of the development site as a whole.

Open space. *See* Section 4500.

Open space ratio. The proportion of a site consisting of open space as defined by Section 4500 and specified in Section 4203, which shall be calculated using the base site area.

Owner. The person or persons having the right of legal title to, beneficial interest in, or a contractual right to purchase a lot or parcel of land.

Parcel. The area within the boundary lines of a development.

Performance guarantee. A financial guarantee to insure that all improvements, facilities, or work required by this ordinance will be completed in compliance with the ordinance, regulations, and the approved plans and specifications of a development.

Pond. *See* Lakes and ponds.

Principal building. *See* Building, principal.

Principal use. *See* Use, principal.

Public improvement. Any improvement, facility, or service, together with customary improvements and appurtenances thereto, necessary to provide for public needs as: vehicular and pedestrian circulation systems, storm sewers, flood control improvements, water supply and distribution facilities, sanitary sewage disposal and treatment, public utility and energy services.

Ravine. An area constituting a "young valley" which adjoins a perennial or intermittent watercourse. It includes the bottom lands of the ravine and the ravine side walls to a point where the slope is less than fifteen (15) percent. See the following illustration.

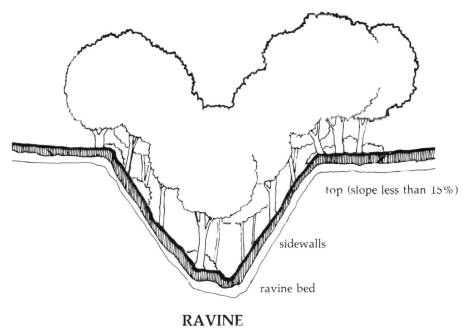

top (slope less than 15%)

sidewalls

ravine bed

RAVINE

Ravine buffer. The area extending one hundred and fifty (150) feet beyond the top of the ravine wall; see the illustration following the definition of Ravine.

Recorded lot. *See* Lot of record.

Recreational vehicle. A vehicle or a unit that is mounted on or drawn by another vehicle primarily designed for temporary living. Recreational vehicles include travel trailers, camping trailers, truck campers, and motor homes.

Recreational vehicle park. A lot on which campsites are established for occupancy by recreational vehicles of the general public as temporary living quarters for purposes of recreation or vacation.

Restrictive, more (less). A regulation imposed by this ordinance is more (less) restrictive than another if it prohibits or limits development to a greater (lesser) extent or by means of more (less) detailed specifications.

Residential street. A roadway so defined by Section 4703.

Restaurant, fast food. An establishment whose principal business is the sale of food and/or beverages in a ready-to-consume state for consumption (1) within the restaurant building, (2) within a motor vehicle parked on the premises, or (3) off the premises as carry-out orders, and whose principal method of operation includes the following characteristics: food and/or beverages are usually served in edible containers or in paper, plastic, or other disposable containers.

Restaurant, standard. An establishment whose principal business is the sale of food and/or beverages to customers in a ready-to-consume state, and whose principal method of operation includes one or both of the following characteristics: (1) customers, normally provided with an individual menu, are served their foods and beverages by a restaurant employee at the same table or counter at which food and beverages are consumed; (2) a cafeteria-type operation where food and beverages generally are consumed within the restaurant building.

Resubdivision. *See* Subdivision.

Rooming house. A dwelling where lodging is provided, for compensation, for from four (4) to ten (10) persons, who are not members of a family occupying that dwelling unit and who do not occupy the dwelling as a simple housekeeping unit.

Sedimentation. The deposition of soil that has been transported from its site of origin by water, ice, wind, gravity, or other natural means as a result of erosion.

Shopping center. A group of commercial establishments planned, developed, and managed as a unit with off-street parking provided on the property.

Shopping center, regional. A shopping center having in excess of seven hundred and fifty thousand (750,000) square feet of gross floor area.

Site area. *See* Base site area.

Stable, commercial. A building or land where horses are kept for remuneration, hire, sale, boarding, riding, or show.

Stable, private. Any building, incidental to an existing residential, principal use, that shelters horses for the exclusive use of the occupants of the premises.

Steep slopes. Land area where the inclination of the land's surface from the horizontal is twelve (12) percent or greater. Slope is determined from on-site topographic surveys prepared with a two-foot contour interval.

Street line. *See* Lot line, front.

Structural alteration. Any change in the supporting members of a building, such as the bearing walls, beams, or girders, or any change in the dimension or configuration of the roof or exterior walls.

Structure. *See* Building.

Structure, accessory. *See* Building, accessory.

Subdivision. Any subdivision or redivision of a subdivision, tract, parcel, or lot of land into two (2) or more parts by means of mapping, platting, conveyance, change or rearrangement of boundaries. All subdivisions are also developments.

Temporary use. *See* Use, temporary.

Use. The purpose or activity for which land or any building thereon is designed, arranged, or intended, or for which it is occupied or maintained.

Use, accessory. An accessory use is one which (1) is subordinate to and serves a principal structure or a principal use, (2) is subordinate in area, extent, and purpose to the principal structure or use served, (3) is located on the same lot as the principal structure or use served except as otherwise expressly authorized by provisions of this ordinance, and (4) is customarily incidental to the principal structure or use. See also Section 5501.

Use, principal. The specific primary purpose for which land is used.

Use, temporary. A temporary use is one established for a fixed period of time with the intent to discontinue such use upon the expiration of such time. Such uses do not involve the construction or alteration of any permanent structure.

Variance. Permission to depart from the literal requirements of this ordinance granted pursuant to Article IX.

Wetland. An area of one-quarter (.25) acre or more where standing water is retained for a portion of the year and unique vegetation has adapted to the area. Wetlands include all areas designated as "marsh" in the *Hydrologic Investigations Atlas* of the U.S. Geologic Survey and all areas designated as "Peotone wet," "Houghton muck, wet," and "Houghton peat, wet" in the *Soil Survey of (County)* of the Soil Conservation Service.

Woodland. An area of planted material covering one (1) acre or more and consisting of thirty (30) percent or more canopy trees having an eight (8) inch or greater caliper, or any grove consisting of eight (8) or more trees having a ten (10) inch or greater caliper.

Woodland, mature. An area of plant material covering one (1) acre or more and consisting of thirty (30) percent or more canopy trees having a sixteen (16) inch or greater caliper, or any grove consisting of eight (8) or more trees having an eighteen (18) inch or greater caliper.

Woodlands, young. An area of plant material covering one (1) acre or more and consisting of seventy (70) percent or more canopy trees having a two and one-half (2.5) inch caliper or greater, or a tree plantation for commercial or conservation purposes where seventy (70) percent or more of the canopy trees have a two and one-half (2.5) inch or greater caliper.

Yard. The space between a lot line and building line.

Yard, front. A yard extending the full width of the front of a lot between the front (street) right-of-way line and the front building line.

Yard, rear. A yard extending the full width of the lot in the area between the rear lot line and the rear building line.

Yard, side. A yard extending the full length of the lot in the area between a side lot line and a side building line.

Article III. Establishment of Zoning Districts

Section 3000. Establishment of Zoning Districts.

(Municipality), (State) is hereby divided into zoning districts of such number and character as are necessary to achieve compatibility of uses within each district, to implement the Official (Municipality) Land Use Plan and related official plans and the Official Zoning Map of (Municipality), and to serve the other purposes of this ordinance which are detailed in Article I.

Section 3100. Zoning Districts.

For the purpose of this ordinance, all land and water areas in (Municipality) are hereby divided into zoning districts which shall be designated as follows: agricultural (AG) district, rural (R) district, estate (E) district, neighborhood conservation (NC) district, development (D) district, urban core (UC) district, heavy industrial (HI) district, holding (HD) district.

Section 3200. Map of Zoning Districts.

Zoning districts established by this ordinance are bounded and defined as shown on the Official Zoning Map of (Municipality), which, together with all explanatory materials contained thereon, is hereby made a part of this ordinance.

Section 3201. Interpretation of District Boundaries.

The following rules shall be used to determine the precise location of any zone boundary shown on the Official Zoning Map of (Municipality):

A. Boundaries shown as following or approximately following the limits of any municipal corporation shall be construed as following such limits.

B. Boundaries shown as following or approximately following streets shall be construed to follow the centerlines of such streets.

C. Boundary lines which follow or approximately follow platted lot lines or other property lines as shown on the (Municipality) Tax Maps shall be construed as following such lines.

D. Boundaries shown as following or approximately following section lines, half-section lines, or quarter-section lines shall be construed as following such lines.

E. Boundaries shown as following or approximately following railroad lines shall be construed to lie midway between the main tracks of such railroad lines.

F. Boundaries shown as following or approximately following shorelines of any lakes shall be construed to follow the mean high waterlines of such lakes, and, in the event of change in the mean high waterline, shall be construed as moving with the actual mean high waterline.

G. Boundaries shown as following or approximately following the centerlines of streams, rivers, or other continuously flowing water courses shall be construed as following the channel centerline of such water courses taken at mean low water, and, in the event of a natural change in the location of such streams, rivers, or other water courses, the zone boundary shall be construed as moving with the channel centerline.

H. Boundaries shown as separated from, and parallel or approximately parallel to, any of the features listed in paragraphs A through G above shall be construed to be parallel to such features and at such distances therefrom as are shown on the map.

Section 3300. Statement of Purpose and Intent of Zoning Districts.

The following sections specify the purpose and intent of the zoning districts established by this ordinance.

Section 3301. Agricultural District.

This district is intended to protect and preserve areas of prime agricultural soils for continued agricultural and agriculturally oriented uses. These areas consist of the most agriculturally productive soils. Their loss cannot be readily compensated, since these soils are relatively scarce, particularly on the national level, and poorer soils require more capital energy and nutrients to provide equal productivity. For these reasons, land should not be converted from the agricultural to another zoning classification unless and until there is no other land available in (Municipality) to accommodate the nonagricultural use. The standards and densities prescribed for this district are intended to preserve the open character of the area and thereby to protect the business of agriculture. Mindful of the statutory prohibition of (Municipality) regulation of agricultural uses, this district is intended not

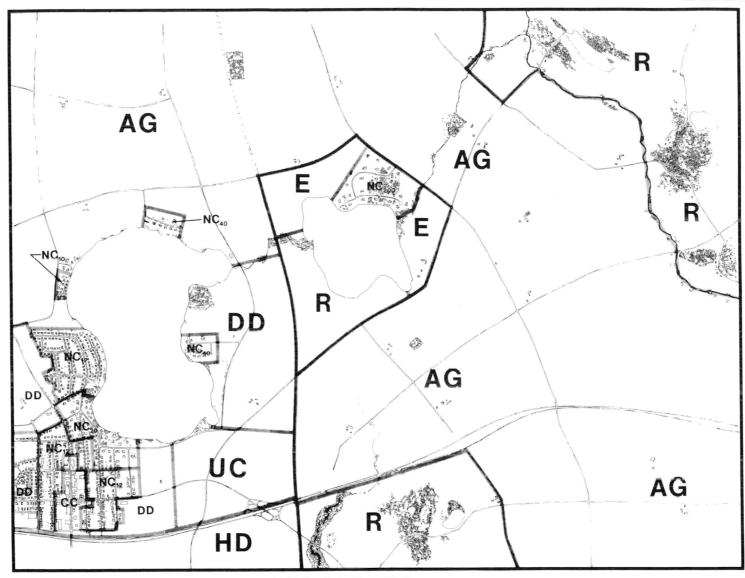

ZONING MAP

ZONING DISTRICTS

AG	Agricultural District	UC	Urban Core
R	Rural District	NC	Neighborhood Conservation
E	Estate District	CC	Commercial Conservation
DD	Development District	HD	Holding District

to regulate agricultural uses, but to regulate those uses which threaten agriculture.

Commentary: It is necessary that agriculture be protected by the creation of this district because of its importance to (Municipality), the nation, and the world. Food production is an essential industry. Throughout the nation, however, agricultural lands are under intense pressure and thousands of acres are converted to urban uses yearly. Moreover, urban areas threaten the productivity of farmlands by competing with them for water.

Agricultural areas play an important role in the purification of water, because they are generally flat and not hydrologically active compared to other soils. The vast majority of the sediments and pollutant loads in lakes and rivers come from hydrologically active areas. Conservation of agricultural land contributes to water quality; any displacement of prime lands that requires a shift of farming operations to hydrologically active areas may be detrimental to water quality.

Agricultural land also functions to maintain air quality. The quality of air in (Municipality), which heavy urbanization has rendered poor, could easily be much less acceptable than it presently is. Farm crops help to cleanse the air and facilitate its movement, which sweeps away pollutants.

Lastly, the open space characteristic of farms is important to nature and carries with it a number of social amenities. Thus, agriculture provides a healthful and stabilizing influence on many natural systems, provides food supply, and has important cultural value.

It should be noted that (Municipality) can serve all projected growth demands past the year 2000 with the land in the development district and available lands within cities and villages. Thus, there is no present need to replace agriculture with some urban use. There simply does not exist a situation in which land for development is in such short supply that prime agricultural land should be converted to urban or urban sprawl uses. At the present, it is simply wasteful, and not in the public interest, to convert prime agricultural land to these uses.

The prior five-acre agricultural zoning has done little to protect agricultural land and has, in fact, accelerated the conversion of agricultural land to residential use. This has had detrimental consequences for (Municipality) both in terms of fiscal expenditure and loss of agricultural and open space. The business of agriculture is intolerant of even relatively low density

development. Development alters the natural environment in areas surrounding it by causing, for example, erosion, runoff, sedimentation, and flood damage, all of which render areas less suitable (or unsuitable) for agriculture. Because it is intended to protect agriculture, the agricultural zone is limited to areas of productive agricultural soils.

Limited residential and other uses which are directly related to or supportive of agriculture or which would not jeopardize the integrity of the agricultural purpose of the district are permitted. While these uses are not completely compatible with agriculture, permitting them recognizes the desire of many landowners to have some development potential. These uses have limited adverse impacts, yet still protect agriculture to the greatest extent possible.

Section 3302. Rural District.

This district is intended to protect and preserve areas of (Municipality) which are presently rural or agricultural in character and use. The qualities of its soils generally do not allow these areas to be classified as prime agricultural land.

These areas are not presently required for urban development and, according to existing population projections, will not be required until the year 2000 at the earliest.

The standards developed for these areas are designed to permit development compatible with the preservation of their rural character and agricultural use while not permanently foreclosing future (post-year 2000) development. When population pressures necessitate conversion of land from nonurban to urban uses, the conversion should first be made from the existing stock of rural land rather than from productive agricultural land.

Commentary: The value of agricultural lands, woodlands, wetlands, and other resources which characterize this district are important to clean water and air and to many natural cycles. Some small areas are also valuable agriculturally, but others are not appropriate for farming. Together with the agricultural district, these lands provide much of the character that makes (Municipality) an attractive place in which to live. Since this land is not needed for development until after the year 2000, permitting rural and exurban uses which do not destroy the land's value is logical.

It should be understood that, although the rural character and natural resources features of these areas are important, the regulations are not intended solely to preserve these characteristics. The most important factor is that the regulations permit a present use of land that will not prematurely preempt more appropriate uses in the future. The district serves to encourage the orderly transition of land from agricultural to low density residential uses and prohibits any uses incompatible with this objective.

Section 3303. Estate District.

The estate district is intended to provide low-density, limited-growth residential areas. It is designed to accommodate residential development opportunities for those who desire exurban, low-density, or estate living and are willing to live in more remote locations and to assume the costs of providing many of their own services and amenities. The public provision of these amenities is precluded because (Municipality) must concentrate its limited resources in areas where more intense future development is logical. The low intensity allowed in this district is similarly necessitated by (Municipality's) need to preserve and support the existing public infrastructure. Accordingly, capital improvements such as highways and major sewer interceptors should be directed away from the estate district. The low intensities permitted in this district generally permit on site septic systems and wells, thereby reducing public capital expenditures.

Commentary: This district complements the development district, in that it houses a specific segment of the population, those who desire estate-type living. Although the land use is residential, it is exurban rather than suburban in character. For example, keeping horses on these residential lots is permitted. The district is intended to house approximately five (5) percent of the required increase in housing stock projected by the year 2000. To this extent, it is more like the development district than the rural district. Unlike the rural district, this district is not expected to be subject to rezoning to higher intensities in the future. It is intended to be built as zoned, while much of the rural area is anticipated to remain vacant for the foreseeable future.

Section 3304. Neighborhood Conservation District.

The neighborhood conservation district is intended to preserve the character of existing neighborhoods and developments under construction at the time of adoption of this ordinance. It is designed to prevent these neighborhoods and subdivisions from becoming nonconforming under the terms of this ordinance. This district is also intended to provide for minor in-filling of existing neighborhoods consistent with their zoning and character at the time of enactment of this ordinance. Such neighborhoods are relatively uniform in character and stable. The regulations permit future development consistent with the existing character. Areas identified as having a stable and fixed character will be allowed to continue to exist and develop under the general regulations governing their design and construction or the actual plat plans previously approved.

Commentary: This district is designed to avoid the creation of large areas of nonconformities as a consequence of the enactment of this ordinance. Large residential properties have been subdivided or largely developed pursuant to the previous zoning ordinance. The legal, administrative, and individual problems that would be created by making these areas nonconforming are not justifiable, and it is largely for this reason that the neighborhood conservation district exists. Only where neighborhoods are in transition would another district designation be used.

It is important that the designation of an area as a neighborhood conservation district not be interpreted to reflect an unconditional decision by (Municipality) that the uses and regulations of the district are ones which would have been prescribed had there not yet been significant development. No new neighborhood conservation districts or expansion of same shall be allowed following the adoption of this ordinance. This district is not considered appropriate for new development. Because there were a number of different lot sizes permitted under the previous zoning ordinance, a similar variety shall appear on the zoning map with the letters (NC) subdesignated by a number. The number indicates the minimum lot size in thousands of square feet. For example, NC_{40} indicates that forty thousand (40,000) square feet is the minimum lot size for the district so designated.

Section 3305. Development District.

This district is intended to accommodate most of the growth expected in the unincorporated areas of (Municipality) during the next twenty-year period. It is to be provided with all public facilities (schools, sewers, water, highways) and will allow most uses by right. It is intended to provide the zoning and capital improvements which attract development. It consists of the areas where development should logically locate as a consequence of planned public facilities and associated capital expenditure. This district provides regulations which permit development of a generally suburban character. It provides for moderate density residential development and for necessary commercial, institutional, and industrial uses. Excluded are uses of higher density or intensity or of major industrial importance.

Commentary: The development district is designed to minimize the costs of extending or expanding public services. It is a planned, logical accommodation of (Municipality) growth intended to serve areas suitable for development and to avoid unsuitable areas. The planning of the size of this district is based on population forecasts. These projections have been converted into projected demands for residential, industrial, commercial, and other land uses of suburban character sufficient to accommodate an estimated two decades of growth. At the time of enactment of this ordinance, most of the land within the development district will be either vacant or undeveloped. Some smaller discontinuous areas of developed land within these districts will be zoned as neighborhood conservation districts.

Uses that would be characterized as being urban or high density rather than suburban have been excluded as have heavy industrial uses. Likewise, uses that are so large as to be of regional importance are not permitted because these uses require specialized and different evaluation and have special locational considerations which make a separate zoning district appropriate.

Unlike the prior (Municipality) zoning ordinance, which segregated different land uses, this development district allows many and varied uses while placing the emphasis on minimizing or buffering any nuisances between uses. Segregation of uses has never provided adequate protection, especially at the boundaries of use districts. This ordinance anticipates the likelihood—and desirability—of considerable mixing of land uses and imposes standards to resolve any possible problems and eliminate the negative impacts of juxtaposing unlike land uses.

Section 3306. Urban Core District.

This district is intended to serve as a community focal point: either as a business and service center or as a transportation center in the form of a commuter rail stop.

In general, the district provides for centers and uses of regional importance. It is intended to be an area of high intensity use on which a full range of

public facilities (including water, sewer, schools, police, fire protection) will generally be focused. The standards and high densities prescribed for the district are designed to optimize utilization of in-place facilities and thus to reduce the fiscal burden of new infrastructure construction on all citizens of (Municipality).

Commentary: Urban core districts are areas which are presently, or will inevitably become, urbanized. In (Municipality), most such areas are within incorporated cities or villages. These districts are the focus of growth in the area immediately surrounding them; their fringes attract growth like a magnet. It is from these districts that public facilities are likely to be extended to accommodate growth. Accordingly, existing commuter rail stops and regional shopping centers serve as focal points for these districts; they supply the type of infrastructure capable of supporting high-intensity development.

These districts must be served by either a major arterial road and commuter rail stop or by two major arterials. Without this type of access there will be substantial disruption of the surrounding neighborhoods. Further, there is need to provide ready access for people of the larger region who support the uses of this district.

Section 3307. Heavy Industrial District.

This district is intended to accommodate those industrial areas which must be segregated because of major negative impacts which cannot be made compatible with other uses through the application of performance standards. The creation of this separate district for heavy industrial use recognizes not only nuisance-type but also infrastructure and operational incompatibilities between its permitted uses and those of other districts. Accordingly, the standards for this district are designed to accommodate very intensive industrial uses having severe nuisances which either cannot be handled by technology or which are nearly impossible to police. Locational criteria for the heavy industrial district focus on transportation, requiring that sites have access to two (2) or more rail lines, or a rail line and either an airport or a major expressway.

Commentary: This ordinance recognizes the possible compatibility of light industry and other land uses within the development districts, so long as the neighboring uses have similar characteristics and can meet performance standards. Linking heavy industrial uses to locations with appropriate transportation amenities is a sound planning approach, and requiring intensive buffers will minimize the impact of these nuisances on any nearby, less-intensive uses. Further, the locational requirements of heavy industry make it important to use a district designation to set aside land for these uses and prevent their being preempted by less-intensive uses.

Section 3308. Holding District.

This district is an interim zoning classification. Because of the annexation laws of (State), much development of urban character occurs in incorporated areas. This district provides transitional zoning in areas in which the County and governments of incorporated areas have signed binding intermunicipal agreements regarding future use of land annexed to an incorporated municipality. Its purpose is to allow some residential use without foreclosing future options if for some reason development is necessary prior to annexation. A precondition for the designation of an area as a holding district is an intermunicipal agreement.

Commentary: In many instances suburban and urban uses are more appropriate in villages and cities than in unincorporated areas. This district provides for cooperative planning between (Municipality) and incorporated municipalities. The district is mapped only where both governments have agreed on the future growth area and the boundaries of rural and agricultural areas. This district is intended to accommodate a significant portion of the growth projected to take place within incorporated areas by the year 2000.

corporated municipalities by strictly defining the growth area of the municipalities and providing a reasonable transitional zoning for such lands. This will result in better planning for (Municipality) as a whole than has been the case under previous zoning schemes which zoned many areas for very low density in spite of general knowledge that a future rezoning would be sought and, in all probability, granted. The prior system provided no guidance to the landowner about whether proposed development should occur at all and, if so, whether it should proceed in the incorporated or in the unincorporated area. Further, by initially establishing artificially low-density zoning, it fostered the emergence of two opposing constituencies: those who built in the zone and disapprove of any change in density (to bring it to realistic levels) because they believe the low-density zoning must continue to protect the character of the area and those who believe they have a right to rezoning upon demand.

Article IV. Regulations.

Section 4000. Introduction.

The purpose of the regulations contained in this article is to allow maximum utilization of land while insuring against detrimental impacts on the environment, neighboring properties, and the public interest. This insurance is provided by separating the unincorporated area of (Municipality) into eight zoning districts and permitting specified land uses within each, provided that a use meets all the additional criteria specified in this ordinance. This regulatory approach has been termed "performance zoning" because it permits a use to be developed on a particular parcel only if that use on that parcel meets "performance" standards which have been enacted to insure against the use causing (or having the potential to cause) the negative impacts mentioned above.

The format of the regulations in this ordinance (and particularly in this article) differs somewhat from that of traditional zoning ordinances because performance zoning requires that consideration be given to site (parcel) characteristics and the range of impacts which any use (such as "office" or "light industry") may have.

Commentary: The following step-by-step guide is provided as an aid for the property owner or prospective developer. It is intended to be a summary of the process by which one can determine what may or may not be permitted on a specific site and, if permitted, the limits that will be placed on its development.

Step 1: Identify the zoning district in which the particular parcel is located. Zoning districts are defined in Article III of this ordinance, and the Official Zoning Map of (Municipality) delineates the boundary of each zoning district.

Step 2: Determine the general use category for the proposed use(s) by referring to Section 4103. Section 4102 (Table of Permitted Uses) identifies the general permitted and conditional use categories which may be established in each zoning district.

Step 3: Determine the maximum performance standards possible for the zoning district in which the parcel is located by referring to Section 4203 (Table of District Performance Standards). The standards specified are for open space ratio, density factor, floor area factor, impervious surface ratio, minimum site area, minimum lot area, and maximum number of lots per development. These terms are defined either in Article II or in this article.

Step 4: Calculate site capacity, base site area, and net buildable site area by following the directions in Sections 4300 through 4305. The principal factors determining site capacity are the natural features and environmental characteristics of the site. If the site includes any natural features or limitations such as floodplains, steep slopes, wetland, woodlands, or others listed in Sections 4400 through 4415, these sections should be referenced in order to determine how such features may operate to restrict development of the site. The open space standards of these sections protect environmentally sensitive features by limiting impervious surface coverage. These standards operate equally across all zoning districts because they are designed to improve the compatibility of development with natural functions of the land and to regulate the resulting impact that any such particular use will have upon existing or future neighborhood uses.

Step 5: Select a land use intensity class from Section 4602 (Table of Land Use Intensity Class Standards). Under this ordinance, the intensity at which a use is developed on a particular parcel is not solely a function of the zoning district in which the parcel is located, except that the maximum performance standards for each zoning district set in Section 4203 may not be exceeded. This ordinance recognizes that uses of a single type (e.g., freestanding commercial) may generate widely different nuisance impacts depending on the intensity at which they are developed. Consequently, a use has the option to develop at an intensity which will minimize nuisances to neighbors or to provide more protection for those neighbors (e.g., a denser bufferyard) as the land is developed at greater intensities. The range of intensity classes open to a use affects only how it can develop on a lot, not whether it can locate on a lot. Several performance standards are specified for each intensity class. These include limits on impervious surface ratio, gross density, trips per acre, height and floor area ratio, signs, and landscaping. All standards in each land use intensity class apply for that class; exceeding any single standard in a class moves a use to the next higher intensity class. Uses may not exceed the standards specified for the highest class in which the use is listed.

Step 6: Determine the required bufferyard (which corresponds to the intensity class of the use) by referring to Section 4606 (Table of Bufferyard Requirements). As a use develops at a greater intensity, the bufferyard necessary to protect neighboring uses increases in size and amount of plant materials and fences. Detailed bufferyard illustrations and standards are contained in Sections 4603 through 4607.

Step 7: Sections 1612 through 1619 contain performance standards for design elements such as landscaping, parking lot landscaping, exterior lighting, and signs. Sections 4700 through 4710 deal with road standards, including types of roads, their widths, access requirements for certain types of roads (when a transportation impact report is required), access for fire vehicles, and clear views at intersections.

Section 4100. Use Regulations.

Sections 4101 through 4108 specify which uses are permitted in each zoning district and define the use categories used in this ordinance.

The purpose of this section is to indicate which land uses may locate in each zoning district and which uses may not locate therein. A further distinction is made between uses which may locate in a given district only upon obtaining a conditional use permit to do so. The uses generally described in Sections 4101 and 4102 are specifically listed in Sections 4103 through 4108.

Section 4101. Uses Permitted by Right, Uses Permitted with Conditional Use Permits, and Uses Not Permitted.

Except as otherwise provided by law or in this ordinance, no building, structure, or land shall be used or occupied except in the zoning districts indicated and for the purposes permitted in this section. The general use categories specified by Section 4102 are defined in Sections 4104 through 4108.

A. A use listed in Section 4102 in any district denoted by the letter "Y" is a use permitted by right, provided that all other requirements of state law and this ordinance have been met and provided that a zoning certificate has been issued in accordance with Article IX.

B. A use listed in Section 4102 may be permitted as a conditional use in any district denoted by the letter "C," provided that the requirements of Article IX have been met.

C. A use listed in Section 4102 is not permitted in any district denoted by the letter "N."

D. Uses permitted by right or as a conditional use shall be subject, in addition, to use regulations contained in this ordinance, to all performance criteria and other regulations governing yards, lot size, lot width, building area, easements, provisions of off-street parking and loading, and to such other provisions as are specified in other articles herein. In particular, the laws of the state and the regulations of the (Municipality) Department of Health regarding water supply and waste disposal shall be adhered to. Further, no zoning permit shall be issued until approval is obtained from the (Municipality) Department of Health for water supply and sewage disposal, unless the premises are served by public water and/or sewage facilities.

E. All solar access developments are permitted as a conditional use in every district.

F. Uses not listed in Section 4102 are not permitted in any district except pursuant to Article IX, which provides for interpretation of uses, or Article VI, which provides for nonconformities.

Although a use may be indicated as permitted or conditionally permitted in a particular district, it does not follow that such a use is permitted or permissible on every parcel in such district. No use is permitted or permissible on a parcel unless it can be located thereon in full compliance with all of the performance standards and other regulations of this ordinance applicable to the specific use and parcel in question.

Section 4102. Table of Permitted Uses. (See page 118.)

Section 4103. Use Categories Defined.

The categories of use utilized by this ordinance are defined in Sections 4104 through 4108. The uses not enumerated in these sections are not necessarily excluded. Article IX empowers the zoning officer to make interpretations of use.

Section 4104. Agricultural Uses.

A. **Agriculture.** Agricultural uses include farms (and farm residences), fish or poultry hatcheries, fur-bearing animal ranches, orchards, raising of livestock, horses, or poultry, truck farming, and all other agricultural uses. Specifically excluded are nurseries and forestry operations.

Commentary: This use category includes all purely agricultural uses. It does not include uses which may be accessory to agriculture, such as retail stores, nor does it include industries or businesses which support or are supported by agriculture.

Section 4102. Table of Permitted Uses.

General Use Category	Agricultural	Rural	Estate	Development	Urban Core	Neighborhood Conservation	Heavy Industrial	Holding District
A. Agriculture								
1. Agriculture	Y	Y	Y	N	N	N	N	Y
2. Forestry	C	C	C	C	C	C	C	C
B. Residential								
1. Conventional subdivision	Y	Y	Y	Y	Y	Y	N	N
2. Performance subdivision	Y	Y	Y	Y	Y	N	N	Y
C. Institutional								
1. Outdoor recreational (except commercial stables)	Y	Y	Y	Y	Y	Y	N	Y
Commercial stables	C	C	C	N	N	N	N	C
2. Institutional, indoor recreation, and special residential	N	N	N	Y	Y	N	N	Y
D. Commercial								
1. Office	N	N	N	Y	Y	N	Y	N
2. Commercial/entertainment	N	N	N	Y	Y	N	N	N
3. Commercial/recreation	N	N	N	Y	Y	N	N	N
4. Recreational rental dwelling	C	Y	N	Y	N	N	N	Y
5. Road service, vehicle service and sales, and fast food	N	N	N	Y	Y	N	Y	N
6. Public service	Y	Y	Y	Y	Y	Y	Y	Y
7. Agricultural support	Y	Y	N	Y	N	N	N	N
8. Nurseries	Y	Y	Y	Y	N	N	N	Y
9. Regional shopping center	N	N	N	N	Y	N	N	N
E. Industrial								
1. Light industry	N	N	N	Y	Y	N	Y	N
2. Heavy industry (except landing strips and heliports	C	C	N	C	N	N	Y	C
3. Extraction	Y	N	N	N	N	N	Y	N

B. **Forestry.** This use includes commercial logging operations, clearing or destruction of forested or woodland areas (as defined by this ordinance, including woodlands, young woodlands, and mature woodlands), selective cutting or clearing for commercial or other purposes, clearing for agriculture or other prospective land uses, and clearing of vegetation in reserved open space or resource protection areas. This does not include authorized clearing in accordance with plans approved pursuant to this ordinance, removal of sick or dead trees, or removal of trees on lots of one (1) acre or less, except where deed restrictions would prohibit this.

Section 4105. Residential Uses.

A. **Conventional residential.** Conventional residential uses include all single-family detached dwelling units in subdivisions built or subdivided prior to enactment of this ordinance and all single-family detached dwelling units in subdivisions subdivided after enactment of this ordinance which are developed to the standards for conventional subdivisions required by this ordinance.

Commentary: This use includes all individual houses, not part of a plat of existing subdivisions, and new single-family subdivisions.

B. **Performance residential.** Performance residential uses consist of all residential subdivisions built or subdivided after enactment of this ordinance except those included within the conventional residential use category.

Commentary: This use category is intended to be the primary mode of residential development. It will permit the residential builder considerable freedom by allowing varied types of dwellings, lot sizes, and design. It also insures adequate open space in each development.

Section 4106. Recreational, Institutional, and Special Residential Uses.

A. **Outdoor recreational.** Outdoor recreational uses include areas for recreational activities (including, but not limited to, picnicing, jogging, cycling, and totlots), arboretums, boat launching ramps, areas for cycling, hiking, and jogging, golf courses (regulation or par 3), outdoor iceskating rinks, nature areas, parks (public or private), picnic areas, playfields, playgrounds, ski or toboggan areas, commercial

stables, outdoor swimming pools, tennis courts, wildlife sanctuaries, and all other outdoor recreational uses. Specifically excluded are outdoor movie theaters, firing ranges, miniature golf courses, golf driving ranges, and marinas.

Commentary: This use is basically an open-space use. Physical structures are permitted, but only as minor, incidental accessories to open-space use.

B. **Institutional, indoor recreational, and special residential uses.** These uses include aquariums, rooming houses, day or youth camps, cemeteries, churches, community or recreational centers, convents or monasteries, daycare centers (day or nursery schools), group dwellings, gymnasiums, halfway houses, libraries or museums, nursing homes, indoor recreational centers, public or private schools, schools or homes for physically or mentally handicapped, indoor skating rinks (ice or roller), indoor swimming pools, tennis, racquetball, handball courts, and all other institutional, indoor recreational, and special residential uses.

Commentary: These uses are all supportive of the residential community: they provide indoor space for recreation, hobbies, meetings, education, and worship, as well as cultural facilities, group quarters for religious groups and the infirm or elderly, and boarding houses. While some uses may be operated for private profit, they duplicate services that are generally provided by public or nonprofit groups.

Section 4107. Commercial Uses.

A. **Office.** Office uses include barbershops (and other personal service uses such as beauty shops), governmental offices, business or professional offices, medical offices or clinics, and all other office uses.

Commentary: This category includes all types of business or governmental offices. It also includes various service-type businesses where service is basically on an individual-to-individual basis as opposed to services which are performed on objects or personal property.

B. **Commercial and entertainment.** These uses include animal shelters, auto accessory stores, banks (and other financial institutions), blueprint and photostat stores, bowling alleys, private indoor clubs, commercial or trade schools (e.g., dance studios, schools for martial arts), currency exchanges, funeral homes, mortuaries, garden supply and/or greenhouses (provided all sales on premises are retail), grocery stores and supermarkets (excluding convenience stores, e.g., "7-Eleven" stores), hospitals, hotels (or motels), ice cream stores or stands, laundries and/or dry cleaners, light mechanical repair stores (e.g., watch, camera, bicycle, TV), stores selling liquor, beer, or soft drinks (in sealed containers, not for consumption on premises), lodges for fraternal orders, package stores, restaurants (standard sit-down, not fast food), retail sales or stores, service businesses or stores (e.g., catering, duplicating, photography, shoe repair, tailoring, travel agency, upholstering), shopping centers, theaters and auditoriums (indoor), upholstery stores, and all other commercial and entertainment uses.

Commentary: This category consists of uses which are varied but share such important land use characteristics as traffic-generation rates and bulk (building) requirements. Accordingly, they have similar impact(s) on other uses in proximity to them.

C. **Commercial recreational use.** These uses include amusement parks, drive-in theaters, fairgrounds, golf driving ranges (including miniature golf), marinas, outdoor theaters (or amphitheaters), race tracks (e.g., auto, dog, go-kart, harness, horse, motorcycle), ranges (skeet, rifle, or archery), sport arenas, and all other commercial recreation uses.

Commentary: This group includes recreational uses which are greater nuisances than conventional outdoor recreational activities because of their size and scale, traffic volumes, noise, lights, or physical hazards such as flying objects or use of weapons.

D. **Recreational rental dwelling uses.** These uses include camps or campgrounds with overnight camping or vacation cottages, rental cabins, vacation cottages, and all other recreational rental uses.

Commentary: These uses are all short-term rental facilities oriented toward leisure activities for the vacationer or organized activities such as summer camps. The users are transient, and much activity is apt to be out-of-doors. Because these uses are leisure-oriented and take place outdoors, they have higher nuisance values than do other residential uses.

E. **Road service.** These uses include arcades or billiard parlors, boat rental and/or storage facilities, body shops, convenience stores (e.g., "7-Eleven" stores), gasoline service stations, garden centers, lawnmower repair stores, fast-food restaurants, recreational vehicle parks, taverns (lounges, night clubs, dance halls), travel trailer parks, commercial vehicle garages, vehicle rentals, vehicle repair (body) shops, vehicle sales, supplies, and service (new or used auto, boat, bus, equipment, motorcycle, truck, snowmobile), and all other road services.

Commentary: Many of these uses have significant nuisance effects because of the types of merchandise sold, most of which require or conventionally involve outdoor storage. They are commonly highway-oriented facilities. The servicing of vehicles and equipment often involves noise, unsightly trash, oil, grease, and dirt, as well as testing and exterior storage. The food and entertainment uses are ones with late hours of operation which often generate excessive litter, traffic, noise, and other neighborhood concerns.

F. **Public service.** These uses include emergency services, service buildings or garages (e.g., ambulance, fire, police, rescue), utility or broadcasting stations or towers, utility service yards or garages, and all other public utility and public service uses.

Commentary: Public service uses are those uses which are essential to the functioning of the community. Most of the impervious surface allowed in these uses will consist of the building's floor area (as opposed, e.g., to parking area). Most often a public service use will be one which supports a public utility (e.g., telephones, electricity). Such utilities usually must be located in residential areas because of the nature of the service they provide. These uses generally do not have employees regularly employed on-site and are consequently not traffic generators. Other than electrical substations, these uses present no public dangers.

G. **Agricultural support.** These uses include farm equipment sales and repair, farm produce sales and supply (feed, grain, fertilizer), farm product processing (cidermill, dairies, poultry, or meat processing) provided that the total number of employees in such processing plants does not exceed five (5), and all other agricultural support uses.

Commentary: These uses are generally supportive of the farm community. Without the presence of such uses, farmers find it increasingly difficult to function. They are fully compatible with agriculture, which distinguishes them from other commercial uses.

H. **Nurseries.** This category includes nurseries with or without retail sales or greenhouses.

Commentary: A nursery is basically an open-space use which generates little traffic and has few nuisances (such as late hours or customer or truck noise) associated with it (see Article II, definition). Nurseries should be distinguished from more intensive garden centers.

I. **Regional center.** This category includes commercial land (use) development consisting of seven hundred and fifty thousand (750,000) or more square feet of gross floor area.

Section 4108. Industrial Uses.

A. **Light industry.** These uses include blacksmith shops, boatworks (custom building and repair), building materials sales or storage yards (excluding asphalt or concrete mixing), bulk materials or machinery storage (fully enclosed), carpet and rug cleaning plants, contractors' offices and equipment storage yards, dry cleaning and laundry plants serving more than one (1) outlet, dyeing plants, extermination shops, food processing and packing plants, fuel oil, ice, coal, and wood sales, furniture cleaning plants, furniture refinishing shops, lumberyards, manufacturing (including the production, processing, cleaning, testing, and distribution of materials, goods, foodstuffs, and products in plants with less than five hundred thousand [500,000] square feet of floor area, or fewer than two thousand [2,000] employees on every shift), mini-warehouses or storage facilities, mirror supply and refinishing shops, monument works, ornamental iron workshops, pilot plants, printing plants, publishing plants, scientific (e.g., research, testing, or experimental) laboratories, trade shops (including cabinet, carpentry, planing, plumbing, refinishing, and paneling), truck terminals, veterinary offices with fully enclosed runs, yards, pens, and kennels, warehouses, wholesale business and storage, and all other light industrial uses.

Commentary. This category contains those industrial uses which are generally not objectionable because of noise, heavy truck traffic, or fumes, or which generate nuisances which may be ameliorated adequately by performance standards.

B. **Heavy industry.** This use category includes landing strips and heliports, asphalt or concrete mixing plants, bulk material or machinery storage (unenclosed), fuel generation plants, grain elevators, meat packing plants or slaughterhouses, resource recovery facilities, motor or rail terminals; also, any industrial use, including those uses listed above as light industry, having five hundred thousand (500,000) or more square feet of floor area or more than two thousand (2,000) employees on any shift, and all other heavy industrial uses.

Commentary: This group contains those uses which have severe potential for negative impact on any uses which would locate relatively close to them. This group differs from light industrial uses in that it includes uses that require unenclosed structures that are large, tall, and unsightly, such as concrete batching plants. These uses also have severe potential for generation of odor and may involve large amounts of exterior storage; because of their scale, they are likely to have a regional impact.

C. **Extraction and junkyard uses.** This category includes junk, scrap, or salvage yards and all extraction uses.

Commentary: These uses create major disruptions to the area's environment, even when carefully regulated. Dust, dirt, noise, and unsightly conditions can be anticipated. None of these uses is an acceptable neighbor in an urban environment.

Section 4200. Zoning District Performance Standards.

Sections 4201 through 4203 delineate the minimum standards for open space, density, impervious surface coverage, and lot area which apply in each zoning district. The purpose of these performance standards is to provide detailed regulations and restrictions by means of minimum criteria which must be met by uses in order to protect neighbors from adverse impacts of adjoining land uses and to protect the general health, safety, and welfare by limiting where uses may be established, insuring that traffic congestion is minimized, controlling the intensity of use, and prescribing other such performance criteria necessary to implement the (Municipality) Comprehensive Plan and to meet the goals and objectives of this ordinance.

Commentary: Prior (Municipality) zoning regulations allowed the juxtaposition of disparate zoning districts (e.g., "highway commercial" adjoining "residential") or permitted incompatible land uses within a single zoning district. Development under that system has demonstrated that traditional zoning does not protect one land use from negative impacts of an adjoining one. Only occasionally, and only for some clear nuisances such as noise, have performance standards previously been used. This ordinance depends on a comprehensive performance evaluation process to insure compatibility between neighboring land uses.

Section 4201. Compliance.

All uses and activities shall comply fully with the provisions of the following standards as a precondition of being permitted pursuant to Section 4102.

Section 4202. Performance Standards.

This section contains the basic standards applicable to the districts and uses allowed by this ordinance. The standards of Section 4203 are minimum standards and shall apply to each district and use therein. All standards must be met. Whenever the standard contained in Section 4203 is different from another performance standard articulated in this article, the strictest standard shall always govern. The density factor (DF) is the maximum density permitted on the buildable portion of the site, as determined in Section 4304. All tracts of land within a district may be developed to the same density factor. The density factor is calculated by dividing the total number of dwelling units by the net buildable site area (Section 4304). Thus, no density factor directly controls actual site capacity. The floor area factor is the amount of floor area of a building compared with the net buildable site area. The minimum site area specifies the minimum total number of acres for which development of a particular use may be proposed. The minimum lot area, on the other hand, specifies the minimum lot size for agriculture, nurseries, and single-family uses.

Section 4203. (See page 123.)

Section 4300. Site Capacity Calculation: Purpose.

Site capacity for any proposed development is equal to the net buildable area of the site multiplied by the density factor (in the case of residential uses) or by the floor area factor or impervious surface ratio, whichever is more restrictive (in the case of nonresidential uses). The site capacity calculation provides the mechanism for subtracting from the base site area all portions of a site inappropriate for development. Consequently, the purpose of this section is to determine the extent to which a site may be utilized given its unique physical characteristics.

Commentary: Because land forms, size, and shape as well as natural or engineered limitations vary significantly from site to site, reasonable development regulations must take account of these variations. The former (Municipality) zoning ordinance did not discriminate on the basis of such site-specific variables as are involved in the site capacity calculations required by this ordinance; this inadequacy resulted in problems such as flooding, erosion, and the loss of valuable resources in (Municipality).

For each tract, the calculations contained in Sections 4301 through 4305 shall be made. If a parcel consists of land in more than a single district, or when it is to be part residential and part nonresidential, calculations shall be done separately for each such part of the total parcel.

Section 4301. Base Site Area (all land uses).

A. Gross site area as determined by actual on-site survey. _____ acres

B. Subtract land constituting roads and land within ultimate rights-of-way of existing roads, rights-of-way of utilities, and easements of access. –_____ acres

C. Subtract land which is not contiguous:

1. A separate parcel which does not abut, adjoin, or share common boundaries with the rest of the development. –_____ acres

2. Land which is cut off from the main parcel by a road, railroad, existing land uses, or major stream, such that common use is hindered or that the land is unavailable for building purposes. –_____ acres

Section 4203. Table of District Performance Standards.

Zoning District and Use	Open Space Ratio (OSR) Minimum (See Section 4500)	Density Factor w/o bonus (DF) Maximum (See Article VIII)	w/bonus	Floor Area Factor (FAF) Maximum	Impervious Surface Ratio (ISR) Maximum	Min. Site Area (*)	Min. Lot Area (*)	Max. No. of lots per Development
Agricultural District								
Agriculture and nursery	—	.025	—	—	—	—	—	—
Conventional subdivision	—	.20	—	—	.09	200,000	**	4
Performance subdivision	.90	6.3	10.0	—	.06	10 Ac	—	—
Institutional	—	—	—	.005	.08	—	—	—
Agricultural support	—	—	—	.55	.80	—	—	—
Other	—	—	—	.35	.50	—	—	—
Rural District								
Agriculture and nursery	—	.025	—	—	—	—	—	—
Conventional subdivision	—	.25	—	—	.10	160,000	**	—
Performance subdivision	.80	5.2	8.0	—	.11	5 Ac	—	—
Institutional	—	—	—	.006	.10	—	—	—
Other	—	—	—	.35	.50	—	—	—
Estate District								
Agriculture and nursery	—	.025	—	—	—	—	—	—
Conventional subdivision	—	.48	—	—	.14	80,000	40,000	—
Performance subdivision	.80	3.55	5.25	—	.08	10 Ac	—	—
Institutional	—	—	—	.008	.10	—	—	—
Other	—	—	—	.12	.20	—	—	—
Neighborhood Conservation								
Conventional subdivision	—	(See Section 5300)		—	—	(See Section 5300)		—
Other	—	—	—	.12	.20	—	—	—
Development District								
Conventional subdivision	—	1.2	1.9	—	.26	40,000	8,500	—
Performance subdivision	.35	6.3	11.5	—	.40	—	—	—
Other uses	—	—	—	1.2	1.0	—	—	—
Conditional uses	—	—	—	.63	.60	30 Ac	—	—
Urban Core District								
Conventional subdivision	—	3.5	4.1	—	.36	10,000	—	—
Performance subdivision	.20	10.65	21.8	—	.52	—	—	—
Other permitted uses	—	—	—	1.2	1.00	—	—	—
Conditional uses	—	—	—	.84	.80	20 Ac	—	—

Zoning District and Use	Open Space Ratio (OSR) Minimum (See Section 4500)	Density Factor (DF) Maximum (See Article VIII) w/o bonus	w/bonus	Impervious Floor Area Factor (FAF) Maximum	Surface Ratio (ISR) Maximum	Min. Site Area (*)	Min. Lot Area (*)	Max. No. of lots per Development
Heavy Industry								
All uses	—	—	—	.94	1.00	—	—	—
Holding district								
Agriculture and nursery	—	.025	—	—	—	—	—	—
Performance zoning	.70	6.3	11.5	—	.18	—	—	—
Other	—	—	—	.35	.50	—	—	—

* The figures specified in this column are minimum square feet unless otherwise specifically expressed in terms of minimum acreage.

** For most areas, the minimum lot area will be 40,000 square feet; on certain soils, it may be 30,000 square feet. See Section 4417.

124

D. Subtract land which in a previously approved subdivision encompassing the same land, as part or all of the subject parcel, was reserved for resource reasons (e.g., flooding or for recreation). –_____ acres

E. Subtract land used or proposed for residential uses, whenever both nonresidential and residential uses are proposed. (In the case of the site capacity calculation for the proposed residential use, subtract the land proposed for nonresidential use.) –_____ acres

F. Subtract land required for bufferyard area by Sections 4603 through 4611. (See commentary below for estimating bufferyard requirement.) –_____ acres

G. Equals base site area. —_____ acres

Commentary: This section makes clear that the area of a parcel which is suitable for development is not conterminus with the gross area of that parcel. The site capacity calculation determines the extent to which a site is developable by "subtracting" land which is unfit for development for any of a variety of reasons.

When a parcel is to be developed for both residential and nonresidential uses, the base site area for each portion must be calculated separately. This is necessary because in the case of residential uses permitted intensity is based on density, whereas in the case of nonresidential uses intensity is based on a floor area factor.

Land constituting easements and rights-of-way of roads must be subtracted because it is literally unavailable for development.

Noncontiguous land consists of areas which are effectively isolated and therefore unavailable for purposes related to the proposed use. For example, if a portion of the parcel is effectively inaccessible from the remainder of the parcel and therefore not buildable, it should be subtracted. If it is large enough to support development independent of the other portion and/or has access to a road, its base site (buildable) area could be calculated separately or could be included in a single, combined calculation.

The site capacity calculation requires the subtraction of the actual calculated bufferyard area. The following table of estimated bufferyard areas has been developed to permit the rapid calculation of base site area before the landowner has decided which bufferyard option will be used. In order to insure that the bufferyard area subtracted from gross site area will be large enough to protect any future adjacent residential uses, the estimates provided assume the "worst case" situation: they assume that the proposed use will develop at the maximum land use intensity permitted and that it will be surrounded by residential uses. Further, the "estimated bufferyard" area is based on a bufferyard wider than the minimum possible option available to the landowner. As a result, the "estimated bufferyard area" may be greater than that which might suffice to meet the minimum requirements of the bufferyards that are actually required.

Estimated Bufferyard Area

General Land Use Category	Estimated Bufferyard Width (feet)
Agriculture Forestry	0
Residential Nursery	20
Indoor Recreation, Institutional, and Special Residential Outdoor Recreation	30
Agricultural Support Commercial Entertainment Office Public Service Road Service Commercial Recreation Light Industry	40
Extraction, Junkyard Heavy Industry	75

Resource Protection and Special Natural Features Land.

Resource/Natural Feature (All Districts)	Open Space Ratio		Acres of Land in Resource	Resource Protection Land (Acres in Resource × Open Space Ratio)
	All Districts except AG District*	AG District*		
Beaches	1.00	1.00	_____	_____
Dunes	.98	.98	_____	_____
Bluffs	1.00	1.00	_____	_____
Ravines	.98	.98	_____	_____
Ravine buffers	.80	.80	_____	_____
Lakes, ponds, or water courses	1.00	1.00	_____	_____
Lake shoreline	.75	.20	_____	_____
Pond shoreline	.75	.20	_____	_____
Wetlands	1.00	1.00	_____	_____
Drainageways	.50	.30	_____	_____
Floodplains	1.00	1.00	_____	_____
Mature woodlands	.85	.60	_____	_____
Woodlands	.70	.40	_____	_____
Young woodlands	.40	.15	_____	_____
Steep slopes (less than 15%)	.60	.30	_____	_____
Steep slopes (16%–30%)	.70	.50	_____	_____
Steep slopes Rodman soils (16%–30%)	.80	.80	_____	_____
Steep slopes (30% or greater)	.95	.95	_____	_____
Rodman soils	.95	.95	_____	_____
Erosion hazard area	1.00	1.00	_____	_____
Prime agricultural soils	—	.85	_____	_____

TOTAL LAND IN RESOURCE   = _____

TOTAL RESOURCE PROTECTION LAND   = _____

*See Section 4500.

126

Section 4302. Resource Protection Land (all land uses).

All land area consisting of the natural resources or natural features listed below shall be measured. The total acreage of each resource shall be multiplied by its respective open space ratio to determine the amount of resource protection land or area required to be kept in open space in order to protect the resource or feature. The sum total of all resource protection land on the site equals TOTAL RESOURCE PROTECTION LAND.

(See table on page 126.)

Commentary: This subsection implements the (Municipality) Natural Resources Plan, which sets minimum levels of protection for different natural resources. All areas within any parcel(s) proposed for development which consist of natural resources or resource limitations shall be protected to the extent that the TOTAL RESOURCE PROTECTION LAND shall be subtracted from that site's buildable area.

This subsection identifies the resources of concern and the proportion of the area encompassing the resource or limitation which must be left in open space and may not be used to calculate a site's buildable area. Sections 4400 through 4419 complement this section by detailing how development of such natural resource areas shall be restricted.

In the agricultural district, a lower level of resource protection is required for certain resources than that which is set in all other districts, because in the agricultural district (which has been so defined and mapped on the basis of its prime agricultural soils) the first priority of (Municipality) is agricultural preservation.

Section 4303. Recreational land (residential uses only).

This calculation is required of all residential land uses with the exception of subdivisions which would be required to provide less than one-quarter (.25) acre by the following calculation. Total recreational land required for residential uses is calculated as follows:

Take	BASE SITE AREA	_____
Subtract	TOTAL ACRES OF LAND IN RESOURCE	−_____
EQUALS	TOTAL UNRESTRICTED LAND	=_____
Multiply	Total Unrestricted Land by one of the following as appropriate:	×_____

Zoning District/Use	Figure to be multiplied by TOTAL UNRESTRICTED LAND	
Agricultural	All subdivisions	0
Rural district	Conventional subdivision	.0065
	Performance subdivision	0
Estate district	Conventional subdivision	.0131
	Performance subdivision	0
Development district	Conventional subdivision without bonus	.0276
	Conventional subdivision with bonus	.0400
	Performance subdivision without bonus	.1018
	Performance subdivision with bonus	.1711
Urban core district	Conventional subdivision without bonus	.0411
	Conventional subdivision with bonus	.0474
	Performance subdivision without bonus	.1085
	Performance subdivision with bonus	.1633

EQUALS	TOTAL RECREATIONAL LAND REQUIRED	=_____
Subtract	Any resource protection land in the categories noted below provided said land is improved, or will be improved, for recreation.	
	Beach	−_____
	Forest	−_____
	Lake shore	−_____
	Pond shore	−_____
EQUALS:	TOTAL RECREATION LAND REMAINING TO BE PROVIDED	=_____

Commentary: One purpose of an open-space requirement is protection of the land's resources; an additional purpose with residential uses is to pro-

vide usable public or common open space as near to each dwelling unit as possible. Thus, there is a need for further control in order to insure that a minimum amount of land not restricted by the two immediately preceding subsections is retained for this purpose.

In the agricultural district and in performance subdivisions in the rural and estate districts, the open space insured by other regulations is adequate, and no additional recreation land is required. The character of the urban core district calls for less recreational space. In the case of neighborhood conservation districts, the areas are so small or are so likely to be fully developed that no useful recreational land would be provided by this specific requirement. An exemption has been created for small residential developments because the recreational land which would have been required by this calculation would be so limited in area as not to provide useful recreational space. The bonus(es) referred to in this section are detailed in Article VIII.

Section 4304. Determination of Site Capacity (all residential land uses).

Individual site capacity is determined by calculating the NET BUILDABLE SITE AREA. For single-family, single-family cluster, or performance subdivisions, the number of dwelling units permitted is determined by multiplying the density factor by the net buildable site area. The calculations are as follows:

Take	TOTAL RESOURCE PROTECTION LAND	_____	acres
Add	TOTAL RECREATION LAND REMAINING TO BE PROVIDED	+ _____	acres
EQUALS	TOTAL OPEN SPACE	= _____	acres
Take	BASE SITE AREA	_____	acres
Multiply by	District open space ratio (see Section 4203)	× _____	acres
EQUALS	MINIMUM REQUIRED OPEN SPACE	= _____	acres
Take	BASE SITE AREA	_____	acres
Subtract	TOTAL OPEN SPACE or MINIMUM REQUIRED OPEN SPACE, whichever is greater	– _____	acres

EQUALS	NET BUILDABLE SITE AREA	= _____	acres
Multiply by	District maximum density factor (Section 4203)	× _____	acres
EQUALS	NUMBER OF DWELLING UNITS (do not round off: use lowest whole number)	= _____	units

Section 4305. Determination of site capacity (all non-residential uses).

Individual site capacity is calculated as follows. Both maximum impervious surface area and maximum floor area must be calculated.

Take	BASE SITE AREA	_____	acres
Subtract	RESOURCE PROTECTION LAND	– _____	acres
EQUALS	BUILDABLE LAND	= _____	acres
Take	BUILDABLE LAND	_____	
Divide by	BASE SITE AREA	÷ _____	
Equals	CALCULATED IMPERVIOUS RATIO	= _____	
Take	IMPERVIOUS SURFACE RATIO (from land use intensity class of proposed use or district maximum, whichever is less)	_____	

If IMPERVIOUS SURFACE RATIO is equal to or less than the CALCULATED IMPERVIOUS SURFACE RATIO, then:

Take	BASE SITE AREA	_____	
Multiply by	IMPERVIOUS SURFACE RATIO	× _____	
Equals	PERMITTED IMPERVIOUS AREA	= _____	
Take	BASE SITE AREA	_____	
Multiply by	FAR (from land use intensity class of proposed use or district maximum, whichever is less)	× _____	
Equals	PERMITTED FLOOR AREA	= _____	

If IMPERVIOUS SURFACE RATIO is more than the CALCULATED IMPERVIOUS RATIO, then:

Take	BASE SITE AREA	_____	

Multiply by	CALCULATED IMPERVIOUS RATIO	×_____
Equals	PERMITTED IMPERVIOUS AREA	=_____
Take	CALCULATED IMPERVIOUS RATIO	_____
Divide by	IMPERVIOUS SURFACE RATIO	÷_____
Equals	REDUCTION FACTOR	=_____
Take	FLOOR AREA RATIO (from Section 4602) or maximum floor area factor (Section 4203) whichever is more restrictive.	_____
Multiply by	REDUCTION FACTOR	×_____
Equals	REQUIRED FLOOR AREA FACTOR	=_____
Multiply by	BASE SITE AREA	×_____
Equals	PERMITTED FLOOR AREA	=_____

Commentary: Certain land which requires protection because of natural resources or limitations must be subtracted from the base site area. Maximum permitted impervious area and floor area are then determined by the above calculations. The maximum intensity of use permitted in a district may not be reached, since a developer may choose to develop within a particular land use intensity class which imposes more restrictive standards than are otherwise applicable in the district.

Section 4400. Natural Resource or Natural Limitation Performance Standards.

A. In addition to the regulations imposed by Sections 4300 through 4303, all development shall be preceded by the identification of any environmental or natural feature described below and shall meet the following standards of environmental protection.

B. Site alterations, regrading, filling, and clearing or planting vegetation prior to submission of the plans for development shall be a violation of this ordinance. Reference in this section to "open space" is intended to mean the term as it is defined by Article II and described in Section 4500.

C. Sections 4402 through 4418 specify the environmental protection standards applicable to each natural resource identified therein unless the feature exists in the agricultural district, in which case the open space ratio contained in Section 4302 shall apply.

D. Sections 4416 through 4419 specify the standards imposed for stormwater runoff, on-site septic systems, and control of soil erosion, sedimentation, and water quality.

Section 4401. Beaches.

A. **Permanent open space.** All such areas shall be permanent open space. No uses or improvements other than those permitted herein shall be permitted in any area consisting of beach as defined by this ordinance.

B. **Permitted uses.** The following uses are permitted on beaches: swimming, boat launching, and recreational uses not involving any permanent structures or movement of sand or earth.

Section 4402. Dunes.

A. **Permanent open space.** At least ninety-eight (98) percent of all such areas shall remain as permanent open space.

B. **Permitted uses.** Since dunes are intolerant of even nonstructural recreational uses, no more than ten (10) percent of the dune area may be used for recreational activities. The following standards shall be utilized in determining the area which shall be counted as constituting the area of a dune, which is used for recreational activities.

1. **Trails.**

a. When the trail is an elevated wooden structure with handrails, the recreational area shall consist of the area occupied by the structure.

b. When the trail is an at-grade wooden walkway without handrails, the recreational area shall consist of the width of the trail plus two (2) feet on either side of the trail.

c. When the trail consists of natural soils or pavement and is used only for pedestrian traffic, the recreational area shall consist of the width of the trail plus four (4) feet on either side of the trail.

d. When the trail consists of natural soils or pavement and is used for horses, the recreational area shall consist of the width of the trail plus six (6) feet on either side of the trail.

e. When the trail consists of natural soils or pavement and is used for motor-driven bikes or vehicles, the recreational area shall consist of the width of the trail plus ten (10) feet on either side of the trail.

2. **Other recreational uses.** All recreational uses shall have the perimeter of the area demarcated by a structure, embankment, or planting which shall be at least two (2) feet high.

a. When the recreational area is demarcated by a structure, embankment, or planting which is four (4) feet or less high, the recreational area shall be the demarcated area plus eight (8) feet beyond the perimeter of the area.

b. When the recreational area is demarcated by a structure, embankment, or planting area which is more than four (4) feet high, the recreational area shall be the demarcated area plus four (4) feet beyond the perimeter of that area.

Section 4403. Bluffs.

A. **Permanent open space.** All such areas shall be permanent open space. No uses or improvements other than those permitted herein shall be permitted in any area consisting of bluff as defined by this ordinance.

B. **Permitted uses.**

1. Only recreational uses consisting of pedestrian access ways shall be permitted.

2. In the erosion hazard area associated with bluffs, any nonstructural recreational use is permitted.

Section 4404. Ravines and Ravine Buffers.

A. **Permanent open space.**

1. At least ninety-eight (98) percent of all ravines shall remain in permanent open space.

2. At least eighty (80) percent of all ravine buffers shall remain in permanent open space. If the area is mature woodlands, woodlands, or young woodlands, at least eighty-five (85) percent of all such areas shall remain in permanent open space.

3. No uses or improvement other than those permitted herein shall be permitted in any area consisting of ravines or ravine buffers as defined by this ordinance.

B. **Permitted uses.** Ravines shall not be the site of any land use or development, with the exception that access to other areas may be provided in ravine areas. In this event an environmental assessment shall provide the basis for location of such access. Minimum damage to the area shall be the guide in location of the access. The protected areas of ravine buffers shall be used only for passive recreation.

C. **Additional regulations.**

1. The streambeds of all ravines shall be kept clear of debris, including leaves and grass clippings, in order to slow undercutting of stream banks.

2. No development shall cause or permit the rate of runoff to ravines and ravine buffer areas to be more than ninety (90) percent of its rate prior to that development.

3. All retention facilities should be set back at least one hundred (100) feet from the top of the ravine wall. All such facilities shall be designed to minimize erosion and maximize measures which stabilize the ravine wall.

Section 4405. Floodplains.

A. The determination of all floodplain boundaries shall be based on the maximum recorded or projected flood elevation applicable. The area constituting a riverine floodplain shall be determined by reference to the following sources in the order indicated below. If the first source is not applicable, the second one shall be used.

1. Certified HUD flood insurance studies and maps;

2. Illinois Department of Transportation Division of Water Resources Regulatory Floodplain maps;

3. *Floodplain Information Maps and Profiles*, prepared by the U.S. Department of Agriculture, Soil Conservation Service;

4. *Hydrologic Investigations Atlas*, prepared by the U.S. Department of the Interior, Geologic Survey—these studies cover the en-

tire area of (Municipality) and show the flood of record, rather than a projected 100-year flood, for each area subject to flooding.

Inland depressional floodplains have an area greater than one-quarter (.25) of an acre or are areas delineated in the *Hydrologic Investigations Atlas* cited above. On-site topographic surveys and stormwater detention calculations (see Section 4416) are utilized to determine the elevations and boundaries of such inland depressional floodplains.

On-site topographic surveys shall be performed to locate the precise floodplain line on a parcel. The survey shall use the flood profile contained in the sources listed above or, if no such profile exists, by performing standard runoff calculations such as those contained in *Standards and Specifications for Soil Erosion and Sediment Control*, prepared jointly by the Northeastern Illinois Planning Commission, Soil and Water Conservation Districts, and the U.S. Soil Conservation Service.

B. **Permanent open space.** All such areas shall be permanent open space. No uses or improvements other than those permitted herein shall be permitted in any area consisting of floodplain as defined by this ordinance.

C. **Permitted uses.** The following uses are permitted within the floodplain as a matter of right:

1. All uses which are permitted in designated open spaces by Section 4500.

2. All uses which are classified as agriculture, nurseries, and outdoor recreation in Sections 4104, 4106, and 4107.

3. Boatlaunching ramp, boat docks, piers, bridge and bridge approaches, marinas, picnic shelters, and stormwater detention facilities, so long as the building permit application shows that a licensed engineer has certified that such structures are designed to withstand the forces exerted by the 100-year flood event at that location.

4. Boat houses, boat storage buildings, and operations, sales, or rental structures (except boat or motor repair buildings) associated with uses permitted in the preceding subsection, where a licensed engineer certifies that such structures are designed to

allow free entrance of floodwaters and structurally to withstand the forces exerted by the 100-year flood event at that location.

5. Operational, rental, or sales shelters associated with uses permitted by this section, drive-in movie screens, provided that their floors or structure are elevated above flood elevation on piles, piers, or other structures designed to permit floodwaters to flow safely underneath.

D. All other buildings or any residential, institutional, office, commercial and entertainment, commercial recreation, recreational rental dwelling, or nursery uses may be permitted pursuant to conditional use permits (see Article VII), provided that all such uses or structures and their access are raised so that no floor, or its structural supports, or any utility line has less than three (3) feet of clearance between its lowest point and the 100-year flood elevation. Vehicular access to such structures shall comply with the same standards in order to insure emergency or fire access during periods of high water. Any reduction of cross-sectional area due to vertical supporting members shall be offset by compensatory storage.

E. **Installation of fill materials.** Fill may be placed within the floodplain only when allowed as a conditional use pursuant to Article VII. An application for such conditional use shall be accompanied by detailed fill plans, showing existing and proposed conditions. If a structure is to be placed on the fill, the plans shall show the structure as well. In considering the application, the Zoning Hearing Board shall determine whether the proposed fill meets the general standards set forth in Article VII and the following additional standards:

1. The cross-sectional area of a riverine floodplain shall not be reduced by more than two and one-half (2.5) percent on either side of the centerline of the watercourse; an inland depressional floodplain may have its location and contours altered through cut and fill over thirty (30) percent of its surface area.

2. Compensatory storage shall be provided to offset the storage lost through the filling.

3. All changes in velocity, depth of flood elevation, or storage shall be limited to the property of the owner doing the filling or those property owners who have been granted flood or flow easements,

provided that in no event shall an increase in flood elevation be permitted if it would affect any existing building or bring any building to within three (3) feet of the flood elevation.

4. In no instance shall the depth of fill in a riverine floodplain exceed three (3) feet, nor shall any fill be placed within twenty-five (25) feet of the stream channel or in a location which might be endangered by or accelerate a meander. In an inland depressional floodplain the depth of fill measured from the natural grade to the new surface shall not exceed five (5) feet.

5. Fill shall consist of soil or rock materials only; sanitary landfills shall not be permitted in the floodplain. Further, all fill areas shall be stabilized with material which will insure and protect against erosion hazards, undercutting, and undermining.

6. Fill on the following soils shall require excavation to a base of clay before any such fill is installed: Marsh; Houghton muck, wet; Houghton peat, wet; Houghton.

F. **Structural anchoring.** Any structure placed in the floodplain shall be anchored firmly to prevent floodwaters from carrying it downstream. Such anchoring shall be sufficient to withstand a flood velocity of six (6) feet per second. The zoning officer shall require the applicant to submit the written opinion of a registered professional engineer that the proposed structural design meets this standard.

G. **Building elevation.**

1. No building or structure or any portion thereof which is located adjacent to a floodplain shall be erected, unless the finished surface of the ground is higher than, or is raised by filling to, an elevation or at least two (2) feet above the elevation of the floodplain.

2. For purposes of this subsection, land adjoining a floodplain shall be defined as perpendicular to the nearest elevation point on riverine floodplains. This excludes all areas downslope from depressional areas.

Section 4406. Wetlands.

A. **Permanent open space.** All such areas shall remain as permanent open space. Wetlands may be dredged for deepening or enlarged, but wetlands shall not be filled.

B. **Permitted uses.** The following buildings or structures are permitted within wetlands as a matter of right:

1. Boatlaunching ramps, boat docks, piers, bridge and bridge approaches, marinas, picnic shelters, and stormwater detention facilities, provided that a licensed engineer has certified that such structures are designed to withstand the forces exerted by the 100-year storm event. Evidence of this certification shall be presented as a precondition to issuance of a zoning certificate.

2. Boat houses, boat buildings, and operational sales or rental structures (except boat or motor repair buildings) associated with uses permitted in the preceding subsection, provided that a licensed engineer certifies that such structures are designed to allow free entrance of floodwaters and structurally to withstand the forces exerted by the 100-year flood event at that location. Evidence of this certification shall be presented as a precondition to issuance of a zoning certificate.

3. Operational, rental, or sales shelters associated with uses permitted by this section; drive-in movie screens, provided that their floors or structures are elevated above flood elevation on piles, piers, or other structures designed to permit floodwaters to flow safely underneath.

All other buildings or any residential, institutional, office, commercial and entertainment, commercial recreation, recreational rental dwelling, or nursery use may be permitted pursuant to conditional use permits (see Article VII), provided that all such uses or structures and their access are elevated so that no floor, or its structural supports, or any utility line has less than three (3) feet of clearance between its lowest point and the 100-year flood elevation. Vehicular access to such structures shall comply with the same standards in order to insure emergency or fire access during periods of high water. Any reduction of cross-sectional area due to vertical supporting members shall be offset by compensatory storage.

Section 4407. Steep Slopes.

In areas of steep slopes, the following standards shall apply:

A. Twelve (12) to less than fifteen (15) percent slope: no more than forty (40) percent of such areas shall be developed and/or regraded or stripped of vegetation.

B. Fifteen (15) to thirty (30) percent slope: no more than thirty (30) percent of such areas shall be developed and/or regraded or stripped of vegetation, with the exception that no more than twenty (20) percent of such areas may be disturbed in the case of Rodman soils.

C. More than thirty (30) percent slope: no more than fifteen (15) percent of such areas shall be developed and/or regraded or stripped of vegetation, with the exception that no more than five (5) percent of such areas may be disturbed in the case of Rodman soils.

Section 4408. Erosion Hazard Areas.

A. All such areas shall remain as permanent open space.

B. Erosion hazard areas may be used to provide access to nonhazard areas, provided that no alternate means or routes of access are feasible.

C. Where structures are provided to protect the property from beach and shoreline erosion, certification of the adequacy of this protection must be obtained from the U.S. Army Corps of Engineers. The area may then be developed as if it were not an erosion hazard area. Additional certification shall be required for any enlargements or extensions of development which was initially permitted pursuant to this section.

Section 4409. Mature Woodlands; Woodlands; Young Woodlands.

A. No more than fifteen (15) percent of any mature woodland may be cleared or developed. The remaining eighty-five (85) percent shall be maintained as permanent open space. No more than thirty (30) percent of any woodlands may be cleared or developed. The remaining seventy (70) percent shall be maintained as permanent open space. No more than sixty (60) percent of any young woodland shall be cleared. The remaining forty (40) percent shall be maintained as permanent open space.

B. **Special woodland protection credit.** When woodlands and/or mature woodlands cover two (2) acres or more of the gross site area of a parcel, and the developer undertakes the following precautions to protect such areas, the portion of the forested area whose canopy or drip line lies beyond fifteen (15) feet from the building construction area but within the lot lines of the property may be added to the net buildable site area in Section 4305. This may increase the number of dwelling units permitted. The canopy or drip line of a tree is that area circumscribed on the ground by a vertical line extended from the outermost extremities of the plant's branches to the ground.

In order to qualify for the right to add to the net buildable site area as provided above, the developer shall:

1. Submit a survey of all trees greater than five (5) inches in caliper, their canopy or drip lines, and the location of all proposed lot lines, buildings, rights-of-way, utility lines and easements, and septic tank filter fields. A line delineating a fifteen (15) foot construction area around all proposed buildings, rights-of-way, utility lines and easements, and septic tank filter fields shall be shown as in the following illustration.

2. Submit in writing the recommendations of a licensed tree expert (as defined by Illinois Revised Statutes) or any person having a college degree in forestry as to which trees may be protected notwithstanding development in close proximity to them, including all recommended protective measures.

3. Employ all recommended tree-protective measures and, in any event:

   a. Erect on-site rope or fence barriers along the line(s) delineated in Subsection (B) (2) and place bales of hay to protect the roots of all trees in excess of five (5) inches in caliper near this line.

   b. Provide a tree-protection supervisor on-site whenever equipment or trucks are placed or are moving near the trees to be protected in order to ensure compliance with all tree-protective measures.

4. Post a bond with (Municipality) in the amount of $4,000 per every acre (or portion thereof) of land in which trees are to be

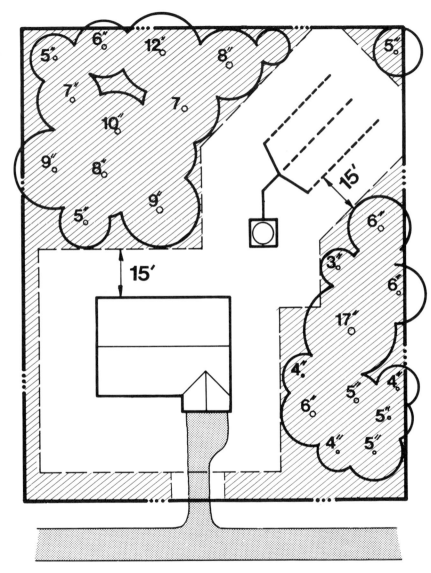

TREE AND DEVELOPMENT SURVEY

preserved. The bond shall be applied to the replacement of any trees which should die within three (3) years of the completion of construction (see Article IX).

5. Submit all of the data as part of the application for a zoning certificate (see Article IX).

C. **Replacement of woodlands credit.** In the case of mature woodlands and/or woodlands, the developer may clear or develop more than the area otherwise permitted to be disturbed by this section, provided that the total mature woodland or woodland area disturbed shall not be increased by more than fifty (50) percent of the area otherwise permitted to be disturbed. No more than twenty-two and one-half (22.5) percent of mature woodlands may be disturbed. No more than forty-five (45) percent of woodlands may be disturbed. In addition:

1. The developer shall designate a new woodland area on a part of the site not forested.

2. The new woodland area shall consist of 1.2 times the surface acreage of the woodland area disturbed pursuant to this subsection.

3. Only plant materials listed in Section 4802 under "woodland" shall be counted as meeting the requirements for replanted woodland pursuant to this subsection. The number and size of plants required is specified in Sections 4801 and 4804.

Section 4410. Lakes and Ponds.

All such areas shall be permanent open space. No development or diverting of these bodies of water shall be permitted except to provide required roads. Filling shall be permitted only in conjunction with deepening the lake and is permitted only if surface area and flood retention remain unchanged or are enlarged.

Section 4411. Lake Shorelines.

The shorelines of lakes, consisting of the area within one hundred (100) feet from the shorelines, shall contain no more than fifteen (15) percent impervious surfaces. At least seventy-five (75) percent of all such areas shall be permanent open space.

Section 4412. Pond Shorelines.

The shorelines of ponds, consisting of the area within fifty (50) feet from the shorelines, shall contain no more than fifteen (15) percent impervious surfaces. At least seventy-five (75) percent of all such areas shall be permanent open space.

Section 4413. Prime Agricultural Soils.

In the agricultural district at least eighty-five (85) percent of all such areas shall remain as permanent open space. Accessory farm structures (e.g., barns, silos) shall be permitted in the open space.

Section 4414. Drainageways.

A. No more than fifty (50) percent of such areas shall be developed.

B. The remaining fifty (50) percent shall remain as permanent open space. Regrading, stripping of vegetation, or filling is permitted in these areas, provided that:

1. The time of concentration of stormwater flows remains unchanged or is lengthened;

2. Stormwater and groundwater storage capacity are unchanged or increased;

3. Natural vegetation is installed (see Section 4800);

4. The resultant new drainageway has less velocity than preexisted or reduces streambank erosion through the provision of erosion control measures, undertaken and contained in Section 4418.

Section 4415. Agriculture District.

Section 4302 specifies natural resource protection standards which apply in the agricultural district. Some open space ratios specified in the agricultural district are less than the ones applicable in other districts. The less strict standard is permitted in the agricultural district as a means of maximizing the protection of prime agricultural soils, an important resource in themselves.

Section 4416. Stormwater Runoff.

A. Each development shall provide for the on-site or off-site detention of excess stormwater runoff resulting from that development. For the purpose of this article, "excess stormwater runoff" shall include all increases in stormwater resulting from: an increase in the impervious surface of the site, including all additions of buildings, roads, and parking lots; changes in soil absorption caused by compaction during development; modifications in contours, including the filling or draining of small depressional areas, alterations of drainageways, or regrading of slopes; destruction of forest; alteration of drainageways or installation of collection systems to intercept street flows or to replace swales or other drainageways; or the alteration of subsurface flows, including any groundwater dewatering or diversion practices such as curtain drains, compared with the site in its natural state.

B. **Limitation on stormwater runoff.** No development shall cause downstream property owners, water courses, channels, or conduits to receive stormwater runoff from proposed developments at a higher peak flow rate than would have resulted from the same storm event occurring over the site of the proposed development with the land in its natural, undeveloped condition, with the exception that in the Lake Michigan watershed the peak flow rate shall be no more than ninety (90) percent of the flow rate that would have resulted from the same storm event occurring on the site of the proposed development with the land in its natural, undeveloped condition. For the purposes of this article, "undeveloped condition" shall mean that all the natural retention areas and drainageways plus existing farm drainage tiles and highway drainage structures shall be included in the flow calculations. For the purposes of the following calculation, all ground covers shall be considered to be meadow or grassland, with the exception that forested areas shall be treated as woodlands. "Channel" or "drainageway channel" shall mean the channels used to convey the 100-year drainage flows between successive retention facilities or to retention facilities or from the property.

C. **Storage capacity.** All stormwater storage facilities shall be designed with sufficient capacity to accommodate all runoff caused by the development in excess of the runoff which would have resulted from the site if left in its natural, undeveloped condition. The storage capacity of all storage facilities shall be sufficient to store one hundred and fifteen (115) percent of the excess flow, in each watershed, which would result from the 100-year storm of 24-hour duration.

Commentary: The excess storage capacity is intended to provide a safety margin for downstream land uses and to provide reserve capacity to offset losses due to the accumulation of sediments and miscellaneous debris.

D. **Detention storage calculation.** The following formula shall be used to calculate the volume of detention required by this ordinance:

$$V = Rd - Rn - Ros - S - GW$$

V = the change in volume (in cubic feet per second) from the site. This is the base volume of excess stormwater flows that would result from the development.

Rd = the volume of stormwater runoff (in cubic feet per second) flowing from the site after its development. This determination shall include runoff from pervious and impervious surfaces, changes in areas of forest, changes in soils due to compaction, and changes in the time of concentration, for a 100-year storm of 24-hour duration.

Rn = the volume of stormwater runoff (in cubic feet per second) flowing from the site in its natural state. This determination shall include runoff from the site with its natural cover, grassland, or woodland for a 100-year storm of 24-hour duration. Farm fields shall be calculated as grassland.

Ros = the volume of stormwater runoff (in cubic feet per second) flowing onto the site from upstream properties in their present state of development for a 100-year storm of 24-hour duration.

S = the change in capacity (in cubic feet per second) of the natural on-site detention areas of the site. This indicates any drainageways, small depressional areas, or other areas which would naturally retain water during a 100-year storm of 24-hour duration. (This calculation may carry either a plus or minus value.)

GW = the change in subsurface flows due to dewatering techniques which would add to the total surface water runoff during a 100-year storm of 24-hour duration. Included here are dewatering devices such as drain tiles, curtain drains, or sump pumps. (This calculation may carry either a plus or minus value.)

Commentary: The detention storage calculation is a comprehensive calculation intended to account for all major factors which alter the runoff characteristics of a site during a 100-year, 24-hour storm. First, the runoff from the site in its developed condition is determined, including all upstream areas. This part of the calculation accounts for the impervious surfaces, ground covers, time of concentration, soil types, and compaction of soils. Then, the runoff from upstream areas, which is a factor beyond the landowner's control, is subtracted from this figure. The runoff from the site in a natural condition is also calculated and subtracted. Natural condition includes all forested areas and assumes a grassland cover for all grasslands and fields, whether cultivated or not. This is done because the natural state of runoff has often been substantially altered causing downstream flood damage. All development must restore runoff characteristics to at least natural condition. Next, change in the site's natural retention capacity is subtracted from the site in its developed capacity. If natural depressional areas are filled or drained, their storage capacity is added to the required detention area. If natural storage capacity is enlarged, it is subtracted from the needed detention storage. Similarly, if groundwater flows are altered so that they reach the streams more quickly, more retention will be needed.

E. **Design regulations.** All detention facilities and improvements required by this section shall comply with the following regulations.

1. **Storage volumes.** Storage may be provided by wet or dry bottom basins or reservoirs or rooftop storage facilities.

2. **Maximum depth.** The maximum planned depth of stormwater stored shall not exceed five (5) feet unless natural ground conditions lend themselves to greater depths.

3. **Outlet control structures.** Outlet control structures shall be designed as simply as possible and shall operate automatically. They will be designed to limit discharges into existing or planned downstream channels or conduits so as not to exceed existing flow of the site in its natural condition.

4. **Spillway.** Emergency overflow facilities shall be provided unless inflow is controlled to divert flows when the basin is at capacity.

5. **Dry bottom basin.** For basins designed without permanent pools:

   a. **Interior drainage.** Provisions must be made to facilitate interior drainage, to include the provision of natural grades to outlet structures, longitudinal and transverse grades to perimeter drainage facilities, or the installation of subsurface drains.

   b. **Multipurpose features.** These may be designed to serve secondary purposes for recreation, open space, or other types of use which will not be adversely affected by occasional or intermittent flooding.

   c. **Cleaning.** The basins shall be designed for periodic cleaning and removal of sediments, which shall be removed from the site or otherwise disposed of in an appropriate manner.

6. **Wet basins.** For basins designed with permanent pools:

   a. **Depth for fish.** If fish are used to help keep the basin clean, at least one-quarter (.25) of the area of the permanent pool must have a minimum depth of ten (10) feet.

   b. **Facilities for emptying.** For emergency purposes, cleaning, or shoreline maintenance, facilities shall be provided or plans prepared for the use of auxiliary equipment to permit emptying and drainage.

   c. **Pollution abatement.** Aeration facilities may be required when the quality of the influent and detention time would result in a lowering of dissolved oxygen content in the basin.

   d. **Slopes.** Approach slopes shall be at least 6:1 but not more than 3:1 and shall be at least four (4) to six (6) feet wide and slope gently toward the basin. The side slopes shall be of nonerosive material with a slope of 1:1 or flatter. The ledge shall be four (4) to six (6) feet wide and slope gently toward the shore to prevent people or objects from sliding into deep water. There shall be a freeboard of twelve (12) to eighteen (18) inches above the high-water elevation on all retention basins. Alternate designs for side slopes may be considered under special circumstances where good engineering practice is demonstrated.

   e. **Cleaning.** The basins shall be designed to include sediment traps in all inlets. Sediment traps shall be designed to permit periodic cleaning and maintenance. A basin maintenance plan shall be developed to insure that the design depths of the basin will remain over time.

7. **Building regulations.**

   a. **Rooftop storage.** Detention storage requirements may be met either in total or in part by detention on flat roofs. Design specifications of such detention shall be a part of the application for a zoning certificate. These specifications shall include the depth and volume of storage, design of outlet devices and downdrains, elevations of overflow scuppers, design loadings for the roof structure, and emergency overflow provisions. Rooftop storage shall not be permitted to drain directly into sanitary sewers or streets.

   b. **Parking lot storage.** Paved parking lots may be designed to provide temporary detention storage of stormwater on a portion of their surfaces not to exceed twenty-five (25) percent. Outlets shall be designed to empty the stored waters slowly, and depths of storage must be limited so as to prevent damage to parked vehicles. Storage areas shall be posted with warning signs and shall be designed to fill to maximum depth in not less than two (2) hours.

   c. **Detention storage.** All or a portion of the detention storage may also be provided in underground detention facilities.

8. Any development which is adjacent to a ravine or ravine buffer and which has in excess of three thousand two hundred (3,200) square feet of impervious surface shall provide evaporative storage to control for a one (1) inch rainfall on those surfaces.

9. Any development which is adjacent to a ravine or ravine buffer and which has an impervious surface ratio in excess of one-half (.5) shall provide evaporative or other storage to control for a two (2) inch rainfall on those surfaces.

10. Retention in floodplains shall be permitted only in depressional floodplain areas. Retention shall not be permitted in riverine floodplains.

F. **Maintenance of facilities.** The developer shall be responsible for the maintenance of all improvements until such time as eighty (80) percent of the development is completed and occupancy permits are issued or until such time as eighty (80) percent of the lots in the development have been sold. The developer shall not, however, transfer these improvements for the purpose of maintenance until he has complied with the above and until he has received final approval, final inspection, and a certificate of compliance from (Municipality). Thereafter, all detention improvements shall be maintained in perpetuity and cannot be developed for any other use which would limit or cause to limit the use for detention.

G. **Inspection of facilities.** The developer's engineer shall be required to inspect all drainage facilities under construction and certify their compliance with approved plans. In addition, a registered engineer, employed by (Municipality), may inspect all drainage facilities while under construction. When facilities are not constructed according to approved plans, (Municipality) has the explicit authority to compel compliance and require correction of any situations which are not according to the approved plans.

Section 4417. Soil Suitability for On-Site Disposal.

On-site septic system disposal shall meet the standards imposed by the (Municipality) Health Department.

A. The minimum site upon which a septic system may be permitted shall not be less than thirty thousand (30,000) square feet in the case of the following soils: Plainfield, Casco, Granby, Boyer, Dresden, Fox, Zurich, Grays.

B. The minimum site upon which a septic system may be permitted shall not be less than forty thousand (40,000) square feet in the case of any soils not specified in Subsection 4419 (A).

Section 4418. Soil Erosion and Sedimentation Control.

A. In order to prevent both soil erosion and sedimentation, a soil erosion and sedimentation control plan shall be required as a part of an application for a zoning certificate (see Article IX) whenever a development will involve any clearing, grading, transporting, or other form of disturbing land by the movement of earth, including the mining of minerals, sand, and gravel (to the extent that such mining is subject to regulation by [Municipality]), provided that any one of the following descriptions applies to said movement of land:

1. Excavation, fill, or any combination thereof will exceed five hundred (500) cubic yards.

2. Fill will exceed three (3) feet in vertical depth at its deepest point as measured from the natural ground surface.

3. Excavation will exceed four (4) feet in vertical depth at its deepest point as measured from the natural ground surface.

4. Excavation, fill, or any combination thereof will exceed an area of five thousand (5,000) square feet.

5. Plant and/or tree cover is to be removed from an area exceeding five thousand (5,000) square feet on any parcel of land.

Specifically exempted from the requirement of a soil erosion and sedimentation control plan are farming or other agricultural uses which (Municipality) is not empowered to regulate.

Whenever any land located in a stream, stream channel, or body of water is disturbed, a soil erosion and sedimentation control plan shall be provided.

B. **Definitions.** For the purposes of this section:

Soil erosion shall mean any removal and/or loss of soil by the action of water, ice, gravity, or wind. Erosion includes both the detachment and transport of soil particles.

Sedimentation shall mean the settling out of the soil particles which are transported by water or wind. Sedimentation occurs when the velocity of water or wind in which soil particles are suspended is slowed to a sufficient degree and for a sufficient period of time to allow the particles to settle out of suspension or when the degree of slope is lessened to achieve the same result.

Erodable slope shall mean all slopes with inclines in excess of four (4) percent.

Large flat surface area (unpaved) shall mean an area which is flat or whose slope is less than four (4) percent and which consists of more than one thousand (1,000) square feet of exposed soil.

C. All measures necessary to minimize soil erosion and to control sedimentation in the disturbed land area shall be provided. Specifically, the following protection shall be provided for all disturbed areas: minimize velocities of water runoff, maximize protection of disturbed areas from stormwater runoff, and retain sedimentation within the development site as early as possible following disturbances. A list of major problem areas for erosion and sedimentation control follows. For each one, the purpose(s) of requiring control is described. Soil erosion and sedimentation control measures for all such areas shall be provided with a view toward achieving the specific purpose listed below for which a control plan is required.

1. Erodable slopes: prevent detachment and transportation of soil particles from slope.

2. Streams, streambeds, streambanks, bodies of water, lake shorelines: prevent detachment and transportation of soil particles.

3. Drainageways: prevent detachment and transportation of soil particles (which would otherwise deposit in streams, bodies of water, or wetlands); promote deposit of sediment loads (traversing these areas) before these reach bodies of water.

4. Land adjacent to streams, ponds, lakes, and wetlands: prevent detachment and transportation of soil particles.

5. Enclosed drainage structure: prevent sedimentation in structure, erosion at outfall of system, and deposit of sediment loads within system or beyond it.

6. Large flat surface areas (unpaved): prevent detachment of soil particles and their off-site transportation.

7. Impervious surfaces: prevent the detachment and transportation of soil (in response to an increase in the rate and/or volume of runoff of the site or its concentration caused by impervious surfaces).

8. Borrow and stockpile areas: divert runoff from face of slopes which are exposed in the excavation process; convey runoff in stabilized channels to stable disposal points; leave borrow areas and stockpiles in stable condition.

9. Adjacent properties: prevent their erosion and/or being deposited with sediment.

D. The table starting on page 140 presents a graphic summary of erosion and sedimentation control measures and indicates, by asterisk, when any such measure may effectively control the problem area. One or more of each such asterisked measure shall suffice to comply with the requirements of this section, provided that the zoning officer specifically determines that it complies with Subsection 4418 (C).

Section 4419. Water Quality Standards.

A. The purpose of this section is to implement the goals and policies of the Federal Water Pollution Control Act. It is the purpose of that act and this section to restore and maintain the chemical, physical, and biological integrity of our waters. It is national policy to prevent, reduce, or eliminate pollution of navigable waters and ground waters and to improve the sanitary condition of surface and underground waters, giving due regard to the conservation of such waters for the protection and propagation of fish and wildlife, recreational purposes, and the use of such water for public water supply, agricultural, industrial, and other purposes.

B. All developments shall comply with the following standard related to nonpoint pollutant loads which leave the site. The amount of nonpoint pollutant loads which leave a site shall be limited to fifty (50) percent of what those loads would have been, as a result of the installation of structures and all other impervious surfaces, had the development been developed conventionally at the same density (in the case of residential developments) or at the maximum impervious surface ratio (in the case of nonresidential uses). In this section, "reference site" is used to describe the development which would have been developed "conventionally."

Commentary: This standard is contained in the Areawide 208 Water Quality Management Plan for Northeastern Illinois *which was developed pursuant to the Federal Water Pollution Control Act Amendment of 1972, as amended. The level of pollution permitted to different land uses was set following analysis of the amount of pollution which would result from typical, existing development in the region. Once this amount of pollution was determined, a standard*

MEASURE	CHARACTERISTICS	ERODABLE SLOPES	WATER BODIES	LAND ADJACENT TO WATER BODIES	DRAINAGEWAYS	ENCLOSED DRAINAGE STRUCTURES	LARGE FLAT SURFACE AREAS	IMPERVIOUS SURFACES	BORROW AND STOCKPILE AREAS	ADJACENT PROPERTIES	INTERIM ROADS AND PARKING AREAS
1. Seeding	Inexpensive and effective, but may require supplemental measures. Stabilizes soil, thus minimizing erosion. Permits runoff to infiltrate soil, reducing runoff volume. Should include prepared topsoil bed.	*	*	*			*		*	*	
2. Seeding with Mulch	Facilitates establishment of vegetative cover. Effective for drainageways with low velocity. Should include prepared topsoil bed.	*	*	*	*				*	*	
3. Hydro Seeding	Effective on large areas. Mulch tacking agent used to provide immediate protection until grass is rooted. Should include prepared topsoil bed and supplemental measures, when necessary.	*		*			*		*	*	
4. Sodding	Provides immediate protection. Can be used on steep slopes where seed may be difficult to establish. Watering until sod is established is desirable. Should include prepared topsoil bed.	*	*	*	*		*		*	*	
5. Mulching	Used alone to protect exposed areas for short periods. Protects soil from impact of rain. Preserves soil moisture and protects germinating seed.	*		*			*		*		
6. Sod Retaining Wall	Protects erodable slopes from sheet erosion. Maximum slope is 1:2. Sod, usually 18″×72″ is piled, tilting slightly toward the slope.	*									

MEASURE	CHARACTERISTICS	ERODABLE SLOPES	WATER BODIES	LAND ADJACENT TO WATER BODIES	DRAINAGEWAYS	ENCLOSED DRAINAGE STRUCTURES	LARGE FLAT SURFACE AREAS	IMPERVIOUS SURFACES	BORROW AND STOCKPILE AREAS	ADJACENT PROPERTIES	INTERIM ROADS AND PARKING AREAS
7. Willow Webs	Protects slopes that are highly susceptible to erosion. Mulch will improve establishment of plant material.	*	*	*	*						
8. Brush and Sod	More expensive than other slope stabilization techniques. Provides a high-quality landscape.	*		*	*						
9. Willow Revetment	Stabilizes cutbanks adjacent to deep water. Aesthetic and wildlife benefits.		*	*	*						
10. Vegetative Buffer	Use grass, prairie or forest. Slows runoff velocity. Filters sediment from runoff. Reduces volume or runoff on slopes.	*		*	*		*		*	*	
11. Reed Banks	Stabilizes streambanks. Provides more visually attractive results than purely structural techniques.		*								
12. Reed Berms	Reduces flow velocity and stabilizes. Breaks wave action. Slightly higher initial costs, but requires little maintenance.		*								

MEASURE	CHARACTERISTICS	ERODABLE SLOPES	WATER BODIES	LAND ADJACENT TO WATER BODIES	DRAINAGEWAYS	ENCLOSED DRAINAGE STRUCTURES	LARGE FLAT SURFACE AREAS	IMPERVIOUS SURFACES	BORROW AND STOCKPILE AREAS	ADJACENT PROPERTIES	INTERIM ROADS AND PARKING AREAS
13. Planter Strips	Traps sediments. Reduces velocity.							*			
14. Reforestation	Intercepts precipitation and reduces runoff. Aesthetic and wildlife benefits.	*		*	*		*			*	
15. Native Prairie	Effective in reducing runoff and capturing sediment. Requires maintenance to continue prairie character.			*	*		*			*	
16. Filters-Strawbale	Filters sediment from runoff. Temporary use for seeded and/or mulched slopes. Staked along contour where slope exceeds 100´	*		*	*				*	*	
17. Grassed Swale or Waterway	Much more stable form of drainageway than bare channel. Grass tends to slow runoff and filter out sediment. Serves as second- and third-order streams.		*	*	*		*	*			
18. Wetland Swale	Lowers runoff velocities. Effectively removes sediment from small- and medium-sized storms. Requires careful design and good maintenance. First-order components of drainage system.		*	*	*		*	*			

MEASURE	CHARACTERISTICS	ERODABLE SLOPES	WATER BODIES	LAND ADJACENT TO WATER BODIES	DRAINAGEWAYS	ENCLOSED DRAINAGE STRUCTURES	LARGE FLAT SURFACE AREAS	IMPERVIOUS SURFACES	BORROW AND STOCKPILE AREAS	ADJACENT PROPERTIES	INTERIM ROADS AND PARKING AREAS
19. Woodland Swale	Canopy intercepts precipitation and roots slow rate of runoff. Greater installation costs, but lower maintenance costs.		*	*	*		*	*			
20. Grading and Shaping	Minimizes exposed areas, thus reducing erosion. Water can be diverted to minimize erosion. Flatter slopes ease erosion problems.	*		*	*		*		*	*	
21. Grubbing Omitted	Saves cost of grubbing. Provides new sprouts. Retains existing root mat system.	*		*	*		*			*	
22. Compaction	Helps hold soil in place, making exposed areas less vulnerable to erosion.										*
23. Rip Rap Slope	Used where vegetation is not easily established. Effective for high velocities or high concentration. Permits runoff to infiltrate soil. Dissipates energy flow.		*			*					
24. Gravel Base	Stabilizes soil surface, thus minimizing erosion. Permits construction traffic in adverse weather. May be used as part of permanent base construction of paved areas.										*

MEASURE	CHARACTERISTICS	ERODABLE SLOPES	WATER BODIES	LAND ADJACENT TO WATER BODIES	DRAINAGEWAYS	ENCLOSED DRAINAGE STRUCTURES	LARGE FLAT SURFACE AREAS	IMPERVIOUS SURFACES	BORROW AND STOCKPILE AREAS	ADJACENT PROPERTIES	INTERIM ROADS AND PARKING AREAS
25. Paving	Provides weather resistant traffic surface, but increases runoff volume and velocity.										✶
26. Benches	Reduces runoff velocity by reducing effective slope length. Collects sediment. Provides access to slopes for seeding, mulching, and maintenance.	✶									
27. Diversion Berm	Diverts water from vulnerable areas. Collects and directs water to prepared drainageways. May be placed as part of normal construction operation.	✶							✶	✶	
28. Diversion Ditch	Collects and diverts water to reduce erosion potential. May be incorporated in permanent project drainage systems.	✶							✶	✶	
29. Dechannelization	Reduces runoff velocities. Increases sediment deposition in floodplain areas.		✶		✶						
30. Roughen Surface	Reduces velocity and increases infiltration rates. Collects sediment. Holds water, seed, and mulch better than smooth surfaces.	✶					✶				

MEASURE	CHARACTERISTICS	ERODABLE SLOPES	WATER BODIES	LAND ADJACENT TO WATER BODIES	DRAINAGEWAYS	ENCLOSED DRAINAGE STRUCTURES	LARGE FLAT SURFACE AREAS	IMPERVIOUS SURFACES	BORROW AND STOCKPILE AREAS	ADJACENT PROPERTIES	INTERIM ROADS AND PARKING AREAS
31. Stockpiling	Topsoil may be stockpiled above borrow areas to act as a diversion. Stockpile should be temporarily seeded.	*					*		*		
32. Pervious Pavement	Permits greater infiltration and reduces runoff. Expensive to install, but can be a permanent site improvement. Lattice concrete pavers permit grass surface where traffic is not excessive.							*			*
33. Protect Work Area	Protects erodible bank areas from stream currents during construction. Minimal disruption when removed.		*								*
34. Retaining Wall	Reduces gradient where slopes are extremely steep. Permits retention of existing vegetation, keeping soil stable in critical areas. Minimizes maintenance.	*									
35. Seepage Control	Prevents piping and soil slippage on cut slopes.	*									
36. Curb	Keeps high velocity runoff on paved areas from leaving paved surface. Collects and conducts runoff to enclosed drainage system or prepared drainageway.	*									

MEASURE	CHARACTERISTICS	ERODABLE SLOPES	WATER BODIES	LAND ADJACENT TO WATER BODIES	DRAINAGEWAYS	ENCLOSED DRAINAGE STRUCTURES	LARGE FLAT SURFACE AREAS	IMPERVIOUS SURFACES	BORROW AND STOCKPILE AREAS	ADJACENT PROPERTIES	INTERIM ROADS AND PARKING AREAS
37. Sediment Trap	May be constructed of a variety of materials. Traps sediment and reduces velocity of flow. Can be cleaned and expanded as needed.		✱	✱	✱						
38. Sediment Basin	Traps sediment. Releases runoff at nonerosive rates. Controls runoff at system outlets. Can be visual amenities.		✱	✱	✱	✱					
39. Sod Filter	Inexpensive and easy to construct. Provides immediate protection. Protects areas around inlets from erosion.					✱		✱			
40. Straw or Rock Filter	Can utilize material found on site. Easy to construct. Filters sediment from runoff.					✱					✱
41. Inlet Sediment Trap	Easy to shape. Collects sediment. May be cleaned and expanded as needed.					✱		✱			
42. Culvert Sediment Trap	Easy to install at inlet. Keeps culvert clean and free flowing. May be constructed of lumber or logs.		✱								✱

MEASURE	CHARACTERISTICS	ERODABLE SLOPES	WATER BODIES	LAND ADJACENT TO WATER BODIES	DRAINAGEWAYS	ENCLOSED DRAINAGE STRUCTURES	LARGE FLAT SURFACE AREAS	IMPERVIOUS SURFACES	BORROW AND STOCKPILE AREAS	ADJACENT PROPERTIES	INTERIM ROADS AND PARKING AREAS
43. Check Dams	Reduces flow velocity. Catches sediment. Can be constructed of logs, straw, hay, rock, lumber, masonry, or sandbags.		*	*	*						
44. Weir	Controls sedimentation in large streams. Causes minimal turbidity.		*	*	*						
45. Windbreak	Minimizes wind erosion. May be snow fence.						*				
46. Stream Pooling	Reduces scoring and dissipates excess energy. "Dams" need not be impermeable. Catches sediment. Provides aquatic habitats.		*	*	*						
47. Slope Drain (chute)	Prevents erosion on slopes when runoff cannot be diverted to edges of slope area. Can be temporary or permanent. Slows velocity of runoff.	*									
48. Slope Drain (pipe)	Prevents erosion on slopes when runoff cannot be diverted to edge of slope area. Usually permanent. Can be constructed as grading progresses.	*									

147

MEASURE	CHARACTERISTICS	ERODABLE SLOPES	WATER BODIES	LAND ADJACENT TO WATER BODIES	DRAINAGEWAYS	ENCLOSED DRAINAGE STRUCTURES	LARGE FLAT SURFACE AREAS	IMPERVIOUS SURFACES	BORROW AND STOCKPILE AREAS	ADJACENT PROPERTIES	INTERIM ROADS AND PARKING AREAS
49. Drop Spillway	Slows velocity of flow, reducing erosive capacity.		*	*	*						
50. Storm Sewer	System removes collected runoff from site, particularly from paved areas. Can accept large concentrations of runoff. Conducts runoff to municipal sewer system or stabilized outfall location. Use catch basins to collect sediment.							*		*	
51. Catch Basin	Collects high-velocity concentrated runoff. May use filter cloth over inlet.							*		*	
52. Energy Dissipator	Slows runoff velocity to nonerosive level. Permits sediment collection from runoff.	*		*	*	*					
53. Level Spreader	Converts collected channel or pipe flow back to sheet flow. Avoids channel easements and construction off project site. Simple to construct.			*	*						
54. Temporary Crossing	Eliminates stream turbulence and turbidity. Provides unobstructed passage for fish and other water life. Capacity for normal flow can be provided with storm water flowing over roadway.		*								*

148

was set which would result in a pollution level equal to fifty (50) percent of that generated by the impervious surfaces in existing developments of similar density.

C. In order to determine whether a development has met the standards imposed by this section, the calculations detailed in Subsection 4419 (E) must be performed. These calculations result in figures for the "actual site pollution index" and the "target pollution index." The "performance index" is equal to the actual site pollution index minus the target pollution index. The target pollution index is equal to the number of "points" that the development must "score" in order to meet the requirements of this ordinance. The difference between the actual site pollution index and this target pollution index, then, indicates whether a subject development has met the standards imposed by this section. If the performance index is a positive number, the water quality standards have not been met, and techniques chosen from among those detailed in Section 4419 (D) must be employed in order to meet these standards.

D. The following table identifies techniques which may be used to meet the water quality standards imposed by this section. It also provides an approximation of the degree to which each of the techniques contributes to water quality improvements. In order to determine the actual impact which utilization of any of the techniques listed below will have on the water quality of a particular site, the calculations required in Subsection 4419 (E) must be performed.

Technique	Approximate Effect on Water Quality
Convert impervious surface to forest	99% reduction in load from each unit of area converted
Convert grassland to forest	90% reduction in load from each unit of area converted
Convert impervious surface to grassland	88% reduction in load from each unit of area converted
Convert impervious surface to porous paving blocks	24% reduction in load from each unit of area converted
Convert impervious surface to porous asphalt	36% reduction in load from each unit of area converted

Stormwater detention basins	30% reduction in load
Use of natural drainage	18% reduction in load
Use of vegetated streamside buffers	8% reduction in load
Use of street sweeping (vacuum - every 7 days)	25% reduction in load
(vacuum - every 3 days)	50% reduction in load
(broom - every 7 days)	25% reduction in load

Commentary: The values in this table for the conversion of one land cover to another interact with each other in a very complex way. For this reason, the figures given in the right-hand column can be taken only as approximations of the effects of quality of water which conversion of a given percentage of a site from one classification to another will produce. The actual impact that any conversion or use technique will have on pollutant loading can only be determined by the calculation in the following section.

E. In order to determine whether a development meets the standards imposed by this section, the target pollution index must be determined. The development will be judged against this. The following calculations are required:

1. Determine reference site coverage and reference pollution index:

    a. Determine REFERENCE IMPERVIOUS SURFACE COVERAGE (residential uses only):

Take	number of dwelling units proposed	_____
Divide by	BASE SITE AREA (from Section 4301)	÷_____
Equals	GROSS DENSITY	=_____
Locate	GROSS DENSITY on the vertical axis of the following graph. Determine the REFERENCE IMPERVIOUS SURFACE COVERAGE by locating the point on the horizontal axis on the graph which corresponds to the development's GROSS DENSITY. Enter this value here:	_____

Commentary: To use the graph, draw line A (shown as example) perpendicular to the vertical axis from the gross density number until it intersects the curved line. Then draw vertical line (B) from the intersection of the curve and line (A) to the horizontal axis and read the impervious surface reference value. This REFERENCE IMPERVIOUS SURFACE COVERAGE figure equals the amount of impervious surface coverage associated with conventional development of that density.

b. Determine REFERENCE IMPERVIOUS SURFACE COVER-AGE (nonresidential only) as follows:

Determine   maximum impervious surface ratio for highest land use intensity class in which the proposed use is permitted (from Section 4602)   _____

Determine   maximum impervious surface ratio for the use in the district in which the use is located (from Section 4203)   _____

Enter   REFERENCE IMPERVIOUS SUR-FACE COVERAGE (the lowest of the two above values) here: _____

c. Determine existing ground cover as follows:

Take   total area of site which consists of woodlands (of all types defined by this ordinance)   _____

Divide by   base site area   ÷ _____

Equals   = _____

Multiply by   × 100

Equals   PERCENTAGE OF SITE IN WOODLAND GROUND COVER   = _____

Locate   the development's DENSITY (for residential uses) or IMPERVIOUS SURFACE COVERAGE (in the case of nonresidential uses) (in

both cases by reference to the vertical axis on the graph)

Determine   REFERENCE LOSS OF FOREST by locating the point on the horizontal access on the graph which corresponds to the development's DENSITY or REFERENCE IMPERVIOUS SURFACE COVER-AGE and enter figure here: _____

Take   PERCENTAGE OF SITE IN WOODLAND GROUND COVER   _____

Multiply by   REFERENCE LOSS OF FOREST   × _____

Equals   REFERENCE PERCENT FOREST   = _____

Take   100

Subtract   REFERENCE PERCENT FOREST   − _____

Subtract   REFERENCE IMPERVIOUS SUR-FACE COVERAGE   − _____

Equals   Reference PERCENT grasslands   = _____

d. Determine reference pollution index:

Take   Percentage REFERENCE Impervious surface condition   _____

Multiply by   × .9

Equals   Impervious surface reference pollution index   = _____

Take   REFERENCE PERCENT FOREST   _____

Multiply by   × .00909

Equals   Forest reference POLLUTION index

Take   Percentage REFERENCE grasslands

Multiply by   × .1

Equals   GRASSLAND REFERENCE POLLUTION INDEX   = _____

Take   IMPERVIOUS SURFACE REFER-ENCE POLLUTION INDEX   _____

| Add | FOREST REFERENCE POLLUTION INDEX | + _____ |

| Add | GRASSLAND REFERENCE POLLUTION INDEX | + _____ |

| Equals | TOTAL REFERENCE POLLUTION INDEX | = _____ |

e. Determine TARGET POLLUTION INDEX as follows:

1. 1. Take | REFERENCE IMPERVIOUS SURFACE COVERAGE | _____

| Multiply by | | × .5 |

| Equals | REDUCTION REQUIRED | = _____ |

| Take | TOTAL REFERENCE POLLUTION INDEX | _____ |

| Subtract | REDUCTION REQUIRED | _____ - |

| Equals | TARGET POLLUTION INDEX | = _____ |

2. Determine ACTUAL POLLUTION INDEX as follows:

a. Determine percentage of site occupied by ground covers listed below.

Ground Cover	No. of Acres	Base Site Area from Section 4301	× 100 =	Percentage of site in this Ground Cover
Woodlands (all types)	__ Acres	_____	× 100 =	_____
Grassland (all remaining pervious)	__ Acres	_____	× 100 =	_____
Impervious (porous paving blocks)	__ Acres	_____	× 100 =	_____
Impervious (porous asphalt)	__ Acres	_____	× 100 =	_____

| Impervious (all remaining impervious) | __ Acres | _____ | × 100 = | _____ |

b. Determine ACTUAL POLLUTION INDEX of site.

1. Take | Percentage Woodlands (all types | _____

| Multiply by | | × .0909 |

| Equals | Actual Forest Pollution Index | = _____ |

2. Take | Percentage Grassland | _____

| Multiply by | | × .1 |

| Equals | Actual Grassland Pollution Index | = _____ |

3. Take | Percentage Impervious–Pervious Paving Blocks | _____

| Multiply by | | × .684 |

| Equals | Actual Porous Paving Block Pollution Index | = _____ |

4. Take | Percentage Impervious–Porous Asphalt | _____

| Multiply by | | × .576 |

| Equals | Actual Porous Asphalt Pollution Index | = _____ |

5. Take | Percentage Impervious | _____

| Multiply by | | × 1.0 |

| Equals | Actual Impervious Pollution Index | = _____ |

6. Take ACTUAL POLLUTION INDEX for the following and sum them:

Woodlands	+ _____
Grasslands	+ _____
Pervious Paving Blocks	+ _____
Porous Asphalt	+ _____

Impervious Surfaces   + _____

Equals ACTUAL POLLUTION INDEX
of site   = _____

Commentary: Different ground covers have different stormwater runoff pollution characteristics. Accordingly, the area occupied by each must be calculated for the purpose of this section. Then the area in each such ground cover is multiplied by a factor indicative of its water quality function.

3. For each of the pollution reduction techniques used and listed below, record the reduction number (in parentheses):

Retention Basin (.30)   _____

Swale Buffer Plantings (.08)   + _____

Seepage Pits (.18)   + _____

Natural Drainage Swales (.18)   + _____

Street Sweeping (.25 or .50, depending on frequency; see Section 4419D)   + _____

Equals (TOTAL REDUCTION FACTOR)   = _____

Take ACTUAL POLLUTION INDEX   _____

Multiply by TOTAL REDUCTION FACTOR   × _____

Equals TOTAL ACTUAL SITE POLLUTION INDEX   = _____

4. Evaluate performance of site design as follows:

Take   total actual site pollution index   _____

Subtract   pollution index   − _____

Equals   Performance Index   = _____

F. If the performance index is a positive number, the nonpoint water quality standards have not been met, and other techniques must be used and the calculation redone in order to insure that a performance index of zero or less has been achieved. If the performance index is zero or a negative number, water quality standards have been met.

Section 4500. Open Space.

A. Land which is required by this ordinance to remain as open space may be used for the recreation, agriculture, resource protection, amenity and other purposes specified in this section. Open-space land shall be freely accessible to all residents of a development with the exception that agricultural land uses shall be permitted to restrict access to that land to those solely engaged in agricultural pursuits. This exception does not apply to all land in the agricultural district, but only to land used for agricultural uses. Open-space land shall not be occupied by nonrecreational buildings, roads, or road rights-of-way except as permitted by Sections 4400 through 4413, nor shall it include the yards or lots of single- or multi-family dwelling units required to meet the minimum standards or parking areas.

B. All developments required by this ordinance to provide open space shall meet the following requirements:

1. Land designated as open space shall be maintained as open space and may not be separately sold, subdivided, or developed except as provided below.

2. An open-space plan shall be submitted as a part of the application for a zoning certificate (see Article IX). This plan shall designate and indicate the boundaries of all open-space areas required by this ordinance. The plan shall:

a. Designate areas to be reserved as open space. The specific design of open-space areas shall be sensitive to the physical and design characteristics of the site.

b. Designate the type of open space which will be provided.

c. Specify the manner in which the open space shall be perpetuated, maintained, and administered.

3. The types of open space which may be provided to satisfy the requirements of this ordinance, together with the maintenance required for each type, are as follows:

a. Natural areas are areas of undisturbed vegetation or areas replanted with vegetation after construction. Woodlands, woodland swamps (hydric soils), prairies, wetlands (hydric prairies), and savannah are specific types of natural areas (see Sections 4800 through 4804 for detailed specifications). Maintenance is limited to removal of litter, dead tree and plant materials, and brush. Natural water courses are to be maintained as free flowing and devoid of debris. Stream channels shall be maintained so as not to alter floodplain levels.

b. Agricultural uses specified in Section 4104. No specific maintenance is required.

c. Garden plots are the division of open space into plots for cultivation as gardens by residents. Maintenance may limited to weeding and fallowing.

d. Recreational areas are areas designed for specific, active recreational uses such as totlots, tennis courts, swimming pools, ballfields, and similar uses. Recreational areas shall be accessible to all residents of the development. Maintenance is limited to insuring that there exist no hazards, nuisances, or unhealthy conditions.

e. Greenways are linear green belts linking residential areas with other open-space areas. These greenways may contain bicycle paths, footpaths, and bridle paths. Connecting greenways between residences and recreational areas are encouraged. Maintenance is limited to a minimum removal and avoidance of hazards, nuisances, or unhealthy conditions.

f. Lawns consist of grass with or without trees. Maintenance is limited to mowing to insure neatness.

g. **Interim open space.** Land intended for future development may be designated as a holding zone and thus remain vacant until such time as this land is annexed or rezoned as a development district.

4. All designated open space shall be large enough to be usable open space. The minimum dimension for usable open space shall be ten (10) feet and the minimum area shall be one hundred (100) square feet.

C. **Preservation of open space.** Open-space areas shall be maintained so that their use and enjoyment as open space are not diminished or destroyed. Open-space areas may be owned, preserved, and main-tained as required by this section by any of the following mechanisms or combinations thereof:

1. Dedication of open space to (Municipality) or an appropriate public agency, if there is a public agency willing to accept the dedication.

2. Common ownership of the open space by a homeowner's association which assumes full responsibility for its maintenance.

3. Dedication of development rights of open space may be made to an appropriate public agency with ownership remaining with the developer or homeowner's association. Maintenance responsibility shall remain with the property owner.

4. Deed-restricted private ownership which shall prevent development and/or subsequent subdivision of the open-space land and provide the maintenance responsibility.

In the event that any private owner of open space fails to maintain same according to the standards of this ordinance, (Municipality) may, in accordance with the Open Space Plan and following reasonable notice and demand that deficiency of maintenance be corrected, enter the open space to maintain same. The cost of such maintenance shall be charged to those persons having the primary responsibility for maintenance of the open space.

D. When the forest preserve district has adopted a greenway, pedestrian, or bike pathway plan, such pathways shall be provided, at the time of development, on all properties on which such pathways are shown.

Section 4600. Land Use Intensity Classification and Bufferyards.

All land uses which are permitted by this ordinance have been assigned a land use intensity class designation (see Section 4602). This classification system separates uses on the basis of the type and degree of "nuisance" or negative impact they are likely to impose on land uses adjacent to them.

In order to minimize any negative effects that a more obnoxious or intensive use will impose on its neighbors, this ordinance requires that bufferyards be provided between uses.

Commentary: Traditional zoning assumes that all uses of a single type (such as an office) always generate the same impacts or have the same levels of nuisance. Based on this assumption, traditional ordinances prescribe a single, unvarying standard for all such uses. Performance zoning recognizes that the traditional assumption is erroneous: the office of an insurance agent with a single employee is clearly much different from a four-story rental office building, for example. In this ordinance, the tremendous variability possible between uses of a single type forms the basis for the land use intensity classification system. Intensity is operationally defined in terms of measurable standards, including impervious surface coverage, building height and bulk, and traffic generation. Each land use intensity class, then, comprises those uses, which, when developed to specified permitted maximum "intensity," have similar "nuisance values."

Bufferyards are required to protect one class of use from adverse impacts caused by a use in another class or to ameliorate the impact two uses in the same class may have on one another. This regulation benefits both the developer and the adjoining landowner(s) because it allows the developer several options from which to choose in developing the property, while insuring each neighbor adequate protection regardless of the developer's choice.

Each land use is listed in one or more use intensity classes. A use must meet all the standards specified for that use in Section 4602. The standards which apply to the highest intensity class for a use shall be the maximum intensity permitted for that use. There are standards which set maximum density, impervious surface ratio, floor area, trip/acre during twenty-four (24) hours, height, exterior storage area, and damaged vehicle storage area. In addition, there are standards for road location and access, hours of operation, and site design (including landscaping, lighting, and signs).

Section 4601. Land Use Intensity Class Standards.

In keeping with the concept that performance should be the relevant measure of any land use regulations, the following section classifies uses according to their respective impact (all uses within a use class are considered to have an equal impact on neighboring uses). A developer may develop at an intensity which will minimize nuisances to neighbors or provide a denser bufferyard if the land is developed at greater intensities. The impacts of greater intensity may include greater impervious surface coverage, with associated increased runoff, heat generation, reduced percolation, and

open space, increased bulk and height of buildings, increased traffic with associated noise and congestion, signs and exterior lighting visible from neighboring property, late hours of operation, and other nuisances. Thus, for example, an office use on any lot may meet the standards at intensity class IV, V, VI, VII, or VIII. The range of intensity classes open to a use does not affect whether it can locate on its lot, but only *how* it can develop on that lot. Performance standards are specified for each intensity class; exceeding any single standard in an intensity class moves a use to the next-higher intensity class. In the event that a use does not appear in the next-higher intensity class, it may not exceed any single criteria in the highest intensity class in which it is listed.

Section 4603. Bufferyards: Purpose.

The bufferyard is a unit of yard together with the planting required thereon. Both the amount of land and the type and amount of planting specified for each bufferyard requirement of this ordinance are designed to ameliorate nuisances between adjacent land uses or between a land use and a public road. The planting units required of bufferyards have been calculated to insure that they do, in fact, function as "buffers."

Bufferyards shall be required to separate different land uses from each other in order to eliminate or minimize potential nuisances such as dirt, litter, noise, glare of lights, signs, and unsightly buildings or parking areas, or to provide spacing to reduce adverse impacts of noise, odor, or danger from fires or explosions.

Commentary: One of zoning's most important functions is the division of land uses into districts which, at least in theory, contain compatible uses. All uses permitted in any district have generally similar nuisance characteristics. In theory, the location of districts is supposed to provide protection, but in practice this is not the case, since uses as diverse as single-family, one-acre lots, highway commercial uses, and general industrial uses can be and are adjacent to one another despite the previous (Municipality) zoning ordinance. Bufferyards will operate to minimize the negative impact of any use on neighboring uses.

Section 4604. Location of Bufferyards.

Bufferyards shall be located on the outer perimeter of a lot or parcel, extending to the lot or parcel boundary line. Bufferyards shall not be located on

Section 4602. Table of Land Use Intensity Class Standards.

Land Use Intensity Class Number and General Use Category	Maximum Density (Gross)	Maximum Impervious Surface Ratio	Maximum Floor Area Ratio	Site Design Standards (See note 1)	Total Trips/Acre per 24 hours	Road Location (See Sections 4701, 4703, 4706)	Maximum Height (feet) (See note 2)	Exterior Storage (See note 3)	Hours of Operation	Damaged Vehicle Storage
Class I										
Agriculture	0.025	.05	n/a	R	n/a	I or II	35/80	n/a	n/a	none
Class II										
Conventional subdivision	0.9	.12	n/a	R	8	I	35	none	n/a	none
Performance subdivision	1.2	.12	n/a	R	10	I	See Section 5200	none	n/a	none
Outdoor recreation	n/a	.05	.003	A	10	I or II	20	none	7 AM 9 PM	none
Class III										
Conventional subdivision	3.2	.26	n/a	R	26	I	35	none	n/a	none
Performance subdivision	5.2	.30	n/a	R	42	I	See Section 5200	none	n/a	none
Outdoor recreation	n/a	.08	.005	A	20	I or II	25	none	7 AM 9 PM	none
Class IV										
Conventional subdivision	5.0	.35	n/a	R	40	I	35	none	n/a	none
Performance subdivision	17.5	.52	n/a	R	140	I	See Section 5200	none	n/a	none
Recreational rental dwellings	10	.25	.15	B	120	II	35	none	24 hr.	none
Outdoor recreation	n/a	.10	.006	A	30	I or II	30	none	7 AM 9 PM	none
Class V										
Outdoor recreation	n/a	.15	.009	A	40	I or II	30	none	7 AM 9 PM	none
Indoor recreation, institutional, and special residential	n/a	.30	.25	A	170	II	35	none	7 AM 10 PM	none
Public service	n/a	.20	.12	A	25	I or II	20	none	n/a	none
Office	n/a	.20	.11	A	150	II	20	none	7 AM 10 PM	none
Nursery	n/a	.03	.05	A	100	II	25	.05	7 AM 9 PM	none
Class VI										
Outdoor recreation	n/a	.25	.01	B	50	I or II	30	none	6 AM 10 PM	none
Public service	n/a	.50	.35	B	50	I or II	30	none	n/a	none
Indoor recreation, institutional, and special residential	n/a	.60	.49	B	350	II	40	none	6 AM 10 PM	none
Office	n/a	.50	.24	B	360	II	60	none	n/a	none
Commercial/entertainment	n/a	.40	.47	B	630	II	25	none	n/a	none
Light industry	n/a	.30	.29	B	105	II	30	none	6 AM 10 PM	none
Nursery	n/a	.20	.20	B	250	II	30	.20	6 AM 10 PM	none
Class VII										
Outdoor recreation	n/a	.40	.02	C	75	I or II	35	none	6 AM 11 PM	none
Public service	n/a	.70	.40	C	75	I or II	40	.10	n/a	none
Indoor recreation, Institutional, and special residential	n/a	.70	.57	C	400	II	45	none	n/a	none
Office	n/a	.70	.36	C	500	II	60	none	n/a	none
Commercial/entertainment	n/a	.65	.77	C	1,000	II	30	none	n/a	none

	Maximum Density (Gross)	Maximum Impervious Surface Ratio	Maximum Floor Area Ratio	Site Design Standards (See note 1)	Total Trips/Acre per 24 hours	Road Location (See Sections 4701, 4703, 4706)	Maximum Height (feet) (See note 2)	Exterior Storage (See note 3)	Hours of Operation	Damaged Vehicle Storage
Agricultural support	n/a	.65	.55	C	250	II	40	none	6 AM 11 PM	none
Light industry	n/a	.50	.48	C	180	II	35	none	6 AM 10 PM	none
Road service	n/a	.50	.19	C	2,000	II	25	none	6 AM 11 PM	none
Class VIII										
Outdoor recreation	n/a	.60	.03	D	110	I or II	40	none	6 AM 12 PM	none
Public service	n/a	.90	.45	D	100	I or II	50	.30	n/a	none
Indoor recreation, Institutional, and special residential	n/a	.80	.65	D	470	II	50	.05	n/a	none
Office	n/a	.90	.50	D	650	II	60	none	n/a	none
Commercial/entertainment	n/a	.90	1.10	D	1,400	II	50	.05	n/a	none
Light industry	n/a	.80	.78	D	280	II	45	.05	n/a	none
Road service	n/a	.80	.31	D	3,200	II	40	.05	n/a	none
Agricultural support	n/a	.80	.80	D	400	II	50	.05	n/a	none
Class IX										
Public service	n/a	1.0	.55	E	200	I or II	50	.80	n/a	.05
Office	n/a	1.0	.70	E	700	II	75	.10	n/a	none
Commercial/entertainment	n/a	1.0	1.2	E	1,600	II	60	.30	n/a	none
Light industry	n/a	.90	.87	E	400	II	45	.50	n/a	.05
Road service	n/a	.90	.35	E	3,600	II	40	.30	n/a	.15
Commercial/recreation	n/a	.70	.30	E	200	II	25/80	none	n/a	none
Agricultural support	n/a	.90	.95	E	600	II	60	.50	n/a	.20

	Maximum Density (Gross)	Maximum Impervious Surface Ratio	Maximum Floor Area Ratio	Site Design Standards (See note 1)	Total Trips/Acre per 24 hours	Road Location (See Sections 4701, 4703, 4706)	Maximum Height (feet) (See note 2)	Exterior Storage (See note 3)	Hours of Operation	Damaged Vehicle Storage
Class X										
Commercial recreation	n/a	.90	.40	E	300	II	40/120	none	no limit	none
Light industry	n/a	1.0	.97	E	600	II	45	.90	no limit	.20
Class XI										
Heavy industry	n/a	.90	.94	E	500	III	60	.90	no limit	.20
Extraction	n/a	.10	.10	E	150	III	30	.80	11 PM	.80

NOTES TO TABLE

1. See Sections 4612 through 4620: Landscaping (Section 4613); Off Street Parking Area Landscaping (Section 4614); Exterior Lighting (Section 4615) and Signs (Section 4616).

2. The figure specified in this column is the maximum permitted height of each permitted structure. When two figures are specified, the latter one is the maximum permitted height of permitted uninhabited accessory structures. The following structures are exempt from the maximum height regulations of this section, except as limited by any height restriction regulation of the Federal Aviation Agency or the Illinois Department of Transportation, Division of Aeronautics, or any height restriction imposed by any airport authority, port district, or other municipal corporation operating an airport.

   a. Agricultural buildings, except residences.
   b. Bulk storage silos and storage towers in all districts except agricultural, provided the maximum permitted height shall not exceed 100 feet.
   c. Concrete batching and mixing towers, provided the maximum permitted height shall not exceed 100 feet.
   d. Gravity feed apparatus in all districts except agricultural; the maximum permitted height shall not exceed 60 feet.
   e. Public utility poles, towers, and wires.
   f. Radio and television antennae and towers.
   g. Towers for mechanical equipment or smoke, provided the maximum permitted height shall not exceed 16 feet above roof line of principal building.
   h. Water tanks and standpipes.

3. Garden centers shall be permitted the following additional exterior storage for plant material only:

   in Class VII–.70
   in Class VIII–.90
   in Class IX–1.00.

any portion of an existing or dedicated public or private street or right-of-way.

Section 4605. Determination of Bufferyard Requirements.

A. To determine the type of bufferyard required between two adjacent parcels or between a parcel and a street, the following procedure shall be followed (see Appendix for sample calculation):

1. Identify the land use category of the proposed use by referring to Sections 4104 through 4108.

2. Identify the use category of the land use(s) adjacent to the proposed use by on-site survey.

3. Identify the land use intensity class of all adjoining land uses by referring to Section 4602. (Municipality) shall supply this information.

4. Classify any street adjacent to the proposed use by referring to Sections 4703 and 4707.

5. Determine the bufferyard required on each boundary (or segment thereof) of the subject parcel by referring to Section 4606.

B. Section 4606 specifies the bufferyard required between adjacent land uses. The requirements are expressed in terms which are further described and detailed in Sections 4606 through 4611 and Sections 4800 through 4806.

C. Bufferyard specifications are detailed and illustrated in Section 4607. The bufferyards illustrated constitute the total bufferyard required between the two adjacent land uses. Any of the options contained in Section 4607 for the required bufferyard shall satisfy the requirement of buffering between adjacent land uses.

D. **Responsibility for bufferyard.**

1. When a use is the first to develop on two adjacent vacant parcels, this first use shall provide the buffer which Section 4606 requires next to vacant land.

2. The second use to develop shall, at the time it develops, provide all additional plant material and/or land necessary to provide the total bufferyard required between those two uses by Section 4606.

E. Existing plant material and/or land located on the preexisting (first developed) land use which meets the requirements of this ordinance may be counted as contributing to the total bufferyard required between it and the second (adjacent) land use to develop.

Section 4606. Table of Bufferyard Requirements.

The letter designations contained in this table refer to the bufferyard requirements and standards contained in Section 4607.

Section 4607. Bufferyard Requirements.

A. The following illustrations graphically indicate the specifications of each bufferyard. Bufferyard requirements are stated in terms of the width of the bufferyard and the number of plant units required per one hundred (100) linear feet of bufferyard. The requirements of a bufferyard may be satisfied by any of the options thereof illustrated. The "plant unit multiplier" is a factor by which the basic number of plant materials required for a given bufferyard is determined given a change in the width of that yard. The type and quantity of plant materials required by each bufferyard, and each bufferyard option, are specified in this section. Sections 4800 through 4806 specify species and size of plant materials. Only those plant materials identified in these sections shall satisfy the requirements of this ordinance.

Commentary: The options within any bufferyard are designed to be equivalent in terms of their effectiveness in eliminating the impact of adjoining uses. Cost equivalence between options was attempted where possible. Generally, the plant materials which are identified as acceptable are determined by the type(s) of soil present on the site. The following illustrations have mathematically rounded the number of plant units required for each option within a given bufferyard. In actual practice, mathematical rounding would be applied to the total amount of plant material required by a bufferyard, not to each one hundred (100) foot length of bufferyard. All of the following illustrations are drawn to scale and depict the bufferyard according to the average projected diameter of plant materials at five (5) years after planting.

Section 4606. Table of Bufferyard Requirements. The letter designations contained in this table refer to the standards contained in Section 4607 of this ordinance.

Proposed Land Use Intensity Class	Adjacent Existing Land Use Intensity Class											Adjacent Vacant Land[2] (District)							
	I	II	III	IV	V	VI	VII	VIII	IX	X	XI	Ag[1]	R	E	NC	DD	UC	HI	HD
I	*	Ag	Ag	Ag	Ag	Ag	*	*	*	*	F	*	*	*	*	*	*	*	*
II	Ag	B	C	D	D	E	G	H	I	J	K	Ag	A	A	A	B	C	J	A
III	Ag	C	B	D	D	E	G	H	I	J	K	Ag	Ag	Ag	B	B	C	J	B
IV	Ag	D	C	B	D	E	G	H	I	J	K	Ag	Ag	C	C	C	A	J	C
V	Ag	D	D	D	*	*	C	D	E	E	F	Ag	Ag	C	C	C	C	D	C
VI	Ag	E	E	E	*	*	*	C	D	D	E	Ag	Ag	D	D	D	D	D	D
VII	*	G	G	G	C	*	*	*	C	C	D	*	A	F	F	F	F	C	F
VIII	*	H	H	H	D	C	*	*	*	B	C	*	A	G	G	G	G	C	G
IX	*	I	I	I	E	D	C	*	*	*	*	*	A	H	H	H	H	B	H
X	*	J	J	J	E	D	C	B	*	*	*	*	B	I	I	I	I	*	I
XI	F	K	K	K	F	E	D	C	*	*	*	F	D	J	J	J	J	*	J

*No bufferyard required.

1. This column applies only in the agricultural district. In any district assume agricultural use is on vacant land in the district in which it is located.

2. Includes land used for agricultural purposes.

Section 4606 (continued).

Proposed Land Use Intensity Class	Expressway[4]	Arterial	Collector[3] Land Use Across Street			Residential Street
			Nonresidential	Vacant	Residential	
I	*	*	*	*	*	*
II	F	D	S_1	S_1	S_1	S_1
III	F	D	S_1	S_1	S_1	S_1
IV	F	D	S_1	B	S_2	S_2
V	*	B	S_1	B	B	C
VI	*	C	S_1	B	D	D
VII	*	D	S_1	C	F	F
VIII	B	E	S_1	C	F	F
IX	C	F	B	D	G	G
X	D	G	C	E	H	H
XI	E	H	C	F	I	I

*No bufferyard required.

3. Residential uses shall provide an E bufferyard against a railroad. The buffer between a residential use and an expressway shall provide a chain link fence as the required structure.

4. Includes frontage roads and internal circulation roads.

B. Each illustration depicts the total bufferyard located between two uses.

C. Whenever a wall, fence, or berm is required within a bufferyard, these are shown as "structure required" in the following illustrations, wherein their respective specifications are also shown. All required structures shall be the responsibility of the higher intensity use. Whenever a wall is required in addition to a berm, the wall shall be located between the berm and the higher intensity use, in order to provide maximum sound absorption.

D. The following plant material substitutions shall satisfy the requirements of this section.

   1. In bufferyards G, H, I, J, and K, evergreen canopy or evergreen understory trees may be substituted for deciduous canopy forest trees without limitation.

   2. In bufferyards, A, B, C, D, E, F, S_1, S_2, and AG, evergreen canopy or evergreen understory trees may be substituted as follows:

      a. In the case of deciduous canopy forest trees, up to a maximum of fifty (50) percent of the total number of the deciduous canopy trees otherwise required.

      b. In the case of deciduous understory, without limitation.

   3. In all bufferyards, evergreen or conifer shrubs may be substituted for deciduous shrubs without limitation.

   4. In all bufferyards required of public service uses, the public service use may substitute evergreen canopy or evergreen understory plant materials for canopy forest trees and understory plant materials, without limitation.

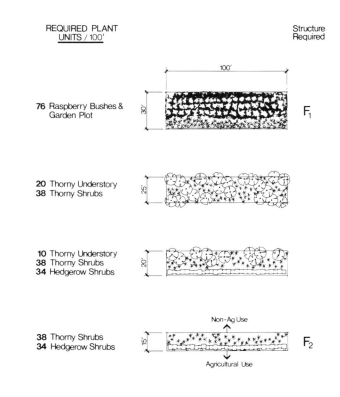

REQUIRED PLANT UNITS / 100'

Structure Required

76 Raspberry Bushes & Garden Plot F_1

20 Thorny Understory
38 Thorny Shrubs

10 Thorny Understory
38 Thorny Shrubs
34 Hedgerow Shrubs

38 Thorny Shrubs
34 Hedgerow Shrubs F_2

Non-Ag Use

Agricultural Use

NOTE:
Required fences and hedges shall be located as close as possible to the property line between the two uses.

BUFFERYARD **Ag**

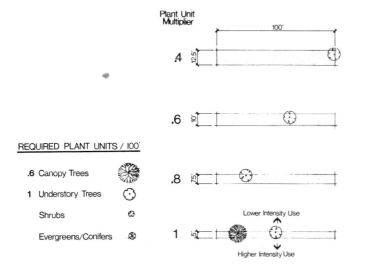

Plant Unit
Multiplier

4   100'

.6

REQUIRED PLANT UNITS / 100'

.6 Canopy Trees

1 Understory Trees

Shrubs

Evergreens/Conifers

.8

Lower Intensity Use

1

Higher Intensity Use

BUFFERYARD **A**

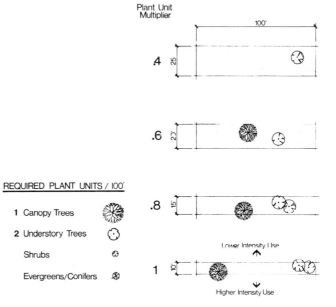

Plant Unit
Multiplier

4   100'

.6

REQUIRED PLANT UNITS / 100'

1 Canopy Trees

2 Understory Trees

Shrubs

Evergreens/Conifers

.8

Lower Intensity Use

1

Higher Intensity Use

BUFFERYARD **B**

Plant Unit
Multiplier

.4

100'
25'

Plant Unit
Multiplier

.4

100
30'

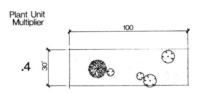

.6

20'

.6

25'

REQUIRED PLANT UNITS / 100'

1 Canopy Trees

2 Understory Trees

3 Shrubs

Evergreens/Conifers

.8

15'

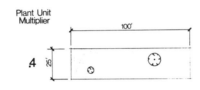

REQUIRED PLANT UNITS / 100'

2 Canopy Trees

4 Understory Trees

6 Shrubs

Evergreens/Conifers

.8

20'

1

10'

Lower Intensity Use

Higher Intensity Use

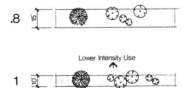

1

15'

Lower Intensity Use

Higher Intensity Use

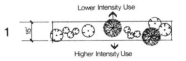

BUFFERYARD C

BUFFERYARD D

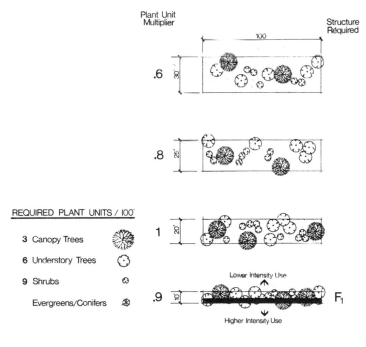

REQUIRED PLANT UNITS / 100'

3 Canopy Trees

6 Understory Trees

9 Shrubs

Evergreens/Conifers

BUFFERYARD E

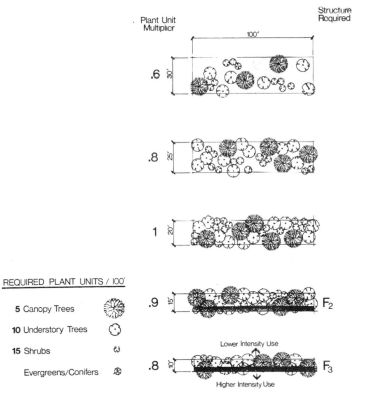

REQUIRED PLANT UNITS / 100'

5 Canopy Trees

10 Understory Trees

15 Shrubs

Evergreens/Conifers

BUFFERYARD F

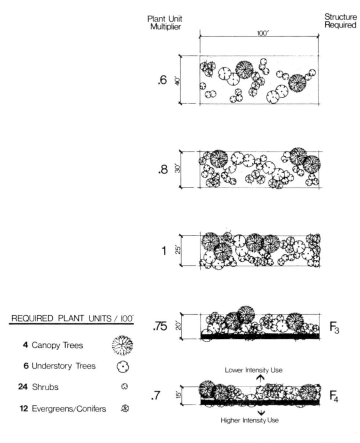

Plant Unit Multiplier

Structure Required

.6

.8

1

.75   F₃

.7   F₄

Lower Intensity Use

Higher Intensity Use

REQUIRED PLANT UNITS / 100'

4 Canopy Trees

6 Understory Trees

24 Shrubs

12 Evergreens/Conifers

BUFFERYARD **G**

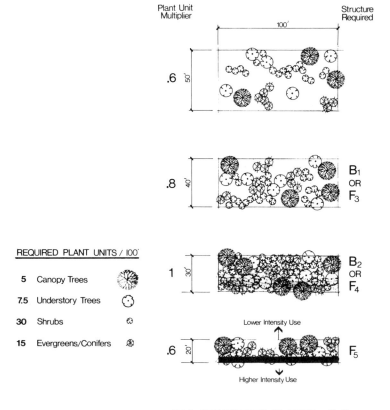

Plant Unit Multiplier

Structure Required

.6

.8   B₁ OR F₃

1   B₂ OR F₄

.6   F₅

Lower Intensity Use

Higher Intensity Use

REQUIRED PLANT UNITS / 100'

5 Canopy Trees

7.5 Understory Trees

30 Shrubs

15 Evergreens/Conifers

BUFFERYARD **H**

164

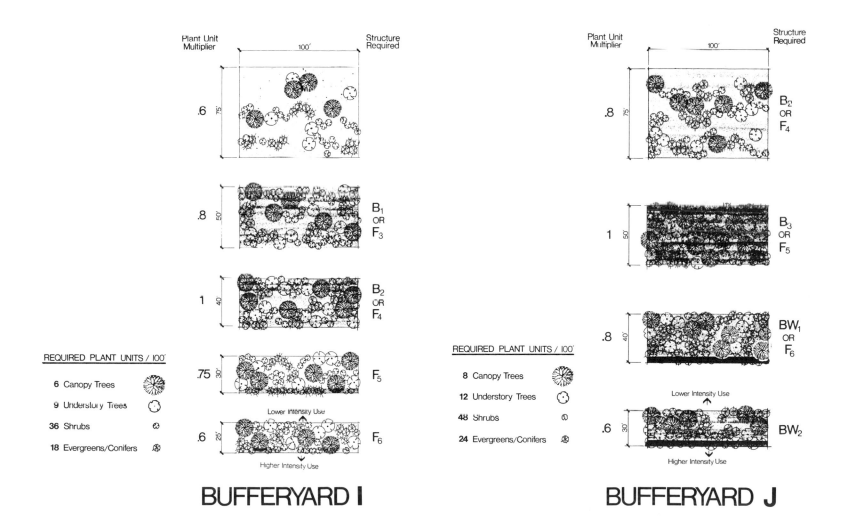

Plant Unit Multiplier

Structure Required

100'

.6 — 75'

.8 — 50' — B_1 OR F_3

1 — 40' — B_2 OR F_4

.75 — 30' — F_5

Lower Intensity Use

.6 — 25' — F_6

Higher Intensity Use

REQUIRED PLANT UNITS / 100'

6 Canopy Trees

9 Understory Trees

36 Shrubs

18 Evergreens/Conifers

BUFFERYARD I

Plant Unit Multiplier

Structure Required

100'

.8 — 75' — B_2 OR F_4

1 — 50' — B_3 OR F_5

.8 — 40' — BW_1 OR F_6

Lower Intensity Use

.6 — 30' — BW_2

Higher Intensity Use

REQUIRED PLANT UNITS / 100'

8 Canopy Trees

12 Understory Trees

48 Shrubs

24 Evergreens/Conifers

BUFFERYARD J

Plant Unit
Multiplier

Plant Unit
Multiplier

Structure
Required

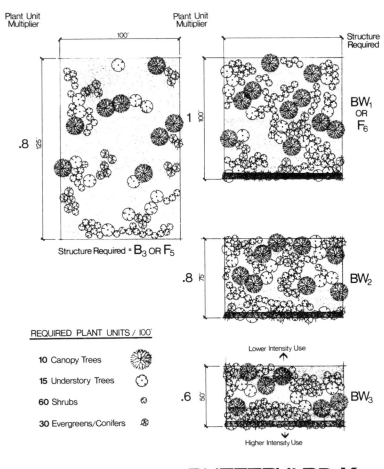

100'

.8

125'

1

100'

BW₁
OR
F₆

Structure Required = B₃ OR F₅

.8

75'

BW₂

REQUIRED PLANT UNITS / 100'

10 Canopy Trees

15 Understory Trees

60 Shrubs

30 Evergreens/Conifers

Lower Intensity Use

.6

50'

BW₃

Higher Intensity Use

BUFFERYARD K

REQUIRED PLANT UNITS / 100'

1 Canopy Tree

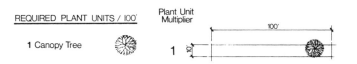

Plant Unit
Multiplier

100'

1

10'

BUFFERYARD S₁

REQUIRED PLANT UNITS / 100'

2 Canopy Trees

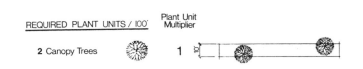

Plant Unit
Multiplier

1

10'

BUFFERYARD S₂

FENCES

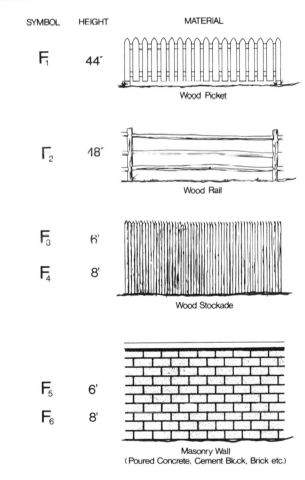

SYMBOL	HEIGHT	MATERIAL
F_1	44″	

Wood Picket

| F_2 | 18″ | |

Wood Rail

| F_3 | 6′ | |
| F_4 | 8′ | |

Wood Stockade

| F_5 | 6′ | |
| F_6 | 8′ | |

Masonry Wall
(Poured Concrete, Cement Block, Brick etc.)

BERMS

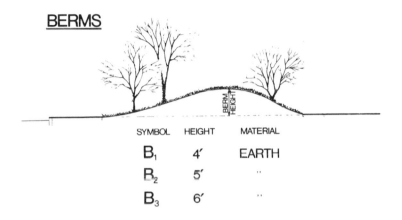

SYMBOL	HEIGHT	MATERIAL
B_1	4′	EARTH
B_2	5′	″
B_3	6′	″

BERM WALLS

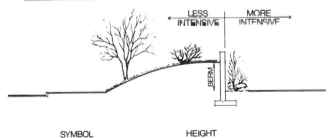

SYMBOL	HEIGHT
BW_1	4′ BERM w/ 6′ MASONRY WALL
BW_2	5′ BERM w/ 7′ MASONRY WALL
BW_3	6′ BERM w/ 8′ MASONRY WALL

E. The following structures are equivalent and may be used interchangeably, so long as both structures are specified in the bufferyard illustrations in this section.

Structure	Equivalent Structure
F_3	B_1
F_4	B_2
F_5	B_3
F_6	BW_1
B_1	F_3
B_2	F_4
B_3	F_5
BW_1	F_6

F. If the development on the adjoining use is existing, planned, or deed-restricted for solar access, understory trees may be substituted for canopy trees where canopy trees would destroy solar access.

G. Any existing plant material which otherwise satisfies the requirements of this section may be counted toward satisfying all such requirements.

H. The exact placement of required plants and structures shall be the decision of each user except that the following requirements shall be satisfied:

1. Evergreen (or conifer) class III and IV plant materials shall be planted in clusters rather than singly in order to maximize their chances of survival.

2. Berms with masonry walls (BW_1, BW_2, and BW_3) required of bufferyard J and K options are intended to buffer more significant nuisances from adjacent uses and, additionally, to break up and absorb noise, which is achieved by the varied heights of plant materials between the masonry wall and the noise source.

   a. When berms with walls are required, the masonry wall shall be closer than the berm to the higher intensity use.

   b. Within a bufferyard, a planting area at least five (5) feet wide containing fifteen (15) percent of the total plant requirements (based on the multiplier = 1) shall be located between the masonry wall and the higher intensity class use. These plants shall be chosen to provide species and sizes to reduce noise in conjunction with the wall.

I. All bufferyard areas shall be seeded with lawn or prairie unless ground cover is already established.

Section 4608. Use of Bufferyards.

A bufferyard may be used for passive recreation; it may contain pedestrian, bike, or equestrian trails, provided that: (a) no plant material is eliminated, (b) the total width of the bufferyard is maintained, and (c) all other regulations of the ordinance are met. In no event, however, shall the following uses be permitted in bufferyards: ice skating rinks, playfields, ski hills, stables, swimming pools, and tennis courts.

Commentary: This section provides flexibility for the use of larger bufferyards. It enables public or private use of bufferyards for limited recreational uses, so long as the total buffer required by the original use is provided.

Section 4609. Ownership of Bufferyards.

Bufferyards may remain in the ownership of the original developer (and assigns) of a land use, or they may be subjected to deed restrictions and subsequently be freely conveyed, or they may be transferred to any consenting grantees, such as adjoining landowners, a park or forest preserve district, (Municipality), or an open-space or conservation group, provided that any such conveyance adequately guarantees the protection of the bufferyards for the purposes of this ordinance.

Section 4610. Excess Bufferyard.

Where the bufferyard required between a land use and vacant land turns out to be greater than that bufferyard which is required between the first use and the subsequently developed use, the following options apply:

A. The subsequent use may provide one half (.5) of the buffer required by Sections 4606 and 4607. The existing use may expand its use into the original buffer area, provided that the resulting total bufferyard between the two uses meets the bufferyard requirements of Sections 4606 and 4607.

B. The existing use may enter into agreements with abutting landowners to use its existing buffer to provide some or all of the required bufferyard of both land uses. The total buffer shall equal the requirements of Sections 4606 and 4607. Provided that such an agreement can be negotiated, the initial use may provide the second use some or all of its required bufferyard and/or extra land on which it might develop. The existing use may reduce its excess buffer by transferring part or all of the excess buffer to the adjoining landowner to serve as its buffer. Any remaining excess buffer area may be used by the existing use for expansion of that use or for transfer by it to the adjoining landowner to expand that adjoining use.

Commentary: Since vacant land may not be developed for years after the first use is established, this provision attempts to address the inevitable uncertainty about the bufferyard which would ultimately be required. It would not be equitable to require that the second use be responsible for all the buffer needed. This provision makes it possible to require buffering from the initial use established and, thereafter, if more buffer exists than is required, makes it possible to utilize land originally set aside for bufferyard.

Section 4611. Contractual Reduction of Bufferyard Abutting Vacant Land.

When a land use is proposed adjacent to vacant land, and the owner of that vacant land enters into a contractual relationship with the owner of the land that is to be developed first, a reduced buffer may be provided by that first use, provided that: the contract contains a statement by the owner of the vacant land of an intent to develop at no greater than a specified land use intensity class; and an agreement by that vacant landowner to assume all responsibility for additional buffer, if needed by the subsequent development of a less intense use than had been agreed upon, is transferred to the owner of the vacant (second in time to be developed) land.

Commentary: This contract mechanism provides a means for avoiding the provision of too large a buffer in areas where the owners of vacant land have relatively firm plans for the ultimate use of their land, which plans do not include land use intensity requiring the greatest bufferyards.

Section 4612. Site Design Standards.

The land use intensity classification standards (Section 4602) regulate landscaping (both on-site and for parking areas), exterior lighting, and signs. The following sections detail the regulations which apply to each of the six standards (R, A, B, C, D, and E) specified in Section 4602.

Commentary: Among nuisances frequently caused by individual uses are too many, too large, or ugly signs, the noise, glare, and unsightliness of parking lots, the massive scale or character of buildings, and the brightness or glare of exterior lighting. It is clear that these nuisance aspects of a use are independent of the use per se: an otherwise tastefully conceived office can be a major nuisance because of large signs, bright lights, and parking areas. Regulatory standards for general landscaping, parking lot landscaping, lighting, and signs are imposed to control adverse impacts on abutting land uses.

Section 4613. General Landscaping Requirements.

This section details the general landscaping required of particular land uses by Section 4602. The number and type of plant units required per three hundred (300) linear feet of nonresidential building(s) perimeter comprising the subject land use are specified for standards R, A, B, C, D, and E. The landscaping requirement specified for residential uses (R) is the requirement per ten (10) dwelling units. The definitions of this ordinance (defining plant units) shall be applicable to the terms utilized in this section.

The requirements of this section shall be applied proportionately when the total linear feet of building(s) perimeter varies from three hundred (300) feet for nonresidential uses or ten (10) residential dwelling units. All required planting shall be located in areas which do not include any bufferyard or right-of-way. Existing plant materials which meet the requirements of this ordinance may be counted as contributing to the total landscaping required by this section.

The following table specifies the type and number of plant units required by this section. Sections 4800 through 4806 further define the species and size of plant materials which may satisfy the requirements of this section.

R

240 S.F./24 Stalls

2 Canopy
3 Shrubs

A

1080 S.F./24 Stalls

5 Canopy
3 Understory
10 Shrubs

B

720 S.F./24 Stalls

3 Canopy
2 Understory
6 Shrubs

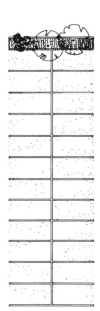

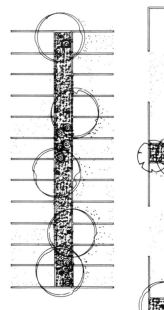

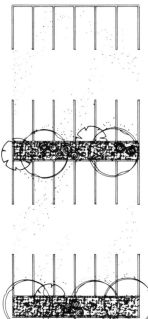

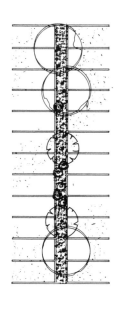

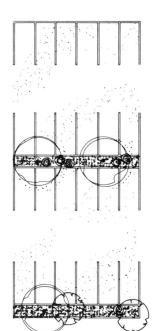

C

360 S.F./24 Stalls

2 Canopy
1 Understory
4 Shrubs

D

240 S.F./24 Stalls

1 Canopy
3 Shrubs

E

240 S.F./24 Stalls

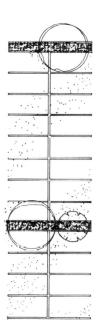

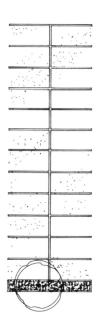

Landscaping Standard (from Section 4602)	Number of Landscaping Units Required (per 300 feet or 10 dwelling units)		
Standard	Canopy	Understory	Shrubs
R	5	5	0
A	5	5	25
B	3	3	15
C	2	2	10
D	1	1	5
E	0	0	0

The planting requirements of standard R need not be provided on any lot which has any area of woodland designated pursuant to Section 4302.

Section 4614. Off-street Parking Landscaping Requirements.

This section details the landscaping required of all off-street parking areas exceeding five (5) parking stalls as specified in Section 4602. The number and type of plant units required per twenty-four (24) automobile spaces is specified for each standard (A, B, C, D, E, or R). Also specified is a minimum area within which the required planting must be provided. Existing plant materials which meet the requirements of this ordinance may be counted as contributing to the total landscaping required by this section. The requirements of this section shall be applied proportionally to any number of spaces other than twenty-four (24). Sections 4800 through 4806 specify the type and quantity of plant materials which satisfy the requirements of this section.

Section 4615. Exterior Lighting Standards.

A. **Purpose.**

This section details the exterior lighting standards specified in Section 4602. The purpose of this section is to regulate the spillover of light and glare on operators of motor vehicles, pedestrians, and land uses in the proximity of the light source. With respect to motor vehicles in particular, safety considerations form the basis of the regulations contained herein. In other cases, both the nuisance and hazard aspects of glare are regulated. This section is not intended to apply to public street lighting.

B. **Definitions.**

1. **Candlepower:** the amount of light that will illuminate a surface one (1) foot distant from a light source to an intensity of one (1) footcandle. Maximum (peak) candlepower is the largest amount of candlepower emitted by any lamp, light source, or luminaire.

2. **Cutoff:** the point at which all light rays emitted by a lamp, light source, or luminaire are completely eliminated (cutoff) at a specific angle above the ground.

3. **Cutoff angle:** the angle formed by a line drawn from the direction of light rays at the light source and a line perpendicular to the ground from the light source, above which no light is emitted.

4. **Cutoff-type luminaire:** a luminaire with elements such as shields, reflectors, or refractor panels which direct and cut off the light at a cutoff angle that is less than ninety (90) degrees.

5. **Footcandle:** a unit of illumination produced on a surface, all points of which are one (1) foot from a uniform point source of one (1) candle.

6. **Glare:** the brightness of a light source which causes eye discomfort.

7. **Luminaire:** a complete lighting unit consisting of a light source and all necessary mechanical, electrical, and decorative parts.

8. **Maximum permitted illumination:** the maximum illumination measured in footcandles at the interior bufferyard line at ground level in accordance with the standards of Subsection (D) below.

C. The following standards are required of all exterior lighting except the outdoor recreational uses specifically exempted below. Many uses have the option of providing a lower light post with a noncutoff type luminaire or a higher pole, up to sixty (60) feet, with a luminaire that totally cuts off light spillover at a cutoff angle smaller than ninety (90) degrees.

The maximum height light post permitted is dependent on amount of cutoff provided. This is designed as a protection against excessive glare and light spilling over to neighboring properties. The exceptions which are permitted provide adequate protection for neighboring residential property.

Exterior lighting shall meet one (1) of the following standards:

1. When light source or luminaire has no cutoff:

Standard	Maximum Permitted Illumination	Maximum Permitted Height of Luminaire
R	0.20	10 ft.
A	0.20	15
B, C, D, E	0.30	20

Illustrations of this type of luminaire are provided below.

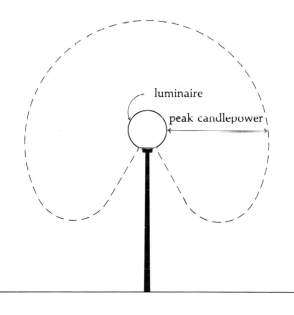

NO CUTOFF LUMINAIRE

Commentary: Exterior lighting fixtures frequently produce unsightly glare. At times, the glare may even result in a safety hazard. The standards imposed by this section are designed to reduce the hazard and nuisance of these fixtures.

2. When a luminaire has total cutoff of an angle greater than ninety (90) degrees, the maximum illumination and the maximum permitted luminaire height shall be:

Standard	Maximum Permitted Illumination	Maximum Permitted Height of Post
R	0.3	15 ft.
A	0.5	20
B	0.75	25
C	1.0	30
D	1.5	35
E	2.0	40

An illustration of this type of luminaire is provided below.

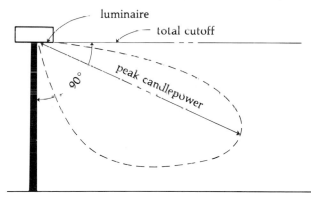

90   CUTOFF LUMINAIRE

Commentary: This standard is designed to insure that no light is emitted above a horizontal line parallel to the ground. In order to achieve total cutoff at ninety (90) degrees, such a luminaire shall emit maximum (peak) candlepower at an angle not exceeding seventy-five (75) degrees. This angle is formed by the line at which maximum candlepower is emitted from the light source and a line perpendicular to the ground from the light source.

3. When a luminaire has total cutoff of light at an angle less than ninety (90) degrees and is located so that the bare light bulb, lamp, or light source is completely shielded from the direct view of an observer five (5) feet above the ground at the point where the cutoff angle intersects the ground, then the maximum permitted illumination and the maximum permitted height of the luminaire shall be:

Standard	Maximum Permitted Illumination	Maximum Permitted Height of Post
R	0.5	20 ft.
A	1.0	25
B	2.0	30
C	3.0	40
D	4.0	50
E	5.0	60

An illustration of this type of luminaire is provided below.

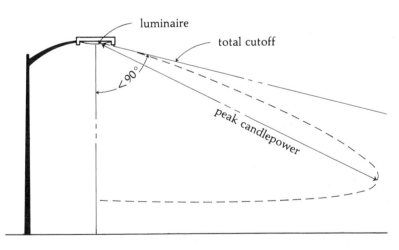

LUMINAIRE WITH LESS THAN 90 CUTOFF

Commentary: This type of light fixture may be taller and provide greater illumination at the property line than the other two types specified above, because the design of this fixture insures that its light source will not be directly visible off-site.

4. **Exemption for specified outdoor recreational uses.**

    a. Because of their unique requirements for nighttime visibility and their limited hours of operation (specified in Section 4602), ball diamonds, playing fields, and tennis courts are exempted from the exterior lighting standards of Subsection (D) above. These outdoor recreational uses must meet all other requirements of this section and of this ordinance.

    b. The outdoor recreational uses specified above shall not exceed a maximum permitted post height of eighty (80) feet.

    c. The outdoor recreational uses specified above may exceed a total cutoff angle of ninety (90) degrees, provided that the luminaire is shielded to prevent light and glare spillover to adjacent residential property. The maximum permitted illumination at the interior bufferyard line shall not exceed two (2) footcandles.

D. **Additional regulations.** Notwithstanding any other provision of this section to the contrary:

1. No flickering or flashing lights shall be permitted.

2. Light sources or luminaires shall not be located within bufferyard areas except on pedestrian walkways.

E. **Measurement.**

1. **Metering equipment.** Lighting levels shall be measured in foot-candles with a direct-reading, portable light meter. The meter shall have a color and cosine-corrected sensor with multiple scales and shall read within an accuracy of plus or minus five (5) percent. It shall have been tested, calibrated, and certified by an independent commercial photometric laboratory or the manufacturer within one (1) year of the date of its use.

2. **Method of measurement.** The meter sensor shall be mounted not more than six (6) inches above ground level in a horizontal position. Readings shall be taken by qualified personnel only after the

cell has been exposed long enough to provide a constant reading. Measurements shall be made after dark with the light sources in question on, then with the same sources off. The difference between the two readings shall be compared to the maximum permitted illumination and property line at ground level in Section 4602. This procedure eliminates the effects of moonlight and other ambient light.

F. **Exterior lighting plan.** At the time any exterior lighting is installed or substantially modified, and whenever a zoning certificate is sought, an exterior lighting plan shall be submitted to (Municipality) in order to determine whether the requirements of this section have been met.

Section 4616. Sign Regulations.

A. **Purpose.** The purpose of this section is to establish minimum regulation for the display of signs for each of the standards specified in Section 4602.

Commentary: There is a significant relationship between the manner in which signs are displayed, on the one hand, and public safety and the value and economic stability of adjoining property, on the other. The reasonable display of signs is necessary as a public service and to the conduct of competitive commerce and industry. The regulations of this section establish minimum standards for signs which directly relate to the use of property and to the intensity of development of each particular land use.

B. *Definitions.*

1. **Sign:** any object, device, display, structure, or part thereof, situated outdoors or indoors, which is used to advertise, identify, display, direct or attract attention to an object, person, institution, organization, business, product, service, event, or location by any means, including words, letters, figures, designs, symbols, fixtures, colors, illumination, or projected images. Signs do not include the flag or emblem of any nation, organization of nations, state, city, religious, fraternal, or civic organization; also merchandise and pictures or models of products or services incorporated in a window display, works of art which in no way identify a product, or scoreboards located on athletic fields. Definitions of particular functional, locational, and structural types of signs are listed in this section.

2. **Arterial sign:** a sign which is located on a site which has frontage on an arterial road (as defined by Sections 4703 and 4704).

3. **Auxiliary sign:** a sign which provides special information such as direction, price, sales information, hours of operation, or warning and which does not include names, brand names, or information regarding product lines or services. Examples of such signs include directories of tenants in buildings, "no trespassing" signs, and signs which list prices of gasoline.

4. **Development sign:** a sign which, by symbol or name, identifies a development. It may also provide an index of uses (tenants) included in the development.

5. **Freestanding sign:** a self-supporting sign resting on or supported by means of poles, standards, or any other type of base on the ground.

6. **Graphic:** a sign which is an integral part of a building facade. The sign is painted directly on, carved in, or otherwise permanently embedded in the facade. Signs in shop windows are included unless they qualify as auxiliary signs.

7. **Marquee:** the sign of a theater, auditorium, fairground, or museum, which advertises present and scheduled events.

8. **Projecting sign:** a sign, other than a wall sign, which is attached to and projects from a structure or building face. The sign face of double-faced projecting signs is calculated by measuring one face of the sign only.

9. **Sign face:** that area of a sign which:

   a. In the case of freestanding, projecting, and marquee **signs** consists of the entire surface area of the sign on which copy could be placed. The supporting structure or bracing of a sign shall not be counted as a part of sign face area unless such structure or bracing is made a part of the sign's message. Where a sign has two display faces back to back, the area of only one face shall be considered the sign face area. Where a sign has more than one display face, all areas which can be viewed simultaneously shall be considered the sign face area.

b. In the case of a sign (other than freestanding, projecting, or marquee) whose message is fabricated together with the background which borders or frames that message, sign face area shall be the total area of the entire background.

c. In the case of a sign (other than freestanding, projecting, or marquee) whose message is applied to a background which provides no border or frame, sign face area shall be the area of the smallest rectangle which can encompass all words, letters, figures, emblems, and other elements of the sign message.

The illustrations below demonstrate how sign face area shall be determined.

Commentary: Some signs consist of a structure or background area on which a message is imposed. The sign face area of these signs consists of that structure or background area. Other signs consist of message areas which constitute only a part of a larger structural or background area. The sign face area of these signs consists of the area which encloses or delineates the boundaries of the message itself.

10. **Sign lighting:** methods of illumination which may be divided into several types:

a. **General:** the sign itself neither is lighted internally nor has an external source of light specifically directed at it. Rather, the sign depends on the general illumination of the area (e.g., parking lot, traffic or pedestrian areas) for its illumination.

b. **Internal:** the sign is made of translucent material with internal lights.

c. **Back lite:** the letters are raised beyond the sign's background and the cover-lighting sources which illuminate the background.

d. **Spot lite:** the sign is lighted by spotlights specifically directed at it.

a.

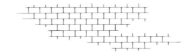

b.

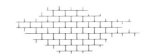
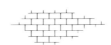

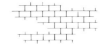

c.

11. **Super graphic:** a sign consisting of a single word which is an integral and permanent part of the facade and which is distinguished only by relief and the shadows thereby created.

12. **Temporary sign:** a sign or advertising display constructed of cloth, canvas, fabric, paper, plywood, or other light material and intended to be displayed for a short period of time (thirty [30] consecutive days). Included in this category are retailers' signs temporarily displayed for the purpose of informing the public of a sale or "special" offer.

13. **Use sign:** the sign(s) permitted for each land use by Section 4618. The size, height, lighting, and other standards applicable to a use sign are specified in Section 4602 and this section.

14. **Wall sign:** a sign mounted parallel to a building facade or other vertical building surface. Parallel signs shall not extend beyond the edge of any wall or other surface to which they are mounted, nor shall they project more than eighteen (18) inches from its surface.

C. **General regulations.**

1. No person shall erect, alter, or relocate within (Municipality) any sign without first obtaining a sign permit (see Article IX), with the following exceptions: (a) memorial signs and tablets displayed on public property or in cemeteries, (b) address numerals and signs not exceeding one (1) square foot in area and bearing the names of occupants of the premises, (c) legal notices, (d) traffic and parking signs which bear no advertising.

2. The repainting, changing of parts, and preventive maintenance of signs shall not be deemed alterations requiring a sign permit.

3. Except for time and/or temperature signs, no flashing, fluttering, undulating, swinging, rotating, or otherwise moving signs shall be permitted.

4. No sign, temporary or otherwise, shall be affixed to a tree or utility pole.

5. No sign shall violate the corner visibility restrictions of Section 4710.

6. No signs including traffic signs and similar regulatory notices except those of a duly constituted governing body shall be allowed within road right-of-way lines.

7. Any spotlights permitted to illuminate signs shall be shielded such that their light source cannot be seen from adjoining roads.

8. **Height.**

   a. The height of a freestanding sign shall be measured from the curb level to the top of the sign.

   b. The height of a projecting sign shall be measured from the base of the sign face to the ground below.

   c. The height of a wall sign shall be measured from the base of the building below the sign to the top of the sign face. The top of the sign shall be no higher than the maximum permitted building height nor shall it be more than three (3) feet higher than the highest ceiling elevation in the building.

   d. The height of a graphic or supergraphic shall be measured from the base of the ground to the top of the sign face.

9. A sign shall not be mounted on a roof.

Section 4617. Table of Sign Performance Standards.

The table on page 178 indicates which sign performance standard (R, A, B, C, D, or E, specified in Section 4602) applies to a particular land use. Subject to any additional applicable requirements of this section, the following table states the specifications for each of the standards as applied to each of the six sign types permitted by this ordinance. For each sign type, the maximum area of the face of the sign, the maximum permitted height, the permitted lighting source, and any additional requirements or limitations are specified.

Section 4618. Detailed Sign Regulations by Sign Type.

A. **Use signs.**

1. Each land use shall be permitted one (1) freestanding sign and one (1) of the following sign types: projecting wall, graphic, supergraphic, auxiliary, as permitted by this section.

Section 4617.
Table of Sign Performance Standards—Sign Standard
(See Section 4617)

	R	A	B	C	D	E
FREE STANDING						
Max. area[1]	$A=.5$ sq. ft.	$A=25$ $A_1=10$ $A_2=2$	$A=35$ $A_1=15$ $A_2=2$	$A=50$ $A_1=20$ $A_2=2$	$A=75$ $A_1=30$ $A_2=3$	$A=100$ $A_1=40$ $A_2=3$
Max. height	Note 2	6 ft.	8 ft.	10 ft.	15 ft.	20 ft.
Lighting	General	Spot	Spot	Spot, internal, back	Spot, internal, back	Spot, internal, back
Other	House no. only					
PROJECTING						
Max. area	2 sq. ft.[2]	12 sq. ft.	15 sq. ft.	18 sq. ft.	24 sq. ft.	30 sq. ft.
Max. height	8 ft.	14 ft.	15 ft.	16 ft.	18 ft. .	18 ft.
Lighting	General	General	General	General	General, internal, back	General, internal, back
Other						
WALL						
Max. area[3]	$A_3=3$ sq. ft.	$A_1=4$ $x=.02$ $A_3=200$	$A_1=4$ $x=.03$ $A_3=300$	$A_1=4$ $x=.04$ $A_3=400$	$A_1=6$ $x=.06$ $A_3=600$	$A_1=8$ $x=.08$ $A_2=800$
Max. height	8 ft.	Max. ht. of building	Max. ht. of building	Max. ht. of building	Max. ht. of building	Max. ht. of building
Lighting	General	Spot, back	Spot, back	Spot, internal, back	Spot, internal, back	Spot, internal, back
Other						
GRAPHICS						
Max. area[4]	6 sq. ft.	12%	16%	20%	28%	38%
Max. height	6 ft.	Max. ht. of building	Max. ht. of building	Max. ht. of building	Max. ht. of building	Max. ht. of building
Lighting	General	Spot, general	Spot, general	Spot, general	Spot, general	Spot, general
Other						
SUPER GRAPHICS						
Max. area		40%	50%	60%	80%	100%
Max. height	Not permitted	Max. ht. of building	Max. ht. of building	Max. ht. of building	Max. ht. of building	Max. ht. of building
Lighting		General	General	General	General	General
Other						
AUXILIARY FREE STANDING						
Max. area[5]		10%	10%	10%	15%	15%
Max. height	Not permitted	4 ft.	5 ft.	6 ft.	8 ft.	10 ft.
Bldg. area		10%	10%	10%	10%	10%
Window area		5%	7%	10%	20%	30%
Other		In display area—not on window				

[1] Choose A or $A_1 + \left(A_2 \times \dfrac{\text{Frontage (ft.)}}{50} \right)$ whichever is greater.

[2] 1 ft. or mounted on house, garage, or mailbox.

[3] Choose A_1 + facade area (sq. ft.)$\times$ (x) or A_3, whichever is less.

[4] In square feet or percent of facade area.

[5] Percent of permissible free standing.

2. When a use takes pedestrian or vehicular access from more than one (1) street or road, one (1) additional sign shall be permitted for each such road to which it has access.

B. **Arterial signs.**

1. Each lot which has a minimum of five hundred (500) feet of frontage on an arterial road, as designated by Section 4704, shall be permitted one (1) arterial sign, in addition to any other sign(s) which may be permitted by this section.

2. An arterial sign shall be a freestanding sign and shall be no more than six (6) square feet in area for each two hundred and fifty (250) feet of arterial road frontage of the lot on which it is to be located. An arterial sign shall be no higher than six (6) feet in height, except when the total area of the sign is one hundred (100) square feet it may be no more than ten (10) feet in height. Such signs may be internally lighted or lighted by spotlights.

3. When more than one (1) lot is to be subdivided or developed as part of a larger land development, there shall be permitted to that development either:

   a. No more than one (1) arterial sign for each arterial road upon which it fronts.

   b. One sign for each two hundred and fifty (250) feet of frontage on an arterial road, provided that the total sign face area thereof shall not exceed the combined sign face area which would otherwise be permitted by this section.

4. Arterial signs shall be located between the arterial road on which they may be permitted and the bufferyard required by the use on the site.

Commentary: An arterial sign is intended to permit the identification of uses located nearby the road. The regulations imposed by this section insure that public highway signs are not rendered ineffective. Arterial signs are adequately sized so that motorists can be informed a safe distance prior to exit of the use(s) located at any roadway exit point.

C. **Development signs.**

1. When a development has in excess of six hundred (600) feet of frontage on an arterial road and consists of more than ten (10) acres, one (1) development sign shall be permitted at each point where a development takes access to an arterial road or on the frontage of the arterial as defined by this ordinance. If the development has in excess of four hundred (400) feet and consists of more than five (5) acres taking access from a collector road, one (1) development sign per collector road upon which it fronts shall be permitted. Development signs are permitted in addition to any arterial sign(s) permitted.

2. A development sign shall be limited in height to no more than six (6) feet above the natural grade in the area, with the exception that, when the width of the sign is less than twenty (20) percent of its height, the sign may be up to twenty-five (25) feet in height.

3. All development signs shall be freestanding.

4. Lighting of a development sign may be by internal lighting, back lighting, the general lighting of the area, or by shielded spotlights.

5. The standards below shall apply to all development signs:

Type of Lighting	Maximum Sign Face Area
General	80 square feet plus 10 square feet for every 100 feet of frontage over 500 feet
Backlighting or spotlighting	60 square feet plus 8 square feet for every 100 feet of frontage over 500 feet
Internal lighting	40 square feet plus 5 square feet for every 100 feet of frontage over 500 feet

6. All development signs shall be located between the arterial or collector roads on which they may be permitted and any bufferyard required by the use on the site.

D. **Additional regulations.**

1. **Marquee signs.** Theaters, museums, auditoriums, and fairgrounds shall be permitted marquee signs up to an additional one hundred (100) percent in area beyond that permitted for freestanding signs,

provided that the area of other signs to which the theaters, museum, auditorium, or fairground may be entitled is reduced. The increase in area permitted the marquee sign shall be equal to the reduction in area of other permitted signs.

2. **Auxiliary signs.** An auxiliary sign may be freestanding, attached to freestanding structures or equipment, or may be attached to the building or windows.

3. **Freestanding signs.** A freestanding sign shall not be located within any bufferyards required by the use of the site on which it is located.

4. **Graphic signs.** A graphic sign shall consist of or be constructed of the same material as the facade of which it is an integral part, with the exception that individual letters or symbols which do not project more than one (1) inch from the facade need not be of the same material as the facade. In the case of a painted graphic, the color of graphic symbols may be different from that of the facade upon which it is painted.

5. **Super graphic.** A super graphic shall consist or be constructed of the same material as the facade of which it is an integral part. No difference in material, color, or tone is permitted.

Section 4619. Temporary Signs.

A. Temporary signs must conform to all regulations of this section but shall not be required to obtain a sign permit.

B. **Political signs.** Temporary signs advertising political parties or candidates for election may be erected or displayed and maintained provided that:

1. The size of any such sign is not in excess of four (4) square feet.

2. The signs shall not be erected or displayed earlier than seventy (70) days prior to the election to which they pertain.

3. The erector of such sign or an authorized agent of the political party or candidate deposits with the zoning officer the sum of twenty-five (25) dollars per each one hundred (100) such signs, or fraction thereof, as a guarantee that all such signs will be removed within twenty (20) days after the date of the election to which

such signs relate. If such signs are not removed at the end of the twenty (20) day period, (Municipality) shall have them removed and keep the full sum deposited to reimburse the expenses thereby incurred.

Section 4700. Transportation and Access Standards.

Sections 4701 through 4707 classify the highway system for the purpose of regulating access, street, and right-of-way standards. In the case of development expected to have significant impact on transportation, a transportation impact analysis is required by Section 4708 to insure that these particular land uses do not adversely impact the highway system. This analysis may result in the developer being required to provide specified highway improvements as a precondition to that development's being permitted. Additionally, Sections 4709 and 4710 impose regulations addressing access for emergency vehicles and areas of unobstructed view at intersections.

Section 4701. Road Classification.

It is the purpose of this section to classify streets and roads on the basis of factors, such as circulation pattern, design speed, and traffic volume, which affect their suitability for particular land uses. There are three basic street types: residential, collector, and arterial. Each basic type is then divided into subcategories for which particularized standards are prescribed. The standards applicable to each are designed to minimize safety hazards, traffic congestion, and other negative impacts which can result when land use development is not carefully coordinated with the street and roadway system. In the case of residential streets, the standards are a function of the dwelling-unit density, average lot size, and average frontage of the residential uses located on the streets. This basis allows the accommodation of different volumes of traffic as well as on-street parking. In the case of nonresidential roads, the standards imposed are a function of the average daily traffic and design speed of each such road.

Commentary: This street classification system separates residential streets from all other types. Residential streets carry significant volumes of foot and bicycle traffic and are used by children. Therefore, design speeds and traffic volumes must remain low in order to provide the necessary safety for residential neighborhoods. Collector roads form barriers between neighborhoods. Their traffic volumes and design speeds are corresponding-

ly greater because their function is to connect major traffic routes. A moderate speed is essential to this function. To control congestion and provide safety, residential properties are not allowed to take direct access to such roads. The arterial roads constitute the highway network upon which most traffic must flow. The efficiency of the system requires that these roads accommodate traffic at high speeds over considerable distances. Whenever these roads become congested, there is pressure to build a bypass to relieve that problem when, in fact, limiting access initially could have prevented congestion.

Section 4702. Definitions.

For the purposes of this article, the following definitions shall apply:

Average daily traffic shall mean (1) the number of vehicles specified as the average traffic using a stretch of road during a twenty-four (24) hour period, either as specified by the Illinois Department of Transportation or a count provided by a professional engineer; or (2) the number of vehicles specified as the average traffic generated by a land use as specified by Section 4708 or from studies of comparable uses conducted by competent professionals.

Average frontage (average lot frontage) shall mean the average front width of lots measured at the street line. This figure shall be calculated separately for each street section, the end points of which shall be a street intersection. This term is applicable only in the case of single-family detached units.

Average lot size shall be calculated by adding the lot size of all lots having direct (or indirect) access to each street section (the end points of which shall be a street intersection) and dividing this total by the number of lots.

Cartway shall mean that portion of a road right-of-way which is paved, exclusive of curbs.

Double-loaded shall mean a residential street having dwelling units that take access from both sides of that street.

Freeway shall mean a highway that accommodates heavy traffic at high speeds with full control of access and no at-grade intersections.

Single-loaded shall mean a residential street having dwelling units that take access from only one side of that street. A single-loaded street includes parkways, one-way loops, and eyebrow roads.

Right-of-way shall mean the road width measured at property lines.

Section 4703. Street Types.

A. **Residential streets.**

1. Residential streets primarily function to provide access to residential uses. All residential streets are intended to accommodate relatively low traffic volumes at slow speeds in order to minimize the basic incompatibility of vehicles and the pedestrians and children who characterize residential neighborhoods. There are five different classes of residential streets created and regulated by this ordinance. Residential streets have historically been considered homogeneous. Depending on the type and density of development served by these streets, however, they are more accurately subcategorized as follows. Even within each subcategory of streets, different standards are applicable depending on whether the streets are one-way or two-way and whether they have curbs. The subcategories are:

    Lane: a residential street or cul-de-sac which serves a maximum of six (6) dwelling units or has an average daily traffic of fewer than forty-nine (49) vehicles.

    Court: a residential street which provides access for individual units. A court serves fewer than fifteen (15) dwelling units or has an average daily traffic of fewer than one hundred and thirteen (113) vehicles (whichever is less). Its design speed is ten (10) miles per hour. Courts may be cul-de-sacs, loops, or small cross streets in a block system.

    Ways: a way is a residential street which provides access to individual dwelling units. It serves fifteen (15) to thirty (30) dwelling units or has an average daily traffic of between one hundred and fourteen (114) and two hundred and forty-two (242) vehicles (whichever is less). The design speed of a way is fifteen (15) miles per hour. Ways may be cul-de-sacs, loops, or minor cross streets. They do not function as collector roads.

Minor street: a minor street serves to collect traffic from courts or ways as well as to give access to individual dwelling units. A minor street serves from thirty-one (31) to one hundred and fifteen (115) dwelling units or has an average daily traffic volume ranging from two hundred and forty-three (243) to nine hundred and twenty-six (926) vehicles (whichever is less).

Major residential street: a street to which individual residential units take direct access. It provides access to minor streets, ways, and courts and serves from one hundred and fifteen (115) to one hundred and sixty (160) dwelling units or has an average daily traffic count of from nine hundred and twenty-seven (927) to twelve hundred and eighteen (1,218) vehicles. Any street serving more than one hundred and sixty (160) units is a collector road to which no direct access by single units is permitted.

2. **Rules for determining number of dwelling units served by residential streets.** The following rules and procedures shall be applied in order to determine the number of dwelling units served by a street. This number shall then be used to determine the residential street subtype and, therefore, the standards which shall be applied.

   a. The standards of Section 4705 apply to street segments. A street segment is the length of a street between intersections or between points which define a change in street configuration (e.g., the length of a street which is one-way is a segment separate from the part of that same street which is two-way).

   b. The number of dwelling units served by a street segment includes all units having frontage on that street segment and all units which have frontage on other segments of that street or other streets which contribute to the traffic volume of that segment.

   c. When more than one route of access is available to a dwelling unit, that unit shall be counted as served by the street segments most likely to provide the access point for that unit. In order to determine this, either of the following methods may be used: (1) a direction-preference analysis shall be conducted to determine directional preferences for trips, or (2) the development shall be divided into trip areas based on the shortest exit route, taking into account any directional preferences.

B. **Collector roads.** Collector roads connect residential streets to the highway system's major and high-speed arterial roads or provide access to nonresidential uses and arterial streets. Collector roads form barriers between neighborhoods and are designed for higher speeds and traffic volumes than are residential streets. Because uncongested traffic flow is necessary for their effective functioning, residential uses are prohibited access to collector roads. Collector roads are classified into three types as follows:

   Minor collector: a minor collector has a maximum design speed of thirty (30) miles per hour and is designed to provide level of service D for a maximum average number of three thousand one hundred and ninety-nine (3,199) vehicle trips per day. A minor collector is a local collector street which may be commercial or industrial in character and on which parking may be permitted. A minor collector also includes any street serving more than one hundred and sixty (160) dwelling units.

   Collector: this road cannot permit on-street parking. It may carry some nonlocal traffic. Average daily traffic is between three thousand two hundred (3,200) and seven thousand (7,000) vehicles. The design speed is thirty-five (35) miles per hour at level of service D.

   Major collector: this road services major regional facilities and may carry nonlocal traffic. Major collectors require four (4) lanes and have average daily traffic in excess of seven thousand (7,000) vehicles. The design speed is thirty-five (35) miles per hour at level of service D.

C. **Arterial streets.** These roads are intended to provide for high-speed travel between or within communities or to and from collectors and expressways. Access is controlled so that only regionally significant land uses may take direct access to these streets. All arterials are designated on the map in Section 4704. The subcategories are:

   Minor arterial: a street which carries some regional traffic and which carries traffic from small areas to regional highways. The design speed of such a road is forty-five (45) miles per hour, and it is designed to provide a level of service C. Traffic flow during peak hours should be at least forty (40) miles per hour, with intersections spaced and controlled accordingly.

Arterials: these roads are regional highways; they may be major state highways as well. The design speed of these roads is fifty-five (55) miles per hour, and access should be controlled to insure forty-five (45) mile per hour traffic at level of service C during peak hours.

Freeways: these roads provide access only to arterials or other freeways. No individual land uses take direct access to such roads. Design speed is sixty-five (65) miles per hour.

Section 4704. Road Classification Map (see page 184).
Section 4705. Road Standards.

The six tables starting on page 185 specify the width requirements for residential streets, collector roads, and arterial roads. There are six charts because standards vary depending on whether a street allows one-way or two-way traffic, whether the street has curbs, and whether it is divided. In addition, the width requirements vary according to the average lot frontage and number of dwelling units located on the street.

Section 4706. Roadway Access.

No use shall be permitted to take direct access to a street or road except as delineated below.

A. **Residential streets.** Only those nonresidential uses shown in Section 4602 as having road location "I" shall be permitted direct access to residential streets. All residential uses may take direct access to residential streets.

B. **Collector streets.** No single individual residential dwelling established pursuant to this ordinance shall be permitted direct access to collector streets. Residential uses gain access to collector roads via residential streets. Only those uses shown in Section 4602 as having road location "II" shall be permitted direct access to collector streets, provided that the following specific criteria are also met.

1. **Minor collectors.** All uses with seventy (70) feet or more of frontage may take direct access to minor collectors. Uses with less than seventy (70) feet of frontage shall not be permitted to take access directly to minor collectors and shall be required to share a common entrance drive. No use shall be permitted to take direct access to a minor collector at any point which is within fifty (50) feet of any intersection. In the case of a minor collector which is entirely within a development, any double aisle of parking may take direct access to that collector.

2. **Collectors and major collectors.** All uses with one hundred and fifty (150) feet or more of frontage may take direct access to collectors and major collectors. Uses with less than one hundred and fifty (150) feet of frontage shall not be permitted to take access directly to collectors or major collectors and shall be required to share common drives. No use shall be permitted to take direct access to a collector or major collector at any point which is within one hundred and twenty (120) feet of any intersection. In the case of a collector or major collector which is entirely within a single development and which provides circulation only within that development, any double aisle of parking may take direct access.

C. **Arterials.** Collector streets shall be permitted direct access to arterial streets only pursuant to the following criteria:

1. **Minor arterials.** A street may take direct access to a minor arterial, provided that the point of such access is more than six hundred (600) feet from any intersection or other point of access to that minor arterial. Whenever access is allowed pursuant to this subsection, it shall be conditioned upon the property (which is permitted access) providing that part of a collector street system required for access to adjoining properties.

2. **Arterials.** A street may take direct access to an arterial, provided that the point of such access is more than one thousand (1,000) feet from any intersection or other point of access to that arterial. Whenever access is permitted pursuant to this subsection, it shall be conditioned upon the property (which is permitted such access) providing that part of a collector street required for access to adjoining properties.

Commentary: This subsection is intended to allow residential streets access to arterial roads in a limited number of places while at the same time requiring planning and provision for the development of a coherent internal

Section 4704. Road Classification Map.

The following map designates all nonresidential roads in (Municipality) according to the foregoing classification scheme.

——— Arterials
——— Collectors

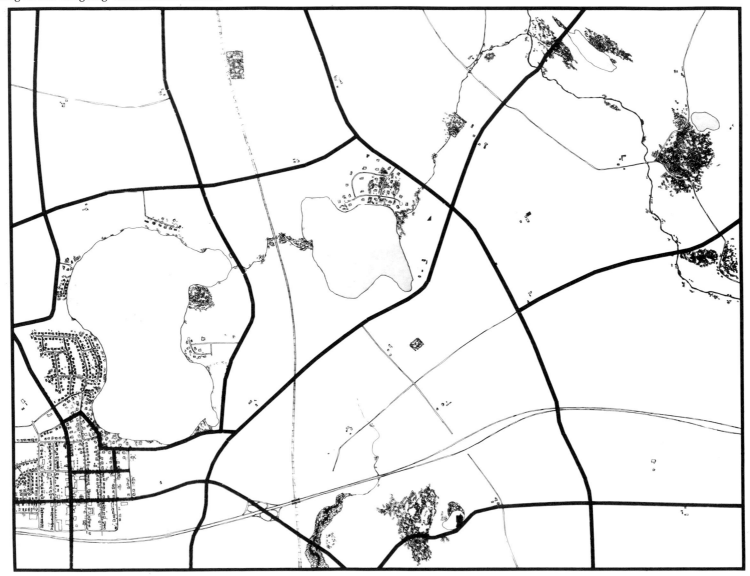

Section 4705. Road Standards.

	ARTERIAL ROADS	
ROAD TYPE design speed	MINOR ARTERIAL 45 mph	ARTERIAL 55 mph
ROAD CONFIGURATION 400 ft. each side of intersections	100 ft. R/W 24 ft.　6 ft.　36 ft.	120 ft. R/W 24 ft.　6 ft.　48 ft.
NORMAL ROAD CONFIGURATION	80 ft. R/W 28 ft.	100 ft. R/W 24 ft.　6 ft.　24 ft.

STREET TYPE	COLLECTOR ROADS		
	MINOR COLLECTOR	COLLECTOR	MAJOR COLLECTOR
maximum ADT	3,199	3,200–7,000	more than 7,000
design speed	30 mph	35 mph	35 mph
UNDIVIDED	60 ft. R/W 24 ft.	66 ft. R/W 28 ft.	80 ft. R/W 48 ft.
DIVIDED	66 ft. R/W 11 ft. 6 ft. 11 ft.	70 ft. R/W 12 ft. 6 ft. 12 ft.	90 ft. R/W 24 ft. 6 ft. 24 ft.

RESIDENTIAL STREETS

STREET TYPE number of du's design speed	**TWO WAY WITHOUT CURBS** 60 feet R/W unless otherwise specified				
	LANE < 7 10 mph	**COURT** 7–14 10 mph	**WAY** 15–30 15 mph	**MINOR STREET** 31–115 20 mph	**MAJOR STREET** 116–160 25 mph
street frontage abutting lots 120 ft or more	40 ft R/W 10 ft	40 ft R/W 13 ft	40 ft R/W 15 ft	44 ft R/W 17 ft	19 ft
90–119 feet	14 ft	17 ft	19 ft	21 ft	23 ft
60–89 feet	17 ft	20 ft	22 ft	24 ft	26 ft
less than 60 feet	23 ft	26 ft	30 ft	32 ft	34 ft
no lots taking direct access	10/17 ft*	13/18 ft*	15/18 ft*	17/21 ft*	20/22 ft*

*The second number is the required width for the forty feet of these roads from where they intersect with a higher order road.

RESIDENTIAL STREETS

STREET TYPE number of du's design speed	**TWO WAY WITH CURBS** 60 feet R/W unless otherwise specified				
	LANE < 7 10 mph	**COURT** 7–14 10 mph	**WAY** 15–30 15 mph	**MINOR STREET** 31–115 20 mph	**MAJOR STREET** 116–160 25 mph
street frontage abutting lots 120 ft or more	40 ft R/W 14 ft	44 ft R/W 16 ft	44 ft R/W 17 ft	19 ft	21 ft
90–119 feet	44ft R/W 16 ft	22 ft	23 ft	25 ft	27 ft
60–89 feet	18 ft	23 ft	24 ft	26 ft	28 ft
less than 60 feet	26 ft	31 ft	32 ft	34 ft	36 ft
no lots taking direct access	16/18 ft*	18/21 ft*	19/22 ft*	20/24 ft*	21/24 ft*

*The second number is the required width for the forty feet of these roads from where they intersect with a higher order road.

RESIDENTIAL STREETS

STREET TYPE number of du's design speed	ONE WAY WITH CURBS 60 feet R/W unless otherwise specified				
	LANE < 7 10 mph	**COURT** 7–14 10 mph	**WAY** 15–30 15 mph	**MINOR STREET** 31–115 20 mph	**MAJOR STREET** 116–160 25 mph
street frontage abutting lots 120 ft or more	40 ft R/W 12 ft	40 ft R/W 14 ft	44 ft R/W 16 ft	18 ft	19 ft
90–119 feet	40 ft R/W 14 ft	18 ft	18 ft	18 ft	20 ft
60–89 feet	44 ft R/W 16 ft	19 ft	20 ft	20 ft	24 ft
less than 60 feet	20 ft	23 ft	24 ft	26 ft	28 ft
no lots taking direct access	40 ft R/W 12 ft	40 ft R/W 14 ft	44 ft R/W 16 ft	18 ft	19 ft

RESIDENTIAL STREETS

STREET TYPE number of du's design speed	ONE WAY WITHOUT CURBS 60 feet R/W unless otherwise specified				
	LANE < 7 10 mph	COURT 7–14 10 mph	WAY 15–30 15 mph	MINOR STREET 31–115 20 mph	MAJOR STREET 116–160 25 mph
street frontage abutting lots 120 ft or more	40 ft R/W 9 ft	40 ft R/W 11 ft	40 ft R/W 14 ft	40 ft R/W 15 ft	44 ft R/W 17 ft
90–119 feet	40 ft R/W 11 ft	40 ft R/W 14 ft	44 ft R/W 16 ft	44 ft R/W 17 ft	44 ft R/W 18 ft
60–89 feet	40 ft R/W 14 ft	44 ft R/W 16 ft	18 ft	20 ft	22 ft
less than 60 feet	44 ft R/W 18 ft	20 ft	22 ft	24 ft	26 ft
no lots taking direct access	40 ft R/W 9 ft	40 ft R/W 11 ft	44 ft R/W 14 ft	44 ft R/W 15 ft	44 ft R/W 17 ft

street system which will ultimately connect each such point of access to the arterial road system.

Section 4707. Temporary Access.

No developer shall be denied a zoning certificate or a building permit for the sole reason that the parcel for which it is sought cannot physically accommodate the requirements of Section 4706 because adjoining segments of the collector road are not yet constructed. In such an event, the use shall be issued a temporary access permit which shall expire when the access required by Section 4706 becomes available to the use.

Section 4708. Transportation Impact Report.

A. **Purpose.** The transportation impact report is designed to identify the transportation (traffic) impacts and problems which are likely to be generated by a proposed use and to identify all improvements required to insure safe ingress to and egress from a proposed development and maintenance of adequate street capacity and elimination of hazardous conditions.

Commentary: The maintenance of a safe transportation network is important to the public safety and welfare. The need to identify all hazards or problems created by a proposed development or the location for which it is proposed is a first essential step for the protection of the public. The transportation impact report allows the identification of roadway and traffic problems which may result from a particular development.

B. **Applicability.** A transportation impact report shall be required in the following cases:

1. Any development which proposes to take direct access to any collector or arterial road.

2. Any residential development which proposes to have more than twenty-five (25) dwelling units.

3. Any use which, according to the table contained in Section 4708(C)(3) or according to a qualified traffic engineer, will generate in excess of either two hundred and fifty (250) trips per acre per day or one hundred (100) trips per day.

Commentary: All uses which, because of size, density, traffic generation rates, or location, can reasonably be expected to pose a traffic problem are required to submit a transportation impact report so that the nature of any such problem can be ascertained and appropriately regulated.

C. **Contents of transportation impact report.** The transportation impact report shall contain the following data and information:

1. **General site description.** A detailed description of the highway network within one (1) mile of the site, a description of the proposed land uses, the anticipated stages of construction, and the anticipated completion date of the proposed land development shall be provided. This description, which may be in the form of a map, shall include the following items: (*a*) all major intersections, (*b*) all proposed and existing ingress and egress locations, (*c*) all existing roadway widths and right-of-ways, (*d*) all existing traffic signals and traffic-control devices, (*e*) all existing and proposed public transportation services and facilities within a one (1) mile radius of the site.

   In addition, any changes to the highway network within one-half (.5) mile of the site, proposed by any governmental agency, shall be described. This description shall include the above items as well as any proposed construction project that would alter the width and/or alignment of the present highway. Such information can be obtained from the (Municipality) Highway Department.

2. **Description of existing traffic conditions.** A report based on the following shall be provided.

   A twenty-four (24) hour traffic count shall be conducted for a period of five (5) weekdays (Monday–Friday) on all roadways which have direct access to a proposed development site. The existing average daily traffic volume and the highest average peak hour volume for any weekday hour between 3 PM and 6 PM shall be recorded. These traffic volumes shall be averaged to determine the average hourly peak traffic volume for the five days between Monday and Friday.

Commentary: This requirement provides accurate data on the traffic condition of roads in the immediate vicinity of a proposal at the time it is actually proposed. The daily figures and peak hour figures are both important. The peak hour traffic volume is the volume that roads are designed to handle, and it is this figure which forms the basis of determining whether any roadway capacity improvements will be necessitated as a result of the traffic impact of the proposed development.

3. **Transportation impact of the development.** The average weekday trip generation rates (trip ends) and the highest average hourly weekday trip generation rate between 3 PM and 6 PM for the proposed use shall be determined from the table contained in this subsection or from figures provided by a qualified traffic engineer. A report shall be made detailing the nature and extent of the trip generation expected to result from the proposed development.

Commentary: For most highways in (Municipality) the peak hour occurs between 3 PM and 6 PM. On such roads the peak transportation impact (the "worst-time" condition of the road) is unlikely to change solely because a single use has a different peak hour. A large development or a development of regional impact may, however, alter this generalization; hence, data for both time periods must be provided.

Table of Average Trip Generation Rate by Land Use Category

Use Category	Land Use	Trip Generation Rates (Trip Origins and Destinations) per 1,000 Square Feet of Gross Floor Area (GFA), Dwelling Unit (D.U.), or Other Specified Unit of Measure	
		Average 24-hour weekday total	Highest average weekday hour between 3 PM–6 PM
Residential	Single family	8.05/D.U.	.81/D.U.
	Multiple family	8.05/D.U.	.81/D.U.
	Condominium	5.6/D.U.	.4 D.U.
	Mobile home	5.2/D.U.	.53/D.U.
	Retirement community & elderly housing	3.3/D.U.	.4/D.U.
	Resort & recreational rental housing	12/D.U.	1.2/D.U.
	All other uses	5.6/D.U.	.5/D.U.
Outdoor Recreation	Boat launching ramp	4.8/ramp	.9/ramp
	Golf course	45.3/hole	7.6/hole
	Park with swimming area	7.4/total acre	1.2/total acre
	Park with hiking, picnicing or camping area	.5/total acre	.08/total acre
	Swimming pool	18.5/100 sq. ft. of water area	1.8/100 sq. ft. of water area
	Tennis court	27/court	5.4/court
	All other uses	6.0/total acre	.9/total acre
Indoor Recreation Institutional, and Special Residential	Church	18.7/GFA	1.5/GFA
	Community or recreation center	25/GFA	4.8/GFA
	Library	42/GFA	6.7/GFA
	Nursing home	2.7/bed	.36/bed
	Schools, elementary	.91/student	.11/student
	high	1.1/student	.29/student
	college	2.2/student	.21/student
	Swimming pool, indoor	18.5/100 sq. ft. of water area	1.8/100 sq. ft. of water area
	Tennis, racquetball or handball court or club	27/court	5.4/court
	All other uses	19/GFA	1.9/GFA
Office	Business or professional office	93/GFA	13.4/GFA
	Medical office or clinic	44/GFA	5.9/GFA
	Office & research park	20.6/GFA	2.4 GFA
	All other uses	20/GFA	2/GFA
Commercial/ Entertainment	Banks and other financial institutions	148/GFA	29.3/GFA
	Bowling alley	33/lane	3.3/lane
	Grocery stores and supermarkets	125.4/GFA	15.7/GFA

	Hospital	12.2/bed	1.3/bed
	Hotel or motel		
	without meeting and/or		
	banquet facilities	9.6/unit	.71/unit
	Restaurant		
	(standard, sit-down)	76/GFA	4.6/GFA
	Retail sales		
	or store	62/GFA	5.8/GFA
	Service business	31/GFA	2.9/GFA
	Shopping centers		
	(under 100,000 sq. ft.)	85.8/GFA	10.5/GFA
	(100,000 to 1,000,000		
	sq. ft.)	49.9/GFA	5.3/GFA
	(over 1,000,000 sq. ft.)	27.1/GFA	3.2/GFA
	All other uses	31/GFA	2.9/GFA
Commercial Recreation	Amusement park		
	fairground	202/acre	20.2/acre
	Outdoor theater		
	Race track		
	All other uses	125/acre	12.5/acre
Road Service	Convenience stores		
	(eg. 7-11 stores)	330/GFA	23.7/GFA
	Fast food		
	restaurants	894/GFA	81.9/GFA
	Gasoline service		
	stations	99.5/GFA	19.4/GFA
	Taverns	133/GFA	26.6/GFA
	All other uses	44/GFA	6.6/GFA
Agricultural Support	All uses	4.01/GFA	.4/GFA
Light Industry	All uses	5.46/GFA	1.18/GFA
Heavy Industry	All uses	4.4/GFA	.8/GFA

Source: Adapted from *Trip Generation Institute of Transportation Engineers*, 1976 and State of California, Department of Transportation, *Sixth, Seventh, Eighth, Ninth, Tenth and Eleventh Progress Reports on Trip Ends Generation Research Counts*, 1970 through July 1976.

4. **Determination of roadway service level.**

a. **Calculate service volumes.** Roadway service volumes shall be calculated at level of service C for roads identified as arterials and at level of service D for roads identified as collectors. Critical elements to be considered in this calculation are: lane width and number of lanes, restricted lateral clearance, the service volume/capacity ratio, percentage of site passing distance greater than one thousand five hundred (1,500) feet, percentage of trucks, grade, and operating and average highway speeds. Data and procedures contained in the *Highway Capacity Manual, Special Report 87*, published by the Highway Research Board, shall be utilized in deriving the data required by the transportation impact report.

Service volume for the given level of service (C for arterials, D for collectors) will be computed directly from capacity under ideal conditions using the adjustment factors for level of service and the critical elements listed above. The specific tables to be used vary, depending on whether the roadway being analyzed is a multi-lane or two-lane highway.

Commentary: The characteristics of each of the different levels of service can be broadly generalized. Definitive service volumes for a given level of service can also be developed for each segment of roadway. Level of service C is generally defined by the Highway Capacity Manual as a road whose flow is stable but where speed and maneuverability are more closely controlled by higher volumes. Most drivers are restricted in their freedom to select their own speed, change lanes, or pass, although a relatively satisfactory operating speed is still obtained. According to the Highway Capacity Manual, forty-five (45) miles per hour has been determined to be a satisfactory operating speed for level of service C for multi-lane highways without access control. Level of service D is defined as a condition approaching unstable flow, with tolerable operating speeds being maintained though considerably affected by changes in operating conditions. Fluctuations in volume and temporary restrictions to flow may cause substantial drops in operating speeds. Drivers have little freedom to maneuver, and comfort and convenience are low; but conditions can be tolerated for short periods of time. Under ideal conditions, an operating speed of thirty-five (35) miles per hour is satisfactory for level of service D on multi-lane rural highways. The roads to which this analysis is to be applied are collector and arterial highways which must be designed to retain these levels of service if they are to fulfill their function of moving people quickly from one part of the region to another.

b. **Calculate whether the roadway is currently operating at the required level of service.** The roadway is considered to be operating at or above level of service C (inclusive of levels A and B) if the service volume computed in Subsection (B) is greater than the hourly peak volume for the period between 3 PM and 6 PM. All arterial roadways operating below level of service C (inclusive of levels D, E, and F) shall be identified as congested locations.

Similarly, the roadway is considered to be operating at or above level of service D (levels A, B, and C) if the service volume computed in Subsection (B) is greater than the hourly peak volume for the period between 3 PM and 6 PM. All collector roadways operating below level of service D (inclusive of levels E and F) shall be identified as congested locations.

Commentary: This section will identify roadways that currently are operating above capacity for levels of service C and D.

5. **Determination of intersection service level.**

   a. **Calculation of intersection capacity at levels of service C and D.** A load-factor analysis shall be conducted for a period of five (5) weekdays (Monday–Friday) on all intersections within one-half (.5) mile of a proposed site. The highest average hourly load factor between 3 PM and 6 PM shall also be recorded. A maximum load factor of three-tenths (.3) will be allowed for intersections involving two (2) arterials or an arterial and one (1) collector roadway. All such intersections with a load factor greater than three-tenths (.3) are operating below level of service C (inclusive of levels D, E, and F) and shall be identified as congested locations.

A maximum load factor of seven-tenths (.7) will be allowed for intersections involving two (2) collector roads. All such intersections with a load factor greater than seven-tenths (.7) are operating below level of service D (levels E and F) and shall be identified as congested locations.

This load factor will represent the highest average for the five (5) days between Monday and Friday. A load-factor analysis is an indicator of the level of service at which an intersection is functioning. The calculation required by this section will identify intersections that are presently operating above capacity for levels of service C and D.

b. **Determine capacity of intersections within one-half mile of proposed site at levels of service C and D.** For intersections which currently are operating with a load factor below three-tenths (.3) during the peak afternoon period, the intersection capacity for level of service C shall be determined. For intersections currently operating with a load factor below seven-tenths (.7) during the peak afternoon period, the intersection capacity for level of service D shall be determined. This calculation will require that a traffic count be conducted for a five (5) day period between Monday and Friday at all affected intersections. Peak hour volume between 3 PM and 6 PM shall also be recorded. The traffic count shall determine: (1) percentage of right-hand turns, (2) percentage of left-hand turns, (3) percentage of trucks, and (4) peak hour factor.

In addition to the traffic survey, an analysis of the intersection shall be undertaken. This analysis will determine the current width of the intersection and the green time to cycle time ratio (G/C ratio). The calculation for determining the capacity at level of service C and D will involve the following assumptions: (1) load factor = .3 (for level of service C) = .9 (for level of service D), (2) metropolitan area over one million (1,000,000) population, (3) outlying business district and residential area, (4) no parking, (5) no bus stops.

To determine intersection capacity at levels of service C and D, figure 6.8 and tables 6.4, 6.5, and 6.6 of the *Highway Capacity Manual* shall be consulted.

This procedure will allow developers and the (Municipality) Highway Department to estimate the additional traffic volume needed to reach capacity at the appropriate levels of service C and D.

6. **Analysis of transportation impact.** The projected total future peak hour traffic demand shall be calculated for all roads fronting on a proposed site and all intersections within one-half (.5) mile of the site. This demand shall consist of an assumed normal increase of traffic volume of one (1) percent per year (unless traffic engineering studies indicate a different rate of increase) and the anticipated traffic that will be generated by the proposed development. An analysis shall be undertaken to determine if roadways and intersections will operate at the appropriate level of service following completion of the development given the future peak hour traffic that will be generated by the proposed development. This analysis consists of the comparison of the total future peak hour intersection and roadway traffic demand with the service volumes for levels C and D computed in Subsection (C) above. All roadways and intersections that would operate below the required level of service following completion of the development shall be considered deficient.

D. **Maintenance of levels of service C and D.** Whenever level of service is determined to be below level C in the case of arterials or below level D in the case of collectors, development is not permitted unless the developer makes the roadway or other improvements necessary to maintain level of service C or D respectively.

Commentary: This section sets forth the method of determining traffic impacts. The developer may choose to reduce what had originally been projected as a development's density in order to avoid having to make any (or as many) roadway or other improvements.

E. **Traffic control devices.** Whenever, as the result of additional traffic generated by a proposed development, the *Manual* determines the need for a traffic signal or regulatory sign, the developer shall be responsible for installing all said devices and signs.

F. **Large developments (over 250 vehicle trips generated per one hour period between 3 PM and 6 PM).**

1. The impact report for developments which will generate between 250 and 1,000 trips during the peak hour shall, pursuant to Section 3A *supra*, involve an analysis of all arterial and collector roadways and all intersections within one (1) mile of the proposed site.

2. The impact report for developments which will generate over 1,000 trips during the peak hour shall involve an analysis of all arterial and collector roadways and all intersections within three (3) miles of the proposed site.

Section 4709. Access for Fire Vehicles and Apparatus.

A. **Purpose.** The purpose of this section is to facilitate rapid and effective extinguishment of fires by ensuring that all premises that a fire department may be called upon to protect in case of a fire shall be readily accessible for effective fire department operations.

B. Every nonresidential use permitted by this ordinance shall provide access for fire vehicles and emergency apparatus from a public street as follows:

1. A dead-end access exceeding three hundred (300) feet in length shall be provided with a turnaround ninety (90) feet in diameter at the closed end.

2. Except as provided by Subsection 4709(B), a fire lane shall be required to provide access to any portion of any structure which is more than: (*a*) one hundred and fifty (150) feet from the nearest street right-of-way when the structure is thirty (30) feet or less in height; (*b*) fifty (50) feet from the nearest street right-of-way when the structure exceeds thirty (30) feet in height.

3. When fire vehicles and apparatus are provided access to any portion of a structure more than the distances from a street right-of-way specified in the subsection above, by means of either bufferyard area or adjoining property, the requirements of Subsection 4709(B)(2) shall not apply.

4. In addition to the situations above which require a fire lane, a fire lane to provide access to any part of a building may also be required if the zoning officer determines that the distance of a structure from the nearest hydrant, the configuration of structures on a

site, or other special characteristics of the site otherwise inhibit rapid, effective fire extinguishment.

5. The zoning officer may determine that public health and safety require fire lanes in addition to private fire protection facilities required by the (Municipality) Building Code for any structure classified by the Building Officials and Code Administrators (BOCA) Basic Building Code (adopted by [Municipality] as its building code) as a high hazard use: any structure to be occupied by uses which involve extreme risks of fire, smoke, explosion, or toxic gas, or structures to be used as places of assembly for large congregations of people susceptible to panic.

C. **Fire lane standards.** A fire lane shall comply with the following standards:

1. The fire lane shall provide clear, unobstructed access for vehicles and apparatus at all times.

2. Signs prohibiting parking or standing of motor vehicles shall be required.

3. Fire lanes shall be eighteen (18) feet in width.

4. The fire lane surface shall be an all-weather roadway.

An alley may contribute all or part of a required fire lane if it meets all other requirements of this section.

D. **Alternatives to fire access lanes.** In lieu of meeting the standards specified above, a developer may substitute alternative means (including but not limited to fire resistant roofs, fire separation walls, space separation, and automatic fire extinguishing systems) of insuring the access necessary for effective fire department operations. Such alternative means shall suffice to meet the requirements of this section, provided that the chief officer empowered to provide fire service in the jurisdiction within which the development is proposed concurs.

Section 4710. Clear View of Intersecting Streets.

A. In order to provide a clear view of intersecting streets to the motorist, there shall be a triangular area of clear vision formed by the two intersecting streets. The size of the triangular area is a function of traffic volume and speed.

B. On any portion of a lot that lies within the triangular area described and illustrated below, nothing shall be erected, placed, planted, or allowed to grow in such a manner as materially to impede vision between a height of two and a half (2.5) feet and ten (10) feet above the grade at the two street center lines.

C. The triangular area shall be formed by a point on each street center line located twenty-five (25), fifty (50), or one hundred (100) feet from the intersection of the street center lines, as indicated below, and a third line connecting the two points.

Road Classification	Distance from Street Center Line Intersection (Feet)
Residential, court or way	25
Residential, minor or major	50
Collector, arterial	100

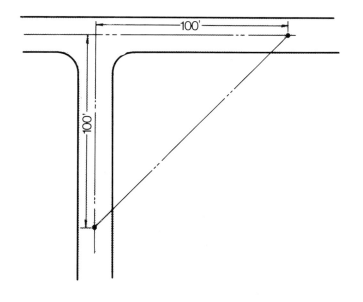

Section 4800. Plant Materials.

Sections 4801 through 4806 specify the plant materials and standards which must be met in order to satisfy the requirements of Sections 4603 through 4611 (bufferyards), 4409 (woodlands), 4419 (water quality), 4500 (open space), 4613 (landscaping), 4614 (off-street parking landscaping), 5002(B)(3) (village house landscaping), and 6007 (nonconforming bufferyards). Included in these sections are regulations relating to the size of plant materials, the soil types which are appropriate for the planting of particular plant materials, the establishment and maintenance of woodlands, prairies, savannah, and preexisting plant materials.

Although these sections do not generally specify the location or spacing of plant material required, all plant materials shall be installed to maximize achieving the purpose(s) for which that planting is required. In the case of bufferyard planting, then, this means that plant materials shall be located so as to achieve the maximum level of protection to the less intense use.

Section 4801. Plant Material Specifications.

A. **Introduction.** The matrix in Section 4802 shall be used to determine which plant materials may be used to satisfy the requirements of this ordinance under specified conditions. The vertical axis of the matrix classifies plant materials by type: canopy trees, understory trees, shrubs, evergreen trees, and ground covers. These plant types correspond to the plant types specified by the sections of this ordinance which require planting.

Only those plant materials identified by an asterisk (*) in the matrix may be counted as satisfying the particular planting requirement. The reason that plant material specifications differ is that they are designed to serve different public purpose functions.

A plant material shall not be counted as satisfying the requirements of this ordinance unless a mark in the matrix indicates it is appropriate as to both its soil type (hydric, mesic, or xeric) and its function (bufferyard, agricultural bufferyard, landscaping, village house landscaping, parking landscaping, woodland, prairie, or savannah), which is indicated on the horizontal axis of the matrix. In the case of planting to establish woodlands, pursuant to Section 4804, the mix of "faster" and "slower" growing plant materials specified in that section shall be provided by selection from among the materials designated as such in the matrix. In the case of planting to establish savannah, only plant materials designated in the matrix as "slower" growing may be counted as satisfying the requirements of Section 4805.

B. **Definitions.** For the purpose of Sections 4800 through 4806, the following definitions apply:

Hydric soils consist of Granby, Harpster, Marsh, Houghton, Montgomery, Pella, Peotone, and Sawmill.

Mesic soils consist of Aptakisic, Ashkum, Barrington, Corwin, Del Rey, Dresden, Elliott, Martinon, Miami, Montmorenci, Morley, Mundelein, Saylesville, Varna, Wauconda, and Zurich.

Xeric soils consist of Boyer, Casco, Fox, Hennepin, Plainfield, and Rodman.

C. **Minimum plant size.** Unless otherwise specifically indicated elsewhere in this ordinance, all plant materials shall meet the following minimum size standards:

| | Minimum Size | |
Plant Material Type	Planting in bufferyards abutting vacant lands	All other plantings
Canopy Tree		
Single Stem	1½ inch caliper	2½ inch caliper
Multi-Stem Clump	6 feet (height)	10 feet (height)
Understory Tree	4 feet (height)	1½ inch caliper
Evergreen Tree	3 feet (height)	5 feet (height)
Shrub		
Deciduous	15 inches (height)	24 inches (height)
Evergreen	12 inches (height)	18 inches (height)

Commentary: In order to deal more fairly with the uncertainty and timing of development of vacant land, the plant material sizes required to buffer against it are less than required against an existing use. This substantially reduces cost and is based on the assumption that a period of approximately three (3) years is expected between buffer planting and occupancy of adjoining property. This assumption allows the smaller plant material time to become established and reach a size comparable to that which is ultimately likely to be necessary to provide adequate protection.

TYPE OF PLANT

Canopy Trees

Scientific Name
Common Name

	Soil Type			Plant Function			Open Space			Growth Rate	
	Hydric	Mesic	Xeric	Bufferyard Landscaping Village House	Ag Buffer	Off Street Parking Landscaping	Woodlands	Savanna	Prairie	Faster	Slower
Acer Negundo — Box Elder	★	★		★	★			★		★	
Acer Platinoides — Norway Maple		★		★	★	★	★				★
Acer Rubrum — Red Maple	★	★		★			★	★		★	
Acer Saccharinum — Silver Maple	★	★	★	★	★	★		★		★	
Acer Saccharum — Sugar Maple		★	★	★	★	★	★	★			★
Aesculus Carnea 'Rubicunda' — Pink Horsechestnut		★	★	★	★	★	★				★
Aesculus Hippocastanum — Common Horsechestnut		★		★	★						★
Ailanthus Altissima — Tree of Heaven	★	★	★	★						★	
Betula Lutea — Yellow Birch		★		★							★
Betula Papyrifera — Paper Birch		★		★							★
Carya Cordiformis — Bitternut Hickory		★		★	★		★				★
Carya Ovata — Shagbark Hickory		★	★	★	★		★	★			★
Catalpa Speciosa — Northern Catalpa		★	★	★	★	★	★				★
Celtis Occidentalis — Common Hackberry	★	★		★	★	★	★			★	★
Fagus Gradifolia — American Beech		★		★	★		★				★
Fraxinus Americana — White Ash		★	★	★	★	★	★				★

Canopy Trees

Scientific Name
Common Name

	SOIL TYPE			PLANT FUNCTION			OPEN SPACE			GROWTH RATE	
	Hydric	Mesic	Xeric	Bufferyard Landscaping Village House	Ag Buffer	Off Street Parking Landscaping	Woodlands	Savanna	Prairie	Faster	Slower
Fraxinus Pennsylvanica — Green Ash	★	★	★	★	★	★	★	★		★	
Fraxinus Quadrangulata — Blue Ash		★		★							★
Ginkgo Biloba — Ginkgo Tree		★	★	★		★					★
Gleditsia Triacanthos Inermis — Thornless Honeylocust	★	★	★	★		★				★	★
Gleditsia Triacanthos — Common Honeylocust	★	★	★	★	★	★	★	★		★	★
Gymnocladus Dioicus — Kentucky Coffeetree		★		★	★	★	★				★
Juglans Cinerea — Butternut		★		★	★		★				★
Juglans Nigra — Black Walnut	★	★		★	★	★	★	★		★	★
Phellodendron Amurense — Amur Corktree		★	★	★		★					★
Platanus Occidentalis — Sycamore Tree		★		★	★		★			★	★
Populas Alba — White Poplar	★	★		★	★		★			★	
Populas Deltoides — Cottonwood	★	★		★	★		★			★	
Populas Grandidentata — Bigtoothed Aspen	★	★		★	★		★			★	
Populas Tremuloides — Quaking Aspen	★	★		★	★	★	★			★	
Prunus Serotina — Black Cherry		★	★	★	★		★	★		★	
Quercus Accitissima — Sawtooth Oak		★	★	★	★		★				★

Canopy Trees

Scientific Name
Common Name

	SOIL TYPE			PLANT FUNCTION			OPEN SPACE			GROWTH RATE	
	Hydric	Mesic	Xeric	Bufferyard Landscaping Village House	Ag Buffer	Off Street Parking Landscaping	Woodlands	Savanna	Prairie	Faster	Slower
Quercus Alba — White Oak		★	★	★	★		★	★			★
Quercus Bicolor — Swamp White Oak	★	★		★	★	★	★	★			★
Quercus Borealis — Northern Red Oak		★		★	★		★	★			★
Quercus Coccinea — Scarlet Oak		★		★							★
Quercus Imbricaria — Shingle Oak		★	★	★	★	★	★				★
Quercus Macrocarpa — Bur Oak		★	★	★	★	★	★	★	★		★
Quercus Muhlenbergii — Chinquapin Oak		★	★	★	★		★				★
Quercus Palustris — Pin Oak		★		★	★		★				★
Quercus Robur — English Oak		★	★	★		★	★				★
Quercus Velutina — Black Oak		★	★	★	★	★	★				★
Salix Amygdaloides — Peach-leaved Willow	★	★		★	★	★	★			★	
Salix Nigra — Black Willow	★	★		★	★		★			★	
Salix Niobe — Weeping Willow	★	★		★	★	★	★			★	
Tilia Americana — American Linden	★	★	★	★	★	★	★	★			★
Tilia Cordata — Littleleaf Linden		★		★	★	★	★				★
Tilia Euchlora — Redmond Linden		★		★	★	★	★				★

Canopy Trees

Scientific Name / Common Name	SOIL TYPE			PLANT FUNCTION			OPEN SPACE			GROWTH RATE	
	Hydric	Mesic	Xeric	Bufferyard Landscaping Village House	Ag Buffer	Off Street Parking Landscaping	Woodlands	Savanna	Prairie	Faster	Slower
Tilia Platyphyllos Bigleaf Linden		★	★	★	★	★	★				★
Ulmus Americana American Elm	★	★	★	★	★	★	★			★	
Ulmus Parvifola Chinese Elm		★		★		★				★	
Ulmus Pumila Siberian Elm		★		★		★				★	

Evergreens

Scientific Name
Common Name

	SOIL TYPE			PLANT FUNCTION			OPEN SPACE			GROWTH RATE	
	Hydric	Mesic	Xeric	Bufferyard Landscaping Village House	Ag Buffer	Off Street Parking Landscaping	Woodlands	Savanna	Prairie	Faster	Slower
Abies Concolor — White Fir		★		★	★		★				★
Abies Balsamea — Balsam Fir		★		★	★		★				★
Juniperus Chinensis — Chinese Juniper		★	★	★	★	★	★				★
Juniperus Virginiana — Eastern Red Cedar		★	★	★	★	★	★	★			★
Larix — European Larch		★		★	★		★				★
Larix Laricina — American Larch	★	★		★	★		★				★
Picea Glauca Alba — White Spruce		★		★	★	★	★				★
Picea Glauca Densata — Blackhill Spruce		★		★	★	★	★				★
Picea Abies — Norway Spruce		★		★	★	★	★				★
Picea Pungens — Blue Spruce		★		★	★	★	★				★
Pinus Banksiana — Jack Pine		★	★	★	★	★	★				★
Pinus Cembra — Swiss Stone Pine		★	★	★	★	★					★
Pinus Nigra — Austrian Pine		★	★	★	★	★	★				★
Pinus Pungens — Table Mountain Pine		★		★	★	★					★
Pinus Resinosa — Red Pine		★	★	★	★	★	★				★
Pinus Strobus — White Pine		★		★	★		★				★

Evergreens

Scientific Name
Common Name

	Soil Type			Plant Function			Open Space			Growth Rate	
	Hydric	Mesic	Xeric	Eufferyard Landscaping Village House	Ag Buffer	Cff Street Parking Landscaping	Woodlands	Savanna	Prairie	Faster	Slower
Pinus Sylvestris / Scotch Pine		★	★	★	★	★	★				★
Pinus Thunbergi / Japanese Black Pine		★	★	★	★						★
Pseudotusuga Tuxifolia / Douglas Fir		★		★	★	★	★				★
Thuja Occidentalis / American Arborbitae		★		★	★						★
Tsuga Canadensis / Canadian Hemlock		★	★	★	★		★				★

Understory Small Trees

Scientific Name / Common Name	SOIL TYPE			PLANT FUNCTION			OPEN SPACE			GROWTH RATE	
	Hydric	Mesic	Xeric	Bufferyard Landscaping Village House	Ag Buffer	Off Street Parking Landscaping	Woodlands	Savanna	Prairie	Faster	Slower
Acer Campestra — Hedge Maple		★		★		★					★
Acer Ginnala — Amur Maple		★		★	★	★					★
Acer Griseum — Paper Bark Maple		★		★	★						★
Aesculus Glabra — Ohio Buckeye		★		★							
Alnus Glutinosa — European Black Alder	★	★		★	★	★	★			★	
Alnus Rugosa — American Alder	★	★		★	★		★			★	
Amelanchier Canadensis — Thicket Serviceberry		★		★	★		★				★
Amelanchier Laevis — Allegany Serviceberry		★		★	★		★				★
Amelanchier Sanguinea — Roundleaf Serviceberry		★		★	★		★				★
Amelanchier Stolonifera — Running Serviceberry		★		★	★		★				★
Betula Lenta — Sweet Birch		★		★	★		★				★
Betula Nigra — River Birch	★	★		★	★	★	★			★	★
Betula Populifolia — Gray Birch		★		★							★
Carpinus Caroliniana — American Hornbeam		★	★	★	★		★				★
Cercidiphyllum Japonicum — Japanese Katsuratree		★		★		★					★
Chionanthus Virginicus — White Fringetree		★		★							★

Understory Small Trees

Scientific Name
Common Name

	SOIL TYPE			PLANT FUNCTION			OPEN SPACE			GROWTH RATE	
	Hydric	Mesic	Xeric	Bufferyard Landscaping Village House	Ag Buffer	Off Street Parking Landscaping	Woodlands	Savanna	Prairie	Faster	Slower
Cornus Alternifolia — Pagoda Dogwood		★	★	★	★	★	★				★
Cornus Mas — Cornelian Cherry		★		★		★					★
Crataegus Crus-Galli — Cockspur Hawthorn		★	★	★	★	★	★	★			★
Crataegus Mollis — Downy Hawthorn		★	★	★	★	★	★	★			★
Crataegus Phaenopyrum — Washington Hawthorn		★	★	★	★	★	★	★			★
Crataegus Punctata — Dotted Hawthorn		★	★	★	★	★	★				★
Crataegus Viridas — Winterking Hawthorn		★	★	★	★	★					★
Elaeagnus Angustifolia — Russian Olive		★		★	★	★					★
Elaeagnus Umbellata — Autumn Olive		★		★	★	★					★
Euonymus Atropurpureus — Eastern Wahoo		★	★	★	★		★				★
Lindera Benzoin — Spicebush		★		★		★					★
Maclura Pomifera — Osage Orange Tree		★	★	★	★	★					★
Magnolia Soulangiana — Saucer Magnolia		★		★							★
Malus Spieces — Crab Apples		★	★	★	★	★	★	★		★	★
Morus Alba — White Mulberry		★	★	★	★	★	★	★		★	
Ostrya Virginiana — Ironwood		★	★	★	★	★	★				★

Understory Small Trees

Scientific Name / Common Name	SOIL TYPE			PLANT FUNCTION			OPEN SPACE			GROWTH RATE	
	Hydric	Mesic	Xeric	Bufferyard Landscaping Village House	Ag Buffer	Off Street Parking Landscaping	Woodlands	Savanna	Prairie	Faster	Slower
Prunus Americana / American Plum		★	★	★	★		★			★	
Prunus Padus / European Birdcherry		★	★	★	★	★					★
Pyrus Communis / Common Pear		★	★	★	★	★	★				★
Salix Interior / Sandbar Willow	★	★		★	★		★	★		★	
Syringa Japonica / Japanese Treelilac		★		★	★	★					★

Shrubs

Scientific Name
Common Name

	SOIL TYPE			PLANT FUNCTION			OPEN SPACE			GROWTH RATE	
	Hydric	Mesic	Xeric	Bufferyard Landscaping Village House	Ag Buffer	Off Street Parking Landscaping	Woodlands	Savanna	Prairie	Faster	Slower
Amorpha Fruiticosa / Indigo Bush		★	★	★	★		★	★	★		★
Aronia Arbutifolia / Red Chokeberry	★	★		★	★	★				★	
Aronia Melanocarpa / Black Chokeberry	★	★		★	★	★	★	★		★	
Berberis Thunbergi / Japanese Barberry		★		★	★	★					★
Calycanthos Floridus / Carolina Allspice		★		★	★	★					★
Caragana Arborescens / Siberian Peashrub		★		★	★	★					★
Caragana Frutex / Russian Peashrub		★		★	★	★					★
Ceanothus Americanus / New Jersey Tea		★		★		★					★
Celastrus Scandens / American Bittersweet	★	★	★	★	★		★				★
Cephalanthus Occidentalis / Button Bush	★	★		★	★		★			★	
Chaenomeles Japonica / Japanese Flowering Quince		★		★	★	★					★
Chaenomeles Lagenaria / Common Flowering Quince		★		★	★	★					★
Cornus Amomum / Silky Dogwood	★	★		★	★	★	★			★	
Cornus Baileyi / Bailey's Dogwood	★	★		★		★	★			★	
Cornus Racemosa / Gray Dogwood	★	★	★	★	★	★	★	★			★

207

Shrubs

Scientific Name
Common Name

	SOIL TYPE			PLANT FUNCTION			OPEN SPACE			GROWTH RATE	
	Hydric	Mesic	Xeric	Bufferyard Landscaping Village House	Ag Buffer	Off Street Parking Landscaping	Woodlands	Savanna	Prairie	Faster	Slower
Cornus Sanguinea Bloodtwig Dogwood	★	★		★	★	★	★			★	
Cornus Stolonifera Redosier Dogwood	★	★	★	★	★	★	★	★		★	
Corylus Americana American Hazelnut		★	★	★	★	★	★	★			★
Cotinus Coggygria Smokebush		★		★		★					★
Cotoneaster Acutifolia Peking Cotoneaster		★		★		★					★
Cotoneaster Multiflora Multiflora Cotoneaster		★		★	★	★					★
Deutzia Gracilis Slender Deutzia		★		★		★					★
Euonymus Alatus Burning Bush		★	★	★	★	★					★
Forsythia Intermedia Border Forsythia		★		★	★	★				★	
Forsythia Ovata Early Forsythia		★		★		★				★	
Forsythia Suspensa Weeping Forsythia		★		★		★				★	
Hamamelis Vernalis Early Witchhazel		★		★		★	★				★
Hamamelis Virginiana Common Witchhazel		★	★	★		★	★				★
Hippophae Rhamnoides Common Seabuckthorn		★		★		★					★
Hydrangea A. Grandiflora A.G. Hydrangea		★		★					★		

Shrubs

Scientific Name / Common Name	SOIL TYPE			PLANT FUNCTION			OPEN SPACE			GROWTH RATE	
	Hydric	Mesic	Xeric	Bufferyard Landscaping Village House	Ag Buffer	Off Street Parking Landscaping	Woodlards	Savanna	Prairie	Faster	Slower
Hydrangea P. Grandiflora / P.G. Hydrangea		★		★						★	
Hypericum Kalmianum / Kalm St. Johnswort		★	★	★		★					★
Hypericum Prolificum / Shrubby St. Johnswort		★	★	★		★		★			★
Ligustrum Amurense / Amur or Cheyenne Privet	★	★	★	★	★	★				★	
Ligustrum O. Regelianum / Regel's Privet		★	★	★	★	★				★	
Ligustrum Vulgare / Common Privet		★	★	★	★	★	★			★	
Loincera / Clavy's Dwarf Honeysuckle		★	★	★		★					★
Lonicera Tatarica / Tatarian Honeysuckle		★	★	★	★	★				★	
Lycium Chinense / Chinese Wolfberry		★		★		★				★	
Myrica Pennsylvanica / Northern Bayberry		★	★	★		★					★
Philadelphus Coronarious / Sweet Mock-Orange		★		★							★
Physocarpus Opulifolius / Ninebark		★		★		★		★			★
Polygonum Auberti / Fleece Flower		★	★	★		★				★	
Potentilla Fruiticosa / Bush Cinquefoil		★	★	★		★		★			★
Prunus Glandulosa / Flowering Almond		★		★						★	
Prunus Triloba / Double Flowering Plum		★		★							★

Shrubs

Scientific Name / Common Name	SOIL TYPE			PLANT FUNCTION			OPEN SPACE			GROWTH RATE	
	Hydric	Mesic	Xeric	Bufferyard Landscaping Village House	Ag Buffer	Off Street Parking Landscaping	Woodlands	Savanna	Prairie	Faster	Slower
Prunus Virginiana / Chokeberry	★	★	★	★	★	★	★	★		★	★
Ptelea Trifoliata / Hope Tree		★		★							
Ribes Americanum / American Black Currant	★	★	★	★		★	★	★		★	
Ribes Alpinum / Alpine Currant	★	★	★	★	★	★					★
Ribes Cynosbati / Pasture Gooseberry	★	★	★	★	★	★	★			★	
Ribes Missouriense / Missouri Gooseberry	★	★	★	★	★	★	★			★	
Ribes Odoratum / Clove Currant	★	★	★	★	★	★					★
Rhamnus Frangula / Buckthorn	★	★		★		★				★	
Rhodotypes Scandens / Black Jetbead	★	★		★		★	★				★
Rhus Aromatica / Fragrant Sumac	★	★	★	★	★	★	★	★	★		★
Rhus Copallina Latifolia / Shining Sumac	★	★	★	★	★	★		★			★
Rhus Glabra / Smooth Sumac	★	★	★	★	★	★	★	★	★		★
Rhus Typhina / Staghorn Sumac	★	★	★	★		★	★	★	★	★	
Rosa Arkansana / Arkansas Rose	★	★	★	★	★	★	★			★	
Rose Palustris / Swamp Rose	★	★		★	★	★	★	★			★
Rosa Setigera / Prairie Rose	★	★	★	★	★	★	★	★	★	★	

Shrubs

Scientific Name
Common Name

	SOIL TYPE			PLANT FUNCTION			OPEN SPACE			GROWTH RATE	
	Hydric	Mesic	Xeric	Bufferyard Landscaping Village House	Ag Buffer	Off Street Parking Landscaping	Woodlands	Savanna	Prairie	Faster	Slower
Rosa Virginiana / Virginia Rose	★	★	★	★	★	★	★	★		★	
Rubus Allegheniensis / Blackberry	★	★	★	★	★	★	★	★		★	
Rubus Idaeus / Raspberry	★	★	★	★	★	★	★	★		★	
Rubus Strigosus / Blackberry	★	★	★	★	★	★	★	★		★	
Sambucus Canadensis / Elderberry	★	★	★	★			★	★			★
Shepherdia Cunadensis / Buffaloberry		★		★		★					★
Spiraea Bumalda / Bumalda Spirea	★	★	★	★		★				★	
Spiraea Chameadrifolia / Germander Spirea	★	★	★	★		★					★
Spiraea Prunifolia / True Bridalwreath Spirea	★	★	★	★		★					★
Spiraea Thunbergi / Thunberg Spirea	★	★	★	★		★					★
Spiraea Vanhouttei / Vanhoutte Spirea	★	★	★	★	★	★					★
Stapylea Trifolia / Bladdernut	★	★	★	★		★	★				★
Stephandra Incisa / Cutleaf Stephandra	★	★	★	★		★					★
Symphoricarpos Alba / Snowberry	★	★	★	★		★					★
Symphoricarpos Orbiculatus / Indian Currant	★	★	★	★		★	★	★			★
Syringa Chinensis / Chinese Lilac	★	★	★	★		★					★

Shrubs

Scientific Name
Common Name

	SOIL TYPE			PLANT FUNCTION			OPEN SPACE			GROWTH RATE	
	Hydric	Mesic	Xeric	Bufferyard Landscaping Village House	Ag Buffer	Off Street Parking Landscaping	Woodlands	Savanna	Prairie	Faster	Slower
Syringa Villosa / Late Lilac	★	★	★	★		★				★	
Syringa Vulgaris / Common Lilac	★	★	★	★		★				★	
Viburnum Acerifolium / Mapleleaf Viburnum		★		★							★
Viburnum Burkwoodi / Burkwood Viburnum		★	★	★							★
Viburnum Carlesi / Korean Spicebush		★	★	★		★					★
Viburnum Cassinoides / Witherod		★	★	★							★
Viburnum Dentatum / Arrowwood	★	★	★	★	★	★	★	★		★	★
Viburnum Lantana / Wayfaring Tree		★	★	★		★					★
Viburnum Lentago / Nannyberry	★	★	★	★	★	★	★	★		★	★
Viburnum Opulus / European Cranberrybush	★	★	★	★	★	★	★				★
Viburnum Prunifolium / Blackhaw Viburnum		★	★	★		★	★				
Viburnum Rhytidophyllum / Leatherleaf Viburnum	★	★	★	★			★				★
Viburnum Sieboldi / Sieboldi Viburnum		★	★	★							★
Viburnum Trilobum / American Highbush Cranberry	★	★	★	★	★	★	★	★			★
Zanthoxylum Americanum / Prickly Ash		★	★	★	★		★				★

Evergreen Shrubs

	SOIL TYPE			PLANT FUNCTION			OPEN SPACE			GROWTH RATE	
Scientific Name Common Name	Hydric	Mesic	Xeric	Bufferyard Landscaping Village House	Ag Buffer	Off Street Parking Landscaping	Woodlands	Savanna	Prairie	Faster	Slower
Juniperus Chinensis Spp. Junipers		★	★	★	★	★					★
Taxus Cuspidata Spreading Yew		★		★	★		★				★
Taxus Cuspidata Upright Yew		★		★							★
Pinus Mugo Mughus Mugho Pine		★	★	★							★

213

Ground Cover: Forbs (satisfies all plant functions)

Scientific Name	Common Name	Hydric	Mesic	Xeric	Woodlands	Savanna	Prairie
Acerates Lanuginosa				X	W	S	P
Acerates Viridiflora							
Echinacea Purpurea	Purple Coneflower						
Liparis Lililfolia	Large Twayblade						
Polygonatum Canaliculatum	Great Solomon's Seal						
Polygonum Scandens	Climbing False Buckwheat						
Achillea Millefolium	Yarrow		M	X	W	S	P
Adiantum Pedatum							
Comularia Majalis	Lily-of-the-Valley						
Galium Boreale	Northern Bedstraw						
Kuhnia Eupatoriodes	False Boneset						
Liatris Aspera	Rough Blazingstar						
Lithospermum Croceum	Hairy Puccoon						
Lithospermum Incisum	Fringed Puccoon						
Silphium Terebinthinaceum	Prairiedock						
Spirea Tomentosa	Harhack Steeplebush						
Thaspium Trifoliatum	Meadow Parsnip						
Veronicastrum Virginicum	Clover's Root						
Viola Sororia	Wood Violet						
Agastache Scrophulariaefolia	Purple Giant Hyssop		M	X	W	S	
Agrimonia Gryposepala	Agrimonies						
Aralia Nudicaulis	Wild Sarsaparilla						
Aralia Racemosa	Spikenard						
Asclepias Exaltata	Poke Milkweed						
Aster Prenanthoides	Crookee-Stemmed Aster						
Aster Saggitfolius	Arrowleafed Aster						
Aster Shortii	Short's Aster						
Athyrium Filix-Feminia							
Botrychium Virginianum							
Brachyelytrum Erectum							
Campanula Americana	Tall Bellflower						
Caulophyllum Thalictroides	Blue Cohosh						
Claytonia Virginica	Spring Beauty						
Conopholis Americana	Squawroot						
Corallorhiza Odontorhiza							
Desmondium Illinoense	Illinois Ticktrefoil						
Dicentra Cucularia	Dutchman's Breeches						
Erigeron Pulchellus	Robin-Plantain						
Erythronium Albidum	White Trout Lily						
Eupatorium Purpureum	Sweet Joe-Pye-Weed						
Eupatorium Rugosum	White Snakeroot						
Galium Aparine	Cleavers						
Galium Circaezans	White Wild Licorice						

Scientific Name	Common Name	Hydric	Mesic	Xeric	Woodlands	Savanna	Prairie
Galium Concinnum	Bedstraw		M	X	W	S	
Goodyera Pubescens	Downy Rattlesnake-Plantain						
Heracleum Lanatum	Parsnip						
Hieracium Scabrum	Rought Hawkweed						
Hydrophyllum Virginianum	Virginia Waterleaf						
Hystrix Patula							
Lactuca Biennis	Blue Lettuce						
Lactuca Spicata	Blue Lettuce						
Lathyrus Ochroleucus	Pale Vetchling						
Lonicera Prolifera							
Mertensia Virginica	Virginia Bluebell						
Orchis Spectabilis	Showy Orchis						
Oryzopsis Racemosa							
Osmorhiza Claytoni	Sweet Cicely						
Osmunda Claytoniana							
Panax Quinquefolium	Genseng						
Parietaria Pensylvanica	Pellitory						
Phryma Leptostachya	Lopseed						
Polygonatum Biflorum	Solomon's Seal						
Polygonatum Canaliculatum	Smooth Solomonseal						
Polymnia Canadensis	Small Flowering Leafcup						
Polemonium Reptans	Greek Valerian						
Podophyllum Peltatum	Mayapple						
Prenanthes Alba	Rattlesnake Root						
Pteridium Aquilinum							
Ranunculus Abortivus	Kidneyleaf Buttercup						
Ranunculus Recurvatus	Hooked Buttercup						
Rubus Occidentalis							
Sanicula Gregaria	Black Snakeroot						
Scrophularia Marilandica	Figwort						
Thalictrum Dioicum	Early Meadow Rue						
Trillium Erectum	Red Trillium						
Uvularia Grandiflora	Large Flowering Bellwort						
Vitis Aestivalis	Summer Grape						
Smilax Hispida	GreenBriar						
Allium Cernum	Wild Onion		M		W	S	
Aquilegia Canadensis	Wild Columbine						
Arabis Canadensis	Sicklepod						
Asclepias Hirtella	Milkweed						
Asarum Canadense	Wild Ginger						
Chara Vulgaris	Stonewort						
Coreopsis Tripteris	Tall Coreopsis						
Erigenia Bulbosa	Harbinger-of-Spring						
Gentiana Flavida	Cream Gentian						
Gentiana Puberulenta							

		Soil Type			Open Space		
		Hydric	Mesic	Xeric	Woodlands	Savanna	Prairie
Oxalis Violacea	Violet Wood Sorrel		M		W	S	
Pedicularis Canadensis	Lousewort						
Polgala Senega	Seneca Snakeroot						
Polygonatum Pubescens	Hairy Solomon's Seal						
Rudbeckia Subtomentosa	Sweet Coneflower						
Taenidia Integerrima	Yellow Pimpernel						
Allium Canadense	Wild Garlic	H	M		W	S	P
Castilleja Coccinea	Indian Paintbrush						
Cirsium Muticum	Swamp Thistle						
Fragaria Virginiana	Wild Strawberry						
Geranium Maculatum	Wild Geranium						
Solidago Gigantea	Late Goldenrod						
Amorpha Canescens	Lead Plant	H	M	X		S	P
Camassia Scilloides	Wild Hyacinth						
Comandra Richardsiana	False Toadflax						
Euphorbia Corollata	Flowering Spurge						
Helianthus Laetiflorus	Snowy Sunflower						
Lespedeza Capitata	Roundheaded Bush Clover						
Lithospermum Canascens	Golden Gromwell						
Ratibida Pinnata	Gray Headed Coneflower						
Rudbeckia Hirta	Blackeyed Susan						
Solidago Rigida	Stiff Goldenrod						
Solidago Speciosa	Showy Goldenrod						
Sporobolus Heterolepis	Prairie Dropseed						
Tradescanthia Ohiensis	Common Spiderwort						
Amphicarpa Bracteata	Hog Peanut	H	M	X	W	S	
Circaea Quadrisulcata	Enchanter's Night Shade						
Cryptotaenia Canadensis	Honewort						
Geum Canadense	White Avens						
Monarda Fistulosa	Wild Bergamot						
Parthenocissus Vitacea							
Polypodium Species	Ferns						
Rhus Radicans	Poison Ivy						
Smilacina Stellata	Starry False Solomon's Seal						
Smilax Ecirrhata	Greenbriar						
Smilax Herbacea	Carrion Flower						
Viola Cucullata	Marsh Blue Violet						
Vitis Riparia	Riverbank Grape						
Anemone Canadensis	Canada Anemone	H				S	P

		Soil Type			Open Space		
		Hydric	Mesic	Xeric	Woodlands	Savarna	Prairie
Apocynum Cannabinum	Indian Dogbane	H				S	P
Cacalia Atriplicifolia	Pale Indian Plantain						
Cacalia Suaveolens	Sweet Scented Indian Plantain						
Galium Tinctorium	Dye Bedstraw						
Gerardia Aspera	Pink Gerardia						
Habenaria Lacera	Orchid						
Helenium Autumnale	Common Sneezeweed						
Heliopsis Helianthoides	Oxeye Sunflower						
Houstonia Caerulea	Innocence						
Liparis Loeseli	Yellow Twayblade						
Lobelia Cardinalis	Cardinal-Flower						
Lobellia Spicata	Pale Lobelia						
Nymphaea Tuberosa	Water Lily						
Oenthera Perennis	Perennial Sundrops						
Pedicularis Lanceolata	Lousewort						
Silphium Lacinatum	Compassplant						
Silphium Perfoliatum	Cup-Plant						
Solidago Ohioensis	Ohio Goldenrod						
Thelyptersis Palustris							
Tofieldia Glutinosa	False Asphodel						
Anemone Cylindrica	Prairie Thimbleweed		M	X		S	P
Anemone Quinquefolia	Wood Anemone						
Anemonella Thalictroides	Rue-Anemone						
Anemone Virginiana	Thimbleweed						
Antennaria Neglecta	Pussytoes						
Apocynum Androsaemifolium	Spreading Dogbane						
Artemsia Caudata	Beach Wormwood						
Artemsia Frigida							
Artemsia Ludoviciana	White Sage						
Artemsia Serrata	Sawtooth Sagebush						
Asclepias Tuberosa	Butterfly Milkweed						
Asclepias Verticillata	Whorled Milkweed						
Aster Azureus	Azure Aster						
Aster Ericoides	Heath Aster						
Aster Laevis	Smooth Aster						
Aster Oblonigfolis	Aromatic Aster						
Aster Pilosus	White Aster						
Aster Ptarmicoides	Stiff Aster						
Aster Sericeus	Western Silvery Aster						
Aster Simplex	White Field Aster						
Astragalus Crassicarpus							
Callirhoe Triangulata	Clustered Poppymallow						
Cassia Fasciculata	Partridge Pea						
Cirsium Altissimum	Tall Thistle						
Cirsium Hilldii	Hill's Thistle						

		Soil Type			Open Space	
		Hydric	Mesic	Xeric	Woodlands	Savanna	Prairie

Species	Common Name	Hydric	Mesic	Xeric	Woodlands	Savanna	Prairie
Cirsium Undalatum			M	X		S	P
Coreopsis Palmata	Prairie Coreopsis Tickseed						
Delphinium Virescens	Prairie Larkspur						
Erigeron Strigosas	Daisy Fleabane						
Gentiana Quinquefolia	Stiff Gentian						
Hackelia Virginiana	Stickseed						
Hedeonva Hispida	Rought Penyroyal						
Helianthus Occidentalis	Naked Sunflower						
Helianthus Strumosus	Pale Leaved Sunflower						
Lactuca Ludoviciana	Wild Lettuce						
Liatris Punctata	Dwarf Blazingstar						
Lithospermum Latifolium	Gromwell						
Microseris Cuspidata	Prairie Dandelion						
Oenothera Biennis	Common Evening Primrose						
Orobanche Fasciculata	Broom-rape						
Parathenium Integrifolium	Wild Quinine						
Petalostemum Canadidum	White Prairie Clover						
Petalostemum Purpureum	Purple Prairie Clover						
Physalis Virginiana	Lanceleaved Ground Cherry						
Plantago Rugelli	Plantain						
Polygala Senega	Seneca Snakeroot						
Potentilla Arguta	Prairie Cinquefoil						
Prananthes Aspera	Rought White Lettuce						
Ranunculas Thomboides	Prairie Buttercup						
Scutellaria Leonardi	Small Skullcap						
Solidago Altissima	Tall Goldenrod						
Solidage Canadensis	Canada Goldenrod						
Solidago Nemoralis	Field Goldenrod						
Sporobolus Asper	Rought Dropseed						
Verbena Hastata	Blue Vervain						
Viola Pedata	Pansey Violet						
Viola Pedatifolia	Larkspur Violet						
Linum Sulcatum	Grooved Flax						

Species	Common Name	Hydric	Mesic	Xeric	Woodlands	Savanna	Prairie
Anemone Patans	Pasqueflower			X		S	P
Arabis Lyrata	Lyre-leaved Rockress						
Castilleja Sessiliflora	Downy Yellow Paintbrush						
Desmodium Nudiiflorum	Naked-Flowered Tick-Trefoil						
Geum Triflorum	Prairie Smoke						
Helianthemum Bicknelli	Rockrose						
Hieracium Longipilum	Long-Haired Hawkweed						
Liatris Cylindracea	Cylindric Blazing-Star						
Oenothera Rhombipetala	Sand Primrose						
Physalis Heterophylia	Clammy Ground Cherry						
Physalis Longifolia	Tall Ground Cherry						
Potentilla Simplex	Common Cinquefoil						

		Soil Type			Open Space	
		Hydric	Mesic	Xeric	Woodlands	Savanna	Prairie

Species	Common Name	Hydric	Mesic	Xeric	Woodlands	Savanna	Prairie
Verbena Stricta	Horny Blue Vervain			X		S	P

Species	Common Name	Hydric	Mesic	Xeric	Woodlands	Savanna	Prairie
Astragalus Canadensis	Canadian Milk Vetch		M			S	P
Bapitisa Leucophaea	Cream Wild Indigo						
Ceanothus Americanus	New Jersey Tea						
Ceratophyllum Demersum	Hornwort (Coontail)						
Echinacea Pallida	Pale Purple Coneflower						
Erynigium Yuccifolium	Rattlesnake Master						
Eupatorium Altissimum	Tall Boneset						
Eupatorium Maculatum	Joe-Pye Weed						
Gaura Biennis	Biennial Gaura						
Gentiana Puberula	Downy Gentian						
Gentiana Saponaria							
Hypericum Canadense							
Hypericum Mutilum							
Lathyrus Venosus	Snowy Wild Pea						
Lespedesa Hirta	Hairy Bush Clover						
Liatris Ligulistylis	Rocky Mountain Blazingstar						
Lilium Philadelphicum	Wild Lily						
Penstemon Digitalis	Beardtongue						
Psoralea Esculenta	Prairie Turnip						
Silphium Integrifolium	Wholeleaf Rosinweed						
Solidago Juncea	Early Goldenrod						
Solidago Missouriensis	Missouri Goldenrod						
Solidago Ulmifolia	Elm-leaved Goldenrod						
Vicia Angustfolia							
Zizea Aptera	Heartleaved Meadow Parsnip						

Species	Common Name	Hydric	Mesic	Xeric	Woodlands	Savanna	Prairie
Apios Americana	Groundnut	H			W	S	
Chelone Glabra Linifolia	Turtlehead						
Cinna Arundinacea							
Dracocephalum Formosius							
Pilea Pumila	Clearweed						
Rudbeckia Laciniata	Greenheaded Coneflower						
Rumex Altissimus	Pale Dock						
Salix Longifolia							
Scutellaria Lateriflora	Mad-Dog Skullcap						
Stachys Hispida							
Teucrium Canadense	Wood Sage						

Species	Common Name	Hydric	Mesic	Xeric	Woodlands	Savanna	Prairie
Polygonum Spiecs	Smartweed	H	M	X	W	S	P

		Soil Type			Open Space		
		Hydric	Mesic	Xeric	Woodlands	Savanna	Prairie
Potamogeton Crispus	Crisp Pondweed	H				S	P

Arenaria Lateriflora	Grove Sandwort	H	M		W	S	
Asclepias Incarnata	Swamp Milkweed						
Aster Lateriflorus	Starved Aster						
Boehmeria Cylindrica	Boghemp						
Botrychium Dissectum							
Cassia Marilandica							
Chaerorhyllum Procumbens							
Cornus Purpusi							
Cuscuta Gronovii	Dodder						
Dodecatheon Meadia	Midland Shootingstar						
Echinocystis Lobata	Wild Cucumber						
Galium Triflorum	Giant Bedstraw						
Impatiens Biflora	Spotted Jewelweed						
Laportea Canadensis	Wood Nettle						
Leersia Virginica							
Lycopus Uniflorus	Water Horehound						
Menispermum Canadensis	Canada Moonseed						
Onoclea Sensibilis							
Osmunda Regalis							
Smilacina Racemosa	False Solomonseal						
Stelronema Ciliatum							
Sympolocarpus Foetidus							
Viola Pubescens	Downy Yellow Violet						

Arenaria Stricta	Rock Sandwort			X	W	S	
Asclepias Ovalifolia	Milkweed						
Coreopsis Lanceolata	Lance-Leaved Coreopsis						
Cynoglossum Virginianum	Wild Comfrey						
Desmodium Cuspidatum	Large-Bracted Tick-Trefoil						
Euphorbia Corollata							
Festuca Obtusa							
Lonicera Dioica	Honeysuckle						
Lupinus Perennis	Wild Lupine						

Arisaema Dracontium	Green Dragon	H	M		W		
Heuchera Richardsonii	Midland Alumroot						
Spiranthes Cernua	Nodding Ladies Tresses						

Arisaema Triphyllum	Small Jack-in-the-Pulpit		M	X	W		
Sanguinaria Canadensis	Bloodroot						
Trillium Gleasoni	Trillium						

Triosteum Perfoliatum	Feverwort		M	X	W		

Asclepias Purpurascens	Purple Milkweed	H	M			S	P
Asclepias Syriaca	Common Milkweed						
Aster Novae-Angliae	New England Aster						
Baptisia Leucantha	White Wild Indigo						
Blephilia Ciliata	Downy Wood Mint						
Caltha Palustris	Marsh Marigold						
Cicuta Maculata	Spotted Cowbane						
Cirsium Discolor	Pasture Thistle						
Cypripedium Candidum	Small White Ladyslipper						
Desmondium Canadense	Snowy Ticktrefoil						
Dryopteris Thelypteris	Marsh Fern						
Gentiana Andrewsii	Bottle Gentian						
Gentiana Crinitia	Fringed Gentian						
Habenaria Flava	Orchid						
Habenaria Leucophaea	White Fringed Orchid						
Helianthus Grosserratus	Bigtooth Sunflower						
Hypericum Punctatum	Spotted St. Johnswort						
Lactuca Canadensis	Canada Wild Lettuce						
Lathyrus Palustris	Wingstemmed Wild Pea						
Liatris Pycnostachya	Prairie Blazingstar						
Lobelia Siphilitica	Great Lobelia						
Lythrum Alatum	Winged Loosestrife						
Napaea Dioica	Glade Mallow						
Oenothora Pilosella	Prairie Sundrops						
Osybaphus Nyctaginea							
Osypolis Rigidior	Cowbane						
Phlox Glabirrima	Smooth Phlox						
Phlox Pilosa	Downy Phlox						
Polytaenia Nuttalli	Prairie Parsley						
Prenanthes Crepidinea							
Prenanthes Racemosa	Smooth White Lettuce						
Pycnanthemum Virginianum	Common Mountainmint						
Sagitaria Latifolia	Arrowhead (Duck Potato)						
Salix Humilis	Prairie Willow						
Saxifraga Pensylvanica	Swamp Saxifrage						
Cacalia Tuberosa	Tuberous Indian Plantain						
Solidago Graminfolia	Narrowleaf Goldenrod						
Spiranthos Ochraleuca							
Spiria Alba	Meadow Sweet						
Thalictrum Dasycarpum	Purple Meadowroe						
Vernonia Fasciculata	Common Ironweed						
Vicia Americana	American Vetch						

| | | Soil Type | | | Open Space | | |
		Hydric	Mesic	Xeric	Woodlands	Savanna	Prairie
Zizea Aurea	Golden Alexander	H	M			S	P
Asclepias Sullivanti	Sullivant's Milkweed	H	M		W	S	
Bidens Frondosa	Beggar-Ticks, Stickright						
Blephilia Hirsuta	Hairy Wood-Mint						
Calopogon Pulchellus	Grass-Pink Calopogon	H			W	S	P
Filipendula Rubra	Queen-of-the-Prairie						
Iris Shrevei	Wild Blueflag Iris						
Lilium Superbum	Turk's-Cap Lily						
Convolvulus Sepium	Wild Morning Glory		M		W	S	P
Krigia Biflora	Two-Flowered Cynthia						
Phlox Divaricata	Blue Phlox						
Tephrosia Virginiana	Goatsrue Hoary Pea						
Cypripedium Pubescens	Yellow Ladyslipper			X	W		
Pyrola Elliptica	Shineleaf						
Dioscorea Villosa	Wild Yam		M		W		
Heptica Triloba	Three Lobed Hepatica						

Grass and Grasslike Groundcover:

| Scientific Name | Common Name | Soil Type | | | Open Space | | |
		Hydric	Mesic	Xeric	Woodlands	Savanna	Prairie
Carex Foenea	Sedge			X	W	S	P
Danthonia Spicata	Junegrass						
Eragrostis Spectabilis	Purple Love Grass						
Andropogran Scoparius	Little Bluestem		M	X	W	S	P
Bromus Purgans							
Carex Bicknellii	Sedge						
Carex Hitchockiana	Sedge						
Carex Jamesii	Sedge						
Carex Pensylvanica	Sedge						
Carex Richardsonii	Sedge						
Elymus Villosus							
Muhlenbergia Cuspidata	Stonyhills Muhly Grass						
Muhlenbergia Racemosa	Upland Wild Timothy						
Panicum Latifolium	Panicum Grass						
Panicum Oligosanthes	Scribner Panic Grass						
Panicum Virgatum	Switchgrass						
Sisyrinchium Campestre	Blue-eyed Grass						
Stipa Spartea	Porcupine Grass						
Panicum Perlongum	Longstalked Prairie Grass						
Bromus Latiglumis	Brome Grass	H	M		W	S	P
Carex Acquatilis	Sedge						
Carex Alopecoides	Sedge						
Carex Amphibola	Sedge						
Carex Bromoides	Sedge						
Carex Cephalophora	Sedge						
Carex Crinita	Sedge						
Carex Cristatella	Sedge						
Carex Debilis	Sedge						
Carex Gracillima	Sedge						
Carex Grisea	Sedge						
Carex Molesta	Sedge						
Carex Projecta	Sedge						
Carex Rosea	Sedge						
Carex Sparganioides	Sedge						
Carex Sprengelii	Sedge						
Carex Stipata	Sedge						
Carex Suberecta	Sedge						
Carex Tuckermani	Sedge						
Elymus Canadensis	Canada Wildrye						
Equisetum Laevigatum	Kansas Horsetail						
Equisetum Avense	Common Horsetail						
Koeleria Cristata	Junegrass						
Muhlenbergia Frondosa							
Panicum Leibergii	Prairie Panic Grass						

		Soil Type			Open Space		
		Hydric	Mesic	Xeric	Woodlands	Savanna	Prairie
Sorghastrum Nutans	Indian Grass	H	M		W	S	P
Spartina Pectinata	Prairie Cordgrass						
Typha Latifolia	Cattail						
Andropogran Gerardi	Big Bluestem	H	M	X		S	P
Carex Meadii	Sedge						
Bouteloua Curtipendula	Side Oats Grama Grass			X		S	P
Bouteloua Hirsuta	Hairy Grama Grass						
Eleocharis Compressa	Flatstemmed Spikerush	H	M			S	P
Eliocharis Obtusa	Spike Rush						
Calamagrostis Candensis	Bluejoint Reed Grass						
Carex Bebbi	Sedge	H			W	S	P
Carex Grayii	Sedge						
Carex Lupilina	Sedge						
Carex Muskingumensis	Sedge						
Carex Normalis	Sedge						
Carex Retrorsa	Sedge						
Carex Tribuloides	Sedge						
Carex Typhina	Sedge						
Carex Vesicaria	Sedge						
Carex Vulpinoidea	Sedge						
Hierochloe Odorata	Holy Grass						
Hypoxis Hirsuta	Golden Stargrass						
Panicum Capillare	Witchgrass		M		W	S	P
Scirpus Americanus	Bulrush						
Sisyrinchium Albidum	White Blue-eyed Grass						
Sisyrinchium Albidum	White Blue-eyed Grass						
Sisyrinchium Angustifolium	Branched Blue-Eye Grass						

Section 4803. Existing Plant Material.

Existing, healthy plant material may be counted as contributing to the total plant material required by this ordinance except in the case of establishment of new woodlands or savannah.

Whenever an existing area meets the definition of woodland, it shall satisfy any planting required by this ordinance regardless of the mix of plant materials otherwise required by Section 4607, provided that understory trees and shrubs constitute at least seventy (70) percent of the individual trees and shrubs present. If understory trees and shrubs constitute less than seventy (70) percent of the trees and shrubs present, additional plant material shall be installed in order to meet the requirements otherwise imposed by Section 4607 through 4806.

No tree greater than five (5) inch caliper shall be counted if more than one-eighth (.125) of the area under its canopy or drip line is closer than fifteen (15) feet from a building, parking area, or road.

Section 4804. Establishment and Maintenance of Woodlands.

A. **Establishment.** The establishment of a woodland for the purposes of Section 4409 (woodlands), 4419 (water quality standards), or 4500 (open space) shall conform to the following standards:

1. The minimum area shall be one and one-half (1.5) acres.

2. No area of woodland shall be less than fifty (50) feet wide.

3. The following plant material shall be provided per acre of woodland to be established. Fractional requirements (resulting from fractions of acres to be established) shall be rounded up.

Plant Materials Required per Acre	Minimum Size Plant Materials
5 slower canopy trees	4 inch caliper
10 canopy trees	2.5 inch caliper
20 faster growing canopy trees	1 inch caliper
30 slower growing canopy trees	5 feet (height)
10 understory trees	1 inch caliper
100 shrubs	3 feet (height)

4. All existing healthy trees shall be preserved to the maximum extent possible.

5. All areas of a newly established woodland shall be seeded as lawn or prairie unless ground cover has already been established.

B. **Maintenance of newly established woodland areas.** Additional plants established by natural succession shall be retained. Dead trees shall be removed where they adjoin roads or buildings. Debris and litter shall be cleaned on an annual or semiannual basis. Damage to fifteen (15) percent or more of the stand due to disease, wind, or fire shall require the replacement of all such damaged trees.

Section 4805. Establishment and Maintenance of Prairie.

A. **Establishment.** The establishment of a prairie for the purpose of Sections 4603 through 4611 (bufferyards) or 4500 (open space) shall conform to the following standards:

1. Plant material shall be ground cover selected from Section 4802.

2. No area of prairie shall be less than fifty (50) feet wide.

3. **Ground preparation.** All areas to be established as prairie shall be tilled to a shallow depth within twenty-four (24) hours prior to seeding. When less than forty-one (41) percent of the area to be established as a prairie consists of vegetated area, a minimum of four (4) inches of topsoil shall be required. This topsoil shall be scarified to a minimum depth of two (2) inches prior to seeding. All installed topsoil shall be final-graded prior to seeding.

4. **Seeding.**

   a. Seeding shall consist of a minimum of three (3) different types of ground cover. The ground cover types are: forbs, grass and grass-like species, and cover grass (see Section 4802). No one type of plant material shall comprise more than forty-five (45) percent of the total prairie plant materials planted. Cover grasses shall comprise no more than six (6) percent and no less than three (3) percent of the total planting. Cover grasses shall be annual grass species.

b. All seed mixtures shall have at least forty (40) to sixty (60) live seeds per square foot.

c. Seeds shall be sown at a rate greater than twenty (20) pounds per acre.

d. Seeds shall be raked into the soil.

e. Seeded areas shall be rolled with a roller weighting approximately one hundred (100) pounds per lineal foot.

B. **Maintenance.** Commencing in the third year following establishment, prairies shall be burned to clear accumulated debris and plantings which choke prairie plant materials. Burning shall be repeated at two- to three-year intervals to achieve this. All such burning shall be done in the spring after all accumulated snow has dissipated. Where burning is not permitted, the prairie shall be mowed to a height greater than six (6) inches and the thatch shall be harvested. Prior to the third year following establishment of a prairie, maintenance is limited to mowing the weeds to a height of no less than six (6) inches. A prairie may also be maintained to allow natural succession towards savannah. The maintenance required of savannah areas depends on the type of plant material present. All savannah areas shall be designated by plant type on the open-space plan (Section 4500) or ground cover specifications (Section 4419). The following maintenance shall be provided:

1. When savannah is designated to be a natural succession, the maintenance specified for prairies in Section 4805 shall be provided, with the exception that a savannah area shall not be mowed or burned.

2. When succession is to be arrested at the savannah stage, the plan shall designate areas to be mowed as grassland. Regular mowing, periodic reseeding, and measures to control weeds shall be provided as required to maintain the character of the savannah.

Article V. Detailed Use Regulations.

Section 5000. Purpose.

The purpose of this article is to specify the detailed regulations, including bulk, layout, yard size, and lot area, that apply to specific land uses. Standards over and above those imposed by other sections of this ordinance are necessary for certain land uses which, although permitted as of right in certain districts, have characteristics that might have negative impacts on nearby uses without these additional regulations. This article also specifies the regulations applicable to temporary and accessory uses, and it details the off-street parking and loading requirements of permitted land uses.

Section 5100. Standards Applicable to Certain Permitted Uses.

In addition to compliance with other regulations imposed by this ordinance, the following standards are required of the specific uses enumerated below.

A. **Golf driving range.**

   1. The site plan required pursuant to Article IX shall show the layout of the property and indicate the location of all driving ranges, putting greens, fences, and structures.

   2. Accessory uses permitted shall be limited to a refreshment stand, a maintenance shed, a miniature golf course, and a pro shop.

B. **Junk, scrap, or salvage yards.**

   1. The site plan required pursuant to Article IX shall show the location of all buildings and the location of storage areas designed or used for automobiles and other vehicles, parts, lubricants, fuel, and other storage.

   2. Any outdoor display of vehicles shall be at least forty (40) feet from any street right-of-way.

   3. All lubricant and fuel oil substances which are to be stored on the site shall be stored with all necessary precautions taken to prevent their leakage and/or surface or subsurface drainage into streams, creeks, or other bodies of water. A plan detailing how these materials will be stored in compliance with this requirement shall be submitted with the application for a zoning certificate.

   4. All hazardous materials shall be stored in a safe manner and, where required, shall be in receipt of a permit for such storage.

C. **Nursery, with or without retail sales or greenhouses.**

   1. No more than twenty-five (25) percent of the retail stock of a nursery shall be of materials not grown on the premises.

   2. No power equipment, such as gas or electric lawn mowers and farm implements, may be sold wholesale or retail.

D. **Outdoor theater, drive-in theater.** Accessory uses permitted shall be limited to the use by patrons of the principal use and shall be limited to a refreshment stand or booth, a souvenir stand or booth, and/or a "kiddy-land."

E. **Public service.** Because of their public necessity, public service uses are permitted in all zoning districts. If the zoning officer determines that the use may cause either a possible hazard to nearby residents or passersby or an interference with the development, use, or enjoyment of surrounding property, the zoning officer may require fencing or screening with densely planted materials to a greater extent than the required bufferyard.

F. **All road service uses.**

   1. Any outside display of vehicles for sale or storage shall be at least forty (40) feet from any street right-of-way.

   2. All activities involving the production, processing, cleaning, servicing, testing, or repair of materials, goods, or products shall conform to all applicable requirements of this ordinance.

   3. All repair, painting, and body work activities shall take place within a building.

G. **Mobile home parks.**

   1. Each mobile home shall be located on a lot conforming to the standards in the table below.

   2. Table of Dimensional Requirements:

| | Length of mobile home | |
	Less than 61 ft.	61 ft. or more
Minimum lot area	3600	4500
Minimum lot width at setback line	42	42
Minimum street setback	10	10
Minimum spacing between units	30	30
Off-street parking spaces	2	2

3. All mobile home parks shall be separated from other residential land uses by a G bufferyard pursuant to Section 4607.

H. **Gas stations.**

1. All services except fuel sales shall be performed within a completely enclosed building.

2. When within seventy-five (75) feet of a residential use, a gas station shall store all refuse and vehicle parts within a completely enclosed building or within an area which is completely visually screened from the view of those residences.

I. **Miscellaneous.**

1. Outdoor structures (bleachers, movie screens, permanent rides) and outdoor seating areas shall be at least twenty-five (25) feet from any lot line, exclusive of bufferyards.

2. Campsites and recreational vehicle sites are subject to building setback regulations.

3. Any outdoor display of vehicles for sale or storage shall be at least forty (40) feet from any street.

4. Any pumps, underground fuel storage tanks, and islands, including any canopies, shall be at least twenty (20) feet from any street or lot line. Entrances and exits to streets shall be at least one hundred (100) feet from any intersection.

5. Chainlink, barbed-wire-topped screening and/or fencing is required for high-voltage transformers and any other utility structures or equipment of potential hazard to residents or passersby.

J. **Exceptions to minimum yard requirements.** The following structures shall be allowed to project into or be constructed on any minimum required yard as follows: awnings and canopies, not to exceed three (3) feet; bay windows, not to exceed two (2) feet; clotheslines; driveways and their curbs, fences, walls, and hedges may be constructed in minimum yard areas, provided that their installation does not violate any other provision of this ordinance.

Section 5200. Residential Use Regulations.

This section specifies the minimum lot dimensions and other requirements for each type of residential unit permitted by this ordinance except in the neighborhood conservation district (see Section 5300).

The regulations provide for lot sizes that vary with the number of bedrooms or size of house and with the type of housing. This gives the developer considerable freedom. For example, in areas where the site is best suited to smaller lots or dwellings, these can be accommodated without a zoning change so long as the overall intensity is balanced by the use of larger lots on other portions of the site.

Any type of single-family detached dwelling unit for which particular standards are not specified in this section shall comply with the requirements of a single-family house.

When a lot size exceeds the minimum permitted area, all other standards applicable to the minimum lot area shall nevertheless apply. The figures specified in the tables of this section are expressed in terms of square feet, feet, or a ratio, whichever applies. The off-street parking figures specify minimum number of off-street parking spaces. When the off-street parking is to be provided entirely on a lot and the required number of spaces is not a whole number, the number of required spaces shall be rounded up to the next higher whole number.

Reduction in number of off-street parking spaces: when a development is specifically designed to be used for senior citizens, all such units shall be required to provide one (1) parking space for each such unit.

A. **Conventional subdivisions.** A conventional subdivision consists of single-family dwellings on individual lots requiring no public or community open space. Section 4203 specifies the minimum site area, minimum lot area, density, and a maximum number of lots in a subdivision. A conventional subdivision is characterized by division of the entire subject parcel into lots. In no event shall the ratio of average lot width to average lot depth exceed 1:2.75. The following table specifies the minimum standards for conventional subdivision units.

Minimum Lot Area	Minimum Lot Width at Setback Line	Maximum Impervious Surface Ratio	Street	Minimum Yards Side (ea.) (feet)	Side Total (feet)	Rear (feet)
40,000	130	.14	35	15	50	50
30,000	110	.17	30	15	48	50
10,000	70	.35	30	8	20	30
8,500	60	.35	30	6	15	20

B.   **Performance subdivision.** Performance subdivisions may contain one or more of the housing types that are specified in this subsection. Such subdivisions shall contain the minimum amount of open space specified in Section 4203. The following subsections specify the standards and requirements for each dwelling type.

1.   **Single-family house.** This dwelling type consists of a single-family residence located on a privately owned lot which has private yards on all four (4) sides of the house. The following table specifies the minimum standards for single-family homes in a performance subdivision.

	2 Bedrooms	3 Bedrooms or More
Minimum Lot Area	6,600 sq. ft.	7,400 sq. ft.
Maximum On-Lot Impervious	16%	22%
Maximum Floor Area Ratio	.16	.24
Minimum Yards – Street	25	25
Side	8	8
Rear	25	30
Minimum Lot Width	60	70
Off-street Parking Spaces	2	3

2.   **Lot-line house.** This dwelling type consists of a single-family, fully detached residence located on an individual lot which is set on the lot line. House windows are prohibited in that wall of the house on the lot line. Either a five (5) foot maintenance easement shall be provided for the neighboring property, or the lot line house may be set back five (5) feet from the line and a recreation, planting, and use easement may be granted to the adjacent lot owner. In addition, the following table specifies the minimum standards for a lot-line house.

	2 Bedrooms	3 Bedrooms or More
Minimum Lot Area	5,500 sq. ft.	6,200 sq. ft.
Maximum On-Lot Impervious	22%	28%
Maximum Floor Area Ratio	.20	.27
Minimum Yards – Street	20	20
Rear	30	30
Side*	28	30
Minimum Building Spacing**	28	30
Minimum Lot Width	55	60
Off-street Parking Spaces	2	3

*This standard applies when units are located on the lot line.

**This standard applies when units are set back from the lot line and the easement described above is provided.

Commentary: Placing a house against one of the side lot lines makes the side yard usable and requires less total land than when the house is centered on the lot. Privacy to adjacent units is insured by the prohibition of windows on the wall of the unit closest to the lot line.

3.   **Village house.** This dwelling type is a single-family residence which is fully detached from neighboring structures. The village house is distinguished by very small front and side yards. The placement of the unit close to the street requires special landscaping or architectural treatment, specified in detail below. The required landscaping is a definitional element of the unit. The following table and text specify the minimum standards for a village house.

	2 Bedrooms	3 Bedrooms or More (1-car garage)	(2-car garage)
Minimum Lot Area	4,200	4,600	5,000
Maximum On-Lot Impervious	23%	23%	27%
Maximum Floor Area Ratio	.26	.28	.34
Minimum Yard – Street	15	15	15
Side	5	5	5
Rear	25	30	30
Minimum Lot Width	46	50	55
Off-street Parking Spaces	2	3	3

The yards of village houses that front on streets shall be landscaped or the units built to include the installation of at least two (2) of the following seven (7) landscaping or architectural treatments:

a. Two (2) canopy trees and three (3) evergreen or understory trees or six (6) evergreen or understory trees.

b. A porch which is roofed but not enclosed and extends across three-fourths (.75) of the front of the house and is at least seven (7) feet in width.

c. A front yard raised above the grade of the sidewalk by at least twenty-four (24) inches and four (4) flowering or evergreen shrubs along each street face.

d. An ornamental fence or wall between twenty-four (24) and thirty-six (36) inches in height, and five (5) flowering shrubs or evergreen shrubs per street face.

e. Twenty (20) flowering or evergreen shrubs or ten (10) flowering or evergreen shrubs, twenty (20) hedge plants, and two (2) understory trees.

f. A hedge consisting of shrubs planted on eighteen (18) inch centers and two (2) understory or evergreen trees.

g. A berm or raised area averaging eighteen (18) inches above the average grade of the rest of the yard and covering forty (40) percent of such yard, with four (4) understory or evergreen trees and six (6) flowering or evergreen shrubs.

Commentary: The landscaping regulations imposed by this subsection are required because, without them, a feeling of overcrowding results when housing is built on lots as small as those allowed for this housing type. Further such material shall not be counted towards the requirement of Section 4613.

4. **Twin house.** This dwelling type consists of a semi-detached dwelling for a single family. It has only one (1) dwelling unit from ground to roof and only one (1) wall in common with another dwelling unit. The following table specifies the minimum standards for a twin house.

			Number of Bedrooms			
	1	2	3 (1-car garage)	3 (2-car garage)	4	5
Minimum Lot Area	2,700	3,200	3,400	3,900	4,000	4,400
Maximum On-Lot Impervious	33%	33%	32%	40%	41%	40%
Maximum Floor Area Ratio	.29	.32	.32	.29	.32	.35
Minimum Lot Width	36	40	40	45	45	50
Minimum Yards–Street	20	25	25	25	25	25
Side	8	10	10	10	10	10
Rear	20	20	20	20	20	20
Off-street Parking Spaces	2	2	2	3	3	4

5. **Patio house.** This dwelling type is a detached or semi-detached unit, for a single family, with one (1) dwelling unit from ground to roof. Each dwelling unit's lot shall be fully enclosed by a wall located at the lot line, thus creating a private yard between the house and the wall. Side and rear walls shall be seven (7) feet in

height, and the front wall shall average six (6) feet in height. That portion of the yard or patio area comprising "minimum patio area" is this housing type's minimum yard area. All living spaces, such as living rooms, dens, and bedrooms, shall face into the yard or patio. The following table specifies the minimum standards for a patio house.

| | *Number of bedrooms* | | | | |
	1	2	3	4	5
Minimum Lot Area					
one story	2,100	2,700	3,300	3,700	4,100
two story	1,800	2,300	2,700	3,000	3,300
Maximum On-Lot Impervious					
one story	46%	51%	53%	53%	52%
two story	32%	36%	37%	37%	36%
Maximum Floor Area Ratio					
one story	.39	.37	.33	.36	.36
two story	.47	.48	.40	.44	.45
Minimum Lot Width	36	38	40	40	45
Minimum Yard Width	6	8	8	8	8
Minimum Patio Area (sq. ft.)	700	750	800	850	900
Minimum Patio Area Width	25	25	25	25	28
Off-street Parking Spaces	1.5	2	2	2.5	3
Height – one story	15	15	15	15	15
two story	25	25	25	25	25

Commentary: The minimum patio area and width requirements are to insure that a reasonably sized yard area exists to support family recreation activities. The whole yard area does not have to have this minimum width. As long as there is a patio area meeting these requirements, then other areas of the yard need only meet the minimum yard width.

6. **Atrium house.** This dwelling type consists of an attached, one-story unit with private individual access for a single family. Each dwelling unit shall have a private yard(s) or atria. The entire lot area of atria and house shall be enclosed by a wall.

The wall shall be at least eight (8) feet in height in the rear or sides of the lot or may average six and one-half (6.5) feet if located in the front. All living spaces, that is, living rooms, dens, or bedrooms, shall face an atrium. The following table specifies minimum standards for an atrium house.

| | *Number of bedrooms* | | | | |
	1	2	3	4	5
Minimum Lot Area					
with on-lot parking	1,800	2,050	2,400	2,600	2,900
with off-lot parking	1,550	1,750	2,000	2,250	2,500
On-Lot Impervious					
with on-lot parking	65%	65%	65%	65%	65%
with off-lot parking	58%	58%	58%	58%	59%
Maximum Floor Area Ratio					
with on-lot parking	.48	.50	.48	.49	.51
with off-lot parking	.58	.58	.58	.58	.59
Minimum Lot Width	36	38	40	40	45
Minimum Atrium Area (sq. ft.)	400	500	500	500	600
Minimum Atrium Width	18	20	20	20	22
Off-street Parking Spaces	1.5	2.0	2.0	2.5	3.0

Commentary: If there is more than one atrium, the secondary spaces need only have a minimum width of six (6) feet and a minimum area of forty-eight (48) square feet.

7. **Weak-link town house.** This dwelling type consists of an attached dwelling unit, a single unit from ground to roof, with individual outside access housing a single family. Each unit shall have both a one- and two-story section. The one-story section shall be at least ten (10) feet wide or thirty (30) percent of the lot width, whichever is greater. A group of attached, weak-link town houses shall average no more than eight (8) dwelling units per group. The following table specifies minimum standards for a weak-link town house.

Number of bedrooms

	1	2	3	4	5
Minimum Lot Area					
with 2-car garage	2,400	2,700	2,800	3,000	3,300
with on-lot parking	2,000	2,300	2,400	2,600	2,900
with off-lot parking	1,700	2,000	2,100	2,300	2,600
Maximum On-Lot Impervious					
with 2-car garage	51%	51%	51%	51%	50%
with on-lot parking	44%	42%	43%	44%	42%
with off-lot parking	35%	33%	35%	36%	36%
Maximum Floor Area Ratio					
with 2-car garage	.36	.36	.38	.42	.46
with on-lot parking	.43	.41	.45	.50	.50
with off-lot parking	.50	.46	.51	.55	.57
Minimum Lot Width					
with 2-car garage	36	38	40	40	42
with on-lot parking	28	30	30	30	32
with off-lot parking	28	28	30	30	32
Minimum Yards –					
Front	15	20	20	20	20
Rear	20	20	22	22	24
Off-street Parking Spaces	1.5	2.0	2.0	2.5	3.0

	1	2	3	4	5
Maximum Floor Area Ratio					
with 2-car garage	.48	.50	.56	.54	.59
with on-lot parking	.57	.57	.62	.58	.60
with off-lot parking	.72	.70	.73	.71	.74
Minimum Lot Width					
with 2-car garage	28	28	28	30	32
with on-lot parking	22	22	24	26	26
with off-lot parking	18	20	22	24	24
Minimum Yards – Front	15	20	20	20	20
Off-street Parking Spaces	1.75	2.0	2.0	2.5	3.0

9. **Multiplex.** This dwelling type may be either a single-family attached dwelling or a multiple family unit. Each unit may take direct access to a private yard or access point, or units may share yards and access. The units may be arranged in a variety of configurations, including back to back, side to side, or vertically; however, no more than six (6) units shall be attached in any single building..

8. **Town house.** This dwelling type consists of a single-family attached unit, with a single unit going from ground to roof, and with individual outside access. Rows of attached town houses shall average no more than ten (10) dwelling units. The minimum amount of exterior walls shall be double the minimum lot width. The following table specifies the minimum standards for a town house.

Number of bedrooms

	1	2	3	4	5
Minimum Lot Area					
with 2-car garage	1,700	2,000	2,000	2,400	2,600
with on-lot parking	1,400	1,700	1,800	2,300	2,500
with off-lot parking	1,100	1,400	1,500	1,800	2,000
Maximum On-Lot Impervious					
with 2-car garage	59%	55%	58%	66%	56%
with on-lot parking	57%	52%	53%	55%	54%
with off-lot parking	45%	42%	43%	41%	42%

Number of bedrooms

	Efficiency	1	2	3	4
Minimum Lot Area	1,450	1,650	1,700	1,750	2,150
Maximum On-Lot Impervious	59%	59%	56%	58%	60%
Maximum Floor Area Ratio	.43	.52	.60	.65	.61
Minimum Lot Width (per structure)	60	70	70	75	75
Minimum Yards –					
Street	25	25	25	25	25
Side	5	5	5	5	5
Off-street Parking Spaces	1.5	2.0	2.0	2.0	2.25

10. **Apartment buildings.** Apartment buildings are buildings comprising multiple dwelling units which share common access to individual units and yards. The yard required shall be the sum of the areas required for each unit within the structure. Apartments shall contain three (3) or more units in a single structure. The following table specifies the minimum standards for apartment buildings.

	Number of Stories				
	2	3	4	5–6	7–8
Minimum Lot Area per Dwelling Unit (D.U.)					
Efficiency	1,050	1,100	1,050	850	750
1 Bedroom	1,450	1,400	1,250	1,000	950
2 Bedrooms	1,650	1,550	1,450	1,100	1,050
3 Bedrooms	1,850	1,600	1,450	1,150	1,050
4 Bedrooms	2,050	1,850	1,600	1,200	1,150
Maximum On-Lot Impervious Surface Ratio					
Efficiency	66%	61%	59%	46%	48%
1 Bedroom	65%	63%	59%	47%	45%
2 Bedrooms	71%	65%	61%	51%	48%
3 Bedrooms	68%	65%	65%	52%	50%
4 Bedrooms	69%	65%	67%	55%	53%
Maximum Floor Area Ratio					
Efficiency	.49	.54	.55	.73	.77
1 Bedroom	.50	.58	.58	.78	.81
2 Bedrooms	.64	.70	.71	.97	.99
3 Bedrooms	.67	.77	.87	1.12	1.15
4 Bedrooms	.69	.76	.88	1.17	1.28
Maximum Height	30	45	60	75	90
Maximum No. D.U.s/ Building	48	48	48	48	48
Minimum Street Frontage of Lot	100	100	100	100	100
Minimum Spacing between Buildings					

	Number of bedrooms				
	Efficiency	1	2	3	4
Off-street Parking Spaces	1.5	1.75	2	3	2.25

Section 5300. Residential Use Regulations: Neighborhood Conservation District.

The table on page 229 specifies the lot area, setback, and bulk requirements for residential uses in the neighborhood conservation district.

Section 5400. Residential Use Design Deviations.

A. **Purpose.** It is the purpose of this section to provide a means of permitting minor deviations from the standards of Sections 5200 and 5300 pursuant to the following criteria and only following review and approval by the planning director pursuant to Article IX.

Commentary: The deviations attempt to reconcile the possibly conflicting goals of a zoning ordinance: to prohibit bad planning and design while promoting good design. Too often, the regulations which operate to prohibit such consequences as overcrowding operate by standardizing design and prohibiting innovation, thereby encouraging mediocrity and precluding good design.

B. **Permitted design deviations: average number of attached units.**

1. The average number of attached units may be increased according to the table at the top of page 230 when the units are clustered in a configuration in which the axes of the buildings intersect with an interior angle greater than sixty (60) degrees and less than one hundred and thirty-five (135) degrees, or, when arranged in an arc, shall form an angle of arc exceeding eighty (80) degrees and not exceeding two hundred (200) degrees. See the illustrations at the bottom of page 229.

Section 5300. Lot Area, Setback, and Bulk Regulations: Neighborhood Conservation District.

	LOT SIZE			SETBACK					BULK	
Zone*	Minimum Lot Area (sq. ft.)	Width (feet)	Front (feet)	Rear (feet)	Total Side (feet)	Minimum Side (feet)	Side Yard Abutting a Street	Impervious Surface Ratio	Height (feet)	Stories
NC$_{200}$	200,000	300	30	150	60	25	30	.05	35	2.5
NC$_{80}$	80,000	190	30	70	48	19	30	.10	35	2.5
NC$_{40}$	40,000	130	30	50	33	13	30	.14	35	2.5
NC$_{20}$	20,000	90	30	30	23	9	30	.20	35	2.5
NC$_{12}$	12,000	70	30	30	17	7	30	.25	35	2.5
NC$_{8}$	8,500	60	30	20	15	6	30	.25	35	2.5

*This column indicates the regulations applicable to the neighborhood conservation district, which has different standards according to the minimum lot size of the particular district. The minimum lot size of a neighborhood conservation district varies and is a function of the character of that district as of the date of enactment of this ordinance. The subscript following the "NC" in each row of this table designates the minimum lot size in thousands of square feet (as the district is designated on the official zoning map). Thus, the minimum lot area in a district designated NC$_{80}$ is 80,000 square feet.

Illustrations for Section 5400 B.

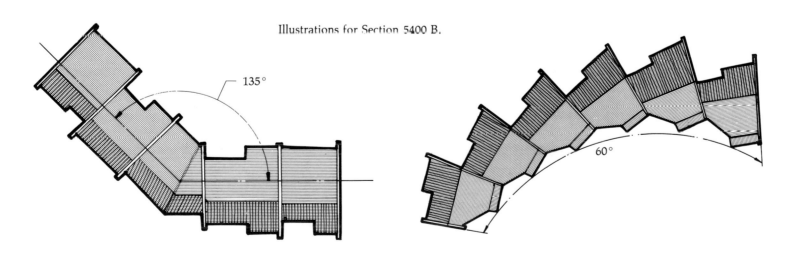

135°

60°

Type of Dwelling Unit	Average Number of Attached Units Permitted per Section 5200	Average Number of Attached Units Permitted per Section 5400
Patio house	7	10
Atrium house	7	10
Weak-line town house	8	12
Town house	10	15

2. The average number of attached units may be increased according to the table below when the dwelling units are clustered into a configuration such that the axes of the buildings form at least two (2) angles in excess of two hundred and twenty (220) degrees each or when arranged in an arc forming an angle exceeding two hundred (200) degrees. See the following illustration.

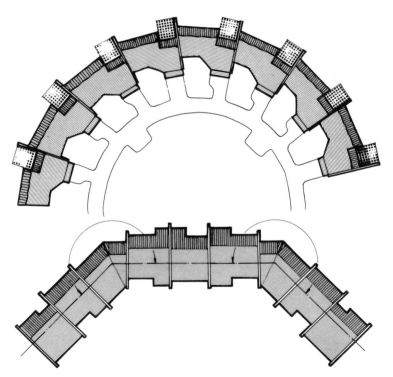

Type of Dwelling Unit	Average Number of Attached Units per Section 5200	Average Number of Attached Units per Section 5400
Weak-link town house	8	16
Town house	10	20

3. The average number of attached units may be increased according to the table below when the units are arranged such that the interior angles formed by the intersection of the axes of the buildings is greater than one hundred and ten (110) degrees and less than one hundred and fifty (150) degrees or where the units are arranged along two (2) or more arcs each of which has an angle exceeding one hundred (100) degrees, and which results in at least one (1) reverse curve. See the following illustration.

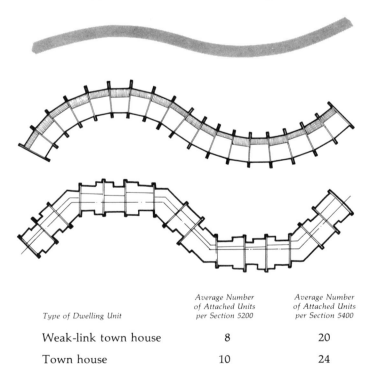

Type of Dwelling Unit	Average Number of Attached Units per Section 5200	Average Number of Attached Units per Section 5400
Weak-link town house	8	20
Town house	10	24

4. The average number of attached units may be increased according to the table below when the units are arranged to enclose a central park or green space which, if rectilinear, shall have a minimum dimension of forty (40) feet and, if circular, shall have a minimum radius of forty (40) feet and, if elliptical, shall have a minimum dimension of fifty (50) feet. See the following illustration.

Type of Dwelling Unit	Average Number of Attached Units per Section 5200	Average Number of Attached Units per Section 5400
Weak-link town house	8	23
Town house	10	32

C. **Permitted design deviations: building spacing.** Minimum side yards between buildings may be varied from the standards imposed by Section 5200, provided that the design standards enumerated below have been met:

1. Where buildings are oriented as illustrated below, the minimum yard between them may be reduced to ten (10) feet, including an eight (8) foot wide paved access area. The area designated as "restricted wall" in the illustration shall not contain windows in excess of four (4) square feet and shall not provide any room facing thereon with more than ten (10) percent of its window area, with the exception that baths, halls, kitchens, and utility areas having windows facing the illustrated yard between buildings

may contain more window area, provided that any such area in excess of four (4) square feet consists of opaque glass.

2. Where buildings are oriented as illustrated below, the minimum yard between them may be reduced to eight (8) feet, including a paved area of that width. The area designated as "windowless" shall not contain windows in excess of four (4) square feet and shall not provide any room facing thereon with more than ten (10) percent of its window area, with the exception that baths, halls, kitchens, and utility areas having windows facing the illustrated yard between buildings may contain more window area, provided that any such area in excess of four (4) square feet consists of opaque glass.

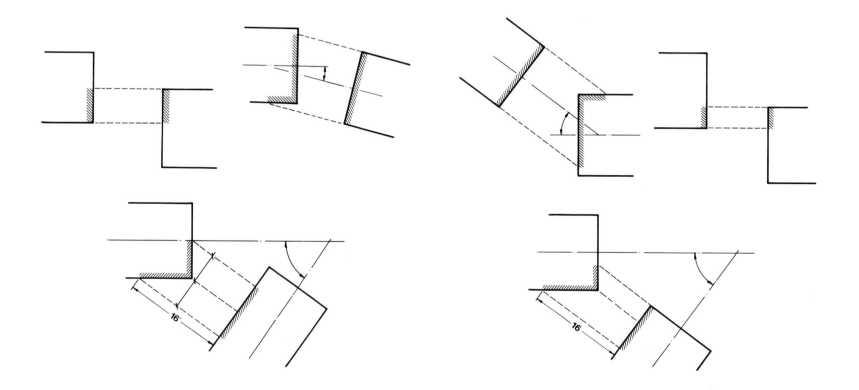

D. **Permitted design deviations: yard requirements.** The minimum front yard requirements of Section 5200 may be reduced according to the following standards:

1. When the dwelling unit types indicated in the following table front on parking areas, pedestrian ways, or open space, rather than directly on streets, the minimum front yard requirement may be reduced as follows. See the following illustration·

2. When the types of dwelling units indicated in the table below have garages which are an attached part of said units, the garage need only comply with the minimum front yard requirement indicated in the table. See the following illustration.

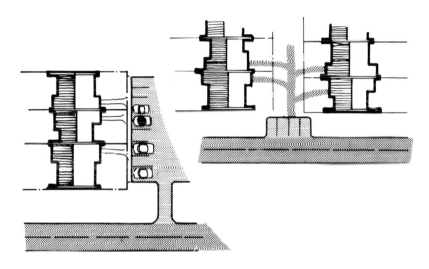

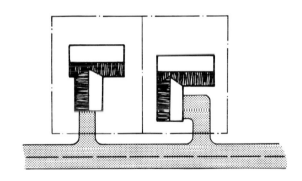

Type of Dwelling Unit	Minimum Yard per Section 5200 (feet)	Minimum Yard Fronting Parking Area per Section 5200 (feet)	Minimum Yard Fronting Pedestrian Way or Open Space per Section 5400 (feet)
Lot-line house	20	15	12
Village house	15	12	9
Twin house	20	15	12
Weak-link town house	15	12	9
Town house	15	12	9
Multiplex	25	20	15

Minimum Front Yard Requirements – Garages

	Minimum Yard per Section 5200	Minimum Yard Fronting Garage Parallel to Street (Illustration A) per Section 5400	Minimum Yard Fronting Garage Perpendicular to Street (Illustration B) per Section 5400
Single-family	30	15	20
Lot-line house	20	8	15
Village house	15	4	10
Duplex	20	8	18
Town house	15	n/a	6
Multiplex	25	12	15

3. Where a building is placed on a parcel such that its entire front is not parallel to the street, as illustrated below, the minimum yard requirements may be met by averaging the yard width from one end of the building (point A in the illustration) to the other end of the building (point B), provided that the yard at its narrowest point is not less than eighty (80) percent of the minimum yard required by Section 5200.

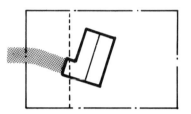 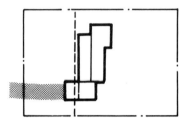

4. Where buildings are aligned to achieve proper solar orientation and units are designed for solar collectors or passive solar heating, the narrowest point of any yard shall not be less than sixty-five (65) percent of the minimum yard required by Section 5200. Further, a shadow plan based on a statement of the degree of solar access to be provided each unit and containing the covenants limiting landscaping shall be submitted.

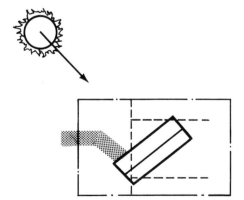

E. **Permitted design deviations: minimum lot width.** In the following situations, lot width on a public or private street required by Section 5200 may be varied as indicated below.

1. Where a dwelling lot is laid out so that it takes access from a common open-space area or pedestrian path rather than from a street, the requirement that a minimum amount of the lot front on a street need not be met. This provision applies to all of the following unit types: single-family, lot-line, village house, patio house, atrium house, and duplex, provided that an alley provides for individual auto access to a garage, carport, or driveway on each lot and that part of a lot shall be within one hundred and twenty (120) feet of a street right-of-way along the open space. (Alternatively, these unit types may be varied by the following subsection.)

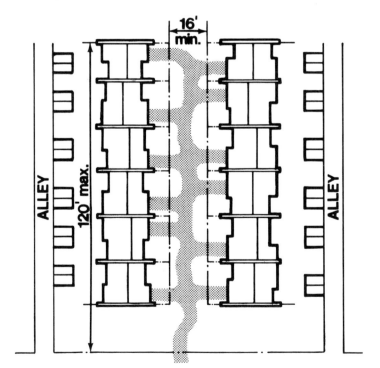

Commentary: In a development oriented toward open space, such access is perfectly acceptable, so long as an automobile can reach each unit. Each unit is assured adequate access, which is the purpose of requiring the frontage on a street. See the following illustration.

2. Where a dwelling lot is laid out so that it takes access from a common open space or pedestrian path, the minimum width of a street required in Section 4705 may be substituted by compliance with the following standards (in the case of patio houses, atrium houses, townhouses, and weak-link town houses). Where the open space or pedestrian area is at least twenty (20) feet wide, units with no frontage or width may be up to ninety (90) feet from the street right-of-way. Where the open space is less than twenty (20) feet wide, the units with no frontage may be up to sixty (60) feet from the street right-of-way. For atrium houses and patio houses reached by pedestrian ways five (5) to ten (10) feet wide, the units may be located up to forty (40) feet from a street right-of-way. See the following illustration.

Commentary: Where units (other than single-family) front on common open space, alleys are not essential, since off-lot parking is more appropriate. The distance a lot can be set back from a street is related to the width of the pedestrian access. Only those units that are surrounded by walls can locate on narrow pedestrian accesses, since the walls afford additional protection to the access.

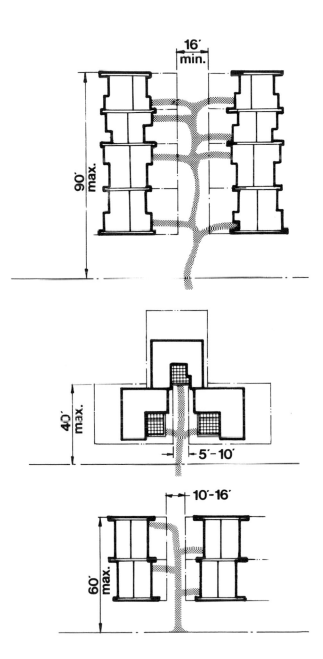

3. Where a street dead-ends, leaving part of a lot fronting on open space (as illustrated below), the lot need only have frontage of ten (10) feet.

4. **Flag lots.** A flag lot is a lot which has minimum frontage on a public or private street, which is reached via a private drive or lane, and whose width some distance back from the street boundary line meets all ordinance requirements. See the following illustration.

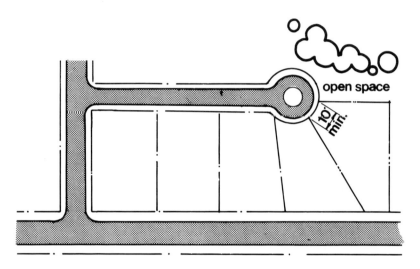

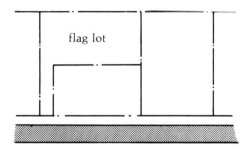

Flag lots shall be permitted, even though they do not meet the minimum lot width requirements at the street boundary line, only in the following instances:

a. Where the flag lot makes it possible better to utilize irregularly shaped properties or areas with resource limitations.

 Commentary: Property irregularities often result in waste of land which could be better utilized through use of the flag lot as illustrated below.

b. Where the flag lots are used to eliminate any accesses to collector or arterial roads.

 Commentary: The use of conventional lots encourages the developer to lose a lot or to seek access to a collector or arterial road. The use of the flag lot may avoid this.

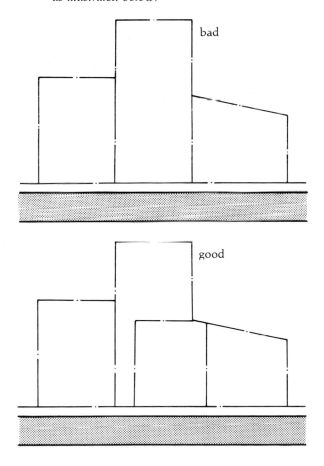

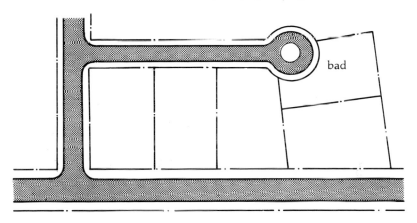

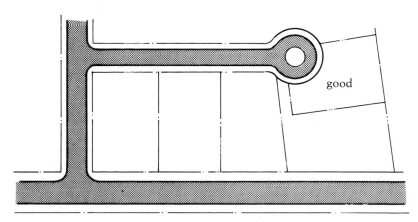

In any event:

a. No more than ten (10) percent of the lots in a subdivision may be flag lots.

b. Flag lots shall not be permitted whenever their effect would be to increase the number of lots taking access to a collector or arterial road.

Commentary: This criterion prohibits one of the most common abuses, the use of flag lots to avoid the developmental costs of roads (see illustration below). These sites are best developed without flag lots, even if the cost of the lots is thereby increased, since controlling access reduces congestion on major roads.

c. That portion of a flag lot shown as shaded in the following illustration shall not be included as a part of the lot area for the purpose of determining average lot area.

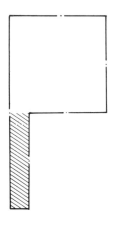

prohibited

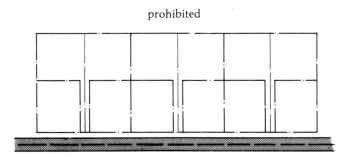

permitted

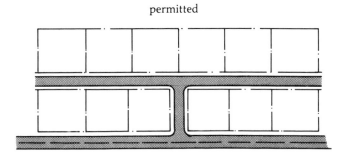

F. **Permitted design deviations: height limitations.** In the case of patio and atrium houses, the height restrictions otherwise imposed by this ordinance may be exceeded provided (1) that any increase in height will not produce an increase in the area covered by the shadow of that building on either its lot or the lot of a neighboring property, and (2) that the shadows shall be projected for the period between 9 AM and 3 PM solar time on 21 December. In no event shall the maximum height be increased by more than eight (8) feet more than otherwise permitted.

Commentary: The principal reason for limiting the height of these dwelling types is to provide adequate light and solar access to the house and yard (patio, atrium). Maintenance of this access is becoming more important as the need to conserve energy grows. The following illustration demonstrates the operation of this provision.

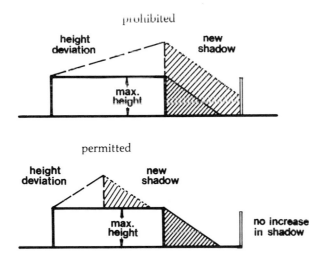

G. **Permitted design deviations: walls.** Minimum side or rear wall requirements otherwise imposed by this ordinance for patio and atrium houses may be reduced where those walls separate the unit from common open space. The graph below may be used to determine the limitations on a reduction of the walls.

Commentary: Where a patio or atrium house opens on an open or forested area, the need for a wall to provide privacy is reduced. The opening of the yard to an increased view is actually desirable. In these cases, the reduction indicated below is permitted.

1. Where the adjoining open space is not woodland as defined in this ordinance:

Percent Reduction in Wall Area

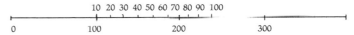

Distance in Feet between Lot Line of Properties or Roads

2. Where the walls of atrium and patio houses front on adjoining open space which is woodland as defined in Section 4409:

Percent Reduction in Wall Area

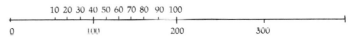

Distance in Feet between Lot Line of Properties or Roads

H. **Permitted design deviations: window restrictions.** The requirements of Section 5200 relating to windows allowed for a particular housing type may be varied as follows. Where the dwelling unit is oriented so as to face a common open space, windows may be installed, provided that in no room other than a bathroom or bedroom shall these be the only windows. In no event shall the windows be sliding doors.

Section 5500. Accessory Uses.

A. **Authorization.** Except as otherwise expressly provided or limited by this ordinance, accessory structures and uses are permitted in any zoning district in connection with any principal use lawfully existing within such district. Any question of whether a particular use is permitted as an accessory use by the provisions of this section shall be determined by the zoning officer pursuant to his or her authority to interpret the provisions of this ordinance.

B. **Zoning certificate required.** No accessory use or structure shall be established or constructed unless a zoning certificate evidencing the compliance of such use or structure with the provisions of this section and other applicable provisions of this ordinance shall have first been issued in accordance with Article IX.

C. **Use limitations.** In addition to complying with all other regulations, no accessory use shall be permitted unless it strictly complies with the following restrictions:

1. The principal use or structure, together with any accessory use or structure, shall not jointly exceed the land use intensity class criteria in any given use class.

2. All signs are subject to the provisions of Sections 4616 through 4619.

3. No accessory structure or use shall be constructed or established on any lot prior to the time of the substantial completion of the construction of the principal structure to which it is accessory.

4. No accessory structure or use on any lot shall cause any impervious surface ratio or exterior storage area more than the maximum permitted on the site by this ordinance.

5. In the case of all commercial and industrial uses: accessory structures shall maintain the same minimum front, side, and rear yard as is required for the principal structure.

6. No accessory structure shall be closer than ten (10) feet to a principal structure or closer than five (5) feet to any other accessory structure, unless it is attached to such principal or other structure.

7. Accessory structures and uses shall comply with all applicable area, bulk, and yard regulations.

The accessory uses and structures specifically mentioned below are subject to the following additional requirements:

D. **Detailed accessory use regulations: home occupations.** It is the intent of this subsection to regulate the operation of home occupations so that the average neighbor, under normal circumstances, will not be aware of their existence other than for a permitted sign.

1. Any resident conducting a home occupation shall apply for and receive a zoning certificate from the zoning officer subject to the following regulations.

2. Any occupation which is customarily, in whole or in part, conducted in a residence may be conducted in any dwelling unit, provided that all of the following criteria are met:

   a. The occupation must be clearly incidental to the use of the dwelling as a residence.

   b. The lot area of the dwelling unit shall be a minimum of twenty thousand (20,000) square feet.

   c. No outdoor display or storage of materials, goods, supplies, or equipment used in the home occupation shall be permitted on the premises.

   d. There shall be no visible evidence that the residence is being operated as a home occupation, except for the permitted sign.

   e. A maximum of two (2) persons other than members of the immediate family residing in the dwelling shall be employed in the home occupation. The total of all employees inclusive of family members shall not exceed six (6) persons.

   f. Off-street parking shall be provided on the premises, as required by Sections 4602 and 5700 or as otherwise necessary.

   g. A home occupation use shall not generate nuisances such as traffic, on-street parking, noise, vibration, glare, odors, fumes, electrical interference, or hazards to any greater extent than what is usually experienced in the residential neighborhood.

E. **Detailed accessory use regulations: private stables.**

1. The minimum lot area shall be two hundred thousand (200,000) square feet for two (2) or more "horses" (includes horses, ponies, mules, donkeys, and other animals used for riding). The minimum lot area shall be one hundred thousand (100,000) square feet when only one (1) horse is kept.

a. When horses are fed by grazing on pasture (at least one season of the year), there shall be one hundred thousand (100,000) square feet of pasture per horse if a single pasture is provided or eighty thousand (80,000) square feet of pasture per horse if two pasture areas are rotated.

b. When horses are not pastured but are fed indoors or in a dry lot, no minimum pasture area per horse shall be required.

c. If horses are kept inside a building, one (1) stall shall be provided for each horse. A tiedown stall shall be a minimum of four (4) feet by eight (8) feet; a box stall shall be a minimum of ten (10) feet by ten (10) feet.

2. The following minimum setbacks shall be provided:

a. Stables, corrals, and piles of manure, feed, and bedding shall be located seventy-five (75) feet from any street or nonresidential lot line and one hundred (100) feet from any residential lot line, in order to minimize odor and nuisance problems. Pasture may extend to the lot line; however, when all of the runoff from a corral or exercise area is controlled and directed over a two hundred (200) foot long grass swale before reaching the property line, the corral or unvegetated exercise area may be located a minimum of forty (40) feet from any street or lot line. Nothing in this subsection shall exempt a use from compliance with Section 4416.

b. Manure piles shall be stored, removed, and/or applied in accordance with (Municipality) Health Department regulations; however, manure shall not be applied on land that is closer than one hundred (100) feet to a residential lot line.

3. A one hundred (100) foot wide area of vegetation cover, exclusive of pasture area, shall be maintained between any corral, unvegetated exercise area, manure pile, or application area and any surface water or well, in order to minimize runoff, prevent erosion, and promote quick nitrogen absorption. Nothing in this subsection shall exempt a use from compliance with Section 4416.

4. In areas with a slope of five (5) percent or less, corrals, unvegetated exercise areas, and manure piles shall be one hundred and fifty (150) feet from a well and two hundred (200) feet from any surface water, unless the water is upgraded or there is adequate diking to comply with the (Municipality) Health Department standards.

5. Corrals, unvegetated exercise areas, manure piles, and manure application are prohibited in areas with slopes greater than five (5) percent, in ten (10) year floodplains, in waterways, and on soils classified as very poorly drained by the Soil Conservation Service Soil Survey for (Municipality), Illinois, September 1970. These soils include Pella, Peotone, Ashkum, Houghton, and Marsh.

6. Manure shall not be allowed closer than seventy-five (75) feet to a well or to any surface water, unless the water is upgraded or there is adequate diking to comply with (Municipality) Health Department standards.

7. Special events, such as shows, exhibitions, and contests, shall only be permitted when a zoning certificate has been granted; such events are subject to the requirements of Section 5600.

F. **Detailed accessory use regulations: private swimming pools and tennis courts.**

1. Pools and courts, including but not limited to aprons, walls, and equipment rooms, shall not protrude into any required yard.

2. They shall be fenced or otherwise protected against intrusion.

3. They shall not be operated as a business or a private club.

G. **Detailed accessory use regulations: residence for caretaker or watchman.**

1. One (1) single-family residence for a caretaker, owner, operator, manager, or watchman and his immediate family is permitted as an attached or detached dwelling for any commercial or industrial use, kennel, stable, or veterinary clinic for purposes of security and protection of the principal use.

2. The standards applicable to a caretaker's residence shall not differ from those imposed by this ordinance on any other housing unit of the same type.

Section 5600. Temporary Uses.

A. **Authorization.** Temporary uses are permitted only as expressly provided in this section and shall comply with the requirements of Article IX.

B. **Zoning certificate required.** No temporary use shall be established unless a zoning certificate evidencing the compliance of such use with the provisions of this section and other applicable provisions of this ordinance shall have first been issued, as provided in Article IX.

C. **Use limitations.**

1. The principal use or structure, together with any temporary uses or structures, shall not jointly exceed the land use intensity class criteria specified in Section 4602 or any standard contained in Article IV.

2. No signs in connection with a temporary use shall be permitted except in accordance with the provisions of Sections 4616 through 4619.

D. **Particular temporary uses permitted.** The following are temporary uses which are subject to the following specific regulations and standards, in addition to the other requirements specified in this ordinance.

1. **Carnival or circus.**

   a. Permitted in any district.

   b. Maximum length of permit shall be fifteen (15) days.

   c. No structure or equipment within five hundred (500) feet of any residential property line.

2. **Christmas tree sales.**

   a. Permitted in any district.

   b. Maximum length of permit for display and open-lot sales shall be forty-five (45) days.

3. **Contractor's office and construction equipment sheds.**

   a. Permitted in any district where use is incidental to a construction project. Office or shed shall not contain sleeping or cooking accommodations.

   b. Maximum length of permit shall be one (1) year.

   c. Office or shed shall be removed upon completion of construction project.

4. **Events of public interest.**

   a. Permitted in any district.

   b. Events may include but are not limited to outdoor concerts, auctions, snowmobile events.

5. **Real estate sales office.**

   a. Permitted in any district for any new subdivision approved in accordance with (Municipality) subdivision regulations. The office may not contain sleeping or cooking accommodations. A model home may be used as a temporary sales office.

   b. Maximum length of permit shall be one (1) year.

   c. Office shall be removed upon completion of the development of the subdivision.

6. **Religious tent meeting.**

   a. Permitted in any district.

   b. Maximum length of permit shall be thirty (30) days.

7. **Seasonal sale of farm produce.**

   a. Permitted in agriculture and rural districts on parcels having a minimum area of eighty thousand (80,000) square feet and a minimum road frontage of one hundred and ninety (190) feet.

   b. If the site is used for growing a minimum of fifty (50) percent of the farm produce sold, the owner or operator of the site may import a maximum of five (5) farm produce products not grown on the site for seasonal sale.

   If the site has a minimum area of two hundred thousand (200,000) square feet and a minimum road frontage of three hundred (300) feet, the owner or operator of the site may import a maximum of ten (10) farm produce products not grown on the site for seasonal sale.

c. Maximum length of permit shall be for six (6) months of each calendar year.

d. Sales areas, including the produce stands, shall be set back a minimum of thirty (30) feet from the nearest right-of-way of any street or highway. Entrances and exits to the parking lot shall be a minimum of thirty (30) feet from any intersection.

8. **Horse show or exhibition.** Permitted for any commercial or private stable for special events, including but not limited to shows, exhibitions, and contests.

9. **Temporary shelter.**

   a. When fire or natural disaster has rendered a single-family residence unfit for human habitation, the temporary use of a mobile home located on the single-family lot during rehabilitation of the original residence or construction of a new residence is permitted subject to the following additional regulations.

   b. Required water and sanitary facilities must be provided.

   c. Maximum length of permit shall be six (6) months, but the zoning office may extend the permit for a period or periods not to exceed sixty (60) days in the event of circumstances beyond the control of the owner. Application for the extension shall be made at least fifteen (15) days prior to expiration of the original permit.

   d. The mobile home shall be removed from the property upon issuance of any occupancy permit for the new or rehabilitated residence. The applicant shall be required to provide express consent and authorization to (Municipality) to remove the shelter at the owner's expense upon termination of the permit.

10. **Tent theater.**

   a. Permitted in any district.

   b. Maximum length of permit shall be five (5) months per calendar year.

F. **Additional regulations.** A carnival or circus, religious tent meeting, tent theater, horse show or exhibition, and events of public interest shall be subject to the following unless otherwise provided in Subsections (A) through (D) above.

1. Documentation from the (Municipality) Health Department that adequate arrangement for temporary sanitary facilities has been insured must be provided.

2. No permanent or temporary lighting shall be installed without an electrical permit and inspection.

3. All uses shall be confined to the dates specified in the permit.

4. Hours of operation shall be confined to those specified in the permit.

5. The site shall be cleared of all debris at the end of the special event and cleared of all temporary structures within thirty (30) days after the closing event. A cash bond for a minimum of twenty-five (25) dollars and not to exceed five thousand (5,000) dollars shall be posted or a signed contract with a disposal firm shall be required as a part of the application for a zoning certificate to insure that the premises will be cleared of all debris during and after the event.

6. Public parking for the exclusive use of the facility shall be provided, and a stabilized drive to the parking area shall be maintained. It shall be the responsibility of the applicant to guide traffic to these areas and to prevent patrons from unlawful parking.

7. Traffic control arrangements required by the (Municipality) Sheriff's Department in the vicinity at major intersections shall be arranged by the applicant.

8. A cash bond for a minimum of twenty-five (25) dollars and not to exceed five thousand (5,000) dollars shall be posted with (Municipality) to insure the repair of any damage resulting to any public right-of-way as a result of the event.

9. Serving of alcoholic beverages shall not be permitted without a permit from the (Municipality) Liquor Commission.

Section 5700. Off-street Parking.

A. The following minimum number of parking spaces shall be required of the nonresidential uses specified below (see Section 5200 for the off-street parking required of residential uses). The minimum size of each parking stall shall be nine and one-half (9.5) feet by eighteen (18) feet, exclusive of aisle width.

Reference herein to "employee(s) on the largest work shift" means the maximum number of employees employed at the facility regardless of the time period during which this occurs and regardless of whether any such person is a full-time employee. The largest work shift may be a particular day of the week or a lunch or dinner period in the case of a restaurant.

The term "capacity" as used herein means the maximum number of persons which may be accommodated by the use as determined by its design or by fire code regulations, whichever is greater.

1. **Agriculture uses:** one (1) space per employee on the largest shift.

2. **Agricultural support uses:** one (1) space per employee on the largest shift, plus one (1) space per two hundred (200) square feet of gross floor area provided for customer sales and service operations.

3. **Commercial and entertainment uses, except as specifically designated below:** one (1) space per hundred fifty (150) square feet of gross floor area of customer sales and service, plus one (1) space per two hundred (200) square feet of storage and/or office gross floor area, or, if the use has at least one hundred thousand (100,000) square feet of gross floor area, five and one-half (5.5) spaces per one thousand (1,000) square feet of gross floor area.

Other commercial and entertainment uses:

Banks: one (1) space per two hundred (200) square feet gross floor area, plus five (5) spaces off-street waiting (loading) spaces per drive-in lane, plus one (1) space per employee on the largest work shift.

Funeral home: one (1) space per four (4) patron seats or twenty-five (25) spaces per chapel unit, whichever is greater.

Grocery or supermarket: one (1) space per one hundred (100) square feet of gross floor area of customer sales and service, plus one (1) space per two hundred (200) square feet gross floor area of storage.

Hospital: two (2) spaces per three (3) patient beds, plus one (1) space per staff doctor and each other employee on the largest work shift.

Hotel or motel: one (1) space per room or suite, plus one (1) space per every three (3) employees on the largest work shift, plus one (1) space per three (3) persons to the maximum capacity of each public meeting and/or banquet room, plus fifty (50) percent of the spaces otherwise required for accessory uses (e.g., restaurants and bars).

Private clubs: one (1) space per three (3) persons to the maximum capacity of the facility.

Repair services: one (1) space per three hundred (300) square feet of gross floor area, plus one (1) space per employee on the largest work shift.

Restaurant, standard: one (1) space per three (3) patron seats or one (1) space per hundred (100) square feet of gross floor area, whichever is greater, plus one (1) space per employee on the largest work shift.

School, commercial or trade: one (1) space per three (3) students, plus one (1) space per employee (including faculty) at capacity class attendance period.

Shopping center, regional: five (5) spaces per one thousand (1,000) square feet of gross floor area.

Theaters and auditoriums: one (1) space per three (3) patrons based on maximum capacity. This requirement may be satisfied on a space-by-space basis by a facility's providing written proof that it has the use of a nearby parking lot available to its patrons (e.g., by contractual arrangement).

4. **Commercial/recreational uses:** one (1) space per four (4) patrons to the maximum capacity of facility, plus one (1) space per two (2) employees on the largest work shift.

Other commercial/recreational uses:

Bowling alley: five (5) spaces per lane, plus one (1) space per employee on the largest work shift.

Drive-in theater: one (1) space per automobile station, plus one (1) space per employee.

Golf driving range: one (1) space per tee, plus one (1) space per employee on the largest work shift.

Marina: one and one-half (1.5) spaces per berth. At least ten (10) percent of the spaces must be large enough to accommodate cars with trailers.

Miniature golf: one and one-half (1.5) spaces per hole, plus one (1) space per employee on the largest work shift.

Outdoor theater: one (1) space per three (3) patrons to the maximum capacity of the facility inclusive of both indoor and outdoor capability.

Skating rink, ice or roller: one (1) space per three hundred (300) square feet of gross floor area.

5. **Extraction uses:** one (1) space per employee on the largest shift.

6. **Heavy industrial uses:** one (1) space per employee on the largest shift, plus one (1) space per company vehicle normally left on the premises.

   Other heavy industrial uses:

   Truck terminal: one (1) space per employee on the largest shift, plus one (1) space per truck normally parked on the premises, plus one (1) space per three (3) patrons to the maximum capacity.

   Junkyards: one (1) space per ten thousand (10,000) square feet of gross land area, plus one (1) space per employee on the largest work shift.

7. **Institutional, indoor, recreational, and special residential uses:** one (1) space per three (3) patrons to the maximum capacity, plus one (1) space per employee on the largest shift.

   Other institutional, indoor, recreational, and special residential uses:

   Camps, day or youth: one (1) space per employee on the largest shift, plus one (1) space per camp vehicle normally parked on the premises.

Cemetery: one (1) space per employee, plus one (1) space per four (4) visitors to the maximum capacity.

Church: one (1) space per four (4) seats of maximum capacity.

Community and recreation center: one (1) space per two hundred and fifty (250) square feet of gross floor area, or one (1) space per four (4) patrons to the maximum capacity, plus one (1) space per employee on the largest shift.

Day or nursery school: one (1) space per teacher/employee on the largest shift, plus one (1) off-street loading space per six (6) students.

Group dwellings: one (1) space per bedroom or sleeping room.

Libraries and museums: one (1) space per two hundred and fifty (250) square feet of floor area or one (1) space per four (4) seats to the maximum capacity, whichever is greater, plus one (1) space per employee on the largest shift.

Monasteries, convents: one (1) space per six (6) residents, plus one (1) space per employee on the largest shift, plus (1) space per five (5) chapel seats if the public may attend.

Nursing homes: one (1) space per six (6) patient beds, plus one (1) space per employee on the largest shift, plus one (1) space per staff member and visiting doctor.

Schools:

a. Elementary and junior high: one (1) space per teacher and staff member, plus one (1) space per two (2) classrooms.

b. Senior high: one (1) space per teacher and staff member on the largest shift, plus one (1) space per five (5) nonbused students.

c. College: one (1) space per staff member on the largest shift, plus one space per two (2) students of the largest class attendance period.

Swimming facility: one (1) space per seventy-five (75) square feet of gross water area, plus one (1) space per employee on the largest shift.

Tennis, racquetball, handball courts: four (4) spaces per court, plus one (1) space per employee on the largest shift.

8. **Light industrial uses:** one (1) space per employee on the largest shift, plus one (1) space per company vehicle regularly stored on premises.

Other light industrial uses:

Mini-warehouse: one (1) space per ten (10) storage cubicles, plus two (2) spaces per manager's residence, plus one (1) space per twenty-five (25) storage cubicles located at the warehouse office.

Veterinary office with enclosed kennels and/or pens: three (3) spaces per doctor, plus one (1) space per employee on the largest shift.

Warehouse: one (1) space per employee on the largest shift, plus one (1) space per four thousand (4,000) square feet of gross floor area.

9. **Nursery uses:** one (1) space per employee on the largest shift, plus one (1) space per two hundred (200) square feet of gross floor area of inside sales or display.

10. **Office uses:** one (1) space per two hundred and fifty (250) square feet of gross floor area.

Other office uses:

Beauty and barber shops: three (3) spaces per operator or one (1) space per one hundred (100) square feet of gross floor area, whichever is larger, plus one (1) space per employee on the largest shift.

Medical offices: five (5) spaces per doctor.

Personal services: one (1) space per two hundred (200) square feet of basement and first floor gross floor area, plus one (1) space per three hundred (300) square feet of any additional floor area for customer service, plus one (1) space per employee on the largest shift.

11. **Outdoor recreational uses:** one (1) space per four (4) expected patrons at capacity.

Other outdoor recreational uses:

Golf courses (nine and eighteen hole): ninety (90) spaces per nine (9) holes, plus one (1) space per employee on the largest shift, plus fifty (50) percent of spaces otherwise required for any accessory uses (e.g., bars, restaurants).

Golf, par three: forty (40) spaces per nine (9) holes, plus one (1) space per employee on the largest shift.

Outdoor swimming pool: one (1) space per seventy-five (75) square feet of gross water area.

Tennis court: three (3) spaces per court.

12. **Public service uses:** one (1) space per employee on the largest work shift, plus one (1) space per company vehicle normally stored on the premises.

13. **Recreational rental uses:** one and one-half (1.5) spaces per site or dwelling unit.

Other recreational rental uses:

Recreational vehicle park: one and one-half (1.5) spaces per each recreational vehicle site, plus one (1) space per employee on the largest shift.

14. **Road service uses:** one (1) space per two hundred (200) square feet of gross floor area, plus one (1) space per employee on the largest shift.

Other road service uses:

Convenient (7-Eleven) grocery: one (1) space per one hundred (100) square feet of gross floor area.

Fast-food restaurant: one (1) space per fifty (50) square feet of gross floor area, plus one (1) space per employee on the largest work shift.

Taverns, dance halls, night clubs, and lounges: one (1) space per fifty (50) square feet of gross floor area, plus one (1) space per employee on the largest shift.

Vehicle sales and service: one (1) space per fifteen hundred (1,500) square feet of gross floor area.

Vehicle repair and maintenance services: one (1) space per four hundred (400) square feet of gross floor area, plus one (1) space per employee on the largest work shift.

B. All parking areas shall be kept in a dust-free condition at all times. In the case of unpaved parking areas, this may be accomplished by oiling or spraying with calcium chloride.

C. **Reduction in the number of required off-street parking spaces for large uses (over 500,000 square feet of gross floor area).** In order to prevent the establishment of a greater number of parking spaces than actually needed to meet the particular needs of those large uses over five hundred thousand (500,000) square feet of gross floor area, a reduction in the number of required off-street parking spaces may be permitted. This reduction shall be permitted subject to the following conditions.

1. A maximum reduction of one (1) parking space per every one thousand (1,000) square feet of gross floor area or twenty (20) percent of the total spaces required can be permitted. The land development plan shall indicate the location and dimensions of the parking area provided.

2. Sufficient area must be reserved to provide for the total number of off-street parking spaces required by Section 5700. The purpose of this reservation is to insure adequate area to meet any future need for additional parking spaces. This reservation shall be provided for by deed-restricting that portion of the site required to provide for the total number of parking spaces on the same property as is being proposed for development. The reserved parking area shall not include areas for required bufferyards, setbacks, or areas which would otherwise be unsuitable for parking spaces due to the physical characteristics of the land or other requirements of this ordinance. The developer shall provide a landscaping plan for the reserved area.

3. The developer shall enter into written agreement with (Municipality) that the additional parking spaces up to the total spaces required shall be provided at the owner's expense should the zoning officer determine that the total required parking spaces are necessary to satisfy the needs of the particular use pursuant to the standards imposed by this ordinance.

Commentary: Certain large uses, such as regional shopping centers, may need fewer parking spaces than are required by this ordinance since their trip generation per one thousand (1,000) square feet of gross floor area is typically less than smaller uses. For example, large industrial users may find, through van-pooling or car-pooling practices, that their parking needs are reduced. This section provides a twenty (20) percent maximum reduction in required parking spaces while at the same time requiring that land be reserved to accommodate future parking needs.

Section 5800. Off-street Loading.

Any use with a gross floor area of six thousand (6,000) square feet or more which requires deliveries or shipments must provide off-street loading facilities in accordance with the requirements specified below.

A. Every retail establishment, industrial or manufacturing use, warehouse, wholesale use, freight terminal, railroad yard, hospital, or sanitarium having an aggregate gross floor area of six thousand (6,000) square feet or more shall provide off-street loading facilities as follows:

Gross Floor Area in Square Feet	Number of Berths
6,000–24,999	1
25,000–79,999	2
80,000–127,999	3
128,000–198,999	4
199,000–255,999	5
256,000–319,999	6
320,000–391,999	7

For each additional seventy-two thousand (72,000) square feet (or fraction thereof) of gross floor area, one (1) additional berth shall be provided.

B. Every public assembly use, such as auditoriums, convention halls, exhibition halls, stadiums, or sports arenas, office buildings, welfare institutions, funeral homes, consisting of twenty (20) units or more, and restaurants and hotels with a gross floor area of greater than thirty thousand (30,000) square feet shall provide off-street berths as follows:

Gross Floor Area in Square Feet	Number of Berths
6,000–29,999	1
30,000–119,999	2
120,000–197,999	3
198,000–290,999	4
291,000–389,999	5
390,000–488,999	6
489,000–587,999	7
588,000–689,999	8

For each additional one hundred and five thousand (105,000) square feet (or fraction thereof) of gross floor area, one (1) additional berth shall be provided.

C. The minimum area for each off-street loading space, excluding area for maneuvering, shall be two hundred and fifty (250) square feet.

D. At no time shall any part of a truck or van be allowed to extend into the right-of-way of a public thoroughfare while the truck or van is being loaded or unloaded.

Article VI. Nonconformities.

Section 6000. Purpose.

It is the purpose of this article to provide for the regulation of legally non-conforming structures, lots of record, uses, and signs and to specify those circumstances and conditions under which such nonconformities shall be permitted to continue. It is necessary and consistent with the regulations prescribed by this ordinance that those nonconformities which adversely affect orderly development and the value of nearby property not be permitted to continue without restriction.

The zoning regulations established by this ordinance are designed to guide the future use of (Municipality's) land by encouraging appropriate groupings of compatible and related uses and thus to promote and protect the public health, safety, and general welfare. The continued existence of nonconformities is frequently inconsistent with the purposes for which such regulations are established, and thus the gradual elimination of such nonconformities is generally desirable. With limited exceptions, the regulations of this article permit such nonconformities to continue without specific limitation of time but are intended to restrict further investments which would make them more permanent.

This article distinguishes major nonconforming uses, minor nonconforming uses, major nonconforming structures, minor nonconforming structures, nonconforming lots of record, and nonconforming signs. Different regulations are made applicable to each of these categories. The degree of restriction made applicable to each separate category is a function of the degree to which that category of nonconformity is a nuisance or incompatible with the purposes and regulations of this ordinance.

Section 6001. Definitions.

A. A **legal nonconformity** is any land use, structure, lot of record, or sign legally established prior to the effective date of this ordinance or subsequent amendment to it which would not be permitted by or is not in full compliance with the regulations of this ordinance.

B. A **nonconforming use** is an activity using land, buildings, signs, and/or structures for purposes which were legally established prior to the effective date of this ordinance or subsequent amendment to it and which would not be permitted to be established as a new use in a zone in which it is located by the regulations of this ordinance.

1. A **major nonconforming use** is any use listed in the table below for the district in which it is listed (see Sections 4104 through 4108 for definitions of each use category).

Neighborhood conservation   All industrial uses, road service,

Zoning District	Major Nonconforming Uses
Agricultural Rural	Heavy industry
Estate	Heavy industry, road service, commercial recreation
Development Urban core	Extraction
Neighborhood conservation	All industrial uses, road service, commercial recreation
Heavy industrial Holding	None

2. A **minor nonconforming use** is any nonconforming use which is not a major nonconforming use.

C. A **nonconforming structure** is any building or structure, other than a sign, legally established prior to the effective date of this ordinance or subsequent amendment to it, which does not fully comply with the standards imposed by Sections 4203 (district performance standards), 4602 (land use intensity class), 4603 through 4607 (bufferyard requirements), 4706 (roadway access), and Article V (detailed use regulations).

1. A **major nonconforming structure** is any nonresidential building or structure located on a parcel which at any point borders a residential use and which exceeds either the maximum floor area or impervious surface ratio standards in the district in which it is located (see Section 4203) or does not fully comply with the bufferyard requirements of either Sections 4603 through 4607 or the maximum feasible bufferyards provision of Section 6007.

2. A **minor nonconforming** structure is any nonconforming building or structure which is not a major nonconforming building or structure.

D. A **nonconforming lot of record** is any validly recorded lot which at the time it was recorded fully complied with all applicable laws and ordinances but which does not fully comply with the lot requirements of this ordinance concerning minimum area or minimum lot width.

E. A **nonconforming sign** is any sign legally established prior to the effective date of this ordinance or subsequent amendment to it which is not in full compliance with the regulations of this ordinance.

Section 6002. Authority to Continue.

A. Except as otherwise provided in this article, any nonconforming lot, use, sign, or structure lawfully existing on the effective date of this ordinance or subsequent amendment thereto may be continued so long as it remains otherwise lawful. All nonconformities shall be encouraged to convert to conformity wherever possible and shall be required to convert to conforming status as required by this article.

B. No nonconformity shall be enlarged upon, expanded, or extended (including extension of hours of operation) unless such alteration is in full compliance with all requirements of this ordinance. Normal maintenance and incidental repair of a legal nonconformity shall be permitted, provided that this does not violate any other section of this article.

   1. Nothing in this article shall be deemed to prevent the strengthening or restoration to a safe condition of a structure in accordance with an order of a public official who is charged with protecting the public safety and who declares such structure to be unsafe and orders its restoration to a safe condition, provided that such restoration is not otherwise in violation of the various provisions of this section prohibiting the repair or restoration of partially damaged or destroyed structures or signs.

   2. Nothing in this article shall be deemed to prevent an extension for the exclusive purpose of providing required off-street parking or loading spaces, and involving no structural alteration or enlargement of such structure, subject only to the restrictions of Sections 4602, 4614, 5700, and 5800.

C. No nonconformity shall be moved in whole or in part, for any distance whatsoever, to any other location on the same or any other lot unless the entire structure shall thereafter conform to the regulations of the zoning district in which it is located after being moved.

D. Any other provision of this article to the contrary notwithstanding, no use, structure, or sign which is accessory to a principal nonconforming use or structure shall continue after such principal use or structure shall have ceased or terminated, unless it shall thereafter conform to all regulations of this ordinance.

E. The burden of establishing that any nonconformity is a legal nonconformity as defined by this article shall, in all cases, be upon the owner of such nonconformity and not upon (Municipality).

Section 6003. Minor Nonconformities.

A. A minor nonconforming use shall not be changed to any use other than a use permitted in the zoning district in which it is located.

B. **Termination of minor nonconformities.**

   1. **Termination by damage or destruction.** In the event that any minor nonconforming structure or use is destroyed by any means to the extent of more than fifty (50) percent of the cost of replacement of such structure or use new, said structure or use shall not be rebuilt, restored, or reoccupied for any purpose unless it shall thereafter conform to all regulations of this ordinance. When such a nonconforming structure or use is damaged or destroyed to the extent of fifty (50) percent or less of the replacement cost, no repairs or rebuilding shall be permitted except in conformity with Section 6002 and other applicable regulations of this ordinance.

   2. **Termination required by modification.** Whenever there is a minor nonconformity, which is nonconforming with respect to any of the performance criteria and regulations specified in Section 4602 (land use intensity criteria) or Sections 4603 through 4607 (bufferyard requirements), such use shall be required to do the following as a precondition to its receipt of any (Municipality) building permit, zoning certificate, or other (Municipality) permit:

      a. Whenever the nonconformity is a result of bufferyards, exterior lighting, or landscaping which does not comply with all requirements of this ordinance, upon application for any (Municipality) permit related to the subject property, the nonconformity shall as a precondition to issuance of that permit be required to comply fully with all such requirements.

b. In the event that the nonconformity is a result of noncompliance with the bufferyards required by this ordinance and when the land area of the subject property precludes provision of the required bufferyards, the nonconformity shall, as a precondition to issuance of that permit, be required to comply fully with the requirements of Section 6007.

Section 6004. Major Nonconformities.

A. A major nonconforming use shall not be changed to any use other than a use permitted in the zoning district in which it is located.

B. **Termination of major nonconformities.**

1. **Termination by damage or destruction.** In the event that any major nonconforming structure or use is destroyed by any means to the extent of more than twenty-five (25) percent of the cost of replacement of such structure or use new, same shall not be rebuilt, restored, or reoccupied for any use unless it shall thereafter conform to all regulations of this ordinance. When such a nonconforming structure or use is damaged or destroyed to the extent of twenty-five (25) percent or less of the replacement cost, no repairs or rebuilding shall be permitted except in conformity with Section 6002 and other applicable regulations of this ordinance.

2. **Termination required by modification.**

a. Upon application for any building permit or other permit related to the subject property, a major nonconforming structure shall as a precondition to issuance of that permit be required to comply fully with all requirements of this ordinance.

b. In the event that the nonconformity is a result of noncompliance with the bufferyards required by this ordinance and when the land area of the subject property precludes provision of the required bufferyards, the nonconformity shall as a precondition to issuance of that permit be required to comply fully with the requirements of Section 6007.

3. **Termination by amortization.** A major nonconforming use not terminated pursuant to any other provision of this ordinance shall be terminated no later than five (5) years from the effective date of this ordinance unless a variation from this requirement is granted pursuant to Article IX.

Section 6005. Nonconforming Lots of Record.

A. A nonconforming lot of record may be used for any principal use permitted in the zone in which the lot is located, provided that for any use which is to be served by an individual well and/or septic system, the nonconforming lot shall be of a size and design to meet the minimum requirements of the (Municipality) Health Department regulations for such wells and septic systems.

B. If the proposed use is to be a single residential dwelling unit of any of the types specified in Article V, to the extent that the lot is physically unable to provide the open space required by that section, that open space need not be required.

C. If the use is to be a residential dwelling unit of the type designated "Atrium house" by Section 5200, the minimum lot width may be reduced to twenty-five (25) feet, provided that the total minimum lot area shall comply with Section 5200.

Commentary: This provision permits a variety of dwelling-unit types which typically would be permitted in a performance subdivision and requires a minimum area of open space, to be used for the development of a nonconforming lot of record. Most of the nonconforming lots of record in (Municipality) are lots which are twenty-five (25) or fifty (50) feet wide and therefore unable to meet the open-space requirements of this ordinance. This provision recognizes the existence of these lots and permits their development, provided that public sewers and water are available to them where required.

Section 6006. Nonconforming Signs.

A. No nonconforming sign shall be changed, expanded, or altered in any manner which would increase the degree of its nonconformity, or be structurally altered to prolong its useful life, or be moved in whole or in part to any other location where it would remain nonconforming.

B. **Termination of nonconforming signs.**

1. **Immediate termination.** The following signs or sign features shall be terminated within six (6) months after the effective date of this ordinance, except as otherwise expressly permitted by this ordinance. Termination of the nonconformity shall consist of removal of the sign or its alteration to eliminate fully all nonconforming features: flashing signs, animated and moving signs, signs which obstruct free ingress to or egress from a fire escape, door, window, or other required access way, signs which by reason of size, location, content, coloring, or manner of illumination obstruct the vision of drivers or obstruct or detract from the visibility or effectiveness of any traffic sign or control device on streets and roads within (Municipality), and signs which advertise a business no longer conducted or a product no longer sold on the premises where such sign is located.

2. **Termination by abandonment.** Any nonconforming sign structure the use of which as a sign is discontinued for a period of ninety (90) consecutive days, regardless of any intent to resume or not to abandon such use, shall be presumed to be abandoned and shall not thereafter be reestablished except in full compliance with this ordinance. Any period of such discontinuance caused by government actions, strikes, material shortages, or acts of God, and without any contributing fault by the nonconforming user, shall not be considered in calculating the length of discontinuance for purposes of this subsection.

3. **Termination by change of business.** Any nonconforming sign advertising or relating to a business on the premises on which it is located shall be terminated upon any change in the ownership or control of such business.

4. **Termination by damage or destruction.** Any nonconforming sign damaged or destroyed, by any means, to the extent of one-third (.333) of its replacement cost new shall be terminated and shall not be restored.

5. **Termination by amortization.** Any nonconforming sign not terminated pursuant to any other provision of this ordinance shall be terminated no later than the date stated below:

Original Value of Sign as Shown on Building Permit	Time Period (following effective date of this ordinance) by Which Termination of Nonconformity Is Required
Less than $4,000	12 months
$4,001 to $10,000	18 months
More than $10,000	24 months

Section 6007. Minimum Acceptable Bufferyard.

When a nonconformity is a result of noncompliance with the bufferyard required by this ordinance and when that nonconformity makes application for a building permit or other (Municipality) permit related to the subject property, if the property is physically unable, because of its limited land area, to provide the bufferyard otherwise required by this ordinance, the following shall suffice for compliance with Sections 6003 and 6004.

A. If the nonconformity for which a permit is sought is of a higher land use intensity class (see Section 4602) than the property adjacent to it, for each such boundary the minimum bufferyard shall be one which meets the following standards.

1. If the applicant's parcel is able to provide seventy-five (75) percent or more of the land, then that amount shall be provided along with all required structures and a percentage of the plant material equal to that of the land area provided.

2. If the applicant's parcel is not able to provide seventy-five (75) percent or more of the land required for the bufferyard, but the adjacent property owner agrees to an arrangement whereby seventy-five (75) percent of the required land area can be jointly provided by the applicant and that adjacent owner, the applicant shall:

a. Where no structures are required, provide one hundred (100) percent of the required plant material.

b. Where a structure is required, provide the next more intensive structure (see Section 4607) and seventy-five (75) percent of the required plant material.

3. If the applicant is unable to comply with either of the above conditions, the minimum acceptable bufferyard specified in Section 6007 (D) shall be provided.

B. If the nonconformity for which a permit is sought is of a lesser land use intensity class (see Section 4602) than the property adjacent to it, for each such boundary the minimum bufferyard shall be one which meets the following standards.

1. If the adjoining use has adequate undeveloped land to provide seventy-five (75) percent of the required buffer, the applicant shall provide twenty-five (25) percent of the required buffer.

2. If the adjoining property owner cannot provide seventy-five (75) percent of the required bufferyard and the applicant and the adjacent property owner agree to an arrangement whereby at least seventy-five (75) percent of the required land area can be jointly provided, the applicant shall:

   a. After deducting all land available for buffers on the adjoining property, provide all land available for buffer so as to approach the required bufferyard width as nearly as possible and twenty-five (25) percent of the required plant material.

   b. The applicant shall not be required to provide the structures.

3. If the adjoining property owner can only provide a minimum acceptable bufferyard pursuant to Section 6007 (D), the applicant shall provide a buffer equal to twenty-five (25) percent of the land and required plant material.

4. If the applicant is unable to comply with (1), (2), or (3) above because insufficient land is available on the applicant's property, the applicant shall provide forty (40) percent of the planting required for a minimum acceptable bufferyard pursuant to Section 6007 (D).

C. If a nonconformity is unable to comply with the minimum bufferyard requirements of this section, it shall not be entitled to the (Municipality) permit for which it has made application.

D. **Table of minimum acceptable bufferyards for nonconformities.** The following table specifies the minimum acceptable bufferyards required by this section.

Table VIII-1 Minimum Bufferyard Requirements for Non-Conforming Uses

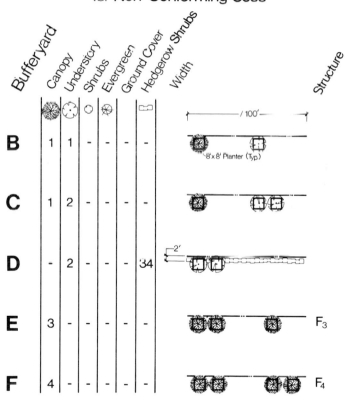

Bufferyard	Canopy	Understory	Shrubs	Evergreen	Ground Cover	Hedgerow Shrubs	Width	Structure
B	1	1	-	-	-	-		
C	1	2	-	-	-	-		
D	-	2	-	-	-	34		
E	3	-	-	-	-	-		F₃
F	4	-	-	-	-	-		F₄

BUFFERYARDS B-F

Table VIII-1 Minimum Bufferyard Requirements for Non-Conforming Uses

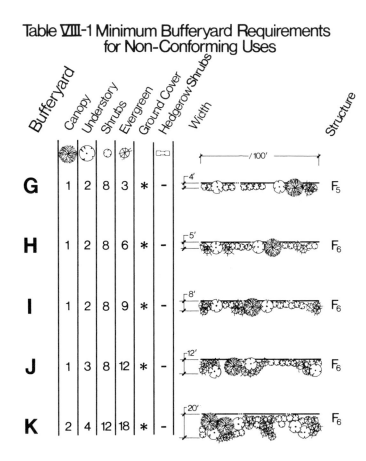

Bufferyard	Canopy	Understory	Shrubs	Evergreen	Ground Cover	Hedgerow Shrubs	Width	Structure
G	1	2	8	3	*	-	4'	F_5
H	1	2	8	6	*	-	5'	F_6
I	1	2	8	9	*	-	8'	F_6
J	1	3	8	12	*	-	12'	F_6
K	2	4	12	18	*	-	20'	F_6

BUFFERYARDS G-K

Section 6008. Inventories and Certificates of Nonconforming Signs.

Within one (1) month after the effective date of this ordinance or any amendment to it, the zoning officer shall inventory all signs subject to termination pursuant to Section 6006 of this article and shall determine the names and addresses of the owners thereof or, in any case where such a determination is impractical, the owner or lessee of the premises on which such sign is located. For each such nonconforming sign, the zoning officer shall determine the nature and extent of the nonconformity and the date on which such nonconformity is required to be terminated pursuant to the provisions of this ordinance.

Upon making such determination, the zoning officer shall notify the aforesaid owner or lessee in writing of his determination. Such inventory and notices shall be kept on file by the zoning officer and be a matter of public record.

Mailing of notice to any party reasonably believed by the zoning officer to be the person required to be given such notice pursuant to this subsection shall be sufficient to commence the amortization periods specified in Section 6006.

Article VII. Conditional Uses.

Section 7000. Purpose.

Conditional uses are those uses which have some special impact or uniqueness such that their effect on the surrounding environment cannot be determined in advance of the use being proposed for a particular location. At that time, a review of the location, design, configuration, and impact is conducted by comparing the proposed use to fixed standards. This review determines whether the proposed use should be permitted by weighing public need for, and benefit to be derived from, the use against the local impact which it may cause. The review considers the proposal in terms of existing zoning and land use in the vicinity of the use, planned and proposed public and private developments which may be adversely affected by the proposed use, whether and to what extent the proposed use at the particular location for which it is suggested is necessary or desirable to provide a development which is in the interest of the public convenience or which will contribute to the general welfare of the area or (Municipality), whether and to what extent all steps possible have been taken by the developer to minimize any adverse effects of the proposed use on the immediate vicinity and on the public health, safety, and welfare in general.

Section 7001. Applicability.

Any use which is permitted as a conditional use by Section 4102 of this ordinance shall comply with this article. Any use which involves filling of a floodplain shall also comply with this article (see Section 4405).

Section 7002. Procedures.

A. Applications for a conditional use shall be submitted simultaneously with an application for a zoning certificate and shall take the form specified by Section 9001.

B. Applications for a conditional use permit shall be processed by the planning director as follows:

1. Copies of the application shall be distributed to the directors and/or superintendents of the Highway Department, Health Department, Building and Zoning Department, Public Works Department, and the Conservation District or their duly authorized representatives.
Author's note: The Conservation District is required by Illinois law and would not be listed otherwise.

2. A public hearing shall be held by the Planning Commission within thirty (30) days of acceptance of the application and after the notice required by law has been provided. Not later than ten (10) days prior to the date set for the hearing on the application, the planning director and each official or consultant to which the application has been referred shall file a written report thereon with the Planning Commission setting forth the recommendations for changes in the plans as submitted and the conditions for approval, if any, necessary to bring such plan into compliance with any applicable ordinance or regulation or to eliminate any adverse effects of the proposed development on those aspects of the general health, safety, and welfare of the community for which such official or consultant has special responsibility.

3. Within thirty (30) days of the public hearing on the application, unless an extension of this time is agreed to by the applicant, the Planning Commission shall render to the (Municipality) Board its recommendation either to grant the application for a conditional use permit, grant it subject to conditions, or deny it. The failure of the Planning Commission to act within this time period shall constitute a recommendation by it that the application be approved.

4. At the next possible regularly scheduled meeting the (Municipality) Board shall either approve or disapprove the application and, where approved, shall establish the specific conditions under which the application is approved. The application shall be denied if the (Municipality) Board finds either that the application and record fail to establish compliance with the standards made applicable to the proposed development by the provisions of this ordinance, or if the proposed use, developed in the proposed manner and at the proposed location, will be inconsistent with the standards applicable to it pursuant to the provisions of this ordinance, or if the adverse impacts of the development, after taking into consideration any proposals of the applicant and any conditions that might be imposed by the (Municipality) Board Commission pursuant to the provisions of this ordinance to ameliorate them, outweigh any public or private benefits of the proposal and require denial of the conditional use approval in the interest of the overall public health, safety, and welfare.

5. The (Municipality) Board may, in approving the application for any conditional use permit, impose such restrictions and conditions on such approval, the proposed use, and the premises to be developed or used pursuant to such approval as it determines are required by the general purposes, goals, and objectives of the Comprehensive Plan and this ordinance to prevent or minimize adverse effects from the proposed use and development on other properties in the neighborhood and on the general health, safety, and welfare of (Municipality). All conditions imposed upon any conditional use permit approval, with the exception of conditions made applicable to such approval by the express terms of this ordinance, shall be expressly set forth in the resolution granting such conditional use permits.

6. In the event a permit for a conditional use is approved or approved subject to conditions, the applicant shall, in writing within ten (10) days following such decision, acknowledge such approval and unconditionally accept and agree to any conditions imposed on the approval. The zoning officer shall then take action to process the application on the zoning certificate for the development to which the conditional use permit applies. In the event such permit is not approved or is approved subject to conditions which are not acceptable to the applicant, the applicant may, within the aforesaid time period, either appeal such decision or abandon the application at the expiration of this ten (10) day period.

Section 7100. Conditions on Conditional Use Approvals.

Every conditional use permit shall be conditioned upon the proposed development fully complying with all requirements of this ordinance and, where applicable, with the (Municipality) Subdivision Regulations. The violation of any condition contained in a conditional use permit shall be a violation of this ordinance.

Section 7101. General Use Standards.

No application for a conditional use permit shall be approved unless the (Municipality) Board shall specifically find the proposed conditional use appropriate in the location for which it is proposed. This finding shall be based on the following criteria:

A. The proposed use shall be in harmony with the general purpose, goals, objectives, and standards of the (Municipality) Comprehensive Plan, this ordinance, or any other plan, program, map, or ordinance adopted, or under consideration pursuant to official notice, by (Municipality).

B. There shall be a community need for the proposed use at the proposed location; in the light of existing and proposed uses of a similar nature in the area and of the need to provide or maintain a proper mix of uses both within (Municipality) and also within the immediate area of the proposed use: (a) the proposed use in the proposed location shall not result in either a detrimental overconcentration of a particular use within (Municipality) or within the immediate area of the proposed use and (b) that the area for which the use is proposed is not better suited for or likely to be needed for uses which are permitted as a matter of right within that district, in light of policies or provisions of the Comprehensive Plan, this ordinance, or other plans or programs of the (Municipality).

C. The proposed use at the proposed location shall not result in a substantial or undue adverse effect on adjacent property, the character of the neighborhood, traffic conditions, parking, public improvements, public sites or rights-of-way, or other matters affecting the public health, safety, and general welfare, either as they now exist or as they may in the future be developed as a result of the implementation of provisions and policies of the Comprehensive Plan, this ordinance, or any other plan, program, map, or ordinance adopted, or under consideration pursuant to official notice, by (Municipality) or other governmental agency having jurisdiction to guide growth and development.

D. The proposed use in the proposed area will be adequately served by and will not impose an undue burden on any of the improvements, facilities, utilities, and services specified in this subsection. Where any such improvements, facilities, utilities, or services are not available or adequate to service the proposed use in the proposed location, the applicant shall, as part of the application and as a condition to approval of the proposed conditional use permit, be responsible for establishing ability, willingness, and binding commitment to provide such improvements, facilities, utilities, and services in sufficient time and in a manner consistent with the Comprehensive Plan, this ordinance, and other plans, programs, maps, and ordinances adopted by (Municipality) to guide its growth and development. The approval of the conditional use permit shall be conditioned upon such improvements, facilities, utilities, and services being provided and guaranteed by the applicant.

Section 7102. Additional Standards for Specified Conditional Uses.

A. No application for issuance of a conditional use permit shall be approved unless the Planning Commission shall find that, in addition to complying with each of the general standards enumerated above, each of the following specific standards applicable to the particular uses enumerated below is met.

B. **Landing strips and heliports.**

1. Landing strips and heliports (accessory hangers and sheds) are classified in the heavy industrial general use category and are subject to the intensity class performance criteria (Section 4602) applicable to that category.

2. The area proposed for this use shall be sufficient and the site otherwise adequate to meet the standards of the Federal Aviation Agency and the Illinois Division of Aeronautics, Department of Transportation, for the class of airport proposed, in accordance with their published *Rules and Regulations*.

3. Any proposed runway or landing strip shall be situated so that any structures, high voltage power lines, towers, chimneys, and natural obstructions within the approach zones shall comply with regulations for height restrictions in airport approach zones of the Federal Aviation Agency and the Illinois Department of Transportation, Division of Aeronautics, or a municipal or other airport authority qualified by law to establish airport hazard zoning regulations.

4. There shall be sufficient distance between the end of each usable landing strip and the airport boundary to satisfy the requirements of the Federal Aviation Agency. If air rights or easements have been acquired from the owners of abutting properties in which approach zones fall, proof thereof shall be submitted with the application.

5. No existing or planned approach areas shall be permitted over existing residential areas or over vacant areas zoned Development District; however, approach areas may be allowed over such vacant areas if deed restrictions or other mechanisms insure that they will not be developed for residential uses.

6. Off-street parking required: one (1) space for every plane space within the hangers plus one (1) space for every tie-down space plus one (1) for every two (2) employees.

7. Building setback: any building, hanger, or other structure shall be at least one hundred (100) feet from any street or lot line.

8. All repair of airplanes and machinery shall be done inside hangers.

9. Residential uses shall not be located within the approach path or the noise zone.

C. **Commercial stables.**

1. Commercial stables are included in the general use category of outdoor recreation and are subject to the land intensity class performance criteria (Section 4602) applicable to that use category.

2. No commercial stable shall be permitted if its existence would be incompatible with surrounding residential land uses and zoning.

3. The minimum lot size area shall be two hundred thousand (200,000) square feet.

   a. If any horses (including horses, ponies, mules, donkeys, and other animals used for riding) are kept outside of any building, the maximum number of horses permitted shall be one (1) per one hundred thousand (100,000) square feet of property.

   b. If all horses (and other riding animals) are kept inside a building, the maximum number of horses permitted shall be limited to the building capacity to house, show, and ride said horses. A stall shall be provided for each horse. The minimum dimension of each stall shall be ten (10) feet by ten (10) feet.

4. The following minimum setbacks shall be provided:

   a. Stables, corrals, and piles of manure, feed, and bedding shall be located seventy-five (75) feet from any street or nonresidential lot line and one hundred (100) feet from any residential lot line, in order to minimize odor and nuisance problems. Pasture may extend to the lot line.

   b. Manure piles shall be stored, removed, and/or applied in accordance with (Municipality) Health Department regulations; however, manure shall not be applied on land that is closer than one hundred (100) feet to a residential lot line.

5. A vegetative strip at least fifty (50) feet wide shall be maintained between any corral, manure pile, or application area and any surface water or well, in order to minimize runoff, prevent erosion, and promote quick nitrogen absorption.

6. In areas with a slope of five (5) percent or less, corrals and manure piles shall be one hundred and fifty (150) feet from a well and two hundred (200) feet from any surface water, unless the water is upgrade or there is adequate diking.

7. Corrals, manure piles, and manure application are prohibited in areas with slopes greater than five (5) percent, in ten (10) year floodplains, in waterways, and on soils classified as very poorly drained by the Soil Conservation Service *Soil Survey* for (Municipality), Illinois, September 1970. These soils include Pella, Peotone, Ashkum, Houghton, and Marsh.

8. Manure shall not be applied closer than seventy-five (75) feet to a well or to any surface water, unless the water is upgrade or there is adequate diking as determined by the (Municipality) Health Department.

9. Parking stalls required are one (1) stall per every two (2) horses (or other riding animals), based on the number of horse stalls or maximum horses allowed on the property, plus one (1) per every employee on the largest shift.

10. Special events such as shows, exhibitions, and contests shall only be permitted when a zoning certificate has been granted and are subject to the requirements of Section 5600 (temporary uses).

D. **Filling of floodplain.** The filling of the floodplain shall be granted only where plans and specifications have been submitted that meet all requirements of Section 4405 and where the following conditions exist which necessitate the filling of the floodplain.

   1. The property would otherwise be able to accommodate at least one residential dwelling with a lot meeting all requirements of Articles IV and V but cannot, because of the floodplain, accommodate even one single-family unit, or,

   2. That the location and/or configuration of the buildable land as calculated in Sections 4301 through 4305 is such that the intensity of land use permitted by Section 4305 cannot be realized without filling in the floodplain. In no event shall the filling of the floodplain be permitted to increase the buildable area calculated by Section 4305.

E. **Recreational rental.** In the agricultural district, recreational uses shall be permitted upon a finding that no more than twenty (20) percent of the site on which they are located comprises prime agricultural soils as defined by this ordinance.

F. **Heavy industrial.** Heavy industrial uses (except landing strips and heliports) shall be permitted in the development district upon a finding that:

   1. The use must be located in a district other than one zoned for heavy industrial purposes, or that no land zoned for heavy industrial use is either available or suitably located.

   2. All existing adjoining uses are permitted in a heavy industrial district, or, if existing uses are not permitted in a heavy industrial district, that either physical barriers, such as expressways or floodplains, or a combination of such barriers and additional buffers shall be provided.

   Commentary: All heavy industrial districts have been mapped (located) to insure that they are adequately buffered from incompatible abutting districts by elevated roads, rail lines, or other forms. It is not intended, therefore, that heavy industrial uses will locate near considerably less intense uses, especially residential uses. This section requires that heavier buffers be installed when such uses do propose to be located in a development district, in which abutting uses may be incompatible.

3. The performance criteria upon which the use shall be conditioned cause no noise, dust, vibration, odor, or other nuisance problems beyond the interior bufferyard line of the use. Data demonstrating this shall constitute a part of the application for the use permit.

H. **Solar access.** The purpose of requiring a conditional use permit for any use which intends to utilize solar access is to insure that that access will be adequately protected by the provisions of this ordinance. Developments planned to permit and protect solar access are in the best interest of (Municipality) in that they reduce dependence on foreign sources of energy. Thus, such developments fully meet the criteria of Sections 7101 (A) and (B). The requirements of Section 7101 (D) shall be presumed to have been met by any such development. The minimum yard and lot width requirements of Article V may be altered provided that such alteration is necessary solely to provide solar access. In other words, the alterations are the minimum required to provide such access, and they do not decrease either total lot area or total usable yard area. Solar access developments shall be permitted upon a finding that:

1. The use, absent its solar aspects, is permitted in the zone for which it is proposed.

2. The proposed plans for solar access best serve to protect the degree and location of that access and do not, or will not, require the restriction of development on adjoining properties with respect to their existing zoning classification. All such plans shall be made a condition of the use permit.

Section 7200. Amendments to Permits for Conditional Uses.

Following the issuance of a conditional use permit pursuant to the provisions of this ordinance, such permit may be amended, varied, or altered only pursuant to the standards and procedures established by this article for its original approval.

Article VIII. Development Alternatives and Bonuses.

Section 8000. Purpose.

One purpose of this article is to provide flexibility to encourage the protection of farmland and prime agricultural soils which other sections of this ordinance do not absolutely protect. The transfer of development potential from a site having a resource deserving protection to another which requires less protection accomplishes this. In addition, this article provides an incentive for the development of housing for persons of low or moderate income. These are the only cases in which the "density factor (with bonus)" column contained in Section 4204 applies.

Commentary: This article attempts to reconcile two conflicting views of land which have long posed a dilemma for planners, elected officials, and the courts. The first view defines land as a public resource which is limited in quantity or which has unique characteristics that require its protection by governmental regulation. The other view is that land is a commodity which the owner has a right to develop—unhampered by regulation. Traditionally, zoning has necessitated a choice between one view and the other, with no attempt to achieve the best balance of competing interests as applied to each parcel of land. The transfer of development rights provides a system which allows (Municipality) to preclude development of particular pieces of property when the public interest necessitates this yet still allows the owner of that land the "rights" to development. These rights, when applied to another piece of land, allow its development at a greater intensity than would otherwise be permitted and insure the owner ample economic return in spite of the fact that some land may be severely restricted from development.

Transfer of development rights is used to protect agricultural areas and/or to provide the owners of property an alternative to development. It is an option to the other zoning regulations of this ordinance which owners may voluntarily choose to exercise. There are two ways in which the transfer of development rights may be allowed. The first is by permitting noncontiguous developments within the agricultural district (see Section 8002), by means of which the total development potential of both sites may be transferred to one site. With the second technique, the development potential for land within the agricultural district may be transferred to land in the development district (see Sections 8003 through 8007).

The second purpose of this article is to provide a bonus or incentive for developers who provide housing for low- or moderate-income persons or households. This is an important national goal and one in which the private sector cannot normally operate without special assistance. It is generally inadequate simply to permit such housing (for example, nothing in this ordinance precludes such housing from being built); in most instances it is simply impossible to build housing for this sector of the market without a subsidy.

Section 8001. Definitions.

The following definitions shall be applicable to this article.

A. **Development rights.** One of a series of rights inherent in fee simple ownership of land (others include air rights or mineral rights) which may be separated from the land. In the context of this article, development rights are the rights to build dwelling units on one's land.

B. **Certificates of development rights.** A certificate entitling the owner to build one (1) dwelling unit. The certificate may be used only as indicated in this article.

C. **Transfer of development rights.** A procedure set forth in this article which permits owners of land in the agricultural district to be compensated for restrictions which are subsequently imposed on their land by selling certificates of development rights, which rights may be applied to the development of the separate parcel of land.

Section 8002. Noncontiguous Development.

With the agricultural district a landowner or group of landowners whose properties are not contiguous may file a development plan in the same manner as the owner of a single property, pursuant to Article IX. Under this option, the following exceptions to other provisions of this ordinance are expressly permitted; all other provisions of the ordinance must be complied with.

A. Section 4302 (C) shall not apply except to a parcel of land less than five (5) acres which has not been actively farmed for the past three (3) or more years. All other provisions of Section 4300 through 4306 shall apply.

B. The open-space requirements of the district or the calculation in Section 4301 shall apply to the site in its entirety rather than to each noncontiguous parcel separately, provided that the following conditions are met.

1. All property owners execute an agreement restricting the use of all property pursuant to an overall plan, stating that they have been fully compensated for any restrictions placed on their respective lands and insuring that the restrictions run with the land.

2. The open space required on any single noncontiguous parcel shall in no event be less than would be required by Section 4204 for the development district.

C. No noncontiguous property which is to remain in agricultural use need have a detailed site plan prepared for it. The property need only be designated as restricted to agricultural use.

D. The density factor on any noncontiguous property shall not exceed that permitted in Section 4204 (under the column headed "density factor with bonus").

E. The calculation of site capacity (Sections 4300 through 4306) requires that base site area have subtracted from it land which is not contiguous to the parcel proposed for development. This shall not be applicable to land developed pursuant to this article which is greater than three (3) acres in area and which has been actively farmed at any time during the preceding three (3) years.

Commentary: The purpose of allowing noncontiguous site area to be calculated as part of the base site area is to provide a means for the development of pieces of property to protect agricultural areas but not necessarily to protect the small pockets of land which exist in the agricultural district but which are not devoted to agricultural use.

Section 8003. Certificates of Development Rights.

(Municipality), by adoption of this ordinance, creates certificates of development rights, subject to provisions of this article.

Section 8004. Creation, Distribution, and Sale of Development Rights.

A. Certificates of development rights shall be held by (Municipality). These rights are available to all landowners (who are not governmental agencies) owning a parcel of ten (10) or more acres in the agricultural (AG) district, which at the time of the adoption of this ordinance is unimproved or in agricultural use or contains one single-family residence. Each landowner owning such a parcel shall be given notice by registered mail of the number of certificates available to him within six (6) months of the adoption of this ordinance. The certificates shall remain in the office of the (Municipality) Clerk and shall be acted upon only when a landowner in the agricultural district actually requests that these development certificates be transferred to a specific parcel of land in which bonus density is permitted by Section 4204 and to which said development rights shall immediately attach to and run with the land.

B. The number of certificates available to the aforementioned landowners is established by multiplying the number of acres constituting the property by the number shown in the table below (according to township), subject to the following limitations.

1. The number of development certificates available to the landowner shall be reduced by one (1) for every residential structure situated on the property at the time of the adoption of this ordinance.

2. Development certificates are not available for any parcel or portion thereof subject to an easement or restrictive covenant prohibiting or preventing development.

Township	Number of Development Certificates per Acre
Antioch	.85
Benton	1.20
Avon	1.00
Cuba	2.40
Ela	2.40
Fremont	1.40
Grant	1.00
Lake Villa	1.00
Libertyville	1.70
Newport	.85
Shields	3.00

Township	Number of Development Certificates per Acre
Vernon	2.40
Warren	1.70
Wauconda	1.00
Waukegan	1.50
West Deerfield	3.70

C. Development certificates may be issued and sold to a person, corporation, partnership, or other legal entity in (Municipality) designated by the landowner, pursuant to the following:

1. The submission to the Planning Director of an agreement of sale for said certificates, duly executed by the parties, which shall be recorded with the (Municipality) Recorder of Deeds.

2. The agreement of sale shall include the following provisions:

   a. The landowner selling said development rights shall file with the Recorder of Deeds a restrictive covenant running with the land, as set forth herein, affecting the parcel of land of said landowner from which the development rights have been transferred. The restrictive covenant shall be as follows:

   "Said premises [legally described] shall not be used at any time for any uses except those specified and indicated in Article IV of the (Municipality) Zoning Ordinance for Agriculture or otherwise permitted by Article VIII. . . . And the grantee, for himself, his heirs, and assigns by the acceptance of this indenture agrees with the grantor, heirs, and assigns that said restrictions and conditions shall be a covenant running with the land, and that in any deed of conveyance of said premises or any part thereof, said restrictions and conditions, when modified pursuant provisions contained herein, shall be incorporated by reference to this indenture and the record hereof or as fully as the same are contained herein."

   b. The seller's parcel shall be designated "restricted" and shall be subject to the limitations and restrictions imposed by this or-

dinance as well as to the limitations and restrictions imposed on said land by virtue of any restrictive covenants.

   c. The use of restricted land shall be limited to agricultural uses detailed in Sections 4100 and 4101 or for a single residential dwelling which may not be subsequently subdivided.

Section 8005. Marketability of Certificates of Development Rights.

The creation of a market for certificates of development rights is essential if the transfer of such certificates is to be a real alternative to development. Such a market is provided by the following provisions:

A. In any district in which bonus density is permitted, the permitted density factor on a property may be increased as specified in Section 4204.

B. Development at the higher density specified in Section 4204 shall be permitted, provided that all other provisions of this ordinance and the subdivision regulations are followed, and provided that the applicant owns certificates of development rights in an amount equal in number to the increase in dwelling units over that permitted without certificates.

C. Development proposals consistent with the requirements of this ordinance shall be approved without the purchase of development rights. Nothing in this ordinance, other than the incentive to increase the density on one's property, shall require a landowner to purchase development certificates.

Section 8006. Taxation.

Certificates of development rights, when applied to an identifiable parcel of land, shall be considered real property. Upon being issued pursuant to Section 8004, certificates shall be recorded in the (Municipality) Recorder of Deeds Office and notification shall be given to the (Municipality) Supervisor of Assessments.

Section 8007. Appeal on Marketability.

(Municipality), recognizing that marketability is essential to the fairness of the system of development rights transfer, will institute special appeal procedures for those parcels whose development rights cannot be marketed under this system at fair market value. (Municipality) believes that it has created a system in which sales between willing buyers and willing sellers will result in fair compensation to owners of development rights. In order to protect landowners and to give (Municipality) an opportunity to study in detail the impact and effectiveness of the transfer of development rights, the following appeal procedure is provided:

A. A landowner who claims that development rights are unmarketable may appeal to the Zoning Board of Appeals which shall hold a public hearing on said appeal. The landowner shall be required to submit to the Zoning Board of Appeals information on asking price, length of sale period, and names of prospective buyers and their offers.

B. The Department of Planning, Zoning and Environmental Quality shall introduce evidence of other land or certificate sales, the number of properties or certificates for sale, a professional appraisal of the certificates' value, and an evaluation of the market conditions in the same municipality and region.

C. The Zoning Board of Appeals shall hear all evidence and submit its recommendation on the requested variation to the (Municipality) Board for action.

D. The (Municipality) Board shall evaluate the marketability of the certificates. If it finds that the certificates are unmarketable, the (Municipality) shall:

1. Purchase the certificates and/or the parcel or a part thereof at a fair market value; or

2. Make an exception for the individual property; or

3. If the evidence clearly indicates a need, change the allocation of development certificates, or the size of development area, or the bonus achieved by using the development certificates, or some combination thereof to make certificates marketable.

Section 8008. Biennial Review.

In order to assess any unexpected problems which may arise from the implementation of this article, (Municipality) shall conduct a periodic review of the operation of the transfer of development rights scheme and report on it to the public. This review shall summarize all activity relative to transfer of development rights and shall consider: (1) Is the system functioning? (2) Is the concept of fair compensation being realized under the system? (3) Is the marketability still present as a result of developments in the past year? (4) Is the tax situation working against the goals of development rights? (5) Comments from the general public. Whenever an amendment to this article appears warranted, a public hearing on the proposed amendment shall be considered. The first review under this section shall be within one (1) year of the effective date of this ordinance.

Section 8009. Low- and Moderate-Income Housing Bonus.

A. In order to encourage the production of housing for low- and moderate-income households, density factor may be increased to the maximum specified in Section 4204 (for density factor with bonus), pursuant to the following regulations.

1. **Low-income subsidized units.**

   a. Any unit subsidized by federal, state, or local government shall earn a bonus of one (1) additional dwelling unit.

   b. In no event shall this bonus be permitted where subsidized units constitute more than twenty (20) percent of a development, except in the case of a development of less than ten (10) dwelling units.

   c. There shall be no limitation on the proportion of subsidized dwelling units for developments of ten (10) dwelling units or less.

2. **Moderate-income units.**

   a. Any unit offered for sale for no more than two and one-half (2.5) times the most current median income value issued by the U.S. Department of Housing and Urban Development's area office for the (Municipality's) metropolitan area shall earn a bonus of two (2) additional dwelling units. (Municipality) shall require from the developer a guarantee that all such units proposed to be developed pursuant this section shall be offered for sale within these price guidelines.

   b. In no event shall this bonus be permitted where moderate income units constitute more than twenty (20) percent of a development, except in the case of a development of less than twenty (20) dwelling units.

c. In no event shall this bonus be permitted where moderate-income units constitute more than forty (40) percent of the total number of dwelling units of a development consisting of less than twenty (20) units.

B. **Design regulations.**

1. All bonus units built pursuant to this section shall be integrated into the overall design of the development. They shall be scattered throughout the development and their design and exterior materials and appointments shall not differ from those of other units in the project.

2. The units built pursuant to these regulations may, however, have less square footage than similar units built for the regular market, provided that the minimum standards of this ordinance are met.

C. **Management.**

1. All governmentally subsidized units shall be managed in accordance with applicable regulations of the subsidizing agency.

2. All moderate-income units developed pursuant to Section 8009 (A) (2) shall be required to insure that they will continue to be available for rental or sale to persons with moderate income levels. This may be insured by providing for their acquisition by the (Municipality) housing authority, by placing restrictions on their resale (restrictions which limit price increases and/or which make them available for sale only to persons with moderate income levels), or by management agreements or other means acceptable to (Municipality).

Commentary: Since moderate income units are likely to be priced below market value, these assurances are required to insure that these units will continue to be available to eligible persons or facilities.

Article IX. Administration and Enforcement.

Section 9000. Purpose.

This article sets forth the procedures required for obtaining zoning certificates, certificates of occupancy, sign permits, and conditional use permits. The powers and duties of the following officers and boards are specified herein insofar as administration of this ordinance is concerned: the Department of Building and Zoning; the Department of Planning, Zoning and Environmental Quality; the Zoning Board of Appeals; the Regional Planning Commission; the zoning officer; the planning director, and the building and enforcement officer. This article also specifies the requirements for amendments, variances, administrative appeals, and interpretations of this ordinance.

Section 9001. Zoning Certificates Required.

No development permitted by this ordinance, including accessory and temporary uses, may be established or changed, no structure shall be erected, constructed, reconstructed, altered, razed, or removed, and no building used, occupied, or altered with respect to its use after the effective date of this ordinance until a zoning certificate has been secured from the zoning officer. Nothing herein shall relieve any applicant of the additional responsibility of seeking any permit required by any applicable statute, ordinance, or regulation in compliance with all of the terms of this ordinance.

Section 9002. Sign Permits Required.

A. Unless specifically exempted by Section 4616, no sign shall be erected, altered, or relocated after the effective date of this ordinance until a sign permit has been secured from the zoning officer. Sign permits shall be renewed prior to their expiration dates as specified below.

B. **Expiration of permits.**

1. Permits for each sign, except temporary signs, shall expire on 31 December of the second year following the year of issuance. All renewals of such permits shall be for three (3) years.

2. Permits for temporary signs shall expire ninety (90) days from the date of issuance of such permit unless otherwise provided by Section 4616.

Section 9003. Application Requirements for Zoning Certificates.

A. All applications for zoning certificates shall be made in writing by the owner of the property for which it is sought on a form supplied by (Municipality) and shall be filed with the zoning officer. The application shall include four (4) copies of the following information, except as provided in Section 9004.

1. The legal descriptions of the parcel(s) for which the certificate is sought.

2. A map (or maps) of the subject property showing (a) its boundaries; (b) total acreage; (c) contours at two (2) foot intervals; (d) location, width, and name of all existing or previously platted streets, railroad, and utility rights-of-way; (e) parks and other public open spaces, or permanent easements, and section and municipal boundary lines within five hundred (500) feet of the tract; (f) the location of existing sewers, water mains, culverts, and other underground facilities within the tract, indicating pipe sizes, grades, manholes, and location.

3. A statement of the proposed use of each parcel, together with a site plan of the layout of the proposed development drawn to scale showing the location and exterior dimensions of all existing and proposed buildings and uses in relation to parcel and street lines. The following information shall be provided:

a. Provisions planned for treatment and disposal of sewage and industrial wastes, water supply, and storm drainage.

b. A site capacity calculation in conformance with Sections 4301 through 4305.

c. The size and arrangement of all buildings used or intended to be used for dwelling purposes, including the proposed density factor.

d. An open-space plan showing the location, dimensions, and arrangements of all open spaces, yards, and bufferyards, including specification of all plant materials to be utilized in providing the bufferyards and landscaping required by this ordinance and including the specification of any use planned for open-space or bufferyard areas.

e. The location, height, and composition material of all walls, fences, or other structures to be utilized in providing the bufferyards required by this ordinance.

f. The location and dimension of all existing and proposed vehicular drives, entrances, exits, traffic-circulation patterns, acceleration and deceleration lanes.

g. The location and dimension of all existing and proposed pedestrian entrances, exits, and walkways.

h. The location, size, arrangement, and capacity of all areas to be used for off-street parking and off-street loading.

i. The location, size, height, composition material, illumination, and orientation of all signs.

j. A certification of compliance with Section 4615 (exterior lighting) signed by the applicant's engineer or plans and specifications of the proposed lighting, if required by Section 4615.

k. Any other data deemed necessary by the zoning officer to determine the compliance of the proposed development with the terms of this ordinance.

l. If the application relates to property scheduled for phased development, the proposed layout of the total projected development shall be indicated and each phase's projected scope and time period indicated to the extent possible.

B. When a zoning certificate is sought for a development which is a part of a plat of subdivision which has received final plat approval or which has been issued a conditional use permit, the plat, or conditional use permit, together with any covenants, conditions, or other restrictions related thereto, shall be submitted as a part of the application for the zoning certificate.

C. Application for a conditional use permit shall be made at the same time or prior to application for a zoning certificate for the same development.

D. In the case of any development which is required to develop pursuant to a plat of subdivision, said development shall have received and properly recorded a finally approved plat before an application for a zoning certificate will be accepted for processing by the zoning officer. If the development for which a zoning certificate is sought is required by this ordinance to submit to site plan review, the approved site plan shall be made a part of the application for a zoning certificate and shall suffice as the statement of proposed use required by this subsection.

E. A temporary use and an accessory use shall require a zoning certificate as a precondition to their lawful establishment. The zoning officer may establish regulations governing the application requirements for a zoning certificate in the case of either a temporary or accessory use which is established at any time other than simultaneously with a principal use, in which case all information specified in Section 9003 (A) shall be submitted. The purpose of the information required to be submitted is to provide the zoning officer with a sufficient factual basis to determine whether all requirements of this ordinance applicable to temporary and accessory uses have been fully complied with.

F. No application shall be accepted by the zoning officer until it is complete as described above and until all fees established by (Municipality) for processing same have been paid in full.

Section 9004. Application Requirements for Sign Permits.

All applications for sign permits shall be made in writing on a form supplied by (Municipality) and shall contain or have attached thereto the following information:

A. Name, address, and telephone number of applicant.

B. Location of building, structure, or lot to which or upon which the sign is to be attached or erected.

C. Two blueprints or ink drawings of the plans, specifications, and method of construction and attachment (i.e., either to a building or in the ground) of all proposed signs.

D. A certified copy of the zoning certificate issued to the use(s) to which the sign is related together with a complete copy of the application required for that zoning certificate. When a sign permit is sought for a use which was existing at the effective date of this ordinance, the zoning officer shall specify the information required to show full compliance with the sign regulations of this ordinance, but in no event shall information not required by this section or an application for a zoning certificate be required.

Section 9005. Procedures.

A. Developments consisting of a single lot of record or a single dwelling unit or a single nonresidential unit shall be reviewed for compliance with this ordinance, and within three (3) days after the application for a zoning certificate has been accepted the zoning officer shall inform the applicant whether the application has been granted.

  1. In any case where the application is granted, the zoning officer shall issue a zoning certificate which shall state on its face: "This certificate does not signify building codes review or approval nor subdivision review or approval and is not authorization to undertake any work without such review and approval where either is required. Before any structure to which this certificate is applicable may be occupied or used for any purpose a certificate of occupancy must be obtained."

  2. In any case where an application is denied, the zoning officer shall state the specific reasons and shall cite the specific chapters, articles, and sections of this ordinance upon which denial is based. If relief of such denial would be available by special permit or variance, the zoning officer shall so state and shall refer the applicant to the appropriate sections of this ordinance.

B. Development consisting of more lots, uses, or structures than described above shall be reviewed for compliance with this ordinance in as timely a manner as possible. The zoning officer shall inform the applicant whether the application has been granted within thirty (30) days after the application for a zoning certificate has been accepted by the zoning officer.

C. Applications for sign permits shall be reviewed for compliance with this ordinance, and within two (2) days after acceptance of same the zoning officer shall inform the applicant whether the permit has been granted.

Section 9006. Site Plan Review.

A. Site plan review shall be required, as a precondition to the issuance of a zoning certificate, in the following instances:

  1. The establishment of any land uses which will take direct access to a collector or arterial road as determined by Section 4706.

  2. The development of any single land use consisting of ten (10) or more acres.

  3. The development of any nonresidential land use consisting of two (2) or more such uses.

  4. The development of any residential land use consisting of more than two (2) residential units.

B. The planning director shall review and approve all site plans subject to the procedures, standards, and limitations set forth herein, and review or disapprove said plan. No development required to submit to site plan review shall be entitled to a zoning certificate until and unless the planning director has approved said site plan.

Commentary: The site plan review process recognizes that the developments to which it is made applicable, even though generally suitable for location in a particular district or on a particular site, are, because of their nature, size, complexity, or other indicators of probable impact, capable of adversely affecting the purposes for which this ordinance is established unless careful consideration has been given to critical design elements. It is the purpose of this section to insure that all elements are reviewed for compatibility with the regulations and intent of this ordinance. A preliminary site plan, much like a preliminary or tentative plat of subdivision, is intended to serve as a working document for the developer and (Municipality) in the initial phases of the site plan review. It shall contain as much of the information required of an application for a zoning certificate as possible and, in any event, shall provide sufficiently detailed information to allow an informed decision concerning the overall acceptability of the proposed development.

Following review of the preliminary site plan, the planning director shall consult with the developer and detail unacceptable and required, but absent, elements. These comments shall be provided to the developer in writing within ten (10) days of said site plan having been submitted to the director.

A final site plan shall be submitted to (Municipality) following the procedure specified above. Said site plan shall be inclusive of all engineering plans and shall contain all of the information required by Section 9003 of an application for a zoning certificate. The planning director shall review said plan for compliance with this section and, in particular, for compliance with the report on the preliminary site plan. In the event that the director determines the final site plan, or any element thereof, unacceptable, written notice of this decision, including all reasons for it and instructions for making said items acceptable, shall be provided to the developer within thirty (30) days of said final site plan having been accepted by the director. While this ordinance specifies no precise time limits within which the director shall review and report on the elements of a final site plan which the developer must amend as a precondition to approval of said plan, the planning director shall conduct such a review and report as expeditiously as possible on it; and in no event shall the review of any item of a plan exceed the time period imposed by this section for review of the entire plan.

Section 9007. Conditional Use Permit.

An application for any conditional use permit required by this ordinance shall be made by following the procedure detailed in Section 9002.

Section 9008. Certificate of Occupancy.

A. No structure shall be erected, constructed, reconstructed, extended, or moved, and no land or building shall be occupied or used in whole or in part for any use whatsoever after the effective date of this ordinance until the owner, tenants, contract purchaser, or authorized agent thereof has been issued a certificate of occupancy by the zoning officer, indicating that the building or use complies with all zoning requirements of this ordinance.

B. No certificate of occupancy shall be issued until the premises in question have been inspected and found by the zoning officer to comply with the requirements of this ordinance. No fee shall be charged for a certificate of occupancy.

C. No permit for any new use or construction which will involve the on-site disposal of sewage or waste, and no permit for a change in use or an alteration which will result in an increased volume of sewage or waste to be disposed of on the site, or which requires the (Municipality) Health Department's approval shall be issued until said approval has been issued by the (Municipality) Health Department.

D. The issuance of a certificate of occupancy in no way relieves any recipient thereof from compliance with all of the terms of this ordinance and all other applicable regulations.

Section 9009. Change of Use.

Change or alteration of the use of any building, structure, or land shall not be permitted until a zoning certificate and a certificate of occupancy are obtained pursuant to this article.

Section 9010. Zoning Officer: Duties and Powers.

The zoning officer shall be appointed by the (Municipality) Board and shall have the following powers and responsibilities:

A. Receive and review all applications for zoning certificates required herein.

B. Process zoning certificate and conditional use permit applications for all permitted uses.

C. Receive applications for amendments and variances and forward same to the zoning board for action.

D. Following refusal of a permit, receive applications for interpretation and appeals and forward same to the zoning board for action.

E. Record and file all applications for zoning certificates with accompanying plans and documents. All applications, plans, and documents shall be a public record.

F. Revoke any zoning certificate issued under a mistake of fact or contrary to the law or provision of this ordinance.

Further, if by amendment to this ordinance any zone boundary or any other matter shown on the Official Zoning Map is changed by action of the (Municipality) Board, such change shall be promptly indicated on said map by the zoning officer, together with the date of passage of the amendment and sufficient written description to give a precise understanding of the change. Every such change shall be certified by the (Municipality) Clerk.

An up-to-date copy of the Official Zoning Map as amended from time to time shall be available for public inspection in the office of the Building and Zoning Department during its regular business hours.

Section 9011. Building and Enforcement Officer: Duties and Powers.

The building and enforcement officer shall have the following powers and responsibilities:

A. Receive and examine all applications for building permits.

B. Process all building permit applications.

C. Issue permits only where there is compliance with the provisions of this ordinance. Permits for construction of uses requiring a variance shall be issued only upon order of the Zoning Board. Permits requiring approval by the (Municipality) Board shall be issued only after receipt of a certified copy of approval from the (Municipality) Clerk and receipt of a zoning certificate.

D. Conduct inspections and surveys to determine compliance or non-compliance with the terms of this ordinance.

E. Revoke, by writing, a permit or approval issued contrary to this ordinance or based on a false statement or misrepresentation in the application.

F. Stop, by written order, work being done contrary to the building permit or to this ordinance. Such written order, posted on the premises involved, shall not be removed except by order of the building officer. Removal without such order shall constitute a violation of this ordinance.

G. Institute any appropriate action or proceedings to prevent unlawful erection, construction, reconstruction, alteration, repair, conversion, maintenance, or use; restrain, correct, or abate such violation, so as to prevent the occupancy or use of any building, structure, or land; or prevent any illegal act, conduct, business, or use in or about such premises.

H. Record and file all applications for permits with accompanying plans and documents. All applications, plans, and documents shall be a public record.

Section 9012. Duties of the Planning Commission.

A. The Planning Commission shall study and report on all proposed amendments to the text of this ordinance referred to it by the (Municipality) Board. When reviewing any such proposed amendments, the Planning Commission shall, within forty-five (45) days of receipt of same from the zoning officer, submit its recommendations and findings to the (Municipality) Board.

B. The Planning Commission shall review this ordinance and report on same to the (Municipality) Board at least once every five (5) years commencing on the date of enactment of this ordinance. Specifically, the Planning Commission shall:

1. Analyze the extent to which development has occurred in (Municipality) as compared to the projected growth at the time of the last previous mapping of the districts created by this ordinance.

2. Recommend any changes in the mapping of (Municipality), particularly in the mapping of the development district, which would be required in order to accommodate the expected twenty-year growth of (Municipality) for residential, industrial, commercial, and other land uses.

3. Analyze the continued validity of any other regulations imposed by this ordinance in terms of changed conditions since the last review of same.

Section 9013. Duties of the Planning Director.

The Planning Director shall receive and review all site plans whose submission is required by Section 9003 and review all proposed zoning amendments and prepare a report on them for the Zoning Board of Appeals and the (Municipality) Board.

Section 9014. Zoning Board of Appeals: Duties and Powers.

(Author's Note: This section, because it was written pursuant to Illinois Statutes pertaining to counties, cannot be said to represent a model or ideal. Illinois counties must live with Zoning Boards of Appeals that make recommendations on rezonings and have quasi-judicial powers with respect to other matters. It is better to limit Zoning Boards to the quasi-judicial functions and let the planning commissions make advisory recommendations, as is the case in most states.)

The Zoning Board of Appeals heretofore established is continued. It shall be representative of (Municipality) and consist of seven (7) members. No two (2) members shall reside in the same congressional township. Terms, vacancies, and successors to the members shall be appointed by the (Municipality) Board in accordance with the Statutes of (State). Nominations to fill a vacancy shall be submitted to the Zoning Committee of the (Municipality) Board which shall evaluate them and recommend to the (Municipality) Board that candidate whom it considers best qualified. The chairperson and vice-chairperson of the Zoning Board shall be selected by the Zoning Board to serve terms of two (2) years. Vacancies in either of these positions shall be filled for the unexpired term of that office.

All meetings of the Zoning Board shall be held at the call of its chairperson or of any three (3) members, at such times and places within (Municipality) as the Zoning Board may determine to be in compliance with any applicable statute, ordinance, or regulation.

The Zoning Board shall have the authority to compel the attendance of witnesses at hearings and to administer oaths, and in furtherance of its duties shall:

A. File minutes of its proceedings and any written recommendations from the Health Department, Regional Planning Commission, State's Attorney, or other official bodies; show the vote of each member on every question or, if a member is absent or fails to vote, indicate such fact; and keep records of its examinations and other official actions.

B. File immediately in the office of the Zoning Board all rules and regulations and amendment or repeal thereof, and every order, requirement, decision, or determination of the Zoning Board. These shall become public records.

C. Establish rules of procedure, and such other rules as it deems necessary, not in conflict with the laws of (State).

D. Hear and decide appeals from any decisions of the zoning officer made in the performance of his duties.

E. Hear and decide all petitions for variations, as provided in this article.

F. Hear all applications for conditional use permits and make a report and recommendation to the (Municipality) Board, in accordance with Article IV and this article.

G. Hear all petitions for amendments of this ordinance and make a report and a recommendation to the (Municipality) Board as provided in this article.

H. Cause, at its discretion, the posting of notice in the form of a sign on property which is subject to a public hearing for rezoning, a conditional use permit, or other matter.

Section 9015. Interpretations.

A. **Purpose.** The provisions of this section are intended to provide a simple and expeditious method for clarifying ambiguities in the text of this ordinance, the zoning map which it incorporates, and the rules and regulations adopted pursuant to it. It is also intended to provide a simple, yet circumscribed procedure for overcoming the inadvertent rigidities and limitations inherent in the promulgation of finite use lists in a world characterized by infinite permutations of essentially similar uses.

B. **Authority.** The zoning officer may, subject to the procedures, standards, and limitations set forth in this section, render interpretations of any provision of this ordinance or any rule or regulation issued pursuant to it, including interpretations of the various uses in any district not expressly mentioned in this ordinance.

C. **Procedure.**

1. **Written request for nonuse interpretation.** Except as provided below, a request for interpretation of any provision of this ordinance, the zoning map, or any rule or regulation adopted pursuant to this ordinance shall be submitted in writing to the zoning officer. No fee shall be required in connection with any such re-

quest. Each such request shall set forth the specific provision or provisions to be interpreted, the facts of the specific situation giving rise to the request for an interpretation, and the precise interpretation claimed by the applicant to be correct. Before rendering any interpretation, the zoning officer shall receive such further facts and information as are in his judgment necessary to a meaningful interpretation of the provision in question

2. **Application for use interpretation.** Applications for a use interpretation shall be submitted to the zoning officer on a form supplied by (Municipality) and shall in all instances contain at least the following information and documentation:

a. The applicant's name, address, and interest in the subject property.

b. The owner's name and address, if different from the applicant's, and the owner's signed consent to the filing of the application.

c. The names and addresses of all professional consultants advising the applicant with respect to the interpretation.

d. The street address and legal description of the subject property.

e. The zoning classification and present use of the subject property.

f. A complete description of the proposed use.

g. The uses permitted by the present zoning classification which are most similar to the proposed use.

h. Documents, statements, and other evidence demonstrating that the proposed use will comply with all use limitations established for the district in which it is proposed to be located.

i. Such other and further information or documentation as the zoning officer may deem necessary or appropriate to a full and proper consideration and disposition of the particular application.

3. **Zoning officer.** Within thirty (30) days following the receipt by the zoning officer of a completed request or application for interpretation, the zoning officer shall mail a written copy of interpretation to the applicant. The zoning officer shall state the specific precedent, reasons, and analysis on which such interpretation is based. The failure of the zoning officer to render an interpretation within such time, or such longer period of time as may be agreed to by the applicant, shall be deemed to be a rejection of the applicant's proposed interpretation. The zoning officer shall keep a copy of each such interpretation on file and shall make a copy of each such filed interpretation available for public inspection during reasonable hours.

4. **Appeal.** Appeals on interpretations rendered by the zoning officer pursuant to this section may be taken to the Board of Appeals as provided in this article.

D. The following conditions shall govern the zoning officer, and the Board of Appeals on appeals from the zoning officer, in issuing use interpretations:

1. No use interpretation shall allow the establishment of any use which was previously considered and rejected by the Board of Appeals on an application for amendment.

2. No use interpretation shall permit a use listed as a permitted or conditional use in any district in which such use is not so listed.

3. No use interpretation shall permit any use in any district unless evidence shall be presented which demonstrates that it will comply with each use limitation established for the particular district.

4. No use interpretation shall permit any use in a particular district unless such use is substantially similar to other uses permitted in such district and is more similar to such other uses than to uses permitted or conditionally permitted in a less restrictive district.

5. If the proposed use is more similar to a use permitted only as a conditional use in the district in which it is proposed to be located, then any use interpretation permitting such use shall be conditioned on the issuance of a permit for a conditional use permit pursuant to this article.

6. Any use permitted pursuant to this section shall fully comply with all requirements and standards imposed by this ordinance.

E. **Effect of favorable use interpretation.** No use interpretation finding a particular use to be permitted or conditionally permitted in a specific district shall authorize the establishment of such use or the development, construction, reconstruction, alteration, or moving of any building or structure, but shall merely authorize the preparation, filing, and processing of applications for any permits and approvals which may be required by the codes and ordinances of (Municipality) or other governmental agencies having jurisdiction. These permits and approvals include, but are not limited to, zoning certificates, conditional use permits, building permits, and certificates of occupancy.

F. **Limitations on favorable use interpretations.** No use interpretation finding a particular use to be permitted or conditionally permitted in a specified district shall be valid for a period longer than one (1) year from the date of issue unless a building permit is issued and construction is actually begun within that period and is thereafter diligently pursued to completion, or a certificate of occupancy is obtained and a use commenced within that period.

A use interpretation finding a particular use to be permitted or conditionally permitted in a specified district shall be deemed to authorize only the particular use at the particular location for which it was issued, and such permit shall not be deemed to authorize any allegedly similar use for which a separate use interpretation has not been issued. Such permit shall automatically expire and cease to be of any force or effect if the particular use for which it was issued shall, for any reason, be discontinued for a period of six (6) consecutive months or more.

G. **Annual report.** The zoning officer shall keep a record of each use interpretation rendered and shall make an annual report of all such interpretations to the (Municipality) Board. The report shall include any recommendations that this ordinance be amended to add new uses to the various use lists established by this ordinance to reflect each use interpretation given pursuant to this section.

H. **Failure of (Municipality) Board to amend the ordinance.**

1. Any appeals on the ruling of the zoning officer concerning the enforcement and interpretation of any provision of this ordinance

shall be filed with the zoning officer within thirty (30) days after the date of the zoning officer's decision thereon.

2. All appeals and applications made to the Board shall be in writing on forms specified by the Zoning Hearing Board and accompanied by fees prescribed by resolution of the (Municipality) Board.

3. All appeals and applications shall refer to the specific provisions of this ordinance involved.

4. The Board shall select a reasonable time and place for hearing the appeal and give due notice thereof to the parties and shall render a written decision on the appeal without unreasonable delay. The Board may affirm, reverse, wholly or in part, or modify the order, requirement, decision, or determination, as in its opinion it determines ought to be done, and to that end shall have all the powers of the officer from whom the appeal is taken. The Department of Building and Zoning shall maintain complete records of all appeal actions of the Board.

5. Within thirty (30) days after the close of a hearing pursuant to Section 9016 the Zoning Board shall render a written decision giving the reason(s) for its decision.

In any case where, upon the expiration of one (1) year following the receipt of the recommendations of the zoning officer pursuant to the above section, the (Municipality) Board shall have failed to adopt an ordinance amendment with respect to any use interpretation included in such recommendation:

1. Any use authorized pursuant to such interpretation, but not yet established or under construction, shall not be established.

2. Any use authorized and established pursuant to such interpretation shall be allowed to continue but shall be subject to all applicable provisions of this ordinance.

3. No similar use interpretation shall be given in the future.

Section 9016. Amendments.

A. **Amendments.** This ordinance may be amended from time to time as conditions warrant in the following manner. As used herein, the term "application" includes (Municipality) Board Resolution or Petition, as appropriate.

1. **Initiation procedures.** Amendments to either the text or maps of this ordinance shall be made by resolutions of the (Municipality) Board or other appropriate governmental agencies empowered to direct the Zoning Board to conduct public hearings to consider proposed amendments to either the text or maps of this ordinance by petition of a party using forms specified by the Zoning Board of Appeals.

2. **Text amendments.** The application for an amendment to the text of this ordinance shall state in particular the article, section, subsection, and paragraph sought to be amended. The application shall contain the language of the proposed amendment and shall recite the reasons for such proposed change in the text.

3. **Map amendments.**

   a. Applications to rezone any property, or any application which seeks to change or modify the standards and requirements imposed on a particular piece of property by the text and maps of this ordinance, including applications for variations and conditional use permits, shall be instituted by (Municipality) or all the fee owners of the property sought to be affected.

   b. In the case where the fee owner has entered into a contract for the sale of the property sought to be affected, the contract purchaser shall be a copetitioner to the petition or application.

   c. In the case of property that is the subject of a land trust agreement, the trustee of such trust, in his or her capacity as trustee, shall be the petitioner or copetitioner to the petition or application.

   d. When the petitioner or copetitioner is a business entity doing business under an assumed name, the petition or application shall include the name and residence of all true and actual owners of such business or entity.

   e. When the petitioner or copetitioner is a partnership, joint venture, syndicate, or an unincorporated voluntary association, the application shall include the names and addresses of all partners, joint venturers, syndicate members, or members of the unincorporated voluntary association.

4. **Trust disclosures.** Whenever any trustee of a land trust makes application for any benefit, authorization, license, or permit, including applications for rezoning, variations, or conditional use permits, which relates to the land which is the subject of such trust, such application shall identify each beneficiary of such land trust by name and address and define his or her interest therein. All applications shall be verified by the applicant, petitioner, or copetitioner in his or her capacity as trustee. If such application is filed by a body politic or other corporate entity, it shall be verified by a duly authorized officer of such body politic or other corporate entity for whom the application is made.

5. **Public hearing.** Upon application, the Zoning Board, after giving fifteen (15) days notice as provided by law, shall conduct a public hearing in each township affected by the terms of the proposed amendment or in the (Municipality) Court House. When considering general amendments, the hearing may be held in the (Municipality) Court House instead of each township. The Zoning Board shall consider and make recommendations on all proposed amendments, taking into account: (a) the testimony at the hearing; (b) a site inspection of the property in question; (c) the recommendations from interested official bodies; and (d) the standards provided below.

B. **Standards for map amendments.** All map amendments shall be consistent with the goals and policies of (Municipality's) adopted Comprehensive Plan and the intent of this ordinance. Accordingly:

1. No rezoning of land from either the rural (R) or the estate (E) district classification to the development district (DD) classification shall be permitted except upon a specific and documented finding that:

   a. A change in demand which significantly (by a factor of at least twenty-five [25] percent) alters the assumptions of the

Comprehensive Plan has occurred such as: (1) a significant change in migration patterns, family size, or birth rate since the last (Municipality) amendment of the development district or (2) a major change, such as the construction of a major road, the installation of a sewer line, or the provision of a formerly unavailable water supply, which significantly alters the suitability of an area for development.

b. An area designated as a development district has been precluded from development by unanticipated events such as the nonprovision of a sewer plant or interceptor or a sewer ban, and that said area constitutes a significant part of the total amount of the planned development district.

Commentary: The location and sizing of the (Municipality)-designated development districts are explicitly and carefully planned to provide for twenty (20) years of capacity subject to review and revision every five (5) years. This comprehensive and continuing planning scheme should not be upset by an ad hoc (rezoning) decision-making process.

2. No rezoning of land from the rural (R) to the estate (E) district shall be permitted except upon a specific and documented finding that there has been a substantial increase in the demand for estate zoning, and that as a result the supply of land zoned estate within a five (5) mile radius of the subject parcel is inadequate to meet the demands for estate-type housing for the next ten (10) years.

3. No rezoning of land from the agricultural district (AG) shall be permitted except upon a specific and documented finding that:

   a. The soils on the property are not, in fact, accurately classified and the inaccurately classified soils are in excess of fifteen (15) acres.

   b. That ninety (90) percent of all land classified as rural (R) or estate (E) has been utilized for urban uses and the land proposed for rezoning is necessary to accommodate growth, and that the proposed property is found to be the most appropriate site for the proposed rezoning in terms of its environmental and fiscal impact when compared to other possible sites.

Commentary: The agricultural district is intended to preserve prime agricultural land for agricultural use. Only after the land in rural and other nonagricultural districts has been developed should (Municipality) begin converting agricultural land to nonagricultural uses. The general prohibition against conversion of agricultural land is, of course, not applicable to land improperly classified as agricultural in the first place.

4. No rezoning of land to the urban core (UC) district shall be permitted except upon a specific and documented finding that:

   a. Marketing studies demonstrate a demand for the facilities of an urban core which cannot be provided by the districts planned and mapped as urban core on the official zoning map and,

   b. Impact studies of existing urban core districts and their equivalents within incorporated areas, within a five (5) mile radius of the site proposed for rezoning, demonstrate that the proposed rezoning will not have adverse impacts on their economic viability and,

   c. Traffic studies demonstrate that the proposed urban core development will not have adverse impacts on the level of service of arterial roads, both in incorporated and unincorporated areas, within a five (5) mile radius of the site proposed for rezoning and,

   d. That a new mass transit station will be built in the first phase of construction and that public transportation will be provided to the site.

5. No rezoning of land to the heavy industrial (HI) district shall be permitted except on a specific and documented finding that:

   a. There is an inadequate supply of land zoned for these uses or that the proposed use cannot be accommodated by those sites due to a lack of transportation, water, or sewer, or that the market area to be served by the proposed use cannot be efficiently served by the geographical location of the existing HI districts.

   b. That roads, floodplains, or other existing or planned features will insure sufficient buffering to protect surrounding land

and uses from the negative impacts of the proposed industrial use.

6. No rezoning of land from the holding district (HD) classification shall be permitted except pursuant to an intergovernmental agreement consistent with Section 3309.

7. No rezoning of vacant land from the neighborhood conservation (NC) or commercial conservation (CC) classification shall be permitted.

8. No particular findings are required for land to be rezoned to the agricultural (AG) district.

C. **Report of the Zoning Board of Appeals.** In addition to the findings required to be made by Subsection (B) above, findings shall be made by the Zoning Board of Appeals on each of the following matters based on the evidence presented to it.

1. The public need for the proposed use.

2. The extent to which the proposed amendment and proposed use are in compliance with and/or deviate from the adopted Comprehensive Plan.

3. The suitability of the property in question for the uses permitted under the proposed zoning.

4. The adequacy of public facilities, such as sewer and water, and other required public services.

The Zoning Board shall not recommend the adoption of a proposed amendment unless it finds that the adoption of such an amendment is in the public interest and not solely for the interest of the applicant.

D. **Report to (Municipality) Board.** The Zoning Board shall make a report to the (Municipality) Board. No amendment shall be passed except by a majority vote of the members of the (Municipality) Board present. In the following cases, no amendment shall be passed except by the favorable vote of three-fourths (.75) of all members of the (Municipality) Board:

1. If a written protest against the proposed amendment is filed with the (Municipality) Clerk no later than 1 PM of the day before the (Municipality) Board votes on said proposed amendment, signed and acknowledged by the owner of twenty (20) percent or more of: (*a*) the frontage proposed to be altered; (*b*) the frontage immediately adjoining or across an alley therefrom; (*c*) the frontage directly opposite the frontage proposed to be altered.

2. If the land affected by a proposed amendment lies within one and one-half (1.5) miles of the limits of a zoned municipality, and if a protest against the amendment is passed by the governing body of the zoned municipality with limits nearest adjacent and the written objection is filed with the (Municipality) Clerk no later than 1 PM of the day before the (Municipality) Board votes on said proposed amendment.

E. **Time limit and notification.** All proposed amendments shall be decided by the (Municipality) Board as soon as practicable after the public hearing, and the applicant shall be notified in writing whether the amendment has been granted or denied.

Section 9017. Variances.

A. **Purpose.** The purpose of this section is to empower the Zoning Board to vary or adapt the strict application of any of the requirements of this ordinance in the neighborhood conservation (NC) district only. No variation shall be permitted in any zoning district except the neighborhood conservation (NC) district. A variance may be appropriate where, by reason of exceptional narrowness, shallowness, or shape or by reason of other exceptional topographic conditions or other extraordinary and exceptional situations or conditions on a piece of property, the strict application of any regulation enacted under this ordinance would result in peculiar, exceptional, and undue hardship on the owner of such property located in the neighborhood conservation district.

Commentary: The use of performance standards contained in this ordinance has, unlike the prior (Municipality) ordinance, authorized more mixing of land uses and considerable more flexibility in the planning of use location. As a consequence, the variance opportunity supplied in this ordinance is drastically different from and more limited than the one provided in the former and most other conventional ordinances. Traditionally, variance provisions are contained in a zoning ordinance to allow relief from the "strict" application of a regulation (such as a minimum yard width or building setback) which will result in an unnecessary hardship, by virtue of the existence of some unique circumstances or physical condition of a particular parcel, usually related to its topography or shape and not generally applicable to land or buildings in the neighborhood. There exist circumstances or conditions such that the strict application of provisions of the ordinance would deprive the applicant of the reasonable use of the land. The performance standards and regulations of this ordinance do not consist of rigid regulations from which a variation could fashion relief. On the contrary, this ordinance builds in both use and design flexibility.

The standards and regulations of this ordinance are designed to allow the maximum possible development consistent with protecting the public health, safety, and welfare. By design and definition, then, no variation beyond the carefully arrived at maximum development standards can be tolerated, because there could be no reasonable basis for such a variation.

It cannot generally be argued that any variation from the standards or regulations will be necessary, because the standards imposed by the ordinance have been carefully planned and constructed specifically to allow the maximum possible freedom to develop without adverse impacts on nearby land.

Inasmuch as performance standards are specifically designed to protect neighbors and the general community from specific adverse by-products, a contention that there would be no adverse impacts would be unwarranted unless the level of performance was established at an unreasonably low level. If this is the case, a landowner's recourse is to have the level of performance standards amended and, if that is to no avail, to attack the reasonableness of the standards. The existing legal prerequisites for a variance could never be met for a reasonable performance standard and, therefore, variance procedures for performance standards in districts other than neighborhood conservation would be superfluous.

B. **Application.** After denial of a building permit by the zoning officer or without denial, a property owner of land located in a neighborhood conservation (NC) district may apply to the Zoning Board for a variation using forms to be obtained from the Zoning Board.

C. **Standards for variations.** No variance in the strict application of the provisions of this ordinance shall be granted by the Zoning Board unless it finds that the following requirements and standards are satisfied. In general, the power to authorize a variance from the terms of this ordinance shall be sparingly exercised. It is the intent of this ordinance that the variance be used only to overcome some exceptional physical condition of a parcel of land located within the neighborhood conservation district which poses practical difficulty to its development and prevents its owner from using the property as intended by the zoning ordinance. Any variation granted shall be the minimum adjustment necessary for the reasonable use of the land.

The applicant must prove that the variance will not be contrary to the public interest and that practical difficulty and unnecessary hardship will result if it is not granted. In particular, the applicant shall establish and substantiate that the appeal for the variance conforms to the requirements and standards listed below:

1. The granting of the variance shall be in harmony with the general purpose and intent of the regulations imposed by this ordinance on the neighborhood conservation district in which it is located and shall not be injurious to the neighborhood or otherwise detrimental to the public welfare.

2. The granting of the variance will not permit the establishment of any use which is not permitted in the neighborhood conservation district.

3. There must be proof of unique circumstances: there must exist special circumstances or conditions, fully described in the findings, applicable to the land or buildings for which the variance is sought, which circumstances or conditions are peculiar to such land or buildings and do not apply generally to land or buildings in the neighborhood, and which circumstances or conditions are such that the strict application of the provisions of this ordinance would deprive the applicant of the reasonable use of such land or building.

4. There must be proof of unnecessary hardship. It is not sufficient proof of hardship to show that greater profit would result if the variance were granted. Furthermore, the hardship complained of cannot be self-created; nor can it be established on this basis by

one who purchases with or without knowledge of the restrictions; it must result from the application of this ordinance; it must be suffered directly by the property in question; and evidence of variance granted under similar circumstances shall not be considered.

5. That the granting of the variance is necessary for the reasonable use of the land or building and that the variance as granted by the Board is the minimum variance that will accomplish this purpose.

The report of the Zoning Board shall fully set forth the circumstances by which this ordinance would deprive the applicant of any reasonable use of his land. Mere loss in value shall not justify a variation; there must be a deprivation of beneficial use of land.

6. That the proposed variation will not impair an adequate supply of light and air to adjacent property, substantially increase the congestion in the public streets, increase the danger of fire, endanger the public safety, or substantially diminish or impair property values within the adjacent neighborhood.

7. That the granting of the variance requested will not confer on the applicant any special privilege that is denied by this ordinance to other lands, structures, or buildings in the same district.

The Board may prescribe any safeguard that it deems necessary to secure substantially the objectives of the regulations or provisions to which the variance applies.

D. **Public Hearing.** Upon application, the Zoning Board, after giving notice as required by law, shall schedule a public hearing in each township affected by the terms of the proposed variance or in the (Municipality) Court House. The Zoning Board shall consider and decide all proposed variations taking into account the standards enumerated above.

After the close of a public hearing and within thirty (30) days the Zoning Board shall render a written decision, setting forth the reasons for such decision, which shall be accompanied by finding of fact(s) specifying the reason(s) for such decision. All such decisions are final and binding on all parties.

Section 9018. Appeals.

A. Appeals to the Zoning Hearing Board may be taken by any person aggrieved or affected by any provision of this ordinance or by any decision, including Section 8004, or any order to stop, cease, and desist, issued by the zoning officer in enforcing the provisions of this ordinance.

B. **General rules and procedures for appeals.**
1. Any appeals from the ruling of the zoning officer concerning the enforcement and interpretation of any provision of this ordinance shall be filed with the zoning officer within thirty (30) days after the date of the zoning officer's decision thereon.

2. All appeals and applications made to the Board shall be in writing on forms prescribed by the Zoning Hearing Board and accompanied by fees prescribed by resolution of the (Municipality) Board.

3. All appeals and applications shall refer to the specific provisions of this ordinance involved.

4. The Board shall select a reasonable time and place for hearing the appeal and give due notice thereof to the parties and shall render a written decision on the appeal without unreasonable delay. The Board may affirm, reverse, wholly or in part, or modify the order, requirement, decision, or determination, as in its opinion it determines ought to be done, and to that end shall have all the powers of the officer from whom the appeal is taken. The Department of Building and Zoning shall maintain complete records of all appeal actions of the Board.

5. Within thirty (30) days after the close of a hearing pursuant to Section 9016 the Zoning Board shall render a written decision giving the reason(s) for its decision.

6. In rendering a decision with respect to an appeal from any order, decision, or determination the Zoning Board shall strictly interpret the language of the ordinance and shall find that the zoning officer was correct in his decision or in error. However, the Zoning Board shall not render any decision which shall modify an order, decision, or determination which confers rights or

privileges on the appellant than are otherwise permissible under the strict interpretation of the language of this ordinance.

7. Such decision shall be submitted to the appellant and the zoning officer.

8. All decisions rendered by the Zoning Board in case of appeals from orders, decisions, or determinations shall be final and binding on all parties.

9 . Any person aggrieved by any decision of the Zoning Board or the governing body may within thirty (30) days after such decision appeal to the Circuit Court of (Municipality).

Part Three

Theory and
Technical Aspects

Definition and Basic Concerns

Although the term "performance zoning" is current in professional jargon, it is often used without full appreciation of its meaning. Indeed, the concept is commonly confused with such other regulatory approaches as impact zoning, impact assessment, and carrying capacity. As used here, the term refers to a technique in which uses are generally permitted as a matter of right in urbanizing areas. Performance standards, not districting, are employed to protect the public health, safety, and welfare. Districts are used to separate areas with broadly different functions (e.g., rural and urban) rather than to isolate different specific uses (e.g., central business and highway commercial). The performance standards allow the landowner considerable freedom to develop property in several different ways. These standards are based variously on the concepts of carrying capacity and threshold of safety, as well as on principles designed to insure a suitable level of environmental quality.

Because it reduces the opportunity for discretionary action by elected officials, performance zoning counters a pernicious trend in zoning. Variances, conditional uses, special use permits, and planned developments are all discretionary procedures that have been added to zoning ordinances with increasing frequency (and complexity) over the years. These have made zoning less a legislative act and more a continuing process of ad hoc administrative decision. By their nature, ad hoc procedures make the role of planning unclear at best and futile at worst.

Recent court decisions have more closely scrutinized the validity of land use ordinances and regulations and have actually begun to perceive the defects of traditional zoning practices.[4] Instead of almost automatically presuming regulations to be valid, the courts are now examining them for exclusionary impact, "parochial vision," "ineptness," or undue harshness with little compensating public benefit. In many states, enabling legislation mandates that zoning be in accordance with the comprehensive plan of the community. Inherent in this mandate is a charge to the courts to determine whether this requirement has been met. But even in a state which does not have this statutory requirement and which has earned the dubious distinction of being "the only state in which Courts have remained happily stuck in the second period of American Zoning for a period of over 40 years,"[5] the judiciary has recognized that a presumption of validity is not one and the same with a conclusion of validity.

All discretionary zoning techniques were introduced to provide flexibility, achieve better quality control, and provide an escape from excessively rigid regulations. Unfortunately, their administration has been subject to different interpretation as the cast of characters changes over time, and so the results have been inconsistent, highly subjective, and too often politically motivated. Frequently the approval process has been intolerably long—a year or more for conditional use permits or planned unit developments in many jurisdictions. If the discretionary approach is rejected, it must be replaced with other techniques which are flexible yet capable of insuring both the public health and safety and a quality environment. Performance zoning does this by introducing a large number of performance criteria against which every development proposal must be evaluated. There are special purpose regulations, such as site capacity calculations, access controls, and highway capacity analysis. Other criteria set a series of interacting standards which define the function and intensity of districts. A third group specifies standards for uses as a function of their intensity and relate these standards to design. All of the standards interact to provide as much control as is required to protect one land use from negative impacts of another. They permit, however, far more flexibility and many more use and design options for a developer than a conventional zoning ordinance does. The narrowly defined land use district is abandoned in favor of districts with distinctly different functions, characters, and purposes; so long as a development does not upset the balance struck by these regulations, it is permitted.

Unlike performance zoning, impact zoning merely provides a mechanism to identify the effects of a proposed rezoning. Although it provides data for the guidance of the decision-making body which has the discretion to deny the project or to permit it, it does not specify objective minimum standards. With performance zoning, a proposed use which meets the performance criteria may not lawfully be refused a permit.

It is possible to convert an impact ordinance to a performance regulation by restating the criteria required of an impact analysis in terms of minimum regulatory standards. Thus, for example, a planned unit development ordinance which requires the submission of considerable data on the traffic, school children, drainage, and other impacts generated by the proposal may be amended to state: "a PUD not exceeding traffic impact X, generating no more than Y (number) of school children, and installing specified drainage and detention improvements (and complying with all applicable ordinance requirements) shall be permitted."

Impact assessment is a carryover from environmental legislation into the field of land use controls. It need not be an integral part of subdivision or zoning ordinances, but rather merely a requirement of the "standard operating procedure" utilized by the land use decision maker. Impact assessment adds length and complexity to the review process. It is an ad hoc fact-finding process, but the facts found are compared against subjective or vague "standards." The reviewing agency retains the power to exercise its own discretion and to weigh the facts subjectively when evaluating a proposal. In practice, such systems often result in two or more sets of experts drawing opposite conclusions as to whether the standards have been met.

Communities have attempted to utilize the concept of performance to insure better developments. Most of their methods, however, have not involved true performance zoning but rather such mechanisms as "arm-twisting" or the imposition of "primitive" standards. On the most elementary level, the community is concerned with performance and, through the familiar process of arm-twisting, tries to force the developer to perform. There are many problems with this approach, not the least of which may be its illegality: even if sophisticted planning helps to establish a community's goals, there will be no law requiring the implementation of these plans. Moreover, the ad hoc, project-by-project basis of such techniques hinders uniform application and requires the developers to guess what the community is expecting of them. Arm-twisting is thus a major cause of the distrust between developers and government, and schemes which employ this tactic in the name of performance zoning can only jeopardize the legality and theoretical acceptance of the true concept. If local officials have sufficient confidence in a technique or standard, they should adopt it in ordinance form. If they do not have faith in it, then they should not subject any developer to any "standard" that will not be consistently and uniformly applied to all. If the community feels a need to experiment, then it should adopt new standards on an interim basis.

Frequently ordinances incorporate primitive standards which hint at the desire for performance but do not define the level of performance required. Typical of this type of standard is: "In designing a Planned Development particular consideration shall be given to: ...The conservation of significant natural resources..."[6] This regulation may be fairly criticized for several different reasons all of which fall into the general category of vagueness. What constitutes "consideration," for example? What is a "significant" natural resource? In fact, what is the precise definition of "natural resource"?

Other examples of this type of regulation include requirements that "adequate open space" be provided by a development or that a development not cause "traffic congestion." By contrast, a true performance standard might address the first concern in the following manner: "In the county residential district, the minimum open space ratio shall be 40 percent of gross site area; density shall not exceed four (4) dwelling units per acre." Open space would have to be defined precisely so that there would be no disagreement about what it does, and does not, constitute. On the traffic congestion issue, a performance standard might simply prohibit all development which would reduce the level of service on any adjoining arterial road below level C (defined in terms of a specific number of vehicles traveling at specified rates of speed) during the "peak hours" (which would also be defined).

The subjective standards approach can address areas of concern only on a case-by-case basis. So long as the standards are general and subjective, the quality and consistency of results are more dependent on the individuals charged with their administration than on the standards themselves. If a standard is subject to different interpretations, it will inevitably be interpreted differently. Litigation is a probable outcome. The results over any significant period of time are likely to be uneven and unpredictable. A zoning ordinance which uses subjective language, as in the foregoing example, to detail its "standards" remains a conventional zoning ordinance, no matter how vigorously its proponents claim it to be based on measurable performance criteria. Wherever significant differences in interpretation are possible, the local government can always resort to arm-twisting to enforce its interpretation, and the developer's only resource is to "take them to court."

It should be noted that there are two distinct types of performance standards. The original performance standards for industrial districts had to be measured on-site after the use was built. Most of the performance criteria in the model ordinance can be measured on site plans or by calculations before the development begins. This is necessary because efficient administration requires that the ability of a proposal to meet the standards be determined when a permit is sought. As a result, measurements may err somewhat, but such an approach does not sacrifice a very significant degree of accuracy, especially when one considers the legal, administrative, and cost problems it avoids. Administratively, if compliance with the ordinance can be determined only after the fact, in all probability it will often have to be enforced by the courts. Such enforcement may require expensive corrective measures on the part of the landowner. On the other hand, the administrative costs of a pre-permit performance test are often considerably less than an on-site test. The personnel may require less training and usually will spend less time on each test. Field tests may demand registered personnel or specialists; they frequently require long, and very costly, periods of time. Administrative expenses increase accordingly. Also, the developer is asked to risk money on an uncertain event. Corrective measures on a finished building will be far costlier than errors in math or design detected during a permit review. It is instructive to examine the experience of communities in the enforcement of noise and air pollution standards. Most small communities and many larger ones simply cannot justify the cost of qualified full-time inspectors. Many do not even own the equipment needed to make the tests. Such communities depend on the deterrent value of the performance regulations to do the job they cannot. Finally, some measurements can only be taken after the occurrence of a unique event, such as a 100-year storm.

There is an additional difficulty associated with ascertaining compliance only after a project subject to regulation has been completed or substantially begun. If the regulation can only be enforced by a fine or criminal penalty, the offender may be punished, but the property rights of the neighbors or the general public (for whose protection the regulation was designed) are left to suffer. Given the choice between a regulation which may be enforced only after investment by a person having to comply with that regulation and one which may be applied and enforced at an earlier (e.g., permit) stage, justice certainly argues for the latter regulatory approach. Common sense as well as legal requirements dictate that a community should assess the probable (if not the precisely calculated) impacts that a proposed use will have before permitting development of that use to commence. When this can be accomplished economically and with ease, it is all the more clearly desirable.

There is some concern in the literature that performance standards not be confused with standards of design.[7] A performance standard is a regulation which specifies a level of performance that is measured to determine compliance, while a design standard is a regulation which dictates a specific design solution for a given level of performance. If the state of the art in planning were sufficiently advanced so that measures of performance were readily available for all planning concerns, this distinction would be impor-

tant because a pure performance standard approach to design would be possible. In all too many areas, however, planners must rely on art, not science, because proven scientific measures simply are not available. Relevant, but unanswered, questions include: What is the visual opacity of various tree species and how does it vary with the seasons? What is the trip generation rate of a shoe store? Is an office building more or less obnoxious than a restaurant? What, in fact, are the accurate indices of obnoxiousness? For a profession proud of its scientific roots, such unanswered questions are often embarrassing. The model ordinance contained herein is the product of eight years of research, funded with over a quarter of a million dollars. It has been necessary to develop design standards capable of meeting given levels of performance. The principal objection to design standards is that they rarely permit more than a single design solution and thus impose monotony. The model ordinance usually provides several acceptable design standards of equal performance, thereby permitting a variety of design solutions. In many areas, further research may provide infinite flexibility through the conversion of the solutions into a design formula. The question to be asked then is whether that degree of design flexibility is sufficient to warrant the additional complexity and increased costs of administration. Frequently the answer will be negative.

Problems are posed when one seeks to determine whether to use a pure performance standard or a performance-based design standard. Whether the standard is defining an acceptable level of performance for single or multiple goals is one problem. Another is the level of complexity for both designer and administrator. Lastly, there is the question of whether the designer is left the freedom and responsibility to provide acceptable performance for each component. In the end, the drafter of the ordinance must weigh the complexity of the design problem against the flexibility permitted by the standard selected. These issues can be illustrated by the following example.

It is certainly possible to develop a pure performance standard for lot size where septic tanks are to be used (based on spacings, minimum disposal areas, and soils) and to let designers plot all the various dimensions out, allowing the variables to control lot size. This would offer the greatest flexibility and freedom. The designer would be required to develop individual lot plans using these standards, and the result would be varying lot sizes and shapes and substantial design costs. The use of odd shapes might enable considerable land to be saved. But irregularly shaped lots have undesirable features. Ultimately the question the community must ask is whether all this complexity is necessary. For example, would not three to five lot sizes, each tied to soils with similar properties for septic disposal fields, be an easier, quicker, and less expensive approach for all concerned? In this case the answer is probably yes, and a design standard with performance-based criteria is probably the best solution.

Subsequent sections of this book will describe how some of the specific performance criteria in the model ordinance were developed. It is appropriate at this point, however, to address the general questions which always seem to be asked about performance standards: Are they arbitrary? Is there a scientific process which guides the setting of standards? How are the courts likely to interpret the way in which the standards were developed?

It has been suggested that one obstacle to enactment of a performance standard zoning ordinance is that enabling legislation does not authorize it. Local authority to zone is limited by each state's zoning enabling act(s); however, the Standard Zoning Enabling Act, which was developed by the Department of Commerce and has provided the basis for nearly every state's enabling legislation, reveals that the concern about performance zoning not being enabled is unfounded. The act authorizes, but does not require, communities to zone for particular purposes stated in the legislation. More than thirty of the fifty states have copied their statements of purpose verbatim from the Standard Act. The act authorizes zoning regulations regarding the "location and use of buildings, structures and land for trade, industry, residence or other purposes...designed to lessen congestion in the streets; to secure safety from fire, panic and other dangers; to promote health and the general welfare; to provide adequate light and air; to prevent the overcrowding of land; to facilitate the adequate provision of transportation, water, sewerage, schools, parks and other public requirements." To the extent that a performance approach to zoning is more accurate in its assumption that the nuisance and public-cost aspects of a use can be better regulated on an establishment-by-establishment basis, based on measurable differences among or between them, than they can be on a use-by-use basis, it is "more" enabled than the traditional zoning regulations. Because performance zoning refuses to make the clearly false assumption that all offices or commercial uses, for example, generate the same type and quantity of nuisance and impact, it is far more rational than the traditional approach, which does operate on this premise. Further, even the U.S. Supreme Court, which until the mid-1970's had stayed out of zon-

ing disputes, has indicated that innovative methods of land use regulation should be encouraged. In *Erznoznik v. City of Jacksonville* the court stated: "It is not our function to appraise the wisdom of [the city's] decision [to impose the challenged restriction on use].... The city's interest in attempting to preserve the quality of urban life is one that must be accorded high respect. Moreover, the city *must be allowed* a reasonable *opportunity to experiment with solutions to admittedly* serious problems" (emphasis added).[8]

The concern about arbitrariness which characterizes discussions of new techniques such as performance zoning rarely plagues planners when they consider conventional zoning ordinances. Today's conventional zoning ordinances regularly blend a number of traditional zoning regulations, nearly all of which are based on arbitrary judgments. There is no research-based justification for having three separate residential districts which require minimum lot sizes of 8,500, 10,000, and 12,000 square feet, respectively. Similarly, requirements for light, air, privacy, and fire access are not so precisely quantifiable as to provide rational justification for two to five foot variations in side yard standards between different zoning districts. Some ordinances permit doctors' offices in one commercial district but not those of architects or engineers. There are remarkably few studies that help a planner to decide what distinctions can and should be made. Parking patterns in shopping centers have been adequately investigated, but no other land uses have received similar study. Some food and retail chains have good data bases; others do not. A lack of sound research on various types of land use which identifies trip generation rates, floor area, employee ratios, peak hours, peak seasons, how customers are attracted, site coverage, rental rates, and other data is the greatest impediment to developing performance standards. Until more studies are conducted, those who are worried about such problems will have to resolve them as best they can. Nevertheless, standards can be developed, tested, and evaluated to the limits of the state of the art, and planners should not hesitate to move ahead on this basis.

With respect to how standards are set, it should be understood that there are several types of standards: those which require a considerable safety margin, those which allow a politically acceptable level of risk, and others which do not involve physical risk but rather establish a community's character. The first choice to be made is whether the standard should necessitate a safety margin to protect against a failure or disaster by overdesign or whether it should be based on an acceptable level of risk in accordance with the projected frequency or odds of a failure occurring. While science may be of assistance in determining the details, the ultimate choice with the second type of standard is clearly a legislative and political one. There will always be a conflict between the public interest and the individual's desire to do with land whatever he or she wishes. It is both a legislative prerogative and duty to seek a balance between the degree of protection and the cost of protection. The measure of a standard's constitutionality is basically twofold. The objective of the regulation must be within the police power. For most standards this is clearly the case, because they are aimed at public health, safety, and welfare. The second factor is whether the regulation is a reasonable way to provide this protection; if it is not, it is an unconstitutional "taking." Discussion of the costs to the private landowner of the method chosen to achieve a given level of protection will be reserved for later. For the moment, it is sufficient to note that performance zoning is distinctly more reasonable than conventional zoning in the setting of standards, because level of performance is inherent and obvious in the standards. This is not usually the case in conventional zoning. For example, when small, relatively homogenous communities have ten or more zoning districts, the distinctions among them may appear (and actually often be) trivial; consequently, a judicial body may conclude that different regulations for each of these separate districts is an unreasonable exercise of the community's police power. By contrast, performance zoning directly addresses many major issues such as resource protection and traffic control through standards whose impact can be evaluated. It is therefore more defensible as a reasonable regulatory approach.

In setting standards to protect the health, safety, and general welfare of a community, the planner must understand that there is a hierarchy of police power concerns in any area: real safety concerns such as threats to life, health, and property or insuring emergency access, general welfare concerns such as preservation of property values and community fiscal policy, and finally concerns involving a community's character, including aesthetics and design.

Both safety margin and level of risk standards require some rational basis, but each community must determine how detailed a study it can afford in order to supply that basis for any particular standard. A fire lane requirement provides an example of standard-setting issues. The width of the largest fire engine could be determined by contacting manufacturers; consulting local fire chiefs to determine reasonable operating clearances would provide data rapidly and inexpensively. More complicated studies could also take into account the dimensions of the surrounding structures; such dimensions might alter the width of a fire lane. An even more complex and scientific determination might involve case studies of real fires and such variables as the effect of wind, frequencies of walls collapsing, and so forth. None of these information bases is arbitrary. The question the local community must address is whether a significantly more precise and less subjective study at greater cost would result in a significantly different standard. The level of protection will ultimately be tested by determining whether the public protection (the land given to protect fire fighters and neighboring structures) is a reasonable one in terms of the private costs (reduced building area) imposed on landowners.

The decision whether to use a 50-year or a 100-year floodplain is a good example of a level of risk standard that is designed to provide protection "most of the time," but which involves the clearly political decision as to how long that period of time should be. As with many other natural phenomena, there is no known flood safety limit: there may always be a storm or flood of greater intensity. The legislators must determine what level of protection adequately serves the public good and does not exceed the price the public wants to pay.

This decision is more complicated than the case mentioned above where public protection need only be balanced against the private costs. With standards that set an acceptable level of risk to the public, each alternative standard has different benefits as well as different private costs. The higher the standard, the lower and less frequent will be the risk to the public. Thus, designing a dike to protect farm fields from flooding in a 25-year storm may be acceptable. The legislative decision is that the public purse cannot afford to protect the farmer against more severe storms and that the farmer may have to be subject to losses every twenty-five years. For an urban area, a different standard is likely to be required; for example, the dike may be designed to protect against a 100-year storm. With a nuclear power plant, a 500-year storm may be the minimum acceptable level of protection.

Although science may help a community's legislative body to assess the odds of a particular event and the costs of the associated regulation, it cannot accept the responsibility for compelling any particular political decision. Scientific precision may actually cause elected officials consternation

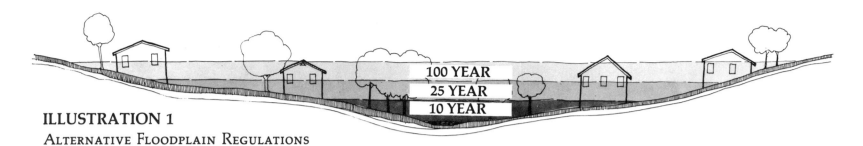

ILLUSTRATION 1
Alternative Floodplain Regulations

if the range of choices is made too explicit. Consider three possible standards for floodplain protection and their political implications (see illustration 1). The first standard, "no building in the 100-year floodplain," will force landowners to forego $300,000 in development potential but result in no deaths and no property damage per hundred years. The second, "no building in the 25-year floodplain," will cost landowners $200,000 and possibly result in two deaths and $1,000,000 in property damage. The third, "no building in the 10-year floodplain," would sacrifice only $100,000 of development potential but result in four possible deaths and $2,000,000 in damages. Providing the elected officials alternatives with this degree of scientific precision is laudable, but elected officials may prefer to make the decision without publicly admitting that a given number of deaths, for example, may be the result of their enactment of a particular standard.

The planner cannot wait until knowledge is complete but must make state-of-the-art judgments. This best-judgment issue should be of no greater concern in performance than in conventional zoning. Several guides for setting standards seem appropriate. Civilization has a long history of destroying its own environment. The great technological and scientific society that has developed since the Industrial Revolution is replete with a history of poisoned soils, contaminated water and air, blighted environments, desertification, flooding, and landslides. While planners cannot identify with precision the critical point for most natural systems, it is still possible to set standards. The proper direction for protection to take is easily identified. The planner should seek to err on behalf of the environment or public interest. Traditionally we have assumed that engineering would take care of all these environmental problems, but history proves that this is a false premise. The planners can inform the elected officials as to the basic conflict between the private rights and public interest. The basis of decisions should be the best information available, which should be documented in plans or even memoranda of record. Only rarely do communities invest in detailed research on zoning. Too often they depend on a search of the literature or on a collection of ordinances from other communities.

The general welfare concerns for preservation of property values and community fiscal stability, if they were dealt with at all by conventional zoning, depended solely on districting. This approach is far too unrefined and insensitive to the myriad variables to be satisfactory. Each separate concern must first be identified and goals with respect to it set. From this the best regulatory approach can be determined. The best approach may involve the use of multiple standards. Urban sprawl, for example, is a traditional concern of planners, because the cost of providing government services dramatically increases when development is widely scattered. Conventional zoning's use of districts to separate urban from nonurban uses is an obvious first step in preventing sprawl, but it will not suffice. Beyond this, intensity standards must be prescribed for the districts to insure the effectiveness of the strategy. In conventional zoning, a fine gradation of districts is used, which makes it difficult to control the economics of land so that growth is encouraged in locations where facilities can be efficiently provided and discouraged in other locations. The use of both districts and intensity standards may be contrasted with the search for standards that protect property values. Property values are maintained in part by protecting uses from the adverse impacts of adjoining uses. Districting has failed to protect, so bufferyards were introduced in performance zoning to do so. This required performance standards for intensity to enable similar nuisances to be grouped together, which in turn permitted the development of standards that would determine the amount of buffer required between uses of different groups.

This procedure of identifying needs, determining the form of the protective measures, and testing them for effect and reasonableness seems to be an adequate scientific basis for standards of the general welfare nature. The courts will often test such regulations in terms of their reasonableness when applied to actual situations. If the community has gone through this same procedure and can demonstrate that the standards provide needed protection at a reasonable cost, then the risk is low.

As in conventional zoning, performance zoning contains a number of regulations intended to set the character or quality of the community. Some of these regulations enhance property values or deal with other general welfare concerns. Often the regulations also have aesthetic or design implications. These standards are intended to insure that a zoning district develops into a community or neighborhood with specific characteristics. Zoning has always been used to create districts of different intensities and character. All state enabling laws permit this. In performance zoning not only the districts but land use intensity classes regulate intensity and character. The standards are more explicit in performance zoning than in conventional zoning ordinances. Performance zoning recognizes that signs, landscape features, lighting, building coverage, building height, building scale, and parking are important factors in determining intensity and character. Other district-wide standards also contribute to character. These standards are at the heart of zoning's central purpose and are therefore more easily understood by the courts. Performance zoning differs from conventional in that performance standards, not district standards, accomplish this goal. This is believed to avoid major problems in the districting approach.

Field observations demonstrate that for nonresidential uses there is often more variability within a given use than between uses permitted in different districts. Therefore, zoning which separates uses by district has led to numerous problems. The speculative zoning change is a good example. If there are too many uses within a conventional zoning district, the variation in nuisance value is too great; hence, petitions for a zoning change are accompanied by sets of pretty renderings and an excellent plan which is less intense than the maximum permitted by the district. This is a familiar phenomenon, as are the fruitless attempts of government to hold the speculator to his word through conditional rezonings. If too much variety is present within a district, the community seeks to prevent being taken in by misleading requests for zoning changes. The historical response to this need has been to seek greater control by adding more districts, conditional or special uses, all ad hoc procedures. The process has not led to increased control, just more zoning changes.

The basic concept of zoning has been that the highest uses, typically residential, need to be separated from the lowest in order to protect them from noise, dirt, and traffic and thus to preserve the character of different neighborhoods. This concept recognizes that land uses can create nuisances that extend beyond their boundaries.

Zoning is in part an exercise of the police power to control the location of nuisances which would adversely affect certain landowners. A very simple theory has been used in conventional zoning to deal with the nuisance problem: that uses can be adequately separated into districts of equal character by arranging them in a hierarchy. This strategy is too simple, and the controversy that often surrounds zoning hearings is an indication that it has failed. A survey of residents, planners, elected officials, and zoning enforcement people in Lake County, Illinois found that the theory works best for uses at the extremes of the hierarchy.[9] There was close agreement on the rating of uses at the top and bottom of the hierarchy. Uses in the middle were subject to a wider variety of rankings. The lack of consensus substantiates the notion that there may be a wider variety of intensities and nuisances within a use than between some uses. Performance zoning utilizes a more complex strategy in which there are fewer general land use types (eighteen versus 283 in the present Lake County ordinance); however, most types of use in performance zoning are further subdivided into several of the eleven land use intensity classifications which determine nuisance potential. Gross density, floor area ratio, impervious surface ratio, total trips per acre in twenty-four hours, and height are some of the criteria used to determine the land use intensity classification. Landscaping, lighting, signs, exterior storage, road location, and hours of operation complete these performance criteria. In combination these standards provide a more precise definition of use intensity than is employed in conventional zoning. They are standards which can be measured with some precision. This classification system provides a definition of uses which more closely approximates the reality of how people actually relate to different land uses. The details of the land use intensity classification system are discussed later.

An issue related to the scientific nature of performance standards is the lack of research on land use. Very little has been done to develop a good data base on various land use types. Such a simple question as how many parking spaces per square foot are needed for a land use type is difficult to answer. Shopping centers alone have been adequately addressed. This issue has been raised previously and should not be ignored. Although John Reps gave zoning its requiem in 1964,[10] it still remains the main tool of local and county planners. Its achievements will and should be questioned, but in the absence of a complete reversal of legal precedent zoning will remain with us for years to come. One reason for zoning's previous ineffectiveness is that the academic community has demonstrated little interest in improving the state of the art. University-related centers for basic research in urban studies and federal funding agencies have never given zoning research a priority. Local or even county agencies cannot afford to take on such research without a significant study subsidy because of the manpower demands of such studies. The studies are hardly exciting, but their importance should not continue to be ignored.

In closing this section it seems appropriate to address another set of commonly asked questions about the administration of performance zoning. Can performance zoning be used by cities and towns? Does performance zoning require larger staffs and more complex administration? Is it possible for small communities to use it?

The model ordinance was developed for use in suburban areas that are undergoing development or are under developmental pressure. It can be used in larger cities with urban renewal areas, but may require significant alteration since the intensities will be higher. Further, there will be many areas that do not need performance zoning because they are built up. Smaller towns and cities may find it quite useful either for in-fill or for growth areas on their fringes.

Performance zoning should not increase staffing, if the community is adequately staffed to administer its current ordinance. Many communities try to muddle through without professional staff; the greater complexity of performance zoning will make this practice more difficult. All too many communities use arm-twisting to achieve their desires. Arm-twisting is much costlier in its demands on staff and developers than is performance zoning, and its results are less predictable. Moreover, a reduction of the number of zoning changes, which are very costly both to local government and to future landowners, may be expected.

Community size is not a critical factor unless the community does not have access to a professional planner. Communities with as few as one thousand residents are using performance zoning. It is only essential that the community be able to obtain the assistance of professional planners to review site plans. Such assistance can come from county, regional, or state planning agencies, or from private consultants. Fee schedules should totally support this activity. Lay planning commissions and elected officials should have access to this assistance in any event.

Having defined performance zoning and reviewed some basic concerns and techniques, we will next discuss the planning base for a model ordinance and then examine the ordinance, covering those sections which differ substantially from conventional ordinances.

Planning for Performance Zoning

Whether zoning is required by statute to be "in compliance with the comprehensive plan" in any state or not, zoning without planning is a means without an end. Foremost among the concerns that brought performance zoning into existence was a sense of frustration over the inability of zoning to meet the goals of planning. Plans are supposed to be implemented, not to be an exercise in utopian thinking, and conventional zoning has done little to implement policy plans. In the area of housing, for instance, conventional zoning has impeded the provision of decent housing. Only a few state courts (Pennsylvania and New Jersey) have held exclusionary zoning to be an illegal practice. There is no question that many communities have avoided their responsibilities to low and moderate income groups by refusing to permit any significant multi-family or attached housing. Further, there is little debate among planners that conventional zoning practices have accelerated the inflation of housing costs. With respect to other important planning objectives such as environmental protection, elimination of traffic congestion, avoiding conflicting land uses, or saving energy, the best that can be said is that conventional zoning has not had much effect, beneficial or otherwise. However much planners object to its specific findings, Siegan's *Land Use without Zoning* presents an indictment of zoning that should not be totally ignored. A comparison of zoned metropolitan areas and rural communities that have never adopted zoning will highlight the conclusion that zoning has contributed little to the creation of well-planned living environments. Some of the most exciting communities, Radburn, New Jersey, the village center in Reston, Virginia, and the plaza in Lake Forest, Illinois, were either built before zoning or created by developers who wrote the zoning to conform to their land plans. Some of the worst strip commercial areas, the most monotonous suburbs, and most insensitive environmental planning have occurred with the blessing and at the mandate of local zoning.

Performance zoning is intended to correct some of these problems. There should be a clear connection between performance zoning and the community's plan. The first and most important issue to be decided is the degree to which a community really wants to plan. Performance zoning, unlike conventional zoning, is capable of managing the community's development over an extended period of time. The model ordinance is designed to exercise considerable control over the location and timing of growth, but does not address the issue of growth versus nongrowth. In an urbanizing community, it can determine where development should take place and therefore where land values will rise, as they have historically done in the suburbs. It also identifies where rural or exurban land values will predominate. There are big capital gains at stake in such distinctions. Thus, opposition to performance zoning may be expected. Opponents will debate the appropriateness of the standards or techniques, but their real criticism is that performance zoning spells an end to ad hoc zoning changes and speculative increases in land value. Vocal opponents are often those who in the past opposed land use controls in the first place, but have been placated by conventional zoning's inability to control a community's future. In suburban situations, those who make money as land speculators or as their agents use the ad hoc system to their advantage and to the detriment of the community as a whole. These people pay lip service to planning. They find it convenient to have the trappings of planning so long as it does not restrict their ability to use their land as they wish. Plans that deal in platitudinous pronouncements and nebulous or general terms frequently fail to specify how the goals are to be achieved and thus are not threatening. Too many individuals want just enough planning to appear progressive or to receive federal monies but not enough to threaten the potential for freewheeling speculation.

Insofar as performance zoning is intended to translate the goals and policies of the plan into a legislative enactment, a first stage in the planning process is for a community to determine what sort of control it wants to exercise over development. In view of the fact discussed above that "support" of a plan often goes little beyond platitudinous statements, it is important for a community, in the first analysis, to understand clearly the role it wants for planning. It is particularly unsettling to those drafting or working with the zoning ordinance to be told repeatedly that the ordinance or plan "is not engraved in stone." It is disturbing because it is a tacit recognition that some elected officials would prefer not to have a meaningful plan. Rather, these officials exhibit only that degree of support needed to give the appearance that they have a plan, which in turn lends credence to their ad hoc decisions.

Performance zoning is flexible; it can adapt to a range of control options but cannot really work efficiently in the ad hoc systems which predominate today. Performance zoning can be used to control where or how growth takes place, and in either case it will eliminate many objectionable elements of the process that now makes these determinations. The decision as to what degree of control a community wishes to exercise should be made early. Performance zoning seeks to be a management device and will not live up to its promise if the community only wishes to react to the pressures around it.

A community land use plan is a prerequisite of performance zoning. An adequate land use plan should differ in detail and format from the models that have been foisted upon us through years of planning under federal programs. Performance zoning is expected to *achieve*; therefore, the familiar, endless sections of data analysis will not suffice as "plans." In most suburban communities growth management is the central issue. The land use plan should contain an estimate of the projected population. A general regional estimate of growth should be available in most areas. Such estimates should be explicit and specify their assumptions (birth and death rates, immigration) so that changing trends can easily be identified and adjustments of the plan made as necessary. Further, where capital investments are likely to dictate the spatial distribution of land uses, alternate spatial configurations should be developed so that inconsistencies between land use and capital facilities planning can be resolved. For example, sewers should be available in an area planned to be urbanized and not in an area that is to remain rural.

Local municipalities in particular should be sensitive to the implications of large-scale, regional capital investment as well as to local investment. Nothing is more pitiful than watching a municipality that is hungry for growth and tax rateables but has been bypassed by new freeways and other transportation improvements. Its own investments in sewer and water will not attract the development it seeks, because it is competitively at such a disadvantage when compared to other locations in the region having good access to transportation facilities.

County and regional agencies should, but probably will not, address these issues to insure that communities do not invest unwisely, Highways, sewers, water supply, airports, and major recreational facilities are all capital investments that will influence where growth goes. Zoning cannot successfully control development if investment decisions regarding land use and facilities by both the community and the region do not coincide. Major changes in the location of capital investment should trigger a comprehensive review of the land use plan and zoning ordinance.

Planning concerns can broadly be divided into three levels. At the macro-level are decisions which channel growth into one area instead of another or which deal with regionally important locational issues. The distinction between rural, suburban, or central cities is certainly a macro-level decision. The location of an airport or a heavy industrial complex or the conservation of wilderness or agricultural areas are likewise decisions of regional importance.

At the intermediate level are decisions needed to achieve a specific purpose or planning goal. Such land use decisions are compatible with the macro-level classifications, but contain important modifying distinctions. The distinction between a rural district and an agricultural district is illustrative. Both districts are designed to permit continued agricultural lands; the rural district gives temporary protection to agricultural use, all the while acknowledging the eventual conversion to urban uses—a distinction of considerable importance. The goal of the rural district is not to preserve a specific resource, prime agricultural land.

The micro-level concerns deal with problems at the interface of a single proposed land use and its neighbors, or with community facilities and physical site characteristics. The protection of adjoining land uses from nuisances generated by the proposed use is an example of a micro-level planning issue.

Comprehensive plans have traditionally laid the groundwork for conventional zoning by focusing on the location of specific land use types, (i.e., central business, highway commercial) and on the intensity of different residential areas. These decisions are primarily intermediate level. Comprehensive plans have usually, and wrongly, ignored the micro-level. Emphasis on the intermediate level has confused or weakened the policies dealing with the macro-level. The conventional zoning ordinance often has several districts within each of the comprehensive plan's land use classifications; this practice weakens or blurs important distinctions further. The Lake County Zoning Ordinance of 1966, for example, has ten districts that are basically residential. In such a framework it is very difficult to implement the land use distinctions, such as those between rural areas and developing suburban centers, called for in a comprehensive plan.

Performance zoning increases the emphasis on macro-level decisions. There are sharp and distinctive breaks between the rural districts and development districts in contrast with the gradation typical of conventional zoning. Further, as part of the rezoning process, the model ordinance requires a review of the assumptions on which the development areas were sized.

sized. Other districts such as heavy industrial or agricultural have unique locational criteria; performance zoning articulates those criteria as the basis on which the districts will be located. Not only does performance zoning deemphasize intermediate decisions by reducing the number of districts and focusing on districts whose purposes are distinctly different, it also shifts the burden of separating uses from each other to the micro-level. This means that the emphasis is on planning criteria at the intermediate level, not on conventional land use types. The micro-level concerns do not involve districting. Specific performance standards address each of these concerns at the time a particular development is proposed, instead of attempting to segregate them into different zoning districts.

There are only four basic classes of land: rural, developing, developed, and special. All of these classes have unique planning problems, and the conversion from rural developing is always a critical land use decision. Each has several possible subcategories, but these should be based on important distinctions which can be validly generalized. The basis of a comprehensive plan is the identification of these basic districts and the zoning and other policies intended to implement the goals of the plan. It is possible to incorporate a short plan right into the introduction or statement of purpose of a zoning ordinance.[11] The following is an outline of the various planning areas.

Rural: an area that should remain rural for the planning period either because it is not needed for development or because it is best suited for rural uses. Such areas must not be provided with urban services or utilities, public sewers, public waters, or major highway extensions. The subcategories are agricultural, wilderness, rural, holding zone, and estate.

Developing: areas intended to handle most of the community's growth needs. The following districts should be sized to handle the community's growth for the entire planning period: development, urban core, heavy industrial, transportation center.

Developed: areas which are already developed. Their intensity runs the gamut from estate to urban core. Unlike the development areas where growth is the driving force, renewal or conservation is the concern to be addressed in the following districts: neighborhood conservation, commercial conservation, and redevelopment.

Special: districts intended to meet special needs which may not be present in all communities. Because of their attributes they may occur in areas which might also be classified in several of the other major categories. Examples of special districts are the conservation and historic districts.

Each of these performance zoning planning areas is significantly different in character and purpose. The purposes and intent of these areas are elaborated in the section which discusses the districts of the model ordinance. If these major areas are planned adequately, a community should be able to achieve the goals of its comprehensive plan. Several examples will point out the necessity for the distinctions which are made. The estate and development districts, though both can be largely residential, place totally different demands on a community. The development district must have urban services, especially public sewers, and its residential population expects and can economically support commercial ventures and services. The estate district cannot be provided with urban-level services in a cost-effective manner, and its character is not generally compatible with commercial developments. The different functions of these two districts should not be confused through an ad hoc rezoning process. An estate area should be viewed as a final land use, not as a holding zone. Similarly, the regionally significant urban cores, whether or not they are primarily commercial in nature, are areas adjoining a transit station, which means that there clearly is justification for substantially more intense development there. A distinction between the urban core and the development district is that the former is of regional importance; thus special locational criteria apply to its location which need not be considered for the development district as a whole.

The planning process is capable of determining the appropriate size and location of each of the development districts. The data needed for these decisions include population growth, family size, and construction and phasing of major public investments. After districts are located and sized, any proposed change is important enough that the elected officials should have to debate publicly its merits in the light of the original assumptions. It is inappropriate to debate whether a zoning change should permit a shoe store or 7-Eleven using the same criteria or process that would be used to determine whether a large tract of land is suitable for a regional shopping center or suburban housing. Conventional zoning makes no distinction between such decisions. Performance zoning is concerned only that the shoe store or 7-Eleven meet all applicable performance standards, but it requires a full legislative review and rezoning when major land use decisions, such as the location of a regional shopping center, are raised.

While a basic comprehensive plan is essential to make performance zoning achieve its purpose, there are selected additional planning studies or elements that may or may not be necessary in every jurisdiction but whose benefits should be considered. Performance zoning is environmentally oriented. A separate study or a section of the comprehensive plan addressing the protection of natural resources is vital. Since these standards are central to the ability of performance zoning to protect the environment, their documentation is of considerable importance from both the planning and legal perspectives. Since different regions of the country contain different environments, this is an element that deserves special attention in tailoring the plan to local needs. This area of concern is more fully discussed on pages 322–25.

If wilderness, conservation, historic, rural, or agricultural districts are to be zoned, a supporting policy plan should be prepared. These are areas in which property rights are most likely to conflict with the public interest because the regulations needed to implement these districts often result in the most extreme break from the traditional land use practices. Because conflict frequently erupts where there are economic implications or major changes, a public airing can be helpful in establishing the policy before any ordinance regulations are drafted.

A traffic element is recommended because the existing highway capacity is increasingly likely to be a limiting factor on development in many areas. If a development district is planned for an area with inadequate roads or if an initial development district will bring roads to capacity, this should be known in advance. A strategy for dedication of road right-of-way and a program for making required improvements should be planned before a zoning ordinance setting land use intensities, which may overburden the highway network, is adopted. Unfortunately, most planners must attempt to protect the capacity of highways by refusing to grant a zoning change. Performance zoning provides a new approach to this issue. A new approach is required because of the failure of transportation plans to address the correct issues. The transportation plans in most metropolitan areas attempt at a regional level to develop major improvements on freeways and mass transit lines to handle a future population. At the local level, the regional plan is likely to be accepted without thought; there is not likely to be a comprehensive arterial improvement plan. Such planning is predicated on the construction of sufficient numbers of freeways. It presumes that arterial congestion will then be tolerable. Traffic congestion is a concern of

local residents, so that assumption is dubious at best. In any event, such plans have proved too ambitious because the required funding has never been available.

A transportation plan which concentrates on preserving the integrity of the existing arterial system is a badly needed planning component. Some notes of caution are in order. Since transportation plans often test a whole network, failure to complete them or even phased development may result in vastly different results from those predicted. A partially complete system that dead-ends in some unlucky community may be worse than no system at all to those located in such a place. A transportation study should concentrate on developing an understanding of where and for how long a road functions below some specified acceptable level. Transportation plans must develop a mechanism for controlling access to, or preserving the integrity of, the existing road network, which would avoid many congestion problems. Finally, a clear understanding of the traffic implications of a land use plan is important if performance zoning is to deal effectively with traffic congestion.

Planners and both appointed and elected officials should strive for a greater understanding of what they are trying to achieve in terms of a living and working environment. While communities are often articulate in voicing their concerns about a development, traffic congestion, environmental protection, noise, dirt, glare, and other nuisances, they frequently adopt plans and ordinances that do not address these concerns. For example, to deal with traffic congestion by creating a district for highway-related uses which generate large numbers of trips per acre fails to confront the issues of road capacity and intensity, access control, and road improvements. Similarly, officials may not understand how zoning districts, lot sizes, density, and other standards relate to the traffic or environmental concerns which they have been able to identify.

Conventional zoning so fails to control land use effectively that it has been characterized as a "game."[12] In this game, for example, the community tries to arm-twist the developer into reducing density. The developer, knowing the community's "game" plan, inflates the density of the original proposal in order to end up with the density actually desired.

Today, the administration of conventional zoning is closer to trench warfare than a game. The failure of many communities to develop ordinances that reflect their concerns or to understand the connection between a standard and an actual piece of construction or development are major reasons that the communities respond as they do. When officials see what their zoning has produced, it too often displeases them. Why else do communities which have worked on a zoning ordinance for years and finally adopted it start the arm-twisting all over again? Perhaps the ordinance does not achieve what they want.

Performance zoning can effectively manage the problems associated with traffic, environment, and community character. If a community is in doubt about the solution to a particular problem, it should take actual sites that represent the problem and lay them out pursuant to different sets of performance standards. This pretesting of regulatory standards can avoid disappointments later by insuring that the standards adopted will, in fact, achieve the desired end.

Legislative Intent

This section explains Article I of the model ordinance. The differences between performance zoning and conventional zoning become apparent in this article. It contains two sections not found in conventional zoning ordinances. The first explains the use of "commentaries." The second is a section on legislative intent and will be the subject of this discussion.

Commentaries are provided throughout the ordinance to explain its reasoning and rationale. The commentary is used to define, for the courts and public, what the legislative body was attempting to do when specific language was included in the text. The purpose and reasoning behind the choice of a standard may also be detailed in the commentary. In yet other cases, the language is explanatory in nature. The purpose is to separate the legislative reasoning from the general text of the ordinance. This is frequently done in legislative documents and is intended to be helpful in the future. The commentary is meant to be a useful part of the body of the adopted ordinance, not just an explanatory guide to the model.

The commentary is a useful technique to provide detail which is not appropriately mixed with the basic text of an ordinance. It is needed because administrators, judges, and developers often do not know the precise intent or rationale of a particular regulation. In most cases, a developer or an official need not read the commentary in order to use the ordinance. It can prove helpful when greater understanding is sought. The commentary may, however, become increasingly valuable with time. For example, it is possible that in the future no official involved in writing the ordinance will be available to explain why something was done. Furthermore, similar discussions are usually absent from conventional ordinances or occasionally buried in the text. Performance zoning seeks to separate, as three distinct textual elements, operational language, discussion of purpose, and the commentary intended to explain or detail regulation. This should make reading the ordinance far easier than when all three elements are mixed together in a single paragraph or statement.

The statement of legislative intent in Article I is a major component of performance zoning. There has always been a tension between the public interest, on whose behalf the police power is exercised, and the individual's freedom and property rights. Unfortunately, most of the discussion of these issues is to be found in legal rather than planning journals. Consequently, planners have with few exceptions tended to ignore these problems. There has been little discussion of how to accommodate the interests of both parties in an ordinance. Transfer of development rights is one of the few exceptions, and the legal profession dominates the literature even in this area. Planners have taken the easy way out and simply chosen to join one side or the other. In conventional zoning, this means a choice between protecting the neighbors or giving the individual the right to build. This has kept the courts busy. But the courts are usually also limited to choosing one side or the other, thereby perpetuating the problem. In conceiving performance zoning, two questions were thoroughly explored. What are the critical elements that zoning must control? How can the inherent conflict between control and freedom best be resolved? Most attempts to improve zoning have sought to deal with such issues, not by developing better standards, but by turning to ad hoc decision making. After sixty years of experience a complete reassessment of that approach was necessary; it led to the rejection of the present system. A new philosophy was developed which can accommodate both community goals and private rights.

The conventional wisdom of the profession maintains that zoning must control land use decisions down to a rather fine scale. Yet the original zoning ordinance in New York had only five zoning districts, and many early zoning ordinances had inclusive zones (that is, all uses were permitted in the least restrictive zone). Over time more and more uses were deleted and new districts created to obtain better control.

Today it is rare to find a zoning ordinance having fewer than ten zoning districts, and many uses are permitted only in one district. The assumption that more districts will result in better control of development in any specific location has proved false. First, it is completely at odds with the reality of the real estate market in America. In addition, the ability of planners to determine accurately the optimal land use for an individual site is doubtful, as the number of requests for zoning changes that are heard documents. Business, even if the cost factor is excluded, does not seek the best site for a new store or plant. It seeks the best *available* site. Availability is a concept that is foreign to planners. Only a fraction of the sites in a community may be for sale at any given time. With a restricted supply of land further broken down into ten or more zoning districts, it should be clear that zoning may create a situation where there are few if any sites available that are properly zoned. It is also erroneous to presume that planners and business use the same criteria for selecting the best locations. It may be valid to say that planners know where development should or should not occur, or what locations are regionally important, and what areas have unique potential due to access, resources, and location; but it is presumptuous for the municipal planner to claim to have similarly accurate criteria for locating a shoe store. Performance zoning accomplishes spatial control of land use with a minimum number of zoning districts. Then, within those districts, control is exercised by making each use pass a series of performance tests.

The cost factor adds more complications. While some uses can afford almost any price for the optimum location, others cannot. Zoning land into increasingly more precise districts can and does drive prices up. That in turn creates business for the speculator. The speculator profits by obtaining a zoning change because he buys land cheap and increases its value by rezoning it. In general, the increased specialization of districts has been accomplished by a declining supply of land for most uses, which makes speculation more attractive. These cost considerations make it more unlikely that land will be appropriately zoned and priced.

In developing zoning districts, one need only be concerned with major forms of land use decisions. A zoning change from rural or agricultural uses to urban, suburban, or exurban uses is such a major land use decision. What land is urbanized is a central concern in land use planning. Decisions of this sort have significant impacts on the cost of government services and therefore should be carefully considered. Urban sprawl or improperly located development can cost the public substantially more than a planned development in the proper location. In many areas, precise land use is not an issue of the same type of importance as whether available capacity exists in the sewer treatment plant or interceptor lines. Other planning concerns such as whether a development can be served by gravity flow or requires a pump station are generally insensitive to land use. Even in measures of performance such as traffic generation there may be differences within traditional land use groupings that are larger than differences between groupings. Where land uses require a different level of governmental service—rural versus urban—there is a legitimate need for a distinction. Areas of special concern—rural, agricultural, historic, wilderness, or conservation—that are determined by their natural or man-made characteristics and need extensive protection are land use categories for which public control is essential.

Areas of regional importance—urban cores, airports, and heavy industrial zones—are areas where planning input is vital to the public interest. Thus, performance zoning deals in terms of zoning districts with very coarse-grained land use distinctions. In this way it permits within developing areas nearly all uses, provided that the uses can meet all the performance criteria. Performance zoning deals with issues of major importance, but leaves landowners a wide range of choices. It thereby attempts to meet the concerns and needs of the general public, while also meeting the needs of the landowner. This does not eliminate conflict, but reduces it to areas where it really counts.

Another way of viewing the conflict between public interest and private rights is as a conflict between those who view land as a commodity to be bought and sold freely and those who believe that land is a finite resource belonging not only to the landowner but to the public and future generations which must be protected. The real estate profession has developed the concept of "highest and best use" based on land as a commodity, with zoning a device to be used to increase land values. The planning profession has a totally different perception of "highest and best use." In many instances the applications of the two views are mutually exclusive. In planning theory, all land is reviewed, and land best suited for particular uses is identified; thus, for the planner "highest and best use" means the use to which a piece of land is best suited. That determination relates to the physical characteristics of the land, to the site's location with respect to regional activities and to other land uses, transportation, and utilities, and to the growth pressures operating on an area. The two theories are in agreement only when the land use identified by the planners is the most economically profitable use or when the only marketable land use is the same as the use for which it has been planned.

The planning profession is guilty of prolonging the conflict between the commodity and resource views of the land. Planners have been reluctant to admit that their proponents have valid concerns. Conventional zoning's evolution toward ever more districts and discretionary procedures has exacerbated the problem by increasing the number of rezoning or discretionary reviews that are conducted. Because the courts have expanded the definition of the police power and have upheld all of the discretionary procedures, the planning profession has little reason to seek a different philosophy. The wisdom of continuing this battle must be questioned. First, it is a battle whose outcome is always unpredictable. The ad hoc nature of the process breeds inconsistency. The plans that are supposed to serve as guides are often vague or ignored. The changing nature of government continually introduces new people and philosophies. The ability to appeal decisions to different groups—planners, elected officials, and the courts—also decreases predictability. If the results are unpredictable, the system has little to recommend it.

The conflict is a costly one. These costs are borne by taxpayers and new residents. Planning staffs must continually review zoning changes, a major job in many communities. This increases staffing requirements and often decreases time available to do planning. The costs of delays, permits, and risks taken by developers are passed on to the final purchaser as higher costs for homes, offices, and business. Zoning is supposed to insure a better future, not to stop the future from coming. Planners are not supposed to be the enemy of development, although there are many citizens who believe this is planning's mission. Zoning should not be obstructionist; all needs should be met in the best possible manner.

As performance zoning has evolved over the years, the need to take into account both views has become increasingly evident. Ignoring the rights of the landowner is counterproductive. Yet land is both a commodity and a resource. Both views have validity, and the world is too complex to attempt to plan for only one of them. In a democracy, legislative bodies are subject to pressures from competing groups; legislation ultimately bears the imprint of compromise. That is the philosophy behind performance zoning. Its goal is to maximize freedom while still protecting the general welfare and providing for a better living environment in the future. The existence of a society with many competing goals is explicitly recognized in performance zoning.

In developing a strategy to implement this general philosophy, the different groups and interests involved must be identified. There are two types of property owners with differing interests: the first landowner seeks to profit from the development or redevelopment of his piece of land, while the owner of developed property has invested his life savings in a house and neighborhood. This second landowner seeks to perpetuate the character of the neighborhood and insure the appreciation of his investment. There are three general groups of individuals and/or communities that have different interests in any prospective development. The community and residents thereof seek to enhance the tax base and character of the area. Other communities of the general region and their residents may be competing for the same ratables and population. Third, individual residents of the greater region are likely to have an interest as future residents of the development. There is a tension between the desires of these different groups. Thus, there

There is a tension between the desires of these different groups. Thus, there is a whole set of needs that should be accommodated. The needs of the present landowner are quite different from the aspirations of the future owners of that land. When development pressures first reach an area, the landowner and his neighbors have similar desires. The neighbors do not object to his developing the land because it will increase their land values. The homeowners and landowners who move to the first development do so because it is a community with open space, low taxes, and a rural character—near a city. Having moved in, the homeowners become the neighbors in subsequent rounds of development. The land that provided the open space and rural character which prompted their move did not belong to them but to others; thus, a conflict exists. The future resident will side with the developer in the first round but join the neighbors for the next.

As it evolved, performance zoning attempted to integrate these competing needs into a single ordinance. For the property owner, freedom, flexibility, and a minimum of delay in obtaining permits are important. Performance zoning seeks to maximize freedom and flexibility by providing the landowner with many options as to how he may develop his land. When compared with conventional zoning, performance zoning inevitably will permit a wider range of choices in a given zoning district. There are often many different uses to choose from and several alternative ways of developing most uses. In the developing area residential, commercial, and most industrial uses will not need a zoning change and thus will be spared expense and delays. But different intensities require different levels of performance, and inevitably the choices have different economic consequences. This is a normal economic fact of life. Consumers and businessmen face these choices daily, so developers and speculators should not be unduly upset if zoning standards explicitly require the same sorts of choices. Landowners, however, cannot do anything they want or develop at any intensity. Land zoned for rural or conservation purposes will be comparatively more severely restricted than land zoned for development. Likewise, there will be individual properties whose locational and site characteristics will restrict their development potential. Performance zoning specifically accounts for such limitations; it is a technique not incompatible with a free market approach.

In a pure free market, the productivity of land would be taken into account. In rural communities, farmers set value in terms of the land's productivity; not all land is of equal value in such a system. An eroded hillside farm on a north slope may have little value compared to a flat site with deep, rich, and well-drained soils. Performance zoning seeks to insure that the more restrictive sites have some potential for development. In designing the standards for the most restrictive zones the intent has been to provide for a reasonable use of the land when it must be developed. Performance zoning provides an additional degree of choice by permitting the land-owner to transfer development rights or to develop in a noncontiguous fashion as options to developing his land in the most restrictive zones.

How does performance zoning protect the interests of the neighbor or the community? First, it provides the public with some forms of protection it does not now have under conventional zoning. Conventional zoning is a win or lose proposition much like Russian roulette. The neighbors' objections, however valid, are thrown to the wind when a zoning change is granted by the municipality or a court. This is hardly fair. The landowner suffers fiscal losses if his petition is denied, but this is not a reason that the neighbors should risk a fiscal loss if the petition is approved. Good legislation seeks to protect both parties; performance zoning provides more opportunities to the landowner, but also sets levels of protection that must be afforded adjoining land uses. An insured level of protection not subject to the outcome of ad hoc proceedings is a new form of protection. The community residents and neighbors will find that performance zoning contains standards that insure protection of the environment, provision of recreational land, and maintenance of highways at a level of service designed to prevent congestion. These are all matters about which neighbors complain during zoning hearings. In conventional zoning, residents must exercise continued vigilance and fight any development that threatens their interest because denial of the right to build is the only protection offered. In both conventional and performance zoning, protection is afforded where no zoning change or other ad hoc proceeding is involved. Where a zoning change occurs, protection of the neighbors will still be guaranteed in performance zoning but not in conventional zoning. It is guaranteed because the standards are built into the ordinance. This is reflected in the presence of standards which are not generally found in zoning ordinances. Performance zoning grants more complete protection to existing residents while still managing to increase freedom of choice for the landowner without requiring ad hoc proceedings—a compromise from which both parties should benefit.

An example of this protection is the bufferyard. While some zoning ordinances require bufferyards between residential districts and industrial districts, there was little research on their adequacy. Further, bufferyards were not required between all districts. In performance zoning a hierarchy of uses based on potential nuisance has been developed and serves, in conjunction with bufferyards, as the basic mode of protecting one use from the adverse impacts of another. The landowner can be certain that whatever use may ultimately be built next door a bufferyard will protect him. The degree of protection required is directly related to the relative nuisance the new use is likely to cause. When compared to conventional zoning this device enables the community to provide protection without the need for an ad hoc decision on the appropriateness of the use.

The need for open space is an important concern. Open space and rural living are among the words used by people in the suburbs to describe why they choose to live in these communities. Yet the open spaces to which they refer are often owned by other landowners and are not their own yards. Years of experience at zoning hearings indicate that vacant parcels in suburban areas, whether they are a straggly field of weeds or a mature forest, are considered an important asset which the neighbors seek to preserve.

Suburbs that were on the urban fringe in the 1950s are now filled up and aging, with the result that people become dissatisfied with overcrowding. Those who moved to suburban or rural environments in the 1950s and 1960s are now surrounded by city. They are seeking homes in new suburbs farther out in order to recapture the rural environment they have lost.

Performance zoning requires significant open spaces and recreational areas and contains standards which protect natural features and resources. This insures the retention of significant open space elements as a community is built. In conventional zoning, open space is land zoned for future development. Zoning which protects community character is good for both the present residents, who rightly feel protective, and for future residents, who will also seek a quality living environment. Unlike conventional large lot zoning, which has been the normal government response to environmental goals, performance zoning achieves this protection without reducing the general value of land.

Performance zoning's attempt to seek a compromise through which valid concerns of both the public and the landowner can be met is unique. This philosophy is reflected in the standards. At each step in the development of standards, the costs and benefits to various groups were examined. The decisions of performance zoning are not win or lose; they are permissive, yet also provide for the protection of the public. This is a new notion. If it can reduce the antagonism between the developers and planners, then performance zoning will have achieved an important goal. By consciously attempting to protect all interests as the standards were developed, performance zoning has broken with the tradition of ad hoc ministerial decisions and made a conscious legislative attempt to resolve fairly basic philosophical differences.

Using this same philosophy, performance zoning has been able to deal comprehensively with conflicts that have proved intractable under conventional zoning. This is important, particularly in the light of the growing dissatisfaction with a long-standing legal precedent, the presumption of validity. A legislative act is presumed to be valid unless the aggrieved party can clearly demonstrate substantial constitutional or legal grounds to declare it void. While the adoption of a zoning ordinance is clearly a legislative act, the courts have recently taken to questioning whether map changes have this same legal standing. In conventional zoning, with its history of more discretionary techniques and finer district distinctions, the courts have correctly characterized such changes as ad hoc administrative decision making. Performance zoning has broken with that tradition. Map amendments in performance zoning are intended to insure that the zoning remain consistent with a community's basic planning goals. The types of small-scale land use decisions which were typical of map amendments under conventional zoning are now decisions which a landowner can make within the framework laid down by the performance criteria. The zoning officer makes the ministerial decision to permit a land use activity solely on the ability of the proposal to meet the performance standard.

The Districts

This section deals with Article III of the model ordinance. The ordinance was prepared for a rapidly growing urban county, Lake County, Illinois, whose population is presently 430,000 and is expected to rise to over 600,000 by the year 2000. Lake County is located along Lake Michigan and borders Wisconsin. The geology is recent glacial till. Performance zoning is also in use in a number of communities in Bucks County, Pennsylvania. These communities represent a more varied and scenic area of coastal plain and piedmont. It can easily be adapted to other environments.

The districts in performance zoning should be districts whose purpose and function are clear and distinct from each other. In most instances, the purpose is to create a district which achieves an important planning goal or which maintains an area with a distinctive character. There remain several districts that are use-oriented, but these are districts where the use has special locational criteria, unique nuisance factors, and/or very different relationships with other land uses. In this section there is a discussion of the districts in the model ordinance and suggestions for other districts which might be useful in other communities. Many of the districts are generic and could be used anywhere; agricultural and development districts are of this type. Others such as the transportation center district are examples of districts in which uses such as residential are best excluded (performance criteria would have this effect) and which must be tailored to unique needs.

Rural Areas.

There are five rural districts. Two of them, the agricultural and wilderness districts, require long-term conservation (twenty years or more), while the rural and holding zone districts envision shorter-term conservation. The estate district is a rural residential area. None of these districts requires urban services such as sewers or water (although private systems serving the development may be required), nor should the residents expect the full range or level of public services provided in cities and towns. A community need not use all of these districts. It is vital that the intensities of use be significantly different from those of the developing areas. Similarly, other district-wide standards should be responsive to rural needs and not easily confused with the standards in the developing or urban areas.

Agricultural district. The purpose of this district is to set aside the land best suited for raising crops and to insure that this land use remains undisturbed by urban disruptions. In order to fulfill its purpose, a high open space ratio is required. For areas where the farms are devoted to general agriculture such as grain, corn, dairy, or livestock, an open space ratio of .85 or .80 is a minimum. Where more specialized crops such as nurseries, wine, or truck gardening are the rule, the open space ratio might be as low as .75 or .70. Lower open space ratios may be tolerated here because such agricultural uses are usually labor intensive and thus require smaller properties. Individual farmers involved in these special crops are more apt to use only their own land, and the movement of equipment from field to field becomes less important. Another exception to the .85 open space ratio would be in agricultural districts where good farmland is often interspersed with significant areas of uncultivatable land. Flat bottom lands with forested ridges are an example. In such situations the site capacity calculation might be used to protect the good soils. A lower open space ratio for the district as a whole would then be reasonable.

The standards for the agricultural district are most difficult to establish fairly in urban counties, where land values for development are significantly higher than the agricultural value. Providing the landowner with a *reasonable* development value for his land is a basic policy of performance zoning. The more rural an area, the less need there will be to address this issue since development values are similar to agricultural values. If one-acre lots on 2 to 10 percent of a farm will provide the landowner with a reasonable return, then performance zoning is similar to many existing agricultural zoning techniques. In more heavily urbanized areas economic pressure requires that the planners give considerable attention to this issue since there is likely to be a significant difference between agricultural and development values. It may be that the differences in values will in some communities be too high to make it possible to preserve farmland using this technique.

Wilderness district. This is the most restrictive type of zoning district. Its purpose is to protect a large area of wilderness—mountains, forests, swamps, or deserts—in its natural state with all of its natural resources, vegetation, and wildlife. Man is an intruder; even his lowest intensity recreational activities such as hiking are often a destructive force in wilderness areas. The desired level of protection requires an open space ratio of at least .98. Gross densities should be lower than that expected with ten-acre zoning. The very high open space ratios should be combined with a density-transfer provision and mandatory noncontiguous development for those properties more than a given distance from existing roads. The intent should be to concentrate all of the minimal development permitted in such districts on their perimeters. The interior of these districts is where the protection from man is most essential.

True wilderness areas will have the native wildlife intact; large predators will still be found in such areas. Areas larger than twenty square miles where roads are three or more miles apart are generally candidates for such zoning. Most such areas will be fairly remote from major urban centers. This should help to reduce the economic problem of providing a reasonable return. Because of the intended purpose and very low intensities, care should be given to designate only legitimate wilderness areas as such. These areas should be recognized as an important regional resource. The pine barrens of New Jersey, mountains, and large swamps are areas that might easily qualify. The uses permitted should be very limited and selected with care.

Rural district. The rural district is not directed at preserving a land use or resource as is the agricultural district. Its purpose is twofold. The rural district seeks to conserve a rural landscape and character; it also is a form of holding district which allows development without permanently precluding a more intensive use in later years. In order to have a district that will preserve a rural character or that can be further developed in the future, a large open space ratio is required. Design studies indicate that rural character will break down as open space ratios fall below .70; an open space ratio of .80 is far better. Illustration 2 demonstrates the impact on an area of varying the open space ratio from .90 open to .60. Only if rugged topography or dense vegetation severely limit the views would open space in the 50 to 60 percent category still provide a rural setting.

Holding zone. This district does what all too many low density residential districts sought to do but failed: to keep land open until its best use can be determined. It should be used where land is suitable for development but is not yet needed during the planning period. The high open space ratio associated with this district permits some use of the land. In addition, there is the provision enabling a portion of the open space to be designated for future development. Through this provision and the net densities permitted, performance zoning—unlike conventional zoning—does not preclude a more intensive use or promote urban sprawl. The use of this district in the model ordinance is unique to communities where annexation is easy or widespread. It is intended to enable a county to coordinate with cities and villages on a single plan. In cities or villages or in counties where annexa-

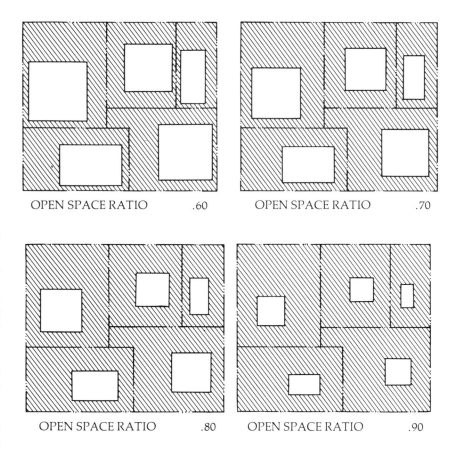

OPEN SPACE RATIO   .60   OPEN SPACE RATIO   .70

OPEN SPACE RATIO   .80   OPEN SPACE RATIO   .90

ILLUSTRATION 2

IMPACT OF VARYING OPEN SPACE

Ratio from .6 to .9

tion is infrequent, it may be used simply to set a priority on which areas are next in line for development. Where the annexation problem is not present, the district serves the same purpose, but references to annexation should be deleted.

The holding zone in any of its forms has advantages over conventional large-lot zoning techniques. It serves notice to all that the district is a transitional or temporary zoning classification. Second, it avoids urban sprawl by preventing premature development at intensities which underutilize the land. In conventional zoning, some development usually occurs at these low densities. When the time for more intensive development arrives, it is inevitable that the residents of those low density developments will strongly oppose the introduction of the higher density uses. In performance zoning, landowners are given notice of the transitory nature of this district. Further, the intent of the district is stated in a straightforward manner, which avoids the problems the courts have had with the use of a large-lot residential district as a holding zone.

The holding zone can appropriately be used as a tool to manage growth in any community that will not be fully developed in the next twenty years. It is flexible enough to be used to stage development. A community could divide its land area into five-year development zones, each tied to a capital program, with the first being a development district and subsequent ones being holding zones. In such a system the zoning ordinance should require the developer to provide the appropriate sewers, water supply, and other improvements as a condition of a premature zoning change. Where rural uses are expected to last for more than twenty years, the holding zone is basically a designation of priority. This is the way in which it is used in the model ordinance, with the exception that the model ordinance anticipates annexation to a city or village as the precondition to proceeding to full development. The holding zone has a higher priority for development than rural or agricultural districts. This order of priority would be used in the evaluation of all zoning changes, with the order of conversion being holding zone land first, rural second, and agricultural as a last resort. Conservation of wilderness zones would have a priority similar to that of agricultural districts. It should be noted that the rural and holding zone districts are quite similar in standards and even purpose. In many communities there may be no need for both.

Estate district. This district provides for low density, estate-type living. Each dwelling is expected to have individual water supply and waste disposal systems. Many communities have several sizes of large-lot zoning districts which provide for larger and larger estates. The largest lot district tends to become a holding zone; development often occurs only when preceded by a rezoning to progressively lower lot sizes. Performance zon-

ing seeks to avoid the need for rezonings and replaces one- to five-acre conventional zoning with a single district. The district has no minimum open space ratio, although natural resources will still be protected by the environmental calculation. The district's density is based on average lot size, not a minimum. The selection of lot size and density for the district is therefore a two-step process, since the two are not directly related. The minimum lot size need only be adequate to provide for on-site wells and septic systems. In most areas, one acre is more than sufficient. Where soils are well suited for septic systems, smaller lots, perhaps only 20,000 square feet, may be used. The density should be based on an average lot considerably larger than the minimum. This permits the developer to work around difficult areas without losing lots. More important, it permits a mix of lot sizes within a single district which meets the needs of districts in the one- to five-acre range. The selection of the density should take into account land values, market potential, and the percentage of the market needing larger lots to keep horses. This district should be designed to permit a maximum number of smaller lots yet accommodate larger lots for the remainder of the market. The area mapped for the estate district should be related to a realistic expectation of use. It should not serve as a holding zone. Estate districts should be located in areas not intended to be served by public services in order to eliminate potential land use conflicts in the future.

Development Areas.

As a group these districts are anticipated to handle most of a community's growth. They deal with the subject that preoccupies suburban planners, growth management. The development districts seek to direct growth into areas where services can be provided in a cost-effective manner while insuring a quality environment. For most suburban areas, the development district will be primary development zone. The three other zones all deal with very specialized areas of regional importance.

Development district. This is the district intended to handle most of the community's growth for the planning period. A key issue will be how much land should be mapped for this district. Two basic approaches may be taken. The first requires an examination of the capacity of critical services, such as sewers and water supply, and a comparison of the available capacity with projected growth rates. In illustration 3, the existing facilities can meet growth needs for seven years.

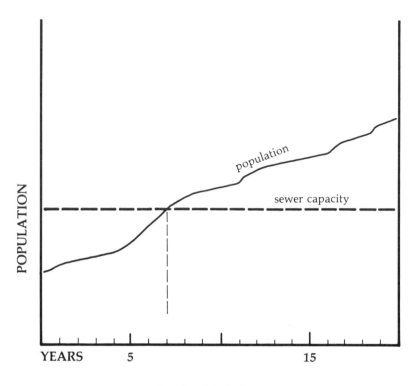

ILLUSTRATION 3

RELATIONSHIP OF SEWER CAPACITY
AND POPULATION FOR A
DEVELOPMENT DISTRICT

A second approach is to set a moderate planning period of five to twenty-five years. A shorter period will result in too little land in the development district and necessitate continual rezoning petitions; beyond twenty-five years there is little accuracy in projections. This approach presumes that the community will be able to provide services or can make the necessary improvements during the planning period. The choice between these methods should be dictated by the realities of facilities planning in the community. In a situation where capacity is limited and a moratorium on hookups is likely, the first method is preferable.

Under either system there is one important concern which the community should address. Is the amount of land zoned sufficiently large to insure that a small number of landowners cannot manipulate the market place and

drive up land prices? Prices are most likely to be driven up when the planning period is short or where the total area needed to accommodate expected development is small. Extending the planning period or intentionally building in a safety margin are the two options for avoiding this. A blend of both may be needed in some communities. It should be noted that this district is predicated on the availability of sewers; without this precondition being met, the district cannot function. One of the most innovative early performance zoning ordinances, Buckingham Township's, has failed to live up to its promise, because four years after its adoption no sewer is available to service the development district.

In rural areas where only a handful of building permits are issued each year but the establishment of an urban community is desired, this problem will be very difficult. The approach used in the rural district may be quite useful. Setting a high open space ratio and permitting urban densities on community septic systems or small package treatment plants while reserving land for future development may be the best approach. This requires a rezoning in later years to permit in-filling of some of the open space and, when it is financially feasible, an extension of public sewers to the development area. The alternative is an oversized development district in which costly central sewer extensions would be needed to serve a few random developments.

Urban core district. This district is intended to create centers of regional activity. It is planned to accommodate a small percentage of a community's residential growth but a large portion of its major commercial and some of its industrial uses. This district is in competition with older downtown or central business areas. Suburban shopping centers have often hastened the collapse of central business areas. Because of its regional impacts on existing commercial areas, roads, and other facilities, a specific urban core district provides the community time to assess the impacts of a regional center before granting the rezoning. Urban cores should be mixed-use areas with high intensity residential as well as commercial and other uses. The intensity of the urban core residential area is more than double that of the development district; it shifts from the single-family densities of the development district to densities that include large percentages of low- and mid-rise multi-family dwellings.

Urban cores should ideally have access to two major regional highways and a commuter rail stop or existing bus route. Centers of regional activity clearly have different locational needs from other suburban uses. In some instances the locations have already been acquired by developers and are so obviously the logical sites that there are no viable alternatives. In this situation the urban core may be designated on the zoning map. In other cases there may be several locations that could serve nearly as well, or the ownership pattern may make it questionable whether adequate land for a regional center can actually be assembled despite locational assets. There is likely to be only one regional center in any one area; hence, if there is doubt about feasibility, it is better not to map the district. All existing urban cores should be so mapped. Performance zoning specifies locational criteria, acreage requirements, and any other factors for which positive findings must be made by elected officials before granting a zoning change. The ordinance reduces the problems associated with zoning changes by setting some qualifying criteria. In granting zoning requests for urban core districts, the municipality should rezone all needed land at the same time rather than proceed on a piecemeal basis. While this may require several public hearings, it will provide more logic to this type of zoning.

Heavy industrial district. Heavy industrial uses have very specific locational requirements such as access to rail systems, major arterial roads, expressways, and, in certain parts of the county, to water transportation. Sites with these attributes are likely to be quite rare. In metropolitan areas heavy industrial districts should not be scattered but concentrated to lessen impacts on other areas. They should be zoned in advance of need. The uses are such that they will face stiff opposition in ad hoc proceedings; further, the danger that such areas will be preempted by less intensive uses is very real. The probability that speculation may drive up the land values is less, since the areas should be large. In addition, competition for heavy industrial sites is quite different in nature from that for residential, light industrial, or commercial uses. It is not a speculative venture. Smaller communities should not provide for this zone unless they have a unique locational advantage or unless identifiable demand for this use is present and an adequate labor pool exists.

Transportation center district. The district is intended to deal with special zoning needs near major transportation nodes such as airports, ports, rail yards, and similar areas. The name of the district reflects the type of center that is to be protected. Such districts should restrict uses to those compatible with and dependent on the transportation center. Special concern for preserving the surrounding area for uses that depend on that node of

transportation should be encouraged. An airport district will serve to illustrate some of the concerns.

Zoning around airports has long been a problem. The FAA regulations governing flight paths and noise levels are well documented. Performance zoning has the unique potential not only to control building heights as in conventional development but, if intensity transfers or development rights are used, to protect areas for runway expansion. Under a properly designed performance district protection of the flight path for an expanding airport should also be possible. This is particularly important in an era when metropolitan airport space is being lost to development. These districts should be sized on optimistic long-term growth projections. Land near such facilities should not be preempted by lower intensity uses, since these sites are generally unique. A community should also review the long-term access needs of these districts and require rights-of-way to be dedicated and roads built.

Developed Areas.

Most communities will have areas of existing development. Many of these areas are stable; little activity may be expected, but the residents of the areas desire to be protected by zoning. The neighborhood and commercial conservation districts seek to conserve what is present in those areas. This is not performance zoning's forte. The only true performance district in this class is the redevelopment district, which applies to areas whose character is to be changed.

Neighborhood conservation district. This district is not a performance district. Pragmatically, it is essential to avoid either making most homes in a community nonconforming or opening up large areas to resubdivision. The standards of the development district in performance zoning will make most existing residential areas nonconforming in terms of open space, bufferyards, and other criteria. Further, since the minimum lot size is so small in performance zoning, the threat of resubdivision is often perceived by local residents of established subdivisions. An early attempt to institute performance zoning by Middletown Township, Pennsylvania in 1972 was repealed because it failed to deal effectively with large areas that were already built up. Where neighborhoods are stable and the only likely development is the addition of rooms or garages, it is a mistake to substitute a completely new performance district. The neighborhood conservation district is intended to conserve preexisting neighborhoods and their zoning. It is not intended to be used for developing new neighborhoods.

A subscript is used on the zoning map to distinguish among different types of neighborhood conservation districts. For example, NC_{40} refers to a district with lots 40,000 square feet in area; NC_{12} refers to a neighborhood with lots of 12,000 square feet (minimum). The permitted uses are residential as in conventional zoning, with the district governing only lot size and density. In performance zoning, the subscript is assigned on the basis of the original lot sizes in the neighborhood.

Commercial conservation district. There are commercial areas that are developed and will not be able to conform to most of the standards in performance zoning. Where such conditions exist, a commercial conservation district may be required. The alternative is to make these areas nonconforming. Uses in this district will be expected to meet as many performance criteria as possible, and special review procedures will set the conditions for development or redevelopment.

Redevelopment (or transitional) district. This is an area that is or was at least partially developed. It may be a fully developed area that has deteriorated and is in need of redevelopment and renewal. It may be an area with sound and substantial buildings which is under economic pressure to develop to higher intensity. It may be an area that was only partially developed and needs incentives for additional development. The common characteristic of such diverse neighborhoods is that they are all neighborhoods whose present character is to be changed.

Of all the districts this is the most difficult to structure. A district that is in transition because its location is so desirable is an easy case to work with, assuming that the intensity desired by prospective developers is compatible with the community's desires. If this is true, the only problem is to determine the design features desired by the community and to include incentives within the system to encourage them. Bonus systems have been used to insure construction of theaters, pedestrian walks, and other amenities in many communities.

Where development must be attracted to an area, the problems are more difficult. These areas often have undesirable features. Increased density alone may not be attractive enough to bring investors back to such areas. There will be many instances where the neighborhoods should not be converted to higher intensities. In some inner cities the higher densities will on-

ly serve to increase an existing concentration of low income or minority families; here higher densities are probably detrimental. Zoning works only when there are economic incentives to develop. A problem in redevelopment areas is that there is often no desire to live or work in such areas. In these situations zoning can only be used as a secondary technique.

Planners attempting to use performance zoning in this type of renewal area have a responsibility to perform an economic and social analysis before developing the zoning standards. If outside economic incentive is required in the form of capital improvements or subsidies, this should be presented with the proposed zoning. All too often plans for these areas have looked beautiful on paper but never materialized because no market exists for that proposal in that location. A number of strategies should be reviewed for use of community development or other government programs for capital improvements.

Tax-increment financing is now permitted in many states and may be an excellent source of funds in some communities.[13] A subsidy to move in middle-class homeowners is also an attractive possibility; this device has been used in Pittsburgh.[14] The planning of measures needed to turn a declining neighborhood around is more important than the form of zoning. Performance zoning is not a cure-all for urban ills. At best, performance zoning is a tool to achieve land use mixes or design qualities once a plan is devised to attract redevelopment. The standards for each such district will have to be tailored individually; thus, in a large city there might have to be a number of such districts.

Special Districts.

These districts do not neatly fit into the rural–developing–developed format because they could exist in two or more of these categories. Conservation areas are usually rural, but they may be found in developing urban areas as well. Historic districts can occur in all three of the major zoning categories, rural, developing, or developed.

Conservation district. This is a district rich in natural resources. Rugged topography, forests, hills, scenic areas, native prairie or desert, stream and river valleys are examples of areas that might be so designated. As with the wilderness, man is an intruder who can damage the topography, vegetation, and wildlife of a conservation district. Unlike the wilderness area, a conservation district may exist quite close to an urban center. It may be much smaller than a wilderness area but should still contain several square miles. Areas much smaller than that can generally be protected by the performance standards for resource protection. Small areas with unique rock formations, nesting sites, or areas of unique vegetation might also be identified as conservation districts. A resource should generally be protected by the natural resource standards if at all possible; however, where the resource is rare and easily mapped, a conservation district may be the best technique.

The conservation district can be created in exurban and suburban situations. This makes the district capable of retaining a high level of protection across a broad range of densities. A minimum open space ratio is probably .70. It is possible to obtain densities as high as 3.0 in development districts, a density comparable to 10,000 square foot lots in conventional zoning; thus, high levels of protection may be attained even in urban settings.

This district may be used for purposes other than conservation. It would be suitable to protect scenic areas or views. The open space ratios and densities would work in the same way as they do for conservation. Certain geological formations and limestone or large aquifer recharge areas might also need similar protection. The name of the district should be expressive of its purpose. The text of the ordinance should fully express that purpose or refer to community plans which do.

Historic district. This class includes districting for areas or neighborhoods that are historic sites of archaeological or historical importance, and some areas of unique cultural importance. Neither performance nor conventional zoning can exert much positive control over architecture. While it is possible to build new buildings in old styles or to make modern buildings that flatter or enhance older ones, this is more often the result of happy accident than of design. Architectural review boards have the ability to avoid the very worst; however, they rarely result in high quality design and often enforce mediocrity. On the other hand, separation and identity are important concerns in historic preservation, and performance zoning can be used to provide open space to separate a historic area. Transfer of development rights may also be used to open up land in and around a historic district. A voluntary system of TDR is used in the model ordinance. It will be of little help if an area is already zoned for much higher densities. Mandatory TDR is legal and would be a great advance over architectural controls.

The Performance Standards

Article IV is the heart of the zoning ordinance. Few of its sections will seem familiar to most zoning practitioners, and it will likely be the form or format rather than the detailed content which is familiar. In a conventional zoning ordinance, the landowner would, at the time development is contemplated, first refer to a zoning map to determine the district classification of the property and would then consult a table or listing of the uses permitted in that district. Next he would check the "bulk," "lot," and "yard" requirements imposed on various uses within the district. The requirements of this traditional system are imposed with no reference to the particular site for which development is proposed. The system virtually ignores such major variables as the uses of the surrounding land and the impact the proposed use will have on them, the environmental constraints, and other limitations of the subject site.

Under performance zoning, the first two steps are identical. The site must be located and its district classification identified in order to know what uses are permitted in that district. At this point, the similarities between the two systems all but vanish. In conventional zoning, the first and second steps narrow the range of development options dramatically. In performance zoning, nearly all options remain open with respect to the development and urban core districts. These districts have been both sized and located to accommodate all growth projected for the community. Therefore, they comprise no small part of the total area zoned. Maximum and minimum standards for the district are assigned by criteria that set a "community character." These are the "general performance standards." Performance zoning then applies site-specific regulations. The landowner is first required to analyze the capacity of the site in terms of its physical suitability for development. Natural resource limitations (such as wetlands or floodplains on the site) and provisions for required open space, for example, are to be taken into consideration at this stage. Next, as the developer refines the plans for the property, a choice of a particular "land use intensity class" must be made. This in turn determines which of several other performance standards and regulations will apply to the proposed use. The logic of this system is both simple and compelling: the more "intense" a land use is, the greater will be its impact on neighboring uses and the community in general. Accordingly, the more intense a land use, the more it must be required (regulated) to ameliorate those impacts. For example, an office may consist of a small insurance sales operation on a small lot or it may consist of a large group of multi-story buildings. In the former case, the office may be reasonably compatible with neighboring residential

uses; therefore, it need not buffer those neighbors nearly so much as the latter use. Traffic impact is also highly variable depending on the size, intensity, and proposed use of a site. A traffic impact analysis is required for all uses above a specified intensity level. Land uses with regional impact are required to carry the analysis beyond the nearest intersections and adequately control their enormous impact on roads at some distance from the site. The analysis is based on sustaining a given level of service on arterial roads and requires the designation of the improvements needed to accommodate the additional traffic. Finally, the ordinance imposes standards to ameliorate any negative effects caused by off-street parking, exterior lighting, signs, and buildings which are incompatible with adjacent uses. These standards, which vary according to the intensity of the use proposed, permit the application of a range of individualized performance criteria.

The developer's choice, then, is to describe at what point the increased intensity is no longer "worth" the increased "performance" required of it. The following sections detail the land use intensity classification system, district performance standards, the site capacity calculation, natural resource protection standards, bufferyards, transportation impacts, and standards for streets, signs, lighting, and landscaping.

Permitted Land Uses and Land Use Intensity Classification.

The typical conventional zoning ordinance may identify well over one hundred individual land uses. The uses are regulated by controlling the districts in which they are permitted. The parcels which are in a zone are mapped, thereby indicating where a selected use may locate. Performance zoning lists only seventeen generalized uses and most of these are permitted in the development districts. In addition, performance zoning contains a land use intensity classification system which divides each land use into one or more of eleven intensity classes. Most land uses appear in several land use intensity classifications as shown in illustration 4.

Why the major shift in classification of land uses? First, too many distinctions in conventional zoning were meaningless or arbitrary, and thus the classification system, while it was the basis of zoning, did not provide the protection it should have. Also, research intended to develop a precise system of classification determined that even within a fairly narrow land use classification there was often greater potential variation between two of the "same" uses than between two supposedly different uses. In seeking to

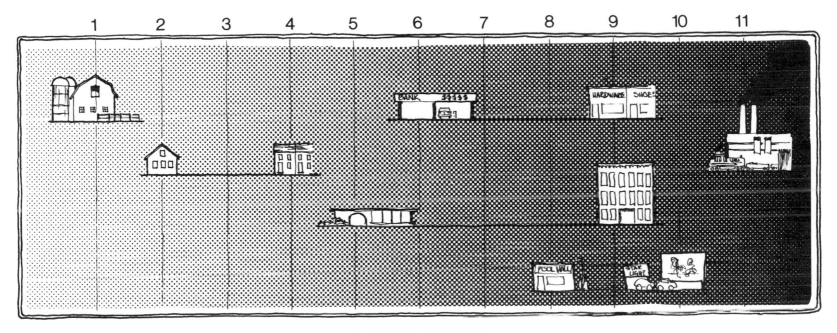

ILLUSTRATION 4

ILLUSTRATION OF LAND USE INTENSITY CLASSIFICATION SYSTEM

eliminate these problems, the development of a new classification system became a necessity.

Traditional zoning assumed that uses could be classified in a hierarchy and that each use occupied only a single position in that hierarchy. In performance zoning, uses may occupy a series of distinct positions depending on their intensity. In developing the new classification system for the model ordinance, a survey was conducted to test some of the concepts on which performance zoning was to be based. Survey results demonstrated that many uses were subject to a wide range of classifications. Although the questionnaire allowed only five possible classifications, nearly two-thirds of the sixty-five land uses had standard deviations of more than one.[15] One explanation is that land uses vary considerably, so that individuals rate a use based on different perceptions of that use. Field surveys gave support to this hypothesis. Restaurants, office facilities, and even housing units may be quite different. Size, scale, signs, lighting, landscaping, and parking are some of the factors that make for a substantial variation from building to building within a land use type.

Identification of nuisance factors is essential to performance zoning. The questionnaire helped to identify many of the particular concerns of citizens. The standards finally chosen for use in the model ordinance are generally quite simple and may be measured or determined from site or floor plans or calculated on the basis of data which the ordinance requires the developer to submit. These data include density, trips/acre, height, floor area ratio, and the presence or absence of exterior and/or damaged vehicle storage. All are obvious measures of intensity. Several of the other factors deserve more discussion.

The impervious surface ratio specifies the portion of the site which may be paved or covered by buildings. Since unlandscaped parking is an important nuisance factor, impervious surface is a much more precise method of evaluating intensity or degree of nuisance than the older, more commonly used measure, building coverage. There was no existing measure of the impact of lighting, landscaping (including the landscaping of parking areas), and signs. The decision, therefore, was to develop six classifications which set specific performance levels for these features.

Traffic noise and congestion were the number one and two ranked nuisances according to the survey. The best way to avoid burdening residential owners with congestion is to segregate uses by the type of street to which they may have access. Accordingly, the model ordinance defines three classes of roads. Residential uses are permitted to locate only on residential streets. Residential access and children can therefore be segregated from busy streets. Most other uses are permitted to front on collector streets or, if they have sufficient frontage, on arterials. Commercial uses and other high traffic generators are prohibited from taking access from residential streets. Thus, each land use intensity standard has a series of performance criteria that clearly limit its nuisance potential.

The decision was made to classify land uses in eleven categories, each having a relatively different level of impact or nuisance value. Specific performance levels were set for each of these categories.

It is appropriate at this point to ask how the standards for the land use intensity classes were developed. First, uses were grouped on the basis of data from survey studies and field observations. Impervious surface was selected as a starting point. For the most part, the impervious surface coverage of a use was observed in the field, from on-site plans, or from aerial photographs. Given the impervious surface ratio and assumptions about building height and parking spaces per unit of floor area, the floor area ratio may be derived mathematically. Once floor area is known, it is then possible to calculate trips per acre for the various uses at different levels of impervious surface. For residential uses, density was the starting point for such determinations. The field survey approach employed to develop the impervious surface ratio was used for both outdoor storage and damaged vehicle storage. The heights were related to actual structures presently existing in the county. The other standards are obvious, with the exception of those for landscaping, signs, and so forth, whose derivation will be covered later.

A use intensity class was thus designed to have a uniform nuisance value. Because it is not based on use alone, it achieves this more precisely than does conventional zoning. It is also a flexible device. Many uses are permitted in three or more land use intensity classes; thus, a landowner has great flexibility about how best to utilize a given site. The use intensity class serves two functions. It classifies uses and sets performance criteria. It is also the major factor in determining the bufferyard requirements between uses. Bufferyards enable performance zoning to mix a wide range of uses in a single district.

Table of District Performance Criteria.

The table of district performance criteria in the model ordinance sets performance standards which control land use intensity from a district perspective. It sets the limits (maximum or minimum) that determine the general character of each zoning district. Note, for example, that a considerably larger open space ratio (OSR) must be maintained in the rural district than in the development district. Similarly, in the urban core a far higher density factor (DF) is used than for the same use in the development district.

Illustrations 5–7 demonstrate the degree to which the character of a site may be changed by significantly altering one of the standards. Character can be changed by altering the density while maintaining open space ratio or by maintaining density while altering the open space ratio. The table of district performance criteria serves the same function as does lot size in conventional zoning ordinances: it sets the character of the district. The three standards provide precision in setting character while leaving the landowner considerable freedom.

The table of alternate performance criteria in this section (table 1) provides a range of residential standards for many districts, including some not used in the model ordinance. This table deals only with conventional and performance subdivisions, not with nonresidential uses. Nonresidential uses should present the planner no difficulty, since both impervious surface and floor area are easily understood. No data are provided for the historic and redevelopment districts because the range of possibilities is so large and must be tailored to site-specific needs rather than general intensities. The table also identifies the average dwelling type on which the maximum density factor is based.

The figures in parentheses represent gross density (GD), that is, the density based on the entire site area, including the open space. The first housing type is for the density factor without bonus; the second is with bonus. In most districts a range of intensities for the district is provided. These intensities bracket those used in the model ordinance. The figures contained in table 1 may be substituted for those in the model ordinance. This permits a planner to choose a development district that is more open with a lower density or less open and higher in density than that proposed in the model ordinance.

TABLE 1
Alternate Performance Criteria

District	OSR	DF without bonus	DF with bonus	ISR	Average dwelling unit type (GD in parentheses)
Wilderness					
Performance sub.	.98	3.55	6.3	.01	SF 10,000 (.06), village house (.09)
Agriculture (rural)					
Performance sub.	.95	3.55	6.30	.03	SF 10,000 (.15), village house (.25)
Agriculture (urban)					
Performance sub.	.85	6.30	12.50	.08	village house (.75), weak-link (1.5)
Rural (rural)					
Conventional sub.	—	.10	—	.06	SF 400,000 (.10)
Performance sub.	.90	2.45	5.60	.05	SF 15,000 (.22), lot line (.40)
Rural (urban)					
Conventional sub.	—	.33	—	.14	SF 120,000 (.33)
Performance sub.	.75	6.30	10.60	.12	village house (1.3), patio (2.2)
Holding zone (rural)					
Performance sub.	.90	4.4	10.6		SF 7,400 (.37), patio (.84)
Holding zone (urban)					
Performance sub.	.70	7.9	12.6		twin (2.1), weak-link (3.3)
Estate (rural)					
Conventional sub.		.25	—	.11	SF 160,000 (.25)
Estate (urban)					
Conventional sub.		.7	—	.17	SF 60,000 (.7)
Development (low density)					
Conventional sub.		1.25	1.90	.29	SF 30,000 (1.25), SF 20,000 (1.9)
Performance sub.	.40	4.40	10.60	.27	SF 7,400 (2.6), patio (6.4)
Development (high density)					
Conventional sub.		1.50	2.45	.33	SF 25,000, SF 15,000
Performance sub.	.30	7.90	12.60	.42	twin (5.5), weak-link (8.8)
Urban Core (low rise)					
Performance sub.	.25	10.60	16.50	.42	patio (8.0), town house (12.3)
Urban core (high rise)	.15	11.50	27.80	.46	atrium (9.7), 4-story apt (23.6)
Conservation (rural)					
Performance sub.	.85	4.1	9.3	.08	SF 8,500 (.53), patio (1.1)
Conservation (urban)					
Performance sub.	.70	4.4	10.6	.14	SF 7,400 (1.2), patio (2.8)

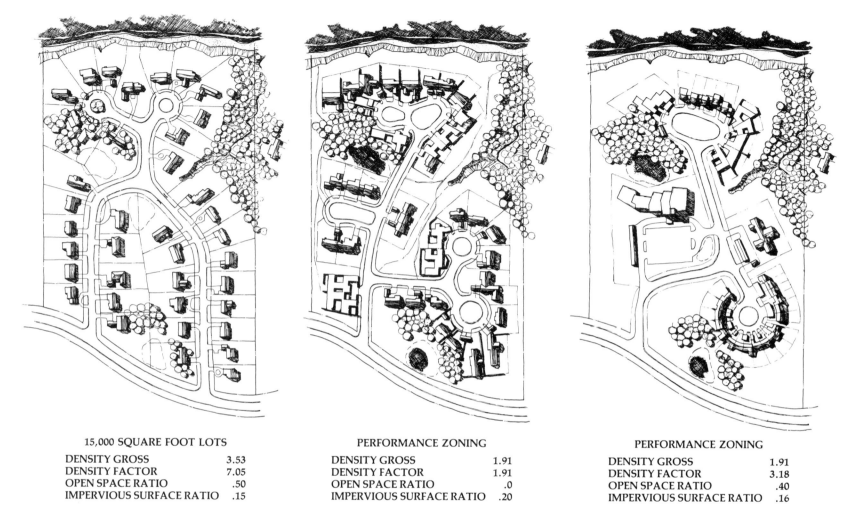

15,000 SQUARE FOOT LOTS		PERFORMANCE ZONING		PERFORMANCE ZONING	
DENSITY GROSS	3.53	DENSITY GROSS	1.91	DENSITY GROSS	1.91
DENSITY FACTOR	7.05	DENSITY FACTOR	1.91	DENSITY FACTOR	3.18
OPEN SPACE RATIO	.50	OPEN SPACE RATIO	.0	OPEN SPACE RATIO	.40
IMPERVIOUS SURFACE RATIO	.15	IMPERVIOUS SURFACE RATIO	.20	IMPERVIOUS SURFACE RATIO	.16

ILLUSTRATIONS 5–7

INTERACTION OF VARIABLES

In developing the standards for residential uses, the procedures used are as follows. First, a district open space ratio is set. This narrows the range of possibilities for the density factor and impervious surface ratio (ISR). Open space was chosen because it, more than anything, was thought to establish the community's character. The next requirement is the determination of gross density for the district, which is a function of the average dwelling unit. The average dwelling unit type in conjunction with open space com-

pletes the definition of neighborhood character. After the average dwelling unit and its associated lot area are determined, gross density and the density factor can be derived. It is insufficient merely to specify a district's gross density because gross density cannot make adjustments for intensity as open space changes; thus, there is a need for the density factor to regulate intensity on the buildable portion of the site. The mix of open space ratio, density factor, average dwelling type, and therefore gross density enables the planner and community to have a precise understanding of the district they have created. Impervious surface ratio follows from the impervious surface of the average dwelling unit. Its frontage determines the area in streets, while setbacks determine the area of drives.

The easiest way to utilize performance zoning is to adopt one of the districts just as they are cited. The standards have been tested to insure that a development meeting all standards is feasible. Caution should be used in altering the numerical values of the standards presented. Even a planner with years of experience should not intuitively make changes. In developing these tables, we attempted to provide a range of alternatives which could be applied to a variety of situations. That planners using this model to prepare zoning ordinances for a variety of communities will need to make small adjustments to tailor the ordinance to local aspirations is understood.

Tables can be generated by a computer to enable a planner to evaluate a wide range of options in minutes. Appendix A outlines the algorithms needed to write such a program. Many small communities may not have access to a computer and will find these calculations too time-consuming to do by hand.

By using table 2, the planner can evaluate a number of alternatives rather quickly and make good estimates of the appropriate standards for each variable. Table 2 provides the density and impervious surface ratio for twenty-eight dwelling unit types or variants. It provides a high and low density, thus bracketing the range that one might expect. A good designer with a fortuitous site will minimize the amount of road per dwelling unit and thus get the most units on his site. A poor designer with a difficult site will maximize the amount of road per dwelling, thus achieving a lower density. Given the range, one may determine the midpoint or any other value that is desired.

The table also introduces a third variable, the floor area of the dwelling unit. In the model ordinance a significant change in intensities results from an increase in floor area, since that triggers an increase in lot size. The table provides data on the minimal unit, 1,100 square feet for most three-bedroom units, as well as for units of 1,800 and 2,400 square feet.

The densities and impervious surface ratio values in table 2 are based on an open space ratio of .00. It should be noted that when there is no open space the density factor and gross density are identical. The first step in making an estimate for another district is to determine the desired open space ratio. With this, one may determine the net buildable site area (NBSA). The desired open space ratio is subtracted from 1.00 to obtain the net buildable site:

$$1.00 - OSR = NBSA.$$

Thus, for a .90 open space ratio, net buildable site area will equal .10. Net buildable site area increases as open space declines; thus, net buildable site area equals .70 where the open space ratio is .30.

The second step is to find in table 2 the dwelling type and size desired and to multiply the values for density and impervious surface ratio for that dwelling type by the net buildable site area. This gives the gross density and impervious surface ratio (ISR') that result when that dwelling unit type is used at the desired open space ratio:

$$GD = DF \times NBSA$$
$$ISR' = ISR \times NBSA.$$

To demonstrate how the calculation might work, hypothesize that a community wants the district to have .40 as the open space ratio. The district standard is to be based on either a twin house or a one-story patio house of 1,800 square feet, with an optimal design [16]

$$1.00 - OSR = NBSA$$
$$1.00 - .40 = .60.$$

According to table 2, rounded high values for the twin house and patio house under the column for units of 1,800 square feet are:

	Twin house	One-story patio house
ISR	.43	.53
DF	6.85	7.16

These values should be multiplied by the constant net buildable site area (.60) to determine the district standards:

	Twin house	One-story patio house
ISR'	.258 (.43 × .60)	.318 (.53 × .60)
GD	4.11 (6.85 × .60)	4.30 (7.16 × .60)

TABLE 2
Conventional Zoning Selection Chart
(Open Space Ratio = .00)

Housing type		Minimum floor area High	Low	(1.7) * Min. floor area High	Low	(2.4) * Min. floor area High	Low
Conventional single family	ISR =	.0455	.0640	.0630	.0847	.0853	.1064
200,000 sq. ft. lot	DF =	.2071	.2019	.2069	.2016	.2067	.2014
Conventional single family	ISR =	.0505	.0687	.0698	.0905	.0922	.1126
160,000 sq. ft. lot	DF =	.2578	.2508	.2575	.2505	.2572	.2501
Conventional single family	ISR =	.0610	.0816	.0849	.1095	.1137	.1381
120,000 sq. ft. lot	DF =	.3409	.3305	.3404	.3298	.3400	.3292
Conventional single family	ISR =	.0792	:0992	.1033	.1228	.1263	.1452
80,000 sq. ft. lot	DF =	.5032	.4841	.5023	.4828	.5013	.4813
Conventional single family	ISR =	.1225	.1483	.1502	.1753	.1781	.2023
40,000 sq. ft. lot	DF =	.9789	.9300	.9756	.9252	.9716	.9200
Conventional single family	ISR =	.1318	.1588	.1599	.1860	.1889	.2141
35,000 sq. ft. lot	DF =	1.1130	1.0547	1.1078	1.0479	1.1028	1.0411
Conventional single family	ISR =	.1458	.1743	.1779	.2053	.2114	.2375
30,000 sq. ft. lot	DF =	1.2883	1.2171	1.2827	1.2090	1.2760	1.2000
Conventional single family	ISR =	.1577	.1885	.1913	.2207	.2259	.2540
25,000 sq. ft. lot	DF =	1.5312	1.4401	1.5216	1.4273	1.5119	1.4148
Conventional single family	ISR =	.1801	.2132	.2205	.2522	.2631	.2923
20,000 sq. ft. lot	DF =	1.8843	1.7609	1.8720	1.7440	1.8577	1.7253
Conventional single family	ISR =	.2064	.2428	.2518	.2858	.2991	.3280
15,000 sq. ft. lot	DF =	2.4777	2.3010	2.4522	2.2686	2.4278	2.2371
Conventional single family	ISR =	.2424	.2815	.2943	.3295	.3517	.3826
12,000 sq. ft. lot	DF =	3.0184	2.7762	3.0184	2.7762	2.9878	2.7345
Conventional single family	ISR =	.1998	.2700	.2791	.3200	.3248	.3557
10,000 sq. ft. lot	DF =	3.5549	3.2457	3.5549	3.2457	3.5039	3.1817
Conventional single family	ISR =	.2176	.2902	.3050	.3437	.3525	.3871
8,500 sq. ft. lot	DF =	4.1220	3.7397	4.1220	3.7397	4.0519	3.6550

Performance Zoning Selection Chart

Housing type		Minimum floor area High	Low	1,800 sq. ft. floor area High	Low	2,400 sq. ft. floor area High	Low
Single family: 2 story, 2 car	ISR =	.2977	.3244	.2885	.3133	.2814	.3045
3 BR, 7,400 sq. ft.	DF =	4.4307	3.9277	3.9139	3.5162	3.5039	3.1817
Lot-line: 1½ story, 2 car	ISR =	.3435	.3658	.3345	.3550	.3274	.3460
3 BR, 6,200 sq. ft.	DF =	5.2687	4.6598	4.5517	4.0900	3.9355	3.5855
Village house: 2 story, 2 car	ISR =	.3420	.3665	.3321	.3547	.3244	.3453
3 BR, 5,000 sq. ft.	DF =	6.3211	5.5279	5.4526	4.8520	4.7916	4.3215
Twin house: 2 story, 2 car	ISR =	.4381	.4503	.4329	.4441	.4320	.4430
3 BR, 3,900 sq. ft.	DF =	7.9808	6.9493	6.8493	6.0753	6.0168	5.3505
Patio house: 1 story, 2 car	ISR =	.5312	.5315	.5308	.5311	.5311	.5312
3 BR, 3,300 sq. ft.	DF =	9.3023	8.0645	7.1633	6.4062	5.9207	5.3333
Patio house: 2 story, 2 car	ISR =	.4248	.4410	.4142	.4290	.4081	.4216
3 BR, 2,700 sq. ft.	DF =	10.6724	9.0744	8.5763	7.5131	6.5402	5.8309
Atrium: on lot, 2,400 sq. ft.	ISR =	.6071	.5954	.6177	.6070	.6222	.6125
3 BR, 1 story	DF =	11.5207	9.6805	8.7489	7.6453	7.4074	6.6007
Weak-link: on lot, 2,400 sq. ft.	ISR =	.4621	.4716	.4555	.4639	.4520	.4600
3 BR, 2 story	DF =	12.6263	10.9170	10.0100	8.9047	8.2034	7.4074
Town house: on lot, 1,800 sq. ft.	ISR =	.5314	.5313	.5306	.5307	.5301	.5308
3 BR, 2 story	DF =	16.5017	14.2450	13.0378	11.5875	11.1607	9.9404

Housing type		Minimum floor area High	Low	1,200 sq. ft. floor area High	Low	1,600 sq. ft. floor area High	Low
Multiplex-A: 2 car, 1,004 sq. ft.	ISR =	.5504	.5420	.5490	.5463	.5509	.5479
2 BR, 2 story	DF =	15.0376	12.3457	12.7389	10.5263	10.1833	8.5616
Apt.: 2 story, 2 car	ISR =	.6988	.6921	.6998	.6948	.7013	.6974
2 BR, 1,000 sq. ft.	DF =	24.6914	23.8663	20.7039	20.0803	15.7233	15.3610
Apt.: 3 story, 2 car	ISR =	.6399	.6368	.6427	.6387	.6434	.6409
2 BR, 1,000 sq. ft.	DF =	25.9067	24.8756	21.7865	21.0084	16.5837	16.1031
Apt.: 4 story, 2 car	ISR =	.6045	.6005	.6066	.6041	.6057	.6038
2 BR, 1,000 sq. ft.	DF =	27.8552	26.8097	23.4192	22.6244	17.7620	17.3010
Apt.: 6 story, 2 level, 2 car	ISR =	.5125	.5119	.5106	.5116	.5115	.5122
2 BR, 1,000 sq. ft.	DF =	35.8423	34.1297	30.2115	28.9017	23.0415	22.2717
Apt.: 8 story, 2 level, 2 car	ISR =	.4869	.4875	.4858	.4880	.4832	.4849
2 BR, 1,000 sq. ft.	DF =	37.4532	35.5872	31.5457	31.1205	24.0385	23.2019

These values should be adequate to set district standards. The calculations provide gross density. The density factor which regulates the model ordinance is the value contained in table 2. Thus, in the example above, in a district with an open space ratio of .40, a twin house with a density factor of 6.85 results in a gross density of 4.11.

There is one caution, however. The one-story patio and atrium houses both have unusually high impervious surface ratios; if the community uses the twin house standards, impervious surface would prohibit the single-story patio house from reaching maximum density even though it has a lot that is 600 square feet smaller. If atrium or single-story houses are desired, this high impervious surface ratio must be taken into account; a calculation for these dwelling unit types should be made. A working set of district standards derived from the example would be:

Open space ratio 40
Density factor 6.85
Gross density (for information only) 4.10
Impervious surface ratio 30

In this example the district requirements are specified using the twin house as the average dwelling unit type. Notice that an allowance was made to accommodate one-story patio houses by raising the impervious surface ratio. In choosing an average dwelling unit type, the idea is to permit the developer a wide range of choices. If the developer desires to use a larger lot and not obtain maximum density by selling more expensive lots, that is his choice. On the other hand, the developer may build using the denser dwelling unit types and, at that density, will be assured of meeting all the other standards (the exception, as noted previously, would be single-story patio or atrium houses which might be limited by impervious surface ratios). If the ordinance is to have flexibility, there should be a number of dwelling types with higher densities than the one used to establish the district standards. If this is not done, the maximum density can only be achieved by using only one or two dwelling unit types, which results in few economically viable mixes of dwelling types and may lead to most developments having similar mixes of dwellings.

A small error is introduced by the calculation. As open space ratios become very large, it is likely that the development will have a long entrance road, thus effectively doubling or tripling the length of road and right-of-way in the development (see illustration 8). It is possible to make an estimate of the percentage of the buildable area in the "extra" right-of-way. If, in a development of .90 open space ratio, it was determined that approximately 10 percent of the buildable area was in extra road and right-of-way, it would be more accurate to calculate gross density based on an open space ratio of .91. Impervious surface would continue to be calculated on an open space ratio of .90. For those interested in a precise determination of the standards, this additional refinement should not add significantly to the time needed to calculate the standards. The estimate of the increase in road lengths should be based on sketches similar to the illustration in order to accommodate the potential development situations the community is likely to face.

Site Capacity Calculation.

This section explains the philosophy, assumptions, and operation of the site capacity calculation. The calculation will be applied to three different, illustrated sites. It should be noted here that the three major elements of the calculation—the natural resource protection standards, the recreational standards, and the bufferyard estimator—will be discussed separately at the end of this section.

The concept of carrying capacity has been borrowed from ecology. It describes a critical point in the interaction of a population with its environment, that point where the population is so large that increases in population cannot be sustained by the environment. Carrying capacity is often defined in terms of density, the population per unit of area, which helps to explain why the concept caught the attention of the planning profession. A natural community moves toward a state of balance. In sensitive communities, where the environment is harsh, there are few species with simple interactions. These populations are often subject to violent oscillations; they grow beyond the carrying capacity and thus crash in bad years. Human populations are not immune to this phenomenon. Overgrazing in Africa has led to large-scale desertification: the edge of the Sahara Desert moved hundreds of miles south in the recent droughts, and thousands died in the resulting famine. The capacity and value of many western rangelands have been reduced by the same process, albeit with less impact on human populations.

Carrying capacity, as the term is used in planning, describes the intrinsic constraints on the development of an area. The concept may be thought of as having three components: environmental, social (population), and economic. Initially, the notion of carrying capacity was applied only to analyses of such natural resource and environmental factors as soils, slopes, and hydrological data; however: "Even a full comprehension of environmental constraints does not obviate the need for hard political choices on how, where and with what intensity resources are going to be used.

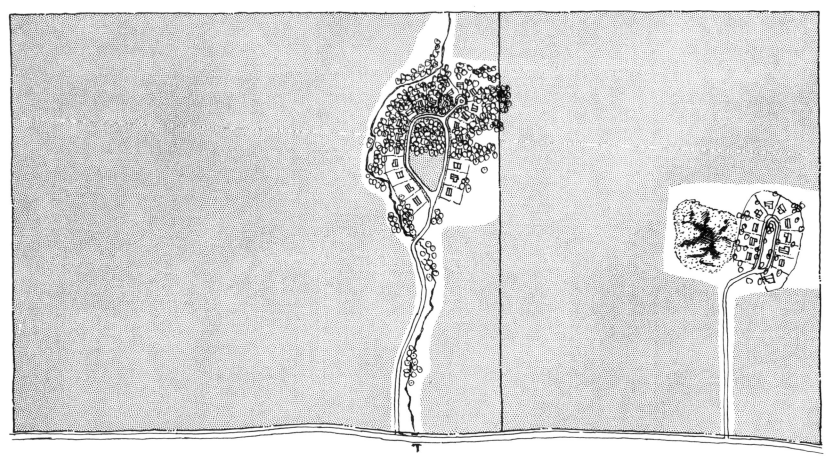

ILLUSTRATION 8

ROAD LENGTH IN DEVELOPMENTS WITH HIGH OPEN SPACE RATIO

These choices involve more than mere compatibility with environmental capacity. They are grounded in social values and preferences....Before an absolute limit on carrying capacity is reached, such as finite land or water supply, overloading may cause unsafe, unhealthy or unpleasant conditions....One can think in terms of a maximum carrying capacity, associated only with a subsistence level of existence, or an optimum density."[17] In addition to the environmental and population or social capacity of a site, an economic "capacity" must be considered. There is a limit to the economic return on any use proposed for a parcel of land. This return varies, of course, with the use.

Carrying capacity has long had a counterpart in land valuation. For example, a farmer who is evaluating the purchase of a farm will assess the soils of several farms. Since soils relate to productivity and indicate areas subject to periodic inundation that may threaten the productivity in some years, the purchaser of a farm can compare the productivity of two farms to determine their value. The farmer is using the concept of carrying capacity, in this case for a selected crop, to determine the value of land. Carrying capacity for regions may be difficult or impossible to establish, although there is ample evidence that water may be a limiting environmental factor in many areas. In the southwest, for example, ground water is being depleted. In the southeast, salt water intrusion results from the withdrawal of too much water from the ground near the ocean. There is certainly good reason to apply carrying capacity to set population limits where such limits can be defined. The ordinance's approach to determining site capacity follows from the points made in this discussion. Site capacity can only be known after one has considered and adjusted for (1) base site area, (2) resource features, and (3) land dedication or restrictive requirements.

Performance zoning relies on the site analysis approach to site capacity in order to ascertain the limits of development. The value of any piece of land is based on objective evaluation of its suitability for development. This system replaces the arbitrary process established by most conventional zoning ordinances. In conventional zoning, basically all land within a single zoning district is of equal value, and significant changes in land value are largely a result of land being reclassified from one zoning district to another.

Certainly there are variations among parcels of land according to their respective sizes, shapes, and natural resource limitations. In addition, the relationship to public infrastructure should play a significant role in com-

parative land valuation. A land valuation system which is much less responsive to governmental whims such as favorable rezonings and much more responsive to actual capacity of a site for development is clearly more sensible and in closer harmony with the public interest. It is, after all, the public which has borne the major cost of calamities such as flooding, water pollution, and sedimentation brought about by the failure of government to preclude inappropriate (we would say "over-capacity") development in the first instance. Performance zoning thus introduces through the site capacity calculation a standard which makes intensity distinctions on a site-by-site rather than on a district basis. Indeed, this logic has been urged by a notable legal scholar who argues that land is, and should be recognized as, "a commodity affected with a public interest...Land is a limited if not depleting commodity which is intimately bound up with our public health and welfare. It is a commodity the use and nuisance of which can impose enormous public and external costs."[18] The site capacity calculation clearly deals with this issue, which conventional zoning has failed to address.

The site capacity calculation takes into account four basic factors which limit development. First, locational and external constraints such as proposed road rights-of-way, utility easements, and other areas which have been otherwise reserved from development are considered. Second, land for bufferyards needed to protect adjoining uses is determined. The third type of constraint is that imposed by sensitive, dangerous, or fragile natural environmental features. Lastly, for residential developments, the calculation takes into account the fact that a certain amount of the site must be reserved for recreational purposes. Each of these limitations on site development, expressed in terms of a certain amount of land area, must be known by a developer in order to calculate the net buildable site area. By multiplying the density factor (or floor area factor in the case of nonresidential development), the developer is able to obtain the maximum use intensity possible on the site. For the purpose of assessing the relative potential of the site, the site capacity calculation may be done in preliminary fashion in ten to fifteen minutes using soil maps as a data base. The calculation required for a building permit must be based on on-site survey data and is therefore more time-consuming.

Illustrations 9–11 and table 3 offer three examples of sites proposed for development. The site capacity calculation is provided for each.

Site A has few capacity limitations; therefore, the standards of the district,

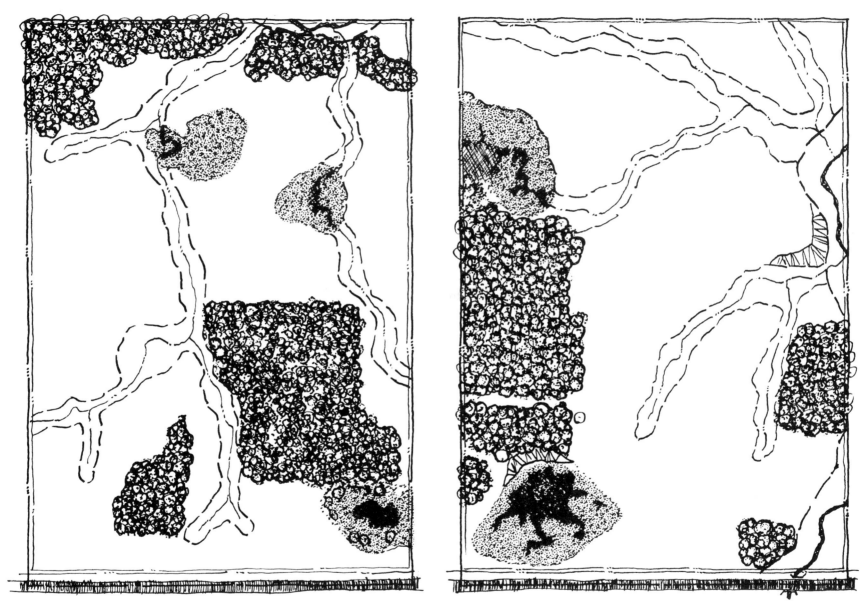

Site A   ILLUSTRATIONS 9–11   Site B

Three Illustrative Sites for Site Capacity Calculation

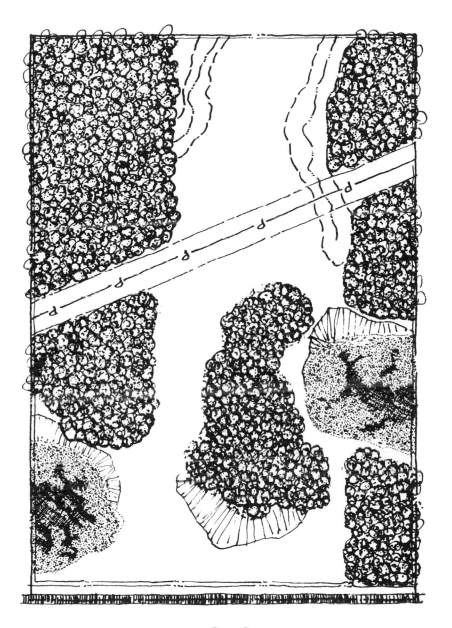

Site C

TABLE 3
Site Capacity Calculation for Three Sites

Base Site Area		Site A	Site B	Site C
a.	Gross site area	44.0	44.0	44.0
b.	Rights-of-way	−1.1	−1.1	−4.1
c.	Noncontiguous land			
d.	Reserved land			
e.	Land for other uses			
f.	Bufferyards	−1.32	−1.32	−1.32
	Base site area	41.58	41.58	38.63

Resource Protection	Open Space Ratio	Site A Acres of Land in Resource	Site A Resource Protection Land	Site B Acres of Land in Resource	Site B Resource Protection Land	Site C Acres of Land in Resource	Site C Resource Protection Land
Natural Resource:							
Floodplain	1.00	.5	.5	2.81	2.81		
Wetlands	1.00	2.19	2.19	3.81	3.81	3.62	3.62
Mature woodlands	.85			6.5	5.52	18.44	15.67
Young woodlands	.40	9.82	3.93				
Slope 12–25%	.60			.5	.3	1.68	1.01
Drainageway	.50	4.37	2.19	4.0	2.0	1.62	.82
Total land in resource		= 16.88		= 17.62		= 25.36	
Total resource protection land			= 8.81		= 14.44		= 21.11

Recreation	Site A	Site B	Site C
Base site area	41.58	41.58	38.63
Total land in resources	−16.88	−17.62	−25.36
Total unrestricted land	=24.70	=23.96	=13.27
Recreation multiplier	× .1008	= .1008	× .1008
Total recreation land required	= 2.49	= 2.42	= 1.34
Recreation land in resource areas	−	− 1.42	− 1.34
Total recreation land remaining to be provided	2.49	1.0	0

Determination of Site Capacity	Site A	Site B	Site C
Total resource protection land	− 8.81	14.44	21.11
Total recreation land remaining to be provided	+ 2.49	+ 1	
Total open space	=11.30	=15.44	=21.11
Base site area	41.58	41.58	38.63
District open space ratio	× .35	× .35	× .35
Minimum required open space	=14.55	=14.55	=13.52
Base site area	41.58	41.58	38.63
Total open space or minimum required open space	−14.55	−15.44	−21.11
Net buildable site area	=27.03	=26.14	=17.52
Density factor	× 6.3	× 6.3	× 6.3
Total number of dwelling units	=170	=164	=110

which are more restrictive, control its intensity, not the site capacity calculation. Site B has substantial limitations, and the calculations limit the site to an intensity somewhat below the maximum permitted use. The third site, C, has severe limitations, and the calculation severely limits use of the site. The three sites illustrate most of the components of the calculations. It is clear from these examples that the site capacity calculation does not limit all sites, nor does it prohibit development of sites having significant limitations. The calculation controls only when the site is more limited than the district standards would otherwise require. It is not self-evident when the site capacity calculation will impose more restrictions than the district standards. The conditions under which the site capacity calculation or district standards control are discussed below.

The calculation makes direct subtractions of nonbuildable areas such as future rights-of-way and easements. All sites, regardless of size, shape, district, or other factors, that have 10 percent nonbuildable lands will suffer a 10 percent loss in intensity compared with a site which has no such areas. These deductions are not uncommon in conventional zoning and are well understood by developers and planners.

The bufferyard factor is also subtracted to arrive at the net buildable site area. As with other nonbuildable lands, if 10 percent of the site is in bufferyards, intensity will be similarly reduced. In addition, there is some predictability regarding the percentage of a site needed for this purpose. Site size is an important factor: the smaller the site, the more of it will be occupied by a bufferyard of a given width. Site shape has a similar direct relationship with the percentage of the site lost; as the irregularity of the site increases, so does the percentage of lost area.

While these factors are likely to result in significant reductions in site area for nonresidential uses, the developer may account for this in the selection of his sites. For most residential uses, such choices are unlikely to result in a significant lowering of the intensity except in the case of very small or irregularly shaped sites. Comparison of the proposed land use with those of its neighbors also assists in predicting buildability. The greater the difference in land use intensity classes, the larger will be the percentage of a site occupied by the buffer. Thus, if an intense industrial use is proposed next to residential uses, one can predict a sizable reduction in buildable site area.

The environmental portions of the calculation have the greatest potential to alter site capacity. It is possible to predict the extent to which the environmental calculation will restrict development below the district maximum, but prediction depends on an understanding of the interrelationship of a number of factors. These are best understood by a graph. When the factors are plotted on a graph, the point at which the calculation takes hold can easily be determined. The major factors affecting this are the type of resource and its level of protection, the percentage of the site covered by a resource, and for residential uses the open space standard of the district.

Illustrations 12 and 13 show the impacts of the environmental and recreational variables in districts with low and moderate open space ratios. Note that the environmental factors are constant: 10 percent floodplain, the rest woodland. They function in the same manner in both districts. The major change is brought about because lowering the district open space requirement lowers the point at which the calculated open space requirement crosses the plot of the district minimum. In the example, illustration 12, where the district requires a minimum open space ratio of .20, the point at which the calculated site capacity takes control is where the site contains 10 percent floodplain and 2 percent woodland. When the district minimum is increased to .40, the woodland can increase to 34 percent of the site before this occurs. Districts with very high open space ratios call for sites that are nearly completely covered by resources requiring high levels of protection before the calculation assumes control.

The level of protection required by a resource determines the slope of the line on the plot of the calculation's impact (illustrations 12 and 13). The lower the open space ratio of the resource, the gentler the slope of the plot. The lower open space ratio of the resource dictates that a greater proportion of the site will have to be covered by that resource before the calculated intensities become controlling. As the level of protection increases, so does the slope; thus, the calculation takes over when less of the site is covered by the resource.

The ordinance requires all residential land developments to provide park or recreational area for future residents of those developments. The recreational calculation is based on the allocation of a percentage of the buildable land to recreation. The addition of the recreational calculation actually decreases the slope of the graphic plot, but it raises the point on the vertical axis of the graph from which it starts. The result is to reduce the percentage of a site that may be covered by a resource without having the site capacity calculation control. The amount of reduction is directly related to the project's density: the higher the density, the more impact the recreational element has on the point at which the site capacity calculation becomes controlling.

The theory of this system makes mathematical sense and survives well a commonsense evaluation. A district based on significant clustering should be less sensitive to the presence of some natural resources, since there is sufficient open space available to work around the resource without impacting

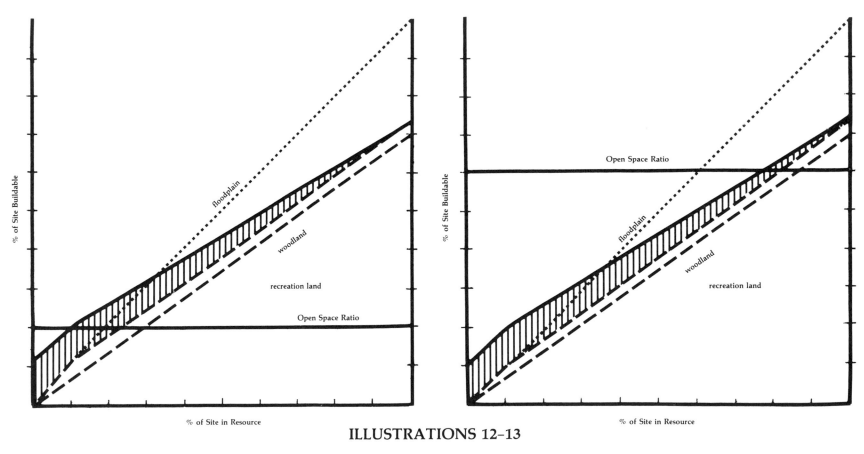

ILLUSTRATIONS 12–13

IMPACTS OF ENVIRONMENTAL AND RECREATIONAL VARIABLES

the total number of units. If no open space is required, as is the case with nonresidential uses, then the presence of unbuildable resource protection land immediately decreases the site's maximum intensity. Thus, the calculation is most restrictive for the highest intensity uses which are most destructive of the environment and which should locate on the best (unrestricted) sites. For residential development, a study of this calculation applied to existing subdivisions determined that the average site in Lake County was 70 percent buildable.[19] Thus, the development district with its .35 open space ratio is more restrictive than the calculation for the average site. Nearly 60 percent of the sites would suffer no reduction for residential development. This provides protection without unreasonable restrictions.

The next three subsections deal with the derivation of standards for bufferyard estimator and the recreational and resource calculations.

Bufferyard area. Land for the installation of a bufferyard required by the ordinance obviously cannot be utilized as any part of a site's buildable area. Accordingly, the amount of this land must be subtracted from a parcel's base site area.

Because a developer may often desire only "ball park" figures in order, for example, to decide whether to pursue consideration of a certain parcel, an alternative to the time-consuming calculation of actual bufferyard requirements was provided. This alternative is included as a table of "bufferyard estimators" in a commentary of the model ordinance.

The explicit subtraction of bufferyard area from site capacity serves three functions. First, it avoids misleading the developer by providing an excessively high estimate of site capacity as a result of not having taken into account land which will, in fact, be unavailable for development. A common fault of conventional zoning is that it may increase expectations to an unrealistic level by not relating development "maximums," such as density, to other ordinance requirements. The result can be additional tension between the municipality and the development community. Second, subtracting land required for bufferyards at this point avoids "double counting" of natural resource protection areas. Whenever such resources are present on a site and can be utilized to provide the bufferyards required, such resources will be protected by the bufferyard, and they should not be "counted" again and deducted in the resource calculation part of the site capacity calculations. Finally, it has generally been the case that small and irregularly shaped parcels are more difficult to develop than larger and

more regularly shaped ones. The bufferyard area automatically lowers the intensity of such sites, thus providing a valuable control. When the bufferyard area is subtracted from base site area, a greater percentage of small or irregularly shaped sites is taken away, resulting in a smaller area available for building; thus, the calculation lowers permitted intensity and thereby provides a more realistic capacity of such sites for development.

Recreational calculations. The recreational land calculation requires that a certain amount of land remain available for recreation in all residential developments. The amount of land varies with the zoning district and density of the proposed development. At the outset, it should be emphasized that "any old land" will not suffice to meet the recreational land requirements. Recreational land must be suitable for recreational activity. It may not, therefore, consist solely of marsh or floodplain, for example.

Increasingly, communities have attempted to impose certain "dedication" requirements on property owners who seek to develop their property. The law on developer donations is inconsistent because there is a great disparity in the nature of, and the procedure whereby, donations have actually been required by various communities.[20] Generally, however, required dedication of land for recreational purposes has been upheld as falling within the police power (or specific standards of enabling legislation, or both). The basis of this conclusion is that increased population together with decreasing open space justifies compulsory dedication "without the necessity of justifying the particular application upon the needs specifically created by an individual builder."[21]

Because land suitable for recreation may also constitute natural resource features, the developer may preserve the resource and satisfy the recreational land requirements simultaneously. For example, areas of forest or shorelines are resources which are restricted from development, but which may be designated and used as the development's recreational land. Other resource land, such as floodplains and wetlands, for example, are not suitable for recreation.

The recreational land requirements for each district are based on the maximum permitted intensity for the district. For example, in the development district, the density (without any bonus) is based on the village house, which is the average dwelling type used in arriving at the density factor and thus determines the maximum population. The .10 of unrestricted land is derived from the amount of recreational land needed for a village house development with no open space.

The ordinance has imposed a recreational land standard of 5.5 acres per one thousand persons. This figure was selected both because it appears to provide an adequate amount of space and because it has survived local court scrutiny.[22] There are a number of standards frequently used in recreational planning from which a standard may be chosen. The recreational calculation cannot set aside the huge land holdings appropriate for a regional usage nor need it attempt to provide for the protection of natural areas, since another element of the site capacity calculation deals with that issue directly. A community may also make a determination of what recreational activities are likely to be engaged in by one thousand people and then estimate the area needed for such activity. It should be noted that the model ordinance uses a lower standard, 3.5 acres per thousand, in the urban core district because the life-styles of urban dwellers and suburban dwellers differ. The method used to determine the standard is a matter of regional concern. The amount of recreational land necessary is a function of local recreational activity and will vary considerably with climate and differences of community "character," for example.

Resource protection land. This element of the calculation adjusts for the presence of land that needs protection from development. This includes land classed as a natural resource or natural feature. Each resource is protected by the open space ratio designated for each such resource. The fifteen resources or features listed in the model ordinance are ones which required regulation in northeastern Illinois. The resources listed and the level of protection need to be adapted to local conditions. For example, other natural resources or features may be appropriate for regulation in other areas; these include alluvial soils, limestone areas, highwater tables (areas with seasonal water tables less than one foot deep), slopes (50 percent or more), rock outcrop areas, erosion hazard or landslide areas, active fault zones, cliffs, cliff buffers, tidelands, buffers for unique areas, wildlife nesting grounds, and aquifer recharge areas.

Several natural features, such as floodplains and watercourses, are so intolerant of development that they must remain 100 percent in open space (see the model ordinance to determine what use this designation permits). Others, such as drainage swales and woodlands, require less protection—or fare less well when the public benefit to be derived from their pro-

tection is balanced against the burden (cost) to the landowner who might otherwise realize considerable economic returns from complete development of such land.

The most severely regulated features tend to be those which, if not regulated, could present some threat to the public safety or health (e.g., floodplains). On the other end of the spectrum are resources which play a less critical role in moderating phenomena (e.g., lakes, pond buffers). Even to the extent that regulation of these latter features is based more on protection of a common good, such as air or water quality, whose degradation poses a potential cost or threat to the public, these regulations are well within the scope of the police power.

Prior to enacting an ordinance which designates resources and features to be regulated and standards applicable thereto, it is recommended that a natural features/resources plan be developed. This document should be the product of a careful study and should delineate the reasons for protecting the resources and the standards needed to do the job. There are numerous examples of such studies. Whether one chooses as a model the techniques of one of the leading landscape architects, such as Ian McHarg or Philip Lewis,[23] or more developer-oriented systems, such as those by Rahenkamp, Sachs, and Wells,[24] is a matter of local choice. The system used to develop the background for the model ordinance was an adaptation of a system developed by Angis Hills[25] which has a rigid scientific and ecological basis since it orders each environmental area from macro- down to micro-detail.

There are four basic classifications in this system: site regions, physiographic complexes, physiographic site classes, and site types (see illustration 6), each of increasingly finer scale. It is a system that can be adapted to a wide variety of purposes without destroying its basic structure. This makes it especially useful as a planning technique.

Site regions are either land or water regions. The boundaries between water and land regions are obvious. Boundaries between site regions on land are defined by macro-climatic differences. Transitions may be abrupt, as is the case in the west where macro-climatic differences closely follow elevation. A transition from a grassland to forested area is often the result of macro-climatic changes. For many jurisdictions there may be only one site region. The boundaries between fresh, brackish, and saltwater environments are logical dividing lines between aquatic site regions. These boundaries should be easily mapped.

Physiographic complexes are distinguished by macro-land forms. A shift in the geology from glacial till to lake-deposited sands distinguishes two site classes. A shift from glacial till to an area with shallow or exposed bedrock is another such divide. The shift from piedmont to coastal plain is a classic divide between two complexes. There will be cases where the geology is unchanged, but a shift in topographic or hydrologic conditions would still require different designations. In Lake County, the glacial till ends with a sharp bluff along the Lake Michigan shoreline. The watershed of Lake Michigan is shallow, rarely more than a mile in depth, and has eroded substantially; thus, the drainage system is well defined with substantial relief, while the rest of the county, despite its identical geology, is characterized by a poorly defined drainage system with numerous depressional areas. The divide between the Lake Michigan watershed with its bluffs and ravines and the Mississippi watershed which is basically flat separates two complexes that are important to distinguish. Most physiographic complexes are quite large and may be easily mapped with high accuracy.

Under the system used in performance zoning, most of the natural features and resources are physiographic site classes. They are characterized by topographic or hydrologic factors, vegetation, soil types, or land form distinctions. Woodlands, prime agricultural land, steep slopes, floodplains, wetlands, and drainageways all constitute physiographic site classes. Each requires an accurate definition to permit mapping, but community-wide mapping of the features is not a prerequisite to enactment of the ordinance. In fact, "pre-mapping" is not recommended for two reasons. First, the process is very time-consuming. Further, the basic sources (such as topographic or soil maps) are generally not sufficiently accurate for the required small-scale application. Accordingly, the mapping of natural features on a parcel-by-parcel basis at the time they are proposed for development is a far more preferable system. The need for definitional precision must be stressed. The features on-site can be regulated only to the extent that they can be accurately (and simply) identified.

For example, "floodplain" has several definitions, some of which are far more encompassing than others. In order for a community to regulate its concept of a floodplain, its ordinance must carefully state what shall (and by implication what shall not) constitute "floodplain." For the same reason that we have not recommended "pre-mapping" (inaccurate basic sources), we caution against ordinance definitions which rely on a single source.

Continuing with the floodplain example, a community may wish to define a floodplain as "any area so designated on X maps, Y maps, or Z maps...whichever is more restrictive."

Some physiographic site classes are such that it makes sense to subdivide them into smaller units, site types, to provide more precise levels of definition. Slopes of different steepness and forests of different types or stages of growth are examples of sensible site types. Site types should only be used when parts of an entire site class require different forms of regulation.

The four categories are illustrated on the hypothetical cross-section of land (illustration 14). Individual communities should develop their own resource studies. Whatever system is chosen for developing the resource protection standards, the analysis is intended to distinguish areas needing significantly different treatment by the zoning regulations. The reason for three types of forest in the model ordinance is the extreme sensitivity of oaks, which are the dominant species in northeastern Illinois. This dictated three levels of protection. Other areas may need only make the distinction between an advanced old field succession and a forest. A distinction between site types should not be made unless a different level of protection is required.

Environmental protection of resources identified in the plan is based on an open space ratio assigned to each resource. Other systems are based on impervious surface ratios or on unique measures for each resource. Open space was chosen rather than impervious surface because it is a better measure of the level of protection. The impervious surface approach fails to control how much resource land is actually disturbed. Yards and rights-of-way are often completely worked over by construction equipment, even though they remain pervious after development. The open space ratio excludes all such areas and is thus more protective. The unique measures approach was rejected because it is too complex.

The open space ratios for different resources are taken from those identified in a natural resources plan which attempts to look at the resources from a variety of perspectives. Unfortunately, there is no handy reference guide with definitive standards for environmental protection. We know all too little about the environment, and even when the knowledge is there, human arrogance and greed continue to plague our ability to interact with the environment without destroying it. We all know that rivers flood, yet we persist in locating in floodplains. It costs about $1,750,000,000 per year for the federal government to provide disaster relief for flooding damage.[26] Anyone who watches television knows that canyons in southern California are subject to fires, flash floods, and mudslides, yet people continue to build and buy expensive homes there. Nevertheless, standards can be set that seek to protect us from the environment and the environment from us. While we do not fully understand how nature balances all its interrelated systems thoroughly enough to model them mathematically as a means of testing alternative protection standards, we certainly understand the importance of various resources and the damage that man can inflict. The standards that must be set should err on the side of safety. In engineering, where tests of structural strength are possible, it is not uncommon to introduce a safety margin of 100 percent or more. Space vehicles, aircraft, and many other vehicles or plants have dual or even triple systems to avert failures and accidents. Good standards can be developed in which the community can have confidence.

There exists no formula for the empirical determination of open space ratios, but there is a tremendous body of knowledge about the environment: the standards must be deduced from that material. First, there is the matter of the importance of the resource itself. Is the resource sufficiently important to the general welfare of the public, to major environmental cycles on which we depend, or to future generations to warrant protection?

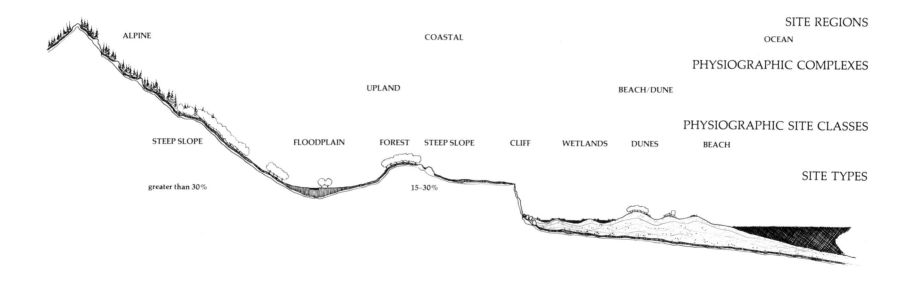

ILLUSTRATION 14

RESOURCE CLASSIFICATION SYSTEM

Numerous factors bear on the issue. Is the resource rare or economically valuable? What are its natural functions? Are those functions important to natural cycles or to the food chain? Does the resource serve as a moderator, protecting or stabilizing a natural cycle? How is the resource involved in geomorphological processes (a question which requires the resource's role and man's role in altering these natural processes to be explored)? There are also health and safety concerns. Is the resource unstable? Can it pose a hazard to life or property? Finally, does the resource provide social or cultural amenities to the community?

The more important the need to protect a resource, the higher its level of protection should be. In addition, there are unique factors about a resource and man's interactions with it which dictate more or less protection. A resource which is easily destroyed, degraded, or rendered unusable requires more protection than a resource that is less easily damaged. Different land uses do different things to resources, and resources have different levels of tolerance for different land uses and the secondary impacts of development. This should be understood. From this body of knowledge standards can be deduced. After they have been tentatively set, they should be reviewed. Are there uses that cannot be located anywhere else but on the resource? Harbors, for example, must be located on lakes. The standards should permit such uses. Are there other ways to protect a resource? If such studies are conducted, the standards will not be arbitrary. The fact that the environmental standards have been deductively derived from careful study removes them from the realm of arbitrariness. While they may not be the result of the direct application of a scientific formula, they are the product of scientifically legitimate thought processes.

In addition to the open space ratio in the site capacity calculation, the ordinance may also prescribe alternative measures to protect particular resources; for example, feature-specific use regulations may be prescribed. In some cases, additional degrees of flexibility in protecting the resources have been provided (see, e.g., the discussion of woodlands).

Lastly, there are standards which relate to all developments. Soil erosion, stormwater detention, and water quality are performance standards which, although designed to protect the watercycle, have such wide application. Of the three only the water quality standards may need explanation. Most areas have or will soon have a water quality plan. Urban stormwater runoff is a major source of water pollution in many areas. As urbanization

continues, this problem grows. It is far easier to deal with the problem through good design than by maintenance activities such as street sweeping or structural measures to purify stormwater runoff. The standards seek a 50 percent reduction in pollutant loads for impervious surfaces. There are a variety of design and landscape measures that reduce loads or trap pollutants; in some cases they can be provided at less cost than traditional designs. The developer has complete flexibility in choosing which techniques to use and gets credit for some techniques that are required for other purposes. This is a new area and further research on techniques is needed.

Bufferyards.

The land use intensity classification system previously described separates uses into groupings of relatively equal nuisance value. Bufferyards are intended to separate uses that are incompatible. Performance zoning is based on a rejection of the assumption made by traditional zoning that widely disparate uses can be kept apart through districting. A proliferation of zoning districts and frequent ad hoc zoning changes have proved this assumption to be false. It is appropriate to note that with the ad hoc proceedings of conventional zoning there is an economic incentive to seek rezonings because large increases in land values typically accrue to the landowner in rezonings from low to high intensity. Making a somewhat larger point, Richard Babcock has written: "Land values often fluctuate substantially because of activities of government in granting favorable zoning, building highways, extending water and sewer mains, or any of a multitude of other factors. The land holder affected by such activities can reap enormous profits simply by having the good fortune to own land in the right place at the right time."[27] Thus, conventional zoning gives positive reinforcement to an individual who seeks to break down the very protection offered by conventional zoning.

The very small number of districts indicates that the performance zoning approach to nuisance regulation is not primarily by districting. Rather, performance zoning allows many different uses to develop within a district (particularly within a development or urban district). It then requires that the more intense or nuisance-producing uses "buffer," literally, their impact on adjacent and neighboring uses.

The bufferyards required by performance zoning serve as an economic disincentive for a considerably more intense use to locate next to a relatively much less intense use. The greater the difference in land use intensity class between two uses, the larger and more densely planted the bufferyard between them must be. A large bufferyard means less buildable area, more intense planting, and increased site improvement costs. On the other hand, performance zoning has provided far more incentive than conventional zoning for a mix of uses which are only "slightly incompatible." So, for example, a small office may locate next to a residential area without having to pay the expensive price of a rezoning. It must, however, "pay the price" of effectively buffering itself from the residences in order to shield them from any "nuisance" or negative impact, including possible diminution of their value.

The key to the bufferyard system is that it offers a landowner a known level of protection. Proponents of conventional zoning would respond that landowners do have protection when adjoining open land is similarly zoned. Unfortunately, the history of zoning (or, more accurately, rezoning) is replete with examples of residentially zoned land being converted to commercial or industrial use. In actuality the theoretical certainty of protection afforded by a zoning map is often not accorded the landowner in reality.

The bufferyard required for a proposed development is determined by reference to a matrix which indicates that, given the land use intensity class of the proposed use and the use adjacent to it, a specified unit of land area and plant material must be provided. It follows from this that the same bufferyard may not be required around the entire perimeter of a parcel. Bufferyards are required against streets, as well as against private property, in certain instances.

Given a system of ranking uses into intensity classes, a study based on existing land use juxtapositions should enable planners to evaluate the effectiveness of proposed bufferyards. In conducting such a study, staff trained in landscape architecture or other design professions are essential. The specifications for bufferyards contained in the model ordinance evolved from numerous tests. The bufferyards were initially developed mathematically so that there would be a regular progression to more intensive buffers. Next, each proposed buffer was drawn in plan and elevation, with plant material sized for both maturity and five years after planting. The illustrations in the model ordinance show the size five years after planting; this is a realistic way to assess the initial effectiveness of plant material. In addition to drawings, a model was built in which the effec-

tiveness of various buffer plantings could be examined visually. The buffers selected from this process were then priced, and additional modifications made. Field trips and photographs were used to obtain further verification of the effectiveness of various bufferyards. Then, the tentatively formulated bufferyard requirements were applied to several actual sites, on each of which several different developments were hypothesized. The bufferyard requirements were scrutinized for their economic consequences and for the extent to which they acted as a physical constraint on the hypothesized development as opposed to what was actually built under conventional zoning. Given the differential between two land use intensity classes, each of the options of the bufferyard class is felt to give equal protection. The variables of distance, intensity of planting, plant material, and land forms are all used in one buffer or another.

The bufferyards in the model ordinance are designed for the climatic conditions of northeastern Illinois. The climate is harsh, characterized by cold winters, often with little snow cover, strong winds, cold wet springs, droughty summers, and dense clay soils. This area is best described as savannah, a transitional area from the eastern deciduous forest to the grasslands of the great plains. Evergreens, except in certain micro-climates, are not native to the region and generally will not regenerate naturally if part of a stand is damaged. The bufferyards in the model ordinance are believed to be the best possible for such a climate, but it was recognized that for some six months of the year the buffer was not visually as effective as possible. In areas where evergreens are native or less sensitive, the substitution of at least 30 percent of the canopy trees and understory plantings with evergreens is recommended. The studies all indicated that evergreens were more effective than canopy or understory trees. Where evergreens do well, consideration of reducing the widths of the buffers may also be in order to reflect the more effective barrier created. One note of caution: some evergreens tend to lose most of their lower branches with age. The mix and selection of species and the use of shrubs can compensate for this condition. The bufferyards and plant materials must be tailored to the climatic conditions of the area.

Transportation.

Surveys conducted as part of comprehensive planning studies or to determine neighborhood needs often find that traffic is a major concern. Similarly, drafters of the model ordinance found that traffic congestion and noise from traffic were the two nuisances most frequently cited in a survey conducted in Lake County. It is surprising that, despite the frequency with which the concern is voiced and our technical understanding of the traffic problem, planning and zoning have failed to provide a remedy. The arterial network is typically ignored in regional transportation plans or regarded as a secondary level of planning. There has also been a failure to integrate traffic concerns into land use and zoning decisions. While the undesirable effects of strip development having free access to roads has been recognized for years, neither local zoning nor state highway departments have seriously addressed the issue of access. Rather, state highway departments almost "automatically" take the view that they cannot prohibit a landowner's access.

This excessive conservatism is not necessitated by legal constraints on the police power. The regulation of traffic congestion and road safety is one which the police power should actively pursue. Instead, planners often find themselves in the embarrassing position of arguing against a new curb cut for a proposed development, explaining the local community's concern for protecting the integrity of a road, only to have the developer display the curb cut permit issued by the state highway department. This occurs despite the fact that standards for curb cuts found in many engineering handbooks generally recommend distances of 600 to 1,200 feet between them. In the past, as one road became congested we built another. Highway construction in most urban areas has always lagged behind need even during the peak years of the federal highway program. Today many states find it difficult to maintain the existing system, much less to build new roads. Concern about access to arterial roads is a vital one, whose time now seems to have come.

There is a second set of concerns related to transportation that performance zoning seeks to address, the environmental impacts of highways. Roads are a major factor in the generation of stormwater runoff. Significant portions of the total impervious areas of a community are in streets. Flooding has often been increased because roads increase the total runoff. Further, the construction of storm sewers speeds the arrival of runoff at rivers and streams. The water coming from streets and roads is very polluted. The per-acre loadings of pollutants are higher for highways than for most other land uses.[28] Pavements absorb heat during the day and radiate it at night. This has undesirable consequences for local climates and for the maintenance of polluted air masses in urban areas. Road construction also disrupts the environment: forests are damaged and drainage patterns are altered; cut and fill results in slopes that cannot be easily revegetated. Roads are the source of noise, vibrations, dirt, litter, and other nuisances. The pedestrian and to a lesser extent motorists are subject to major safety hazards. Dangers are most severe when pedestrian traffic and vehicular traffic intermix, particularly if the pedestrians are children. Residential land uses maximize such intermixing. Lastly, roads cost money. Excessive standards can raise housing costs for no practical reason. The development community frequently complains that excessive residential road standards unnecessarily raise the cost of housing. Thus, environmental and cost concerns both point to narrower residential roads. All of these concerns for the environment and cost are seldom addressed in conventional zoning.

Performance zoning imposes certain specific access requirements for different land uses. Residential uses are most adversely affected by the noise and hazard of a busy road. Further, by their very nature residential uses require the most frequent access to streets. The capacity of a road to handle traffic is adversely affected by the frequency of access. Thus, common sense dictates that individual residential dwellings not be permitted access to major roads: these roads carry the heaviest traffic volumes and frequent access would disrupt them; at the same time, the heavy volumes would be a hazard to the residential areas. Access by individual residential dwellings is restricted to residential streets. Commercial, industrial, and other uses that generate high daily traffic volumes are prohibited from taking access on residential streets. This separation of uses by the type of street they may take access from is important to performance zoning's basic goal of minimizing negative impacts that one use may impose on another.

A second level of access control is introduced on the higher levels of streets, collectors and arterials. On these roads, access is restricted to certain intervals. For most collectors, the restriction is not very limiting, since under performance zoning these roads serve as local access streets for nonresidential uses. As the traffic volume on the roads becomes more intense, the access spacing increases. On arterials access is limited to intervals of 800 or 1,200 feet. This requires the development of a collector road network to provide access to uses within areas bounded by arterials (superblocks). Illustration 15 shows the impact of these requirements on a portion of an arterial road. The number of access points is reduced from fifteen to three by the performance standards.

Arterial roads have been said to form superblocks, a notion that has been

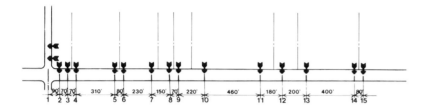

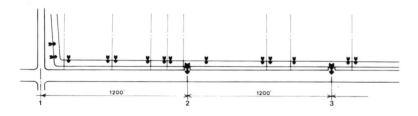

ILLUSTRATION 15

HIGHWAY ACCESS CONTROLS

around since Clarance A. Perry's *The Neighborhood Unit* (1929). Efficient development of a superblock transportation system requires developers to create an internal road network within each superblock that provides access to individual uses. While this notion is often opposed by landowners, there is little basis to conclude that it is a radically new concept. Large residential developers have used this technique since its inception: Radburn, New Jersey in 1929 and Levittown, Pennsylvania in the 1950s are two examples. In more recent new towns such as Reston, Virginia and Columbia, Maryland the concept is applied to residential and nonresidential prop-

erties. There is no legitimate reason that government cannot and should not provide the public the same control that the private sector has long provided when a single owner controlled a development. The need for a comprehensive interior road network holds true whether the land use is residential or commercial.

Most superblocks are developed over time by a series of developers, which is one reason government has had difficulty dealing with access problems. It would be unfair to deny a landowner the right to develop because his property is too close to an existing access point on the arterial highway when the required collector roads do not exist. The problem is not the standards but in the administrative and procedural method of implementing them. How can the standards be applied to permit development of an internal system incrementally? This problem has been partially resolved in residential developments for years. It is not at all uncommon for a community to require stub streets to adjoining properties. Some progressive planning agencies often use their staff to plan a collector street network for an entire area or superblock. The mandated stub street is incorporated into performance zoning. In order to deal better with the problem a further refinement is introduced: temporary access. This enables the community to permit access on a first-come, first-serve basis until the collector road connecting properties is completed. Once properties sharing common frontage roads are linked, the temporary accesses may be closed by the community. This gives the community power regardless of the commitment of the state highway department.

It is unfortunate that an explanation of why such a system of collector roads is necessary still seems required. In many parts of the country the basic arterial network that we have today was established by the farm roads; surprisingly few roads have been added since. In Lake County only 60.27 miles of new arterial or expressway right-of-way have been created since 1939, although the population has gone from 120,000 to 430,000 in those forty years. It is not surprising that the road network is becoming congested. This is true even though the 1950s and 1960s saw frantic highway construction. With increasing concern about government spending, it is unlikely that that level of construction can be achieved again.

What is the capacity of the road network to support new development? For arterial highways, carrying capacity may be defined as level of service C, a traffic condition in which flow is slightly constricted by the volume of traffic, so that flow is relatively free and average speeds of forty-five miles per hour may be maintained. If traffic increases, the flow becomes more constricted and speed declines. Since arterial roads are intended to facilitate travel within or through a region, the maintenance of high speeds is essential. Permitting the arterial networks to become congested and speeds to be lowered cannot be justified unless an expressway system with roads spaced about two miles apart can be developed. Such a condition was never attainable in the best of times and is totally unrealistic today. In Lake County a carrying capacity study based on development in individual superblocks was conducted. Sixteen superblocks were chosen for study, a sample about 5 percent of the total. In three of the sixteen superblocks two or more roads were already at level of service C, so that development could only be accommodated by increasing the number of lanes. The average density of new development permitted without exceeding level of service C in the study was only .75 dwellings per acre. This estimate is optimistic since the study considered only development in the superblocks in question. A sizable portion of available capacity would actually be used by development occurring elsewhere in the region. Given the very low capacity of the existing network to sustain growth, there must be an endeavor to insure adequate capacity. Control of access is an essential first step.

There remain only two ways to increase capacity: double the number of lanes on existing roads or develop new arterial roads. The costs of either approach are beyond the capabilities of government. Thus, performance zoning attempts to regulate development to insure the integrity of arterials by requiring intensive land uses to make improvements on the roads which will provide adequate capacity after development. As a preliminary to this end, a traffic impact report is required by certain proposed developments.

For small developments unlikely to have significant impact on road capacity, no special studies are needed, although the provision of temporary access roads and collectors providing access to adjoining properties is required. Acceleration and deceleration lanes must be provided if the access is to be a permanent access for the superblock.

If the development intensity is above the critical level, a study is required to determine the needed improvements. The developer must make such improvements as center turn-lanes, right-of-way dedications, or additional traffic lanes. Provisions for a cash contribution are available for areas where insufficient frontage is developed to make the improvements worthwhile until more development occurs in the corridor. Regional

developments—those that have not only high trip generation rates but serve regional functions—must study whether the improvements required are needed beyond their own property line or superblock. This is necessary because regional centers may cause congestion several miles from the site. These high intensities can be permitted only if improvements are made to that part of the system impacted by them.

The other major concerns with streets are environmental impact and cost. Standards currently required for residential streets in many communities are excessive. It often seems that engineers, the highway superintendent, snow plow crews, and the fire and police departments would like all roads built to four-lane arterial standards. Environmental, aesthetic, and economic concerns all point toward reduced standards for residential streets. Performance zoning has attempted to deal with these issues.

There are several historic reasons that excessive road standards have been imposed. First, a rural community often makes few demands on developers; thus, inadequate or substandard roads are often accepted only to become a burden in later years. Communities reacting to this often adopt excessive standards. The use of the grid system in many cities and suburbs has also generated problems. The grid system makes it difficult to distinguish among different levels of roads, with the result that through-traffic often occurs on streets that should be completely residential. In many cities streets were built in an era when most people walked or used public transportation and have proved inadequate for automobiles. As local officials responded to these problems, the simplest solution was to increase the standards. A third type of problem has arisen as suburban communities adopted standards developed in large cities. The transfer of city standards to suburban intensities and road patterns was not accompanied by an analysis as to whether the same street widths needed in the city with small, narrow lots and a grid street system were applicable to low density subdivisions with curvilinear streets and cul-de-sacs.

The factors which should determine street width can be easily identified. Traffic volume is certainly one. A road which serves only a few trips per day need not be as wide as a busier one. The need or potential for on-street parking may require additional road width to accommodate parking lanes. On residential streets the need for on-street parking is related to lot frontage and lot size, because as lot size and frontage decrease the chances are that drives and garages will become inadequate for off-street parking and that one or more cars are likely to be parked on the streets. Vehicular speed also affects appropriate road width. Where two vehicles approach each other at a relative velocity of 110 miles per hour (two cars traveling fifty-five miles per hour), the road requires greater width to accommodate safe passing than where the relative velocities are only twenty miles per hour (two cars traveling at ten miles per hour). Lastly, there is the concern that two vehicles traveling in opposite directions will meet at a point where only a single open lane exists. Where the odds of such a meeting are very low, only a single traffic lane may be needed.

The performance zoning hierarchy of standards serves to separate residential streets from collector streets, which are likely to serve nonresidential uses. Since the trip generation rate of most nonresidential uses is several times higher than residential rates, this lowers traffic volume and makes narrower streets feasible. The standards also tend to separate roads by design speed. Within the residential street class, standards vary as a function of traffic volume, which is directly related to the number of dwelling units served and design speed. On residential streets these variables interact with the lot frontage to determine needed width. A range of street or cartway widths is therefore provided.

Minimum road widths in the model ordinance were derived from a detailed analysis. Research by Dr. H. Topps of Frankfurt, Germany furnished the technical methodology.[29] First, street widths adequate to handle peak hour situations without relationship to parking were determined. Traffic counts in several Lake County subdivisions showed that 2.55 was the average number of total trips during the 3 PM to 6 PM period. This figure is higher than older California data, which calculated 2.34 trips for the same time frame.[30] Next, the mix of vehicles on the street during the three-hour peak time period was determined by survey; on Lake County residential streets the mix was 90 percent cars, 5 percent vans, and 5 percent trucks or school buses.

The next step was to determine the number of meetings on a 0.1 mile length of street in the 3 PM to 6 PM time period. Research resulted in the following formula:

$$N = \frac{[(0.5 \times H \times T) - 1.1] \times [H \times T]}{2},$$

where N is the number of vehicular meetings per 0.1 mile of street during peak hours, H is the number of households taking access to the street or its tributaries, and T is the number of trips per household.

Before the results of the calculation can be used to determine minimum street widths, the type of vehicles involved in a meeting must also be determined. There are six possible combinations of the three types of vehicles mentioned above. The percentage of meetings is shown in table 4.

TABLE 4
PERCENT OF TOTAL MEETINGS BY VEHICLE TYPE

Type of vehicle meeting	Percent of total vehicle meetings (from Lake County surveys)
Auto/auto	81.0
Auto/van	9.0
Auto/truck-bus	9.0
Van/van	0.25
Van/truck-bus	0.5
Truck-bus/truck-bus	0.25

The frequency of a meeting of different classes of vehicles is a critical element in determining road width. Having previously determined the number of vehicles involved in meetings during the peak three-hour period on a street, one may calculate the number of meetings involving a particular type of vehicle by multiplying the total number of vehicular meetings by the appropriate percentage of meetings in table 4. Requirements for residential street widths were selected on the basis of the decisional standard that a meeting which occurred at least once every ten days during the peak hours should be easily accommodated. Less frequent meetings could require one vehicle to stop in order to let another pass. For residential streets, table 5 provides the number of dwellings required to have one meeting of each vehicular combination every ten days.

By measuring the width needed for two such vehicles and adding a safety margin for clearance, the minimum width of streets can be determined. One additional category was developed where auto/auto meetings are less frequent than once every twenty days. Parking requirements were then added to the traffic lanes to determine final street widths. It should be noted that these street widths do not include curbs. There are fewer options where curbs must be provided since roads must be sized for the maximum meeting.

TABLE 5

NUMBER OF DWELLING UNITS PRODUCING A
MEETING ONCE EVERY TEN DAYS

Vehicular basis of width standard	Maximum dwellings to which standard applies
Auto/auto	15 dwelling units
Auto/truck-bus	31 dwelling units
Van/truck-bus	116 dwelling units
Truck-bus/truck-bus	161 dwelling units

Landscaping, Parking Lots, Lighting, and Signs.

Many nuisances cited as important in the Lake County survey are not directly related to land use, floor area, or total impervious surface, but rather to other details of the development such as unsightly signs, parking areas, and glare from lights. Standards which deal with these nuisances were incorporated into the land use intensity classification to insure less potential for nuisances from buildings, signs, lighting, or parking areas as bufferyards become more transparent. It is clear that good design can abate or eliminate many of these nuisances. The visual impact of parking lots can be made more pleasant by the use of vegetation and other forms of screening. Lighting can be designed to eliminate glare. Landscaping can soften unpleasant buildings and block or reduce glare. Signs may be scaled down. Performance criteria for both general and parking lot landscaping as well as for exterior lighting and signs are specified in the model ordinance's table of land use intensity classification.

In that table letter designations are used to indicate minimum levels of performance. Subsequent sections on each design feature contain the performance criteria associated with each such designation. The intensity of a land use may change depending on whether it is able to comply with each of these standards. In order to be placed in a particular intensity class, a land use must meet all of the standards for that class; thus, the classification of a use can be determined by the criterion having the greatest nuisance value or worst performance.

There are six design classifications for these factors, despite the fact that there are eleven land use intensity classifications. This is done for pragmatic reasons. First, several intensity classifications permit 100 percent impervious surface coverage of the buildable site area; accordingly, there is no need to create special criteria for these classifications. Residential areas were all given the same standard to avoid increasing the cost of dwelling units.

The landscaping requirements for buildings and parking lots were based on sketch plans for several actual sites in much the same manner as the bufferyards were developed. After tentative development, the standards were checked against the landscaping in actual commercial, office, or industrial situations. The most stringent standards have been found to exist in some commercial developments.

The control of signs posed a real dilemma since signs serve legitimate functions and yet often pose real nuisances. Signs have a communication function which a sign ordinance must recognize and permit. Concurrently, though, regulations must control the nuisances. This is a formidable design problem. The sign industry argues that viewing distance and a large message should set the standards; this would permit huge signs unnecessarily visible for a half mile or more. Strict sign regulation exists in several areas. Most shopping centers exercise control over mall signs and even the design of store fronts. Most new towns and many large mixed-use planned developments also exercise strict control. The argument that business is restricted by strict sign regulation is refuted by such self-imposed controls. If private enterprise successfully regulates signs and can still attract businesses to its developments, the legitimacy of the argument that government regulation of signs will destroy business opportunities is considerably weakened. Further, it seems logical that the general public is entitled to the same level of protection that a developer imposes to protect his investment.

As a preliminary to developing the standards for signs in the model ordinance, the size and coverage of signs in areas with "quality" signage were analyzed. Where possible, photos or actual on-site measurements of these areas were used.

The structure of performance zoning provides a unique opportunity to deal creatively with the conflicting interests involved in sign control. Residential neighbors desire to be screened from commercial land uses partially to prevent nuisances such as signs from being seen. Thus, uses for which the ordinance requires heavy buffering have less need to limit the size or number of signs. In addition, the changing standards provided by the land use intensity classification provide an opportunity for more intense land uses to trade off the need to meet certain standards (e.g., sign regulations) against the flexibility of other development options (intensity class). A special sign for arterial roads was also developed; this is discussed in detail later.

The lighting of developments is of great concern to neighbors and travelers. Bright, glaring lights are an obvious problem. Glare can confuse or annoy drivers; it may also partially blind them. In cities and shopping areas bright lights are intended to prevent crime. On the other hand, many suburban residents desire few lights or low intensity lighting in order to retain the suburban or rural character of the area. One wealthy Chicago suburb still maintains its old gas street lights, although they clearly have little value in providing modern levels of illumination.

Several facts about lighting fixtures should be understood. The first is the term "cutoff." Unless there is some form of shield, light radiates in all directions from the source; consequently, most household lamps have some sort of shade. The same concept is applied to outdoor lighting. Where the source is shielded so that no light can escape in a specific direction, a zone of total cutoff exists. The zone of cutoff is delineated in the vertical plane. Illustration 16 shows how the angle of cutoff is measured. Glare is most pronounced along the line of maximum candlepower, also shown in illustration 16.

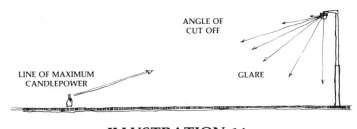

ILLUSTRATION 16

GLARE

It should be fairly obvious that glare occurs when the light source is in direct line with the viewer. Thus, a fixture that is designed so that viewers located on neighboring properties are outside the line drawn from the light fixture to the ground along the angle of total cutoff will fully protect these neighbors from glare. A second measure of protection is to control the illumination at a particular point along the line of maximum candlepower and to insure that total cutoff occurs at ninety degrees. The bufferyards will then provide an additional reduction of glare for light coming out above the line of maximum candlepower. This class of light fixtures should be shorter because they depend more heavily on the bufferyard for protection. A third class of lights has a cutoff angle greater than ninety degrees. In these fixtures the angle of maximum candlepower may be near ninety degrees. The bufferyard and shorter lighting standards are both needed to assist in preventing glare.

The simple standards in the ordinance make it possible to evaluate the performance from drawings and the manufacturers' specifications at the building permit stage. Specifying all three alternatives in this manner makes enforcement reasonably simple. This should minimize the need for on-site testing or verification. It is recommended that the lighting engineer be required to sign and seal a statement indicating that the proposed lighting plan is designed to meet the specifications of the ordinance.

Performance zoning deals with signs along arterial highways in a unique fashion. It requires a bufferyard between various uses and arterial highways and limits direct access. Signs for each land use intensity classification must be located on the other side of the bufferyard where they will not be visible. Gas stations, restaurants, and other uses that depend on casual traffic on the highways to provide business volume may argue that such strict limitation of signs and direct access from an arterial road will negatively affect their businesses. This need not be the case—and will not be if all similar uses are likewise restricted and if the need for directional and locational information is recognized. The arterial sign regulations were designed to meet these needs.

It should be noted that sign and access control increase safety on roads and also reduce visual clutter. Too many signs, seeking to alert people to business locations, tend to reduce legibility. Further, they distract drivers or cause them to drive slowly in order to spot a specific use. Sudden stops, frequent turning movements, and visual distractions reduce safety. The sign industry's arguments that signs are a welcome distraction apply only to interstate traffic, not to arterial roads. In performance zoning, access is limited on arterial roads, leaving collector roads with lower speeds as locations where signs and turning movements are more plentiful and can be safely handled because of the lower speeds and traffic volumes.

Arterial signs must be located between the bufferyard and the arterial highway. Some states have permitted gas stations to display the company symbol on the road right-of-way before the turnoff, thus eliminating the need for a towering sign. This approach guides the development of the arterial sign standards of the model ordinance which regulate those signs needed along major roads to provide directional information. These signs need not be large; many of these uses are chain operations: the logo is all that is needed. A relatively small sign with letters six inches high is both visible[31] and can provide the necessary information without cluttering a highway. In fact, this size of lettering is generally used by state highway departments for their signs. To test the adequacy of arterial type signs, take a phone book and a sample of the longer names in the yellow pages. The method of evaluating standards was to place the size of letters on a sign of the required square footage and to determine whether the message could be displayed using appropriate letters. The arterial sign standard permits a sign of a given size for every 250 feet of arterial road frontage, provided that the area of all signs along a given frontage meet the required area regulations. In order to provide maximum flexibility the number of individual signs, within limits, is the decision of the landowner, so long as the total signage area is not exceeded. A single large sign along a property with substantial frontage is reasonable. Billboards are classified as arterial signs and regulated as described above.

In addition, developments of a certain size which have permanent direct access to the arterial highway are permitted an additional sign identifying the development. These uses would typically be larger, mixed-use developments such as shopping centers or commercial parks. Alternatively, a development that has many small businesses would be able to erect a large number of smaller signs. Burma Shave, after all, was famous for its signs posted along the highways. Those signs that amused decades of auto travelers were about five square feet in area. The arterial sign provides flexibility and choice; it permits essential signage, strictly controls it, and provides great flexibility in how advertising is accomplished.

Standards Applicable to Specific Uses

Article V of the model ordinance should not be unfamiliar to most planners. It contains the myriad of detailed use standards for various permitted uses. The number of required parking spaces is typical of this type of standard. Two sections of this article deserve some explanation: the standards for the various residential dwelling types and the section on design deviations.

Residential Use Regulations.

At first, it may seem inconsistent that an ordinance which seeks to provide a maximum degree of development freedom contains so many detailed regulations governing various forms of residential dwelling unit types. Certainly the traditional zoning ordinance, which typically specifies minimum standards for bulk, setback, lot area, and little else, appears to regulate the residential unit less; however, experience in reviewing plats of subdivisions submitted under a wide range of zoning ordinances reveals the necessity of such detailed regulation. Conventional zoning does nothing to encourage, and in many cases precludes, good design. Further, without continual vigilance on the part of local officials most plans would not even meet many of the standards contained in the applicable codes. Given this generally low level of design, it seems appropriate to set forth standards that will insure a minimal level of achievement. Given the decision to set specific design standards, it becomes appropriate to specify a number of standards for each dwelling type. Off-street parking requirements and unit size, for example, vary with number of bedrooms; therefore, it is reasonable to vary lot size as well. Moreover, such standards can assist in the conservation of land and in encouraging the widest possible housing market. Another major reason for the adoption of comprehensive standards for residential dwelling types is related to maintaining the integrity of the open space requirements. The minimum lot sizes required by this ordinance as well as rights-of-way are excluded from the definition of open space. The standards provide a minimal lot for each unit whether it is sold conventionally or as a condominium or whether it is rented because there is no logical reason for making distinctions on these bases. The yard also defines a minimum area that should be available for private recreation, adequate light and air, and separation of individual dwellings.

A major segment of the population is now unable to purchase a home. This is a problem which zoning should attempt to address. Conventional zoning has exacerbated this problem by requiring ever costlier requirements such as increased lot width, increased lot size, and more frontage improvements, which add substantially to cost and often do not appear to be related logically to the reason that they are imposed in the first place. Often a suburban zoning ordinance requires the landowners to seek a larger lot than would meet the needs of a large segment of the population. This also restricts the market and adds to the cost. The detailed standards of performance zoning are intended to encourage a wider variety of housing types and sizes.

By permitting all types of dwelling units, performance zoning greatly increases the choice of dwelling units which may be constructed as of right (with no need of a zoning change). Since zoning amendments often take many months and increase the cost of land, this can represent a significant financial savings. Further, the flexibility of permitting many different types of residential units as of right enables a developer to shift plans as the market changes without having to become involved in a lengthy and expensive approval process.

Performance zoning also encourages a mix of housing in any particular development. Because the three performance standards, density factor, open space ratio, and impervious surface ratio, interact, it is possible to select a housing type that cannot achieve maximum density while still meeting the minimum open space requirements. The wide range of housing types allows the developer to select several housing types to achieve a mix that permits optimization of the value of the site. The variety of permitted lot sizes enables developers to alter the capacity by selecting units with fewer bedrooms or by shifting dwelling types. Elderly and single-person households, in particular, are likely to benefit from this flexibility.

Performance zoning can also directly address the needs of lower income groups. In the 1950s small "starter" houses were constructed on small lots throughout the nation. Those dwellings provided many families with their first homes. Through the years sizes of both lots and houses have rapidly increased, often because ordinances have required larger lots or instituted minimum square footage requirements. A rule of thumb in the building industry is that the improved lot should not exceed one quarter the total cost of the unit. This has actually accelerated the inflation of housing costs; as square footage has increased, landowners have been able to ask more for a given lot size due to the multiplier effect that is built into the rule of thumb. The result is that more expensive homes must now be constructed on those small lots; consequently, the starter house is disappearing.

The lot size imposed by performance zoning is based on the size of the dwelling. For example, the minimum lot size for a three-bedroom dwelling unit is based on an assumed house size of approximately 1,100 square feet. Dwelling size for a two-bedroom unit is generally near 1,000 square feet. The on-lot impervious surface coverage was designed to accommodate a unit of that size with little room to spare. Thus, as housing size increases or two-car garages are added, the size of the lot must increase, which automatically lowers the density yield of the development, thereby increasing per-lot costs. While this lot size design standard will not cancel out the effects of inflation, it does work to encourage the production of small homes on smaller lots, thus permitting more people to enter the housing market.

The model ordinance recognizes a scale relationship between house and lot. That relationship determined yard to floor area ratios, shadow coverage, building spacing, and other factors. In some areas of the country the size of the average dwelling unit is nearly double that of the 1950s, creating both real and perceived crowding. The standards of performance zoning automatically maintain the scale relationships as the size of dwelling units changes.

In reviewing the lot size standards contained in the model ordinance, planners or builders should recognize that the lot area required for any housing type is somewhat sensitive to climate or latitude. Smaller lots tend to be more viable in warmer climates and lower latitudes where the sun is higher in the sky. The atrium and patio houses are particularly sensitive to latitude since the walled yards are very small and more heavily shadowed. In northern regions larger lots and wider minimum yards are advised in order to insure adequate light during the winter. When reducing minimum yard requirements, planners should also consider the availability of private recreational space and shade.

In the light of the increasing attention being given to solar access, it should be noted that solar access may require that housing be sited in unconventional manners. Solar access often requires east-west streets on which the houses on the south side are best located so that they have no front yard while those on the north side have little rear yard.[32] In order to accommodate solar access, the lot requirements of both conventional zoning and the standards of the model ordinance would have to be substantially revised. Such standards would have to recognize orientation of street and lot.

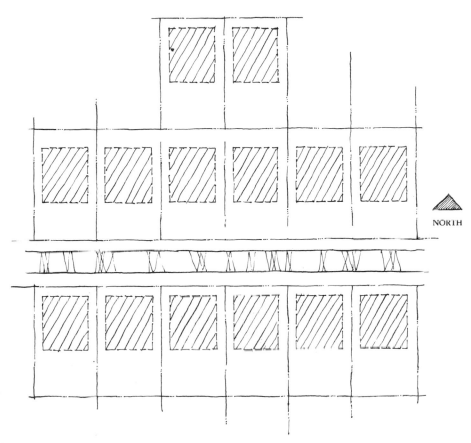

NORTH

ILLUSTRATION 17

Asymmetrical Building Setbacks for Solar Access

While performance zoning is not specifically designed to accommodate solar access, it is clear that some of the dwelling units are well suited to provide it. For example, on small lots single-family houses require an unconventional, asymmetrical layout such as shown in illustration 17. On the other hand, the lot-line house having a side-yard facing south may be an ideal housing type for solar design. Other housing types should be evaluated and lots resized or proportions changed if a community desires to make maximum use of solar access.

Design Deviations.

Designers know that rigid lot standards tend to produce mediocrity rather than encourage good design. For this reason, the model ordinance allows "design deviations"—exceptions to regulations otherwise imposed—in return for certain specified design elements to be provided by the developers.

An example will illustrate the need for such a device. Zoning ordinances adopted in the early 1950s or even 1960s often did little to regulate the design of row houses other than to set lot size, frontage, and setback requirements. Many recent developments have reproduced all the worst features of the traditional Philadelphia or Baltimore row house in the suburbs. In the resulting dissatisfaction and backlash, some creative developer became inspired and suggested that the "row house" be renamed "town house." Accompanying the change in name, communities imposed standards regulating the number of units that could be attached in a single row and requiring that fronts be staggered every so many units or feet. These regulations sought to avert the worst form of such developments. They have achieved that purpose, but also have imposed a rigid barracks appearance which equally discourages good design. Such marvelous historical designs as the Royal Crescent in Bath, England, for example, would be prohibited by most suburban zoning ordinances.

The design deviations are an attempt to provide greater design flexibility while still retaining a minimum degree of control. The standards attempt to identify some of the common design strategies which avoid monotony and to provide the deviations from the standards that allow their implementation. The alternative is to require some form of architectural review or variance proceeding. Neither of these ad hoc proceedings has a successful track record and both can involve expensive time delays. A variance is even less likely to result in desirable design since zoning boards are less schooled in design issues than are architectural review boards.

Nonconformities

Article VI of the model ordinance deals with nonconformities of use, structure, and lot. In both conventional and performance zoning, regulations governing nonconformities are intended to provide relief to owners whose use, building, or lot predates and does not conform to the ordinance or its amendments. Under performance zoning, an existing use may fail to meet many additional standards: intensity, bufferyards, access, signs, or other performance criteria. Since most uses are permitted as a matter of right in development and urban core districts, the problem of nonconforming structures is likely to be more critical than nonconforming uses.

It is senseless to make most of a community nonconforming; accordingly, the first step in performance zoning is to create neighborhood conservation and nonresidential conservation districts. These districts are a continuation of conventional zoning districts. Cities that are built-up should consider using performance zoning in development or redevelopment districts or for PUD's, but probably should not completely revamp their ordinances. A first step in avoiding massive nonconformance is, therefore, a pragmatic approach to those existing neighborhoods that are stable. There is no benefit to be gained from the complete elimination of conventional zoning standards in these areas.

Turning to the issue of nonconforming uses, the introduction of the bufferyard concept is both a great asset and a complicating factor. This concept permits a wide range of uses on adjoining properties, thus reducing the chance that either use will be nonconforming on the basis of the district in which it is located. However, the bufferyards introduce the possibility that present uses in two adjoining structures will become nonconforming solely because there is no buffer between them. Where there is potential to provide the required buffer, the creation of a nonconformity can be avoided. This reduces the administrative costs associated with nonconformities. The bufferyard concept in performance zoning also foresees the possibility that the use of a structure may change in the future. With conventional zoning, once a decision to permit a use was made, the responsibility to protect or buffer the less intensive use became the sole responsibility of the landowner who needed the protection. In performance zoning the more intensive use has most of that responsibility.

There remains the problem of what to do if the required buffer cannot be provided. In order to reduce the number of uncorrectable nonconformities, the maximum feasible buffer is introduced. It does not protect as well as the required buffer. The notion of a maximum feasible buffer may seem to run counter to the principles establishing the bufferyards. It is a pragmatic device to be applied where two uses presently exist side by side and have done so for some years. In such situations, the insertion of the minimum feasible buffer will increase the protection afforded the higher (less nuisance value) use and should increase its value. In return fewer uses will have to face amortization.

Amortization requires the eventual elimination of the nonconformity. In order to balance the public benefits against costs to landowners, different levels of nonconformity are defined. Major nonconformities are so serious that they should be removed within a fixed period of time. This is the strictest amortization requirement. Minor conformities are less serious and do not require amortization within a fixed time period. They cannot, however, be made worse and must take the maximum feasible corrective actions in order to obtain any building or use permit.

The land use intensity classification requires that a land use be classified on the basis of the worst criteria. Special rules are provided which alter this practice when the classification system is applied to preexisting uses. The object is not to create too many problems involving a major nonconformity. This is a means of providing maximum protection for neighbors and the public while still insuring that the landowners' equity interests are considered. Nonconforming uses follow the traditional pattern; they are uses which are not permitted in a district. The model ordinance contains a table that specifies, district by district, uses which are considered to be major nonconformities. All other uses not permitted in a district and not classified as major nonconformities requiring amortization are considered to be minor.

Nonconforming structures are more broadly defined in performance than in traditional zoning. A structure is nonconforming if it fails to meet the performance criteria of the district. A use which is improperly buffered is classified as a nonconforming structure. In many cases there may be several ways of eliminating the nonconformity; the buffer may be installed, or landscaping, lighting, or sign control may put the use in a lower use intensity class where a smaller buffer is permitted. A major nonconforming structure is defined as a nonresidential use which adjoins a residential use, in a development or urban core district, and exceeds the requirements for floor area or impervious surface in those districts, or any use which cannot provide the minimum feasible buffer as defined in the nonconforming use section.

Lastly, there are provisions for nonconforming lots of record. As do many other areas, Lake County has land which was subdivided in the 1920s and 1930s and sold with frontages of twenty-five or fifty feet. Some care in dealing with these areas is needed. In performance zoning, areas of this type which can be provided with sewers should go into the development district. Owners of several properties have substantial freedom to develop. This still leaves the possibility of a nonconforming lot of record. Provided that it is only to be used for one dwelling, there is a wide range of dwelling unit types from which to choose. It is unlikely that a property will be nonconforming in area since an atrium house can be built on a lot as small as 1,850 square feet. It is obvious that regulations which apply to a nonconforming lot of record permit development if certain conditions can be met. The likelihood that nonconforming lots in development districts will not be buildable is small. Where septic tanks must be used, nonconformities may still be a problem; there is no solution except sewers, which do not force a community to make some of these lots unbuildable.

Alternatives and Bonuses

Article VIII of the zoning ordinance is discussed in this section. Much attention has been focused recently on techniques that may be coordinated with zoning in order to achieve goals that have proved elusive in the past. A major criticism of zoning over the years has been that it is a negative tool: it can prohibit what is bad, but is unable to insure that good planning will be implemented. Several aspects of performance zoning seek to minimize this failing. Providing additional choices to the developer is one method of encouraging good land use practices. A second method is the use of bonuses. A bonus is an economic incentive to do something. Performance zoning integrates three such techniques into its framework: noncontiguous development, transfer of development rights (TDR), and a direct bonus.

Bonuses are often contained in planned unit development ordinances which list goals such as superior landscaping or pedestrian ways as means by which extra density may be earned. Such a use of bonuses does not realize their potential. There are other planning goals which the simple permissiveness of an ordinance, whether performance or conventional, is not sufficient to achieve. This type of dilemma is best illustrated by New York City's desire for new theaters in its theater district. The city turned to bonuses to provide economic incentives to meet the goal. Bonuses or development alternatives are also appropriately used to deal with areas where planners find the greatest discrepancy between the goals of competing interest groups or between the public interest and private property rights. Where the tension between such goals is very great, the tendency is to choose one view which will prevail and to sacrifice the other. This leads either to a failure to protect or to a heavy burden on one party. The philosophy of performance zoning is that the needs of both groups can be accommodated to a certain extent. The regulatory result need not be "winner take all." Both noncontiguous development and TDR are used in such situations.

Housing Bonus.

The model ordinance uses this device to make provision for moderate or low income housing, a goal that otherwise is extremely elusive. While some communities have attempted to mandate a mix of low income housing, such an approach has not met with initial success in the courts. A bonus provision can provide a voluntary economic incentive that some will choose to exercise. The use of a bonus leaves the developer freedom of choice and does not raise the same legal questions that a mandatory re-

quirement does. Where federal programs are used, the bonus provisions enable the community to control the intensities of the development and thereby avoid intensities that have all too often resulted in the creation of "projects." The scale of such projects is often so large as to be incongruent with the character of the remainder of the community. Large segments of the population usually oppose them, and their residents suffer a stigma. The bonus in the model ordinance is designed to provide an incentive to scatter individual dwellings throughout a development. Such scattered-site housing is clearly superior to large-scale projects. If the maximum densities permitted in a district are set to encourage a mix of dwelling unit types, a substantial incentive for the provision of modest cost housing can be provided without recreating our past mistakes.

The money available for federal subsidy programs is limited. The bonus system can be used to encourage the private marketplace to meet needs of lower income households without the use of conventional federal subsidy programs. The phenomenon of windfall profits that results from a zoning change is by now well understood by planners and laymen alike. Many techniques have been proposed, particularly in recent years, to recoup the windfalls for the public interest and welfare by requiring that permitted development deliver some elements for the general benefit of society. The oldest and most successful method of harnessing such windfalls is the bonus. Bonuses have been used in PUD's and in New York's zoning ordinance to provide for amenities and land uses that otherwise would not be provided by the private market. The same approach can be used to encourage the provision of moderate income housing. When a zoning change is approved, a petitioner has succeeded in increasing the value of that rezoned land. That increment of increased value is not the result of capital improvements, but of a benefit granted by government. In a traditional zoning system, the landowner alone benefits from the increased value; very little is passed on to the ultimate owner or renter. The government can recapture the windfall if it grants the zoning change subject to conditions which require the developer to do certain things. So long as those demands increase the profit to be made on a project, there is an economic incentive for developers to do what the community has decided to be in its interest—such as the provision of a mix of housing. The developer is asked to make no charge for land and improvements on a portion of the additional lots permitted him by the bonus and to build smaller houses on those lots for sale to families of modest means. This system permits the community to discount the cost of land and improvements in order to provide moderate income housing. It can work on even very expensive land, with only modest intensities being required. Table 6 and illustrations 17, 18, and 19 demonstrate this. Obviously, the mechanism can work better on land that is more modestly priced, but the example was chosen to illustrate what can be done if a community sets its mind to achieve a specific goal.

The development of this bonus system permits a small percentage of units to be built and offered for sale at a cost equal to the cost of the structure. The units will be small units without frills, but they can be priced so as to reach a large segment of the population that is now economically excluded from the housing market. The bonus in the model ordinance does not attempt to deal with these extreme land value situations, but it will nevertheless address the needs of individuals who are at the upper end of the moderate income scale.

Transfer of Development Rights.

The transfer of development rights permits two properties which may or may not abut or adjoin each other to be developed as a single development. It is even possible for two properties which are in different zoning districts to be so developed. One of the two properties is intended to be the site of most or all of the development while the other remains totally or largely in open space. In the noncontiguous development system, no development certificates are issued by the local government. It works like clustering except that now two separate properties are involved. The higher densities that may be achieved through using a noncontiguous development provide the economic incentive by decreasing development costs and developing where market potentials are highest. It serves the public interest by "producing" areas of open space.

If a landowner owns two pieces of land, there are obvious advantages to this system. If two landowners are involved, it will clearly be more difficult to work out the legal and financial arrangements needed to put a project together. The worth of the two respective shares or of the two properties may become an issue of contention. A host of legal relationships must be formalized. It may be too much to expect many developers actively to seek a landowner who is willing to enter into a joint venture. But, despite the complex legal and marketing problems, the noncontiguous development option is thought worthwhile when there is a district in which the community would prefer that development did not occur. In scenic,

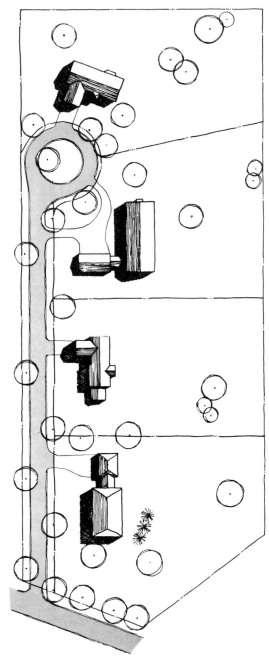

ILLUSTRATION 18
SITE WITHOUT BONUS

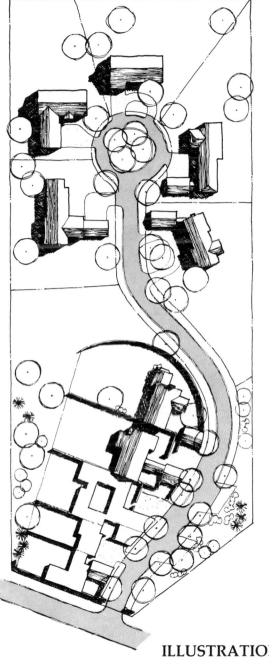

ILLUSTRATION 19
SITE WITH BONUS

TABLE 6
COMPARISON OF SITE DEVELOPMENT
WITH AND WITHOUT BONUS

	Costs		Sales		Sales Value	
	DU/AC with bonus	1 DU/AC without bonus	Improved lots	Per Lot Value	2 DU/AC with bonus	1 DU/AC without bonus
Land:						
5 AC	$150,000	$150,000	4-40,000 sq. ft. lots	$56,000		$224,000
Improvements:			5-20,000 single family			
Roads	18,000	16,500	sq. ft. lots	40,000	$200,000	
Sewer	15,600	14,300	2-Patio house (about 10,000 sq. ft.)	18,000	36,000	
Water	4,700	4,300	1-atrium house (8,000 sq. ft.)	10,000	10,000	
Landscaping ..	8,400	7,700	2-atrium house (5,000 sq. ft.)	0	0	
Total	$196,700	$192,800	Total		$246,000	$224,000

agricultural, or wilderness areas, the standard which would best protect the resource would be a prohibition of any development. In urban areas, the development value of land makes total restrictions against development unreasonable. In the case of agriculture, development is actually a nuisance for the farmer; thus, an option that allows the landowner to transfer his development potential to another piece of land meets both the goal of preserving the resource and providing a use for the land. Noncontiguous development may occur within the agricultural district or be permitted between districts so long as the land left vacant is in the districts requiring the greatest protection.

The densities transferred are determined solely by the densities currently permitted on the two tracts. The only new regulation required is some form of maximum density on the receptor site which prevents it from becoming too dense. This requires a special density ceiling for transfers between districts. If the transfer is within a district, there is no change in the maximum permitted density.

The use of transfer of development rights has been put forward in recent years as an outstanding tool to supplant zoning in situations where preservation is preferred to development. Its potential to deal with large-scale protection is, however, severely limited, since there must be a market capable of absorbing, within a reasonable time, the certificates that have been created. Thus, the transfer system may work best if the amount of land to be protected is small and the potential market for development comparatively large.

Historic preservation and resource preservation on a small scale are ideally suited to this approach. In suburban or rural environments where agricultural, scenic, or wilderness resources are present, the reverse is likely to be true. In these areas there is a need to protect large areas with a small to moderate market for development. This, in fact, is important in the decision to integrate TDR with performance zoning and the choice of TDR system used.

There are four basic forms of TDR. The first, noncontiguous development, is nothing more than an offshoot of cluster zoning, allowing a clustering to take place on two separate pieces of land. Mandatory TDR forbids a landowner to develop his land and enjoins him to sell his development rights to realize the development value of his property. In Voluntary TDR, the landowner may choose to develop and build on his land or to sell his develop-

ment rights. Lastly, there is Permit TDR, in which all development is permitted on the basis of having acquired a sufficient number of development rights.

The combination of voluntary TDR and noncontiguous development was selected as the best combination for most suburban needs. The permit TDR system is the most complicated because it requires that all owners of vacant land be given development rights.[33] It represents a completely different land use control system, which gives all landowners a share in development and requires strict coordination of planning, zoning, and the development rights elements. While parallels may be drawn to other existing transfer of development rights systems, the mandatory permit system requires a completely new legislative base. In contrast, the scheme established by the model ordinance is strictly voluntary. While this may avoid most legal objections, its major drawback is that it operates only when a landowner chooses to exercise an option to sell development rights rather than to build. This may not insure the goals for which the system was enacted such as, for example, preservation of historic buildings or small critical areas. If the areas to be preserved are scenic, agricultural, or wilderness areas rather than historic buildings, neither voluntary nor mandatory TDR can provide total protection because it is impossible to develop a large enough market for the development rights. The voluntary system has the distinct advantage of not being viewed by landowners as an additional restriction on the use of their property. If TDR can only protect a portion of the land, it does not matter from the viewpoint of efficiency whether the system is mandatory or voluntary. Thus, since the voluntary system has other advantages, it is recommended.

The pricing concept of development rights is that the number of certificates of such rights (per parcel) should be equal in value to the difference between the agricultural value and the development value of the land. The equation expressing the seller's view is

Value of certificates per acre = land value − agricultural value.

Obviously, in order to consummate a sale, there must be a buyer. The buyer views a certificate quite differently—from the perspective of the ability of the land to support development. Thus, the buyer values certificates in terms of the new increment of profit that results from an increase in density which will be permitted once they are purchased. For the buyer, the equation is

$$\text{Certificate value} = \frac{\text{value of site @ bonus density} - \text{value of site @ permitted density}}{\text{Bonus density} - \text{permitted density}}.$$

It is probable that the values derived from the two formulas will not be identical. The ordinance has used the allocation of the number of certificates per acre as a means of reconciling two disparate conceptions of the value of the certificates.

If the value of certificates on a per-acre basis equals the value of a certificate to a developer, one certificate per acre will be allocated. If the value of certificates per acre is less than the certificate value, then only a fraction of a certificate will be allocated to each acre. Where raw land costs are very high, the value of certificates on a per-acre basis will exceed the value to a developer. In this instance, more than one certificate will have to be issued per acre. The determination of the appropriate number of certificates per acre must be based on careful analysis of land values in the area.

A major complication in allocating certificates arises when a community is so large that there are major differences in land values in different parts of the community. This raises the question of whether the number of certificates per acre should vary within the community. It should be obvious that even in a small community there is a good chance that there will be some differences in land value. There are also different values for different dwellings, so there is likely to be a range of values on the developer's side as well. If the range of values per acre is small, there will be little trouble in using a single allocation value.

In general, most areas of township size (thirty-six square miles) should be able to get by with a single value for certificates unless there is some capital investment (a sewer, road, or other utility) that makes land in one section of the community substantially more valuable. For larger areas land values may vary by a factor of two or more. In such a case more than one value may be required even though the delineation of the areas will raise a controversy. If a single value is used in the allocation and is based on the lowest land values, TDR simply will not work in the high value areas. On the other hand, if the allocation of certificates is based on the highest land value of the area, more certificates will be given out. That in turn means that less preservation will be possible. It also raises an additional problem: the owners of the lowest valued land would get substantially more certificates than their land values warrant. They therefore get a windfall profit. Owners in low value areas therefore could sell certificates below the calculated rate and still get a windfall, thereby preventing the owners of high-priced land from selling for a fair value. The method of allocating certificates must take these concerns into account and must be based on common sense. It must be remembered that it will do no good to set a value system where there are not both willing buyers and willing sellers. There can be strong pressures to set value to protect all of the resources and ignore the economics. This will lead to an unworkable system. A simple game may easily be developed as a means of pretesting the various values.

Administration

Performance zoning requires a slightly different administrative approach from conventional zoning. Article IX sets out this approach. Because the performance criteria are complex, a detailed site plan review must be conducted before zoning or building permits are issued. As is the case with a planned unit development, it makes considerable sense to integrate the reviews for zoning and plat or land development into a single process. A second major difference is the treatment accorded zoning changes. The last important difference is the use of the variance procedure. With these exceptions this article is mainly boilerplate. Further, it reflects the process as required by Illinois Law and *is not* a procedural model. Illinois is perhaps the only state in which the zoning board of appeals is both an advisory and a quasi-judicial body. In most other states, the planning commission, not the zoning board of appeals, has the responsibility to advise the governing body on zoning changes. Illinois is probably stuck with this procedure, but others should not imitate it, since it further fragments and weakens planning.

Plan Review.

The zoning officer and director of planning are clearly given the powers to review a proposed development in much the same manner as a plat of subdivision would be reviewed. The procedures even permit a preliminary review. This comprehensive review will certainly require a trained staff, but not necessarily a new one. If the community has a professional staff capable of reviewing plats not only for straight compliance but design as well, the community has all the staff it needs to implement performance zoning. In order to shorten the time needed to obtain approvals, the plat, subdivision, or land development review should, as in the model ordinance, be downgraded to a purely ministerial function in which a final plat approval is granted automatically if zoning and building permits can be issued.

Zoning Changes.

Zoning changes in conventional systems are the rule rather than the exception. An ad hoc process takes over that has a life of its own. The reduced number of districts and increased choice within districts under performance zoning should reduce the need for many zoning changes. The lure of big profits to be made from rezoning rural land to urban intensities remains, and so zoning requests may be anticipated. An adequately sized development district may reduce this pressure. The model ordinance is based on a twenty-year development district. It is to be sized initially for twenty-five years and updated every five years. This will insure a large development district and thus an adequate supply of land on the market. No single landowner or small group of landowners will have a corner on the market, and inflation of land prices and speculation will therefore be discouraged. This is important: if sufficient land is not zoned for development, speculative pressures and land values reinforce each other in providing incentives to seek zoning changes. Communities that seek to make the development district as small as possible may be harming their own cause by encouraging requests for zoning changes. Performance zoning seeks to reduce the frequency of zoning changes. To achieve this goal, the community must be liberal in its approach to establishing the development district.

The most important control which can limit requests for zoning changes is the set of standards imposed by performance zoning that must be considered before a zoning change is granted. The developer must demonstrate that either population trends have changed sufficiently to require that the development districts be enlarged or that an area has received new capital facilities sufficient to justify a reclassification. The establishment of a series of conditions that must be present if a zoning change is to be granted should have the effect of reducing the number of requests for changes. These criteria apply to the planning department's mandatory five-year reviews and to requests for rezoning by developers and speculators.

In addition, a set of priorities identifies the order in which various types of land should be rezoned. Clearly, agricultural, scenic, and wilderness lands are the last that should be developed. Rural lands or holding zones are given priority for rezoning from the rural to the development category. This integrates long-range planning with zoning. The order of priority will make it far more difficult to obtain a speculative zoning change, which in turn will reduce the number of requests. Caution should be used in setting out the original zoning. Performance zoning is not to be used to limit growth but rather to control where the growth should occur and how development should proceed in order to insure a quality community. The judiciary will be reluctant to uphold the strict provisions for granting a zoning change if the community has not provided adequate land for development in the first place. A community seeking to utilize performance zoning will do well to demonstrate that it has provided for the community's development by using optimistic estimates of growth potential or by showing that its estimates meet those of the region or state for growth.

Performance zoning should be honest. If a community has reasons for retarding growth, it should adopt a Petaluma-type ordinance which limits the number of building permits issued in a given year. This places the test of legality up front. Further, it does not confuse the purpose of performance zoning, to permit development in a manner consistent with a community's plan, with the growth/no-growth issue.

Variances.

From its inception zoning has contained provisions for granting variances. Conventional zoning standards force a rigid geometric form on the land. Perhaps this is why a rather dull but influential midwestern lawyer thinks that euclidian zoning has something to do with Euclid's geometry. When that rigidity is combined with the doctrine that all land within a district must be equal, it is easy to understand why variances are needed. Except in the neighborhood conservation districts which retain conventional zoning standards, variances are not needed or desirable in performance zoning. There are no reasons that this device should be continued in performance zoning, since site capacity is in fact determined by the presence or absence of environmental or site constraints. A major reason for granting variances has historically been the existence of limiting natural factors on a site.

In conventional zoning, where all lots are to be identical in size and there is but a single position for a residence on a lot, a natural feature may require that these standards be varied. In performance zoning a landowner is not restricted to a single dwelling unit type, but may select one better adapted to the site; units of smaller size may be chosen which demand a smaller lot. The variance is unnecessary. Further, developments built pursuant to performance zoning cannot be laid out in such a manner that a lot is unbuildable. Thus, the variance only applies to lots in the neighborhood or commercial conservation districts.

Notes

1. 272 U.S. 265 (1926).

2. Dennis O'Harrow, *Performance Standards in Industrial Zoning, Planning Advisory Service Information Report* 32 (1951).

3. John W. Reps, "Requiem for Zoning," in *Planning 1964* (Chicago: American Society of Planning Officials, 1964), p. 57.

4. Norman Williams, *American Land Planning Law, Land Use and the Police Power* (Chicago: Callaghan & Co., 1977).

5. Ibid., pp. 103 and 143. Professor Williams describes the second period of zoning law as one in which courts tend to hold restrictive regulations invalid as applied: "the burden of proof was on the municipalities to show why a given restriction should be enforced by a specific indication of the harm to be avoided thereby."

6. Lake County Zoning Ordinance, Lake County Department of Planning, Lake County, Illinois, 1976, pp. 4–49.

7. James R. Pease, "Performance Standards: A Technique for Controlling Land Use," *Oregon State University Extension Service Special Report* 424 (1975): 16.

8. 422 U.S. 205 (1975). The case dealt with a zoning ordinance regulation prohibiting adult theaters in certain locations which was challenged on the ground of the First Amendment.

9. Zoning questionnaire results, Lake County Department of Planning, Zoning and Environmental Quality, Lake County, Illinois, 1977.

10. "Requiem for Zoning," (n. 3), pp. 56–67.

11. The Quakertown Area Zoning Ordinance (Bucks County Planning Commission, Bucks County, Pennsylvania, 1975) provides an actual example of this technique.

12. Richard F. Babcock, *The Zoning Game* (Madison: University of Wisconsin Press, 1969).

13. John Hulkonen, "Tax Increment Financing: A Total Community Approach to Economic Development," *AIDC Journal* 9, no. 2 (April 1979): 49–67.

14. Robert Paternoster, "Pittsburgh Subsidizes New Home Mortgages," *Practicing Planner* 6, no. 5 (December 1976): 40–41.

15. Zoning questionnaire, Lake County Department of Planning, Zoning and Environmental Quality, Lake County, Illinois, December 1977, p. 4.

16. Table 2 provides a high and low value for each floor area standard. The high value is associated with optimal design, that is, the highest density and least street. The low value has the most street and therefore lower density.

17. Rice Odell, "Carrying Capacity Analysis: Useful but Limited," in *Management and Control of Growth*, vol. 3, ed. R. Scott et al. (Washington, D.C.: Urban Land Institute, 1975), pp. 22–23.

18. R.F. Babcock, "Land Use as a Commodity Affected with a Public Interest," *Washington Law Review* (April 1977): 312.

19. "Analysis of Resource Protection Standards" (Lake County, Ill.: Lake County Department of Planning, Zoning and Environmental Quality, 1979), p. 6.

20. See 43 A.L.R. 3d 862 (1972): "Validity and construction of Statute or Ordinance requiring land developer to dedicate portion of land for recreational purposes or to make payment in lieu thereof."

21. Ibid., p. 866.

22. *Krughoff* v. *City of Naperville*, 68 Ill. 2d 352 (1977) (Illinois).

23. Landscape Architecture Research Office, *Three Approaches to Environmental Resource Analysis* (Washington, D.C.: The Conservation Foundation, 1967).

24. *Impact Zoning in Duxbury: A Model for Land Use Control, Development Impact Model* (Philadelphia: Rakenkamp, Sachs, Wells, and Associates, Inc., 1973).

25. *Three Approaches to Environmental Resource Analysis* (n. 23), p. 23.

26. Rutherford H. Platt, "The National Flood Insurance Program: Some Midstream Perspectives," *Journal of the American Institute of Planners*, no. 3 (July 1976): 303.

27. "Land Use as a Commodity" (n. 18), p. 305.

28. Bill Macaitis and Subhash Patel, "Analysis of 208 Nonpoint Stormwater Runoff" (Chicago: Metropolitan Sanitary District of Greater Chicago, 1978).

29. "Determining the Width of Residential Streets," *Traffic Engineering and Control* 16 (November 1975): 481–84.

30. Herman K. Chang, *Eleventh Progress Report on Trip Ends Generation Research Counts* (San Francisco: California Department of Transportation, 1976).

31. A six (6) inch letter is visible at two hundred and fifty (250) feet; see Karen Claus and James Claus, eds., *Visual Communication through Signage* (Cincinnati: Sign of the Times Publishing Co., 1974).

32. Duncan Erley and Martin Jaffee, *Site Planning for Solar Access: A Guidebook for Residential Developers and Site Planners* and *Protecting Solar Access for Residential Development: A Guidebook for Planning Officials* (Chicago: American Planning Assn., 1979).

33. Senate Bill no. 254, State of Maryland, 1972.

Appendix

FORMULAS FOR TABLES RELATING OPEN SPACE RATIO, DENSITY, IMPERVIOUS SURFACE RATIO, DWELLING UNIT TYPE, AND FLOOR AREA

The following formulas supply the full calculations needed to derive specific values for two of the three major variables given knowledge of the value of the third one, and information on the type of dwelling unit and its floor area. The calculations state the given variable, open space ratio, density or impervious surface ratio. The letter references refer to column headings from the table for conventional single family or performance zoning dwelling types.

Given OPEN SPACE RATIO

Step 1

$$100 - (\text{open space ratio} \times 100) = \text{buildable area}$$

Step 2

$$\frac{\text{buildable area}}{\text{lot area B} + (\text{R.O.W. area E} \times \text{open space adjustment})} = \text{dwelling units}$$

Step 3

$$\frac{\text{dwelling units}}{100} = \text{DENSITY}$$

Step 4

dwelling units $\times$ [impervious lot A + (street impervious C $\times$ open space adjustment)]

$$\frac{}{100} = \text{IMPERVIOUS SURFACE RATIO}$$

Given IMPERVIOUS SURFACE RATIO

Step 1

$$100 \times (\text{impervious surface ratio}) = \text{impervious surface}$$

Step 2

$$\frac{\text{impervious surface}}{\text{impervious lot D}} = \text{dwelling units}$$

Step 3

dwelling units $\times$ (lot area B + R.O.W. area E) = buildable area

Step 4
    buildable area $>$ 100   stop, print
    buildable area $\leq$ 100   continue

Step 5
    $$\frac{100 - \text{buildable area}}{100} = \text{open space ratio (temporary)}$$

Step 6
    $$\frac{\text{impervious surface}}{\text{impervious lot A} + (\text{street impervious C} \times \text{open space adjustment})} = \text{dwelling units}$$

Step 7
dwelling units $\times$ [lot area B + (R.O.W. area E $\times$ open space adjustment)] = buildable area

Step 8
    Same as 4

Step 9
    Same as 5 = OPEN SPACE RATIO

Step 10
    $$\frac{\text{dwelling units}}{100} = \text{DENSITY}$$

Given DENSITY

Step 1
    100 $\times$ density = dwelling units

Step 2
    Dwelling units $\times$ (lot area B + row area E) = buildable area (temporary)

Step 3
    If buildable area $>$ 100   stop, print
    If buildable area $\leq$ 100   continue

Step 4
    $$\frac{100 - \text{buildable area}}{100} = \text{open space ratio (temporary)}$$

Step 5
    Dwelling units $\times$ [lot area B + (row area E $\times$ open space adjustment)] = buildable area

Step 6

Same as 3

Step 7

Same as 4 = OPEN SPACE RATIO

Step 8

$$\frac{\text{Number of dwelling units} \times [\text{impervious lot A} + (\text{street impervious C} \times \text{open space adjustment})]}{100} = \text{IMPERVIOUS SURFACE RATIO}$$

OPEN SPACE ADJUSTMENT TABLE

OPEN SPACE RATIO	OPEN SPACE ADJUSTMENT
0– .40	1.0
.401– .50	1.12
.501– .60	1.26
60.1– 70	1.41
70.1– 80	1.59
80.1– 90	1.78
90.1– 95	1.88
95.1– 100	2.0

The following tables contain the data to be used in the above formulas.

HOUSING TYPE	IMP. SUR.	A IMPERVIOUS LOT			B LOT AREA		
		Min. Area	Avg. Area	Large Area	Min. Area	Avg. Area	Large Area
Single Family, 2 story, 3 bdrm, 2 car, 7,400 SF	22%	1,628	1,914	2,200	7,400	8,700	10,000
Lot line, 1½ story, 3 bdrm, 2 car, 6,200 SF	28%	1,736	2,100	2,520	6,200	7,500	9,000
Village house, 2 story, 3 bdrm, 2 car, 5,000 SF	27%	1,350	1,647	1,944	5,000	6,100	7,200
Twin house, 2 story, 3 bdrm, 2 car, 3,900 SF	40%	1,560	1,920	2,200	3,900	4,800	5,500
Patio house, 1 story, 3 bdrm, 2 car, 3,300 SF	53%	1,749	2,491	3,074	3,300	4,700	5,800
Patio house, 2 story, 3 bdrm, 2 car, 2,700 SF	37%	999	1,367	1,889	2,700	3,700	5,100
Atrium, 1 story, 3 bdrm, 2,400 SF	54%	1,560	2,340	2,925	2,400	3,600	4,500
Weaklink house, 2 story, 3 bdrm, 2,400 SF	43%	1,032	1,419	1,806	2,400	3,300	4,200
Town house, 2 story, 3 bdrm, 1,800 SF	53%	954	1,325	1,590	1,800	2,500	3,000
Multiplex A, 2 story, 2 bdrm, 2 car, 1,000 SF	56%	952	1,142	1,523	1,700	2,040	2,720
Apartment, 2 story, 2 bdrm, 2 car, 1,000 SF	71%	1,172	1,406	1,874	1,650	1,980	2,640
Apartment, 3 story, 2 bdrm, 2 car, 1,000 SF	65%	1,008	1,209	1,612	1,550	1,860	2,480
Apartment, 4 story, 2 bdrm, 2 car, 1,000 SF	61%	885	1,061	1,415	1,450	1,740	2,320
Apartment, 6 story, 2 bdrm, 2 car, 1,000 SF	51%	561	673	898	1,100	1,320	1,760
Apartment, 8 story, 2 bdrm, 2 car/2 lev, 1,000 SF	48%	504	605	806	1,050	1,260	1,680

HOUSING TYPE	LOT WIDTH*			BLOCK SIZE FACTOR*						HALF WIDTH	
	Min.	Avg.	Large	Min. Area		Avg. Area		Large Area		Street	R.O.W.
Block size factor				1.15	1.75	1.15	1.75	1.15	1.75		
Single Family, 2 story, 3 bdrm, 2 car, 7,400 SF	70	70	70	81	123	81	123	81	123	16	30
Lot line, 1½ story, 3 bdrm, 2 car, 6,200 SF	60	60	60	69	105	69	105	69	105	16	30
Village house, 2 story, 3 bdrm, 2 car, 5,000 SF	55	55	55	63	96	63	96	63	96	16	30
Twin house, 2 story, 3 bdrm, 2 car, 3,900 SF	45	45	50	52	79	52	79	58	88	16	30
Patio house, 1 story, 3 bdrm, 2 car, 3,300 SF	40	40	45	46	70	46	70	52	79	16	30
Patio house, 2 story, 3 bdrm, 2 car, 2,700 SF	40	40	45	46	70	46	70	52	79	16	30
Atrium, 1 story, 3 bdrm, 2,400 SF	40	40	40	46	70	46	70	46	70	16	30
Weaklink house, 2 story, 3 bdrm, 2,400 SF	30	30	32	35	53	35	53	37	56	16	30
Town house, 2 story, 3 bdrm, 1,800 SF	24	24	26	28	42	28	42	30	46	16	30
Multiplex A, 2 story, 2 bdrm, 2 car, 1,000 SF	30	40	45	40	61	46	70	52	79	16	30
Apartment, 2 story, 2 bdrm, 2 car, 1,000 SF	(3.333)	(3.542)	(3.750)	(3.833)	(5.833)	(6.073)	(6.199)	(4.313)	(6.563)	16	30
Apartment, 3 story, 2 bdrm, 2 car, 1,000 SF	(3.810)	(4.048)	(4.286)	(4.382)	(6.668)	(4.655)	(7.084)	(4.929)	(7.501)	16	30
Apartment, 4 story, 2 bdrm, 2 car, 1,000 SF	(3.333)	(3.542)	(3.750)	(3.833)	(5.833)	(4.073)	(6.199)	(4.313)	(6.563)	16	30
Apartment, 6 story, 2 bdrm, 2 car, 1,000 SF	(3.333)	(3.542)	(3.750)	(3.833)	(5.833)	(4.073)	(6.199)	(4.313)	(6.563)	16	30
Apartment, 8 story, 2 bdrm, 2 car/2 lev, 1,000 SF	(3.333)	(3.542)	(3.750)	(3.833)	(5.833)	(4.073)	(6.199)	(4.313)	(6.563)	16	30

*Figures in parentheses represent the lot's ratio of width to length.

HOUSING TYPE	C STREET IMPERVIOUS						D TOTAL IMPERVIOUS					
	Min. Area		Avg. Area		Large Area		Min. Area		Avg. Area		Large Area	
Block Size Factor	1.15	1.75	1.15	1.75	1.15	1.75	1.15	1.75	1.15	1.75	1.15	1.75
Single Family, 2 story, 3 bdrm, 2 car, 7,400 SF	1,296	1,968	1,296	1,968	1,296	1,968	2,924	3,596	3,210	3,882	3,496	4,168
Lot line, 1½ story, 3 bdrm, 2 car, 6,200 SF	1,104	1,680	1,104	1,680	1,104	1,680	2,840	3,416	3,204	3,780	3,624	4,200
Village house, 2 story, 3 bdrm, 2 car, 5,000 SF	1,008	1,536	1,008	1,536	1,008	1,536	2,358	2,886	2,655	3,183	2,952	3,480
Twin house, 2 story, 3 bdrm, 2 car, 3,900 SF	832	1,264	832	1,264	928	1,408	2,392	2,824	2,752	3,184	3,128	3,608
Patio house, 1 story, 3 bdrm, 2 car, 3,300 SF	736	1,120	736	1,120	832	1,264	2,485	2,869	3,227	3,611	3,906	4,338
Patio house, 2 story, 3 bdrm, 2 car, 2,700 SF	736	1,120	736	1,120	832	1,264	1,735	2,119	2,105	2,489	2,719	3,151
Atrium, 1 story, 3 bdrm, 2,400 SF	736	1,120	736	1,120	736	1,120	2,296	2,680	3,076	3,460	3,661	4,045
Weaklink house, 2 story, 3 bdrm, 2,400 SF	560	843	560	843	592	896	1,592	1,880	1,979	2,267	2,398	2,702
Town house, 2 story, 3 bdrm, 1,800 SF	448	672	448	672	480	736	1,402	1,626	1,773	1,997	2,070	2,326
Multiplex A, 2 story, 2 bdrm, 2 car, 1,000 SF	640	976	736	1,120	832	1,264	1,592	1,928	1,878	2,262	2,355	2,787
Apartment, 2 story, 2 bdrm, 2 car, 1,000 SF	61	93	65	99	69	105	1,233	1,265	1,471	1,505	1,943	1,979
Apartment, 3 story, 2 bdrm, 2 car, 1,000 SF	70	107	74	113	79	120	1,078	1,115	1,283	1,322	1,691	1,732
Apartment, 4 story, 2 bdrm, 2 car, 1,000 SF	61	93	65	99	69	105	946	978	1,126	1,160	1,484	1,520
Apartment, 6 story, 2 bdrm, 2 car, 1,000 SF	61	93	65	99	69	105	622	654	738	772	967	1,003
Apartment, 8 story, 2 bdrm, 2 car/2 lev, 1,000 SF	61	93	65	99	69	105	565	597	670	704	875	911

HOUSING TYPE	E R.O.W. AREA						F TOTAL AREA					
	Min. Area		Avg. Area		Large Area		Min. Area		Avg. Area		Large Area	
Block Size Factor	1.15	1.75	1.15	1.75	1.15	1.75	1.15	1.75	1.15	1.75	1.15	1.75
Single Family, 2 story, 3 bdrm, 2 car, 7,400 SF	2,430	3,690	2,430	3,690	2,430	3,690	9,830	11,090	11,130	12,390	12,430	13,690
Lot line, 1½ story, 3 bdrm, 2 car, 6,200 SF	2,070	3,150	2,070	3,150	2,070	3,150	8,270	9,350	9,570	10,650	11,070	12,150
Village house, 2 story, 3 bdrm, 2 car, 5,000 SF	1,890	2,880	1,890	2,880	1,890	2,880	6,890	7,880	7,990	8,980	9,090	10,080
Twin house, 2 story, 3 bdrm, 2 car, 3,900 SF	1,560	2,370	1,560	2,370	1,740	2,640	5,460	6,270	6,360	7,170	7,240	8,140
Patio house, 1 story, 3 bdrm, 2 car, 3,300 SF	1,380	2,100	1,380	2,100	1,560	2,370	4,680	5,400	6,080	6,800	7,360	8,170
Patio house, 2 story, 3 bdrm, 2 car, 2,700 SF	1,380	2,100	1,380	2,100	1,560	2,370	4,080	4,800	5,080	5,800	6,660	7,470
Atrium, 1 story, 3 bdrm, 2,400 SF	1,380	2,100	1,380	2,100	1,380	2,100	3,780	4,500	4,980	5,700	5,880	6,600
Weaklink house, 2 story, 3 bdrm, 2,400 SF	1,050	1,590	1,050	1,590	1,110	1,680	3,450	3,990	4,350	4,890	5,310	5,880
Town house, 2 story, 3 bdrm, 1,800 SF	840	1,260	840	1,260	900	1,380	2,640	3,060	3,340	3,760	3,900	4,380
Multiplex A, 2 story, 2 bdrm, 2 car, 1,000 SF	1,200	1,830	1,380	2,100	1,560	2,370	2,900	3,530	3,420	4,140	4,280	5,090
Apartment, 2 story, 2 bdrm, 2 car, 1,000 SF	115	175	122	186	129	197	1,765	1,825	2,102	2,166	2,769	2,837
Apartment, 3 story, 2 bdrm, 2 car, 1,000 SF	131	200	140	213	148	225	1,681	1,750	2,000	2,073	2,628	2,705
Apartment, 4 story, 2 bdrm, 2 car, 1,000 SF	115	175	122	186	129	197	1,565	1,625	1,862	1,926	2,449	2,517
Apartment, 6 story, 2 bdrm, 2 car, 1,000 SF	115	175	122	186	129	197	1,215	1,275	1,442	1,506	1,889	1,957
Apartment, 8 story, 2 bdrm, 2 car/2 lev, 1,000 SF	115	175	122	186	129	197	1,165	1,225	1,382	1,446	1,809	1,877

HOUSING TYPE	A IMPERVIOUS LOT						B LOT AREA					
	Min. Area		Avg. Area		Large Area		Min. Area		Avg. Area		Large Area	
Block Size Factor	1.15	1.75	1.15	1.75	1.15	1.75	1.15	1.75	1.15	1.75	1.15	1.75
Conventional Single Family 8,500 SF Lot	1,200	1,700	2,120	2,320	2,590	2,790	8,500	8,500	8,500	8,500	8,500	8,500
Conventional Single Family 10,000 SF Lot	1,250	1,800	2,220	2,470	2,740	2,900	10,000	10,000	10,000	10,000	10,000	10,000
Conventional Single Family 12,000 SF Lot	2,200	2,450	2,950	3,200	3,750	4,000	12,000	12,000	12,000	12,000	12,000	12,000
Conventional Single Family 15,000 SF Lot	2,250	2,500	3,000	3,250	3,800	4,050	15,000	15,000	15,000	15,000	15,000	15,000
Conventional Single Family 20,000 SF Lot	2,500	2,750	3,390	3,640	4,330	4,580	20,000	20,000	20,000	20,000	20,000	20,000
Conventional Single Family 25,000 SF Lot	2,650	2,900	3,540	3,790	4,480	4,730	25,000	25,000	25,000	25,000	25,000	25,000
Conventional Single Family 30,000 SF Lot	2,900	3,150	3,930	4,180	5,010	5,260	30,000	30,000	30,000	30,000	30,000	30,000
Conventional Single Family 35,000 SF Lot	2,950	3,200	3,980	4,230	5,060	5,310	35,000	35,000	35,000	35,000	35,000	35,000
Conventional Single Family 40,000 SF Lot	3,050	3,300	4,230	4,480	5,410	5,660	40,000	40,000	40,000	40,000	40,000	40,000
Conventional Single Family 80,000 SF Lot	3,350	3,360	5,370	5,620	7,290	7,540	80,000	80,000	80,000	80,000	80,000	80,000
Conventional Single Family 120,000 SF Lot	3,650	4,450	6,620	8,020	10,240	11,690	120,000	120,000	120,000	120,000	120,000	120,000
Conventional Single Family 160,000 SF Lot	3,750	4,650	6,920	8,320	10,640	12,040	160,000	160,000	160,000	160,000	160,000	160,000
Conventional Single Family 200,000 SF Lot	4,050	5,400	7,660	9,760	12,270	14,320	200,000	200,000	200,000	200,000	200,000	200,000

HOUSING TYPE	LOT WIDTH*			BLOCK SIZE FACTOR						HALF WIDTH	
	Min. Area	Avg. Area	Large Area	Min. Area		Avg. Area		Large Area		Street	R.O.W.
Block Size Factor				1.15	1.75	1.15	1.75	1.15	1.75		
Conventional Single Family 8,500 SF Lot	(2.367) 60	(2.367) 60	(2.015) 65	69	105	69	105	75	114	16	30
Conventional Single Family 10,000 SF Lot	(2.369) 65	(2.369) 65	(2.043) 70	75	114	75	114	81	123	16	30
Conventional Single Family 12,000 SF Lot	(2.443) 70	(2.443) 70	(2.133) 75	81	123	81	123	86	131	16	30
Conventional Single Family 15,000 SF Lot	(2.660) 75	(2.350) 80	(2.133) 85	86	131	92	140	98	149	16	30
Conventional Single Family 20,000 SF Lot	(2.467) 90	(2.221) 95	(2.000) 100	104	158	109	166	115	175	16	30
Conventional Single Family 25,000 SF Lot	(2.500) 100	(2.260) 105	(2.060) 110	115	175	121	184	127	193	16	30
Conventional Single Family 30,000 SF Lot	(2.480) 110	(2.270) 115	(2.080) 120	127	193	132	201	138	210	16	30
Conventional Single Family 35,000 SF Lot	(2.433) 120	(2.240) 125	(2.069) 130	138	210	144	219	150	228	16	30
Conventional Single Family 40,000 SF Lot	(2.369) 130	(2.193) 135	(2.043) 140	150	228	155	236	161	245	16	30
Conventional Single Family 80,000 SF Lot	(2.216) 190	(2.103) 195	(2.000) 200	219	333	224	341	230	350	16	30
Conventional Single Family 120,000 SF Lot	(2.368) 225	(2.275) 230	(2.196) 235	259	394	265	403	270	411	16	30
Conventional Single Family 160,000 SF Lot	(2.365) 260	(2.275) 265	(2.196) 270	299	455	305	464	311	473	16	30
Conventional Single Family 200,000 SF Lot	(2.223) 300	(2.151) 305	(2.080) 310	345	525	351	534	357	543	16	30

*Figures in parentheses represent the lot's ratio of width to length.

HOUSING TYPE	C STREET IMPERVIOUS						D TOTAL IMPERVIOUS					
	Min. Area		Avg. Area		Large Area		Min. Area		Avg. Area		Large Area	
Block Size Factor	1.15	1.75	1.15	1.75	1.15	1.75	1.15	1.75	1.15	1.75	1.15	1.75
Conventional Single Family 8,300 SF Lot	1,104	1,680	1,104	1,680	1,200	1,824	2,304	3,300	3,224	4,000	3,790	4,614
Conventional Single Family 10,000 SF Lot	1,200	1,824	1,200	1,824	1,296	1,968	2,450	3,624	3,420	4,294	4,036	4,868
Conventional Single Family 12,000 SF Lot	1,296	1,968	1,296	1,968	1,376	2,096	3,496	4,418	4,246	5,168	5,126	6,096
Conventional Single Family 15,000 SF Lot	1,376	2,096	1,472	2,240	1,568	2,336	3,626	4,596	4,472	5,490	5,368	6,386
Conventional Single Family 20,000 SF Lot	1,664	2,528	1,744	2,656	1,840	2,800	4,164	5,278	5,134	6,558	6,170	7,380
Conventional Single Family 25,000 SF Lot	1,840	2,800	1,936	2,944	2,032	3,088	4,490	5,700	5,476	6,734	6,512	7,818
Conventional Single Family 30,000 SF Lot	2,032	3,088	2,112	3,216	2,208	3,360	4,932	6,238	6,042	7,396	7,218	8,620
Conventional Single Family 35,000 SF Lot	2,208	3,360	2,304	3,504	2,400	3,648	3,158	6,560	6,284	7,734	7,460	8,958
Conventional Single Family 40,000 SF Lot	2,400	3,648	2,480	3,776	2,596	3,920	5,450	6,948	6,710	8,256	7,986	9,580
Conventional Single Family 80,000 SF Lot	3,504	5,328	3,584	5,456	3,680	5,600	6,854	8,928	8,954	11,076	10,970	13,140
Conventional Single Family 120,000 SF Lot	4,144	6,304	4,240	6,448	4,320	6,576	7,794	10,754	10,860	14,468	14,560	18,216
Conventional Single Family 160,000 SF Lot	4,784	7,280	4,880	7,424	4,976	7,568	8,534	11,930	11,800	15,744	15,616	19,608
Conventional Single Family 200,000 SF Lot	5,520	8,400	5,616	8,544	5,712	8,688	9,570	13,800	13,296	18,304	19,982	23,000

HOUSING TYPE	E R.O.W. AREA						F TOTAL AREA					
	Min. Area		Avg. Area		Large Area		Min. Area		Avg. Area		Large Area	
Block Size Factor	1.15	1.75	1.15	1.75	1.15	1.75	1.15	1.75	1.15	1.75	1.15	1.75
Conventional Single Family 8,500 SF Lot	2,070	3,150	2,070	3,150	2,250	3,420	10,570	11,650	10,570	11,650	10,750	11,920
Conventional Single Family 10,000 SF Lot	2,250	3,420	2,250	3,420	2,430	3,690	12,250	13,420	12,250	13,420	12,430	13,690
Conventional Single Family 12,000 SF Lot	2,430	3,690	2,430	3,690	2,580	3,930	14,430	15,690	12,430	15,690	14,580	15,930
Conventional Single Family 15,000 SF Lot	2,580	3,930	2,760	4,200	3,940	4,470	17,580	18,930	17,760	19,200	17,940	19,470
Conventional Single Family 20,000 SF Lot	3,120	4,740	3,270	4,980	3,450	5,250	23,120	24,740	23,270	24,980	23,450	25,250
Conventional Single Family 25,000 SF Lot	3,450	5,250	3,630	5,520	3,810	5,790	28,450	30,250	28,630	30,520	28,810	30,790
Conventional Single Family 30,000 SF Lot	3,810	5,790	3,960	6,030	4,140	6,300	33,810	35,790	33,960	36,030	34,140	36,300
Conventional Single Family 35,000 SF Lot	4,140	6,300	4,320	6,570	4,500	6,840	39,140	41,300	39,320	41,570	39,500	41,840
Conventional Single Family 40,000 SF Lot	4,500	6,840	4,650	7.080	4,830	7,350	44,500	46,840	44,650	47,080	44,830	47,350
Conventional Single Family 80,000 SF Lot	6,570	9,990	6,720	10,230	6,900	10,500	86,570	89,990	86,720	90,230	86,900	90,500
Conventional Single Family 120,000 SF Lot	7,770	11,820	7,950	12,090	8,100	12,330	127,770	131,820	127,950	132,090	128,100	132,330
Conventional Single Family 160,000 SF Lot	8,970	13,650	9,150	13,920	9,330	14,190	168,970	173,650	169,150	173,920	169,330	174,190
Conventional Single Family 200,000 SF Lot	10,350	15,750	10,530	16,020	10,710	16,290	210,350	215,750	210,530	216,020	210,710	216,290

DATE DUE

JAN. 17, 1983

GAYLORD

PRINTED IN U.S.A.

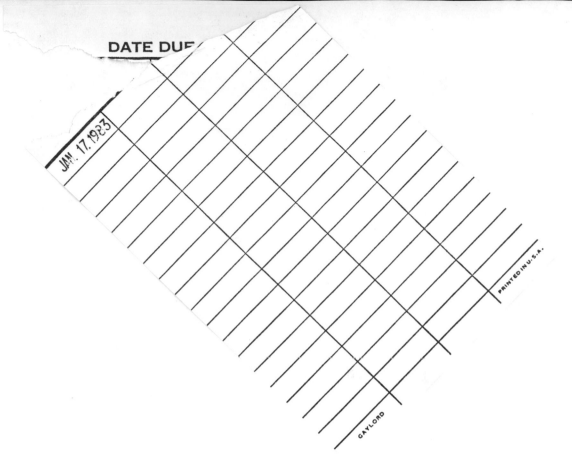

Randall Library — UNCW
HT169.6 .K462   NXWW
Kendig / Performance zoning
3049002694598